Reasoning of State

CW01035172

Scholars and citizens tend to assume that rationality guides the decision making of our leaders. Brian Rathbun suggests, however, that if we understand rationality to be a cognitive style premised on a commitment to objectivity and active deliberation, rational leaders are, in fact, the exception – not the norm. Using a unique combination of methods, including laboratory bargaining experiments, archival-based case studies, quantitative textual analysis, and high-level interviews, Rathbun questions some of our basic assumptions about rationality and leadership, with profound implications for the field of international relations. Case studies of Bismarck and Richelieu show that the rationality of realists makes them rare. An examination of Churchill and Reagan, romantics in international politics who sought to overcome obstacles in their path through force of will and personal agency, show what less rationality looks like in foreign policy making.

BRIAN C. RATHBUN is a professor in the School of International Relations at the University of Southern California. He is the author of *Partisan Interventions* (2004), *Trust in International Cooperation* (2012), and *Diplomacy's Value* (2014), which won the best book award from the Diplomatic Studies Section of the International Studies Association. He has published articles in journals such as *International Organization, World Politics, International Security*, and *International Studies Quarterly*, among others.

Cambridge Studies in International Relations: 149

Reasoning of State

Editors

Evelyn Goh
Christian Reus-Smit
Nicholas J. Wheeler

Editorial Board

Jacqueline Best, Karin Fierke, William Grimes, Yuen Foong Khong, Andrew Kydd, Lily Ling, Andrew Linklater, Nicola Phillips, Elizabeth Shakman Hurd, Jacquie True, Leslie Vinjamuri, Alexander Wendt

Cambridge Studies in International Relations is a joint initiative of Cambridge University Press and the British International Studies Association (BISA). The series aims to publish the best new scholarship in international studies, irrespective of subject matter, methodological approach or theoretical perspective. The series seeks to bring the latest theoretical work in International Relations to bear on the most important problems and issues in global politics.

Series list continues after index.

Reasoning of State

*Realists, Romantics and Rationality
in International Relations*

Brian C. Rathbun

University of Southern California

 CAMBRIDGE
UNIVERSITY PRESS

CAMBRIDGE
UNIVERSITY PRESS

University Printing House, Cambridge CB2 8BS, United Kingdom

One Liberty Plaza, 20th Floor, New York, NY 10006, USA

477 Williamstown Road, Port Melbourne, VIC 3207, Australia

314–321, 3rd Floor, Plot 3, Splendor Forum, Jasola District Centre,
New Delhi – 110025, India

79 Anson Road, #06–04/06, Singapore 079906

Cambridge University Press is part of the University of Cambridge.

It furthers the University's mission by disseminating knowledge in the pursuit of
education, learning, and research at the highest international levels of excellence.

www.cambridge.org
Information on this title: www.cambridge.org/9781108427425
DOI: 10.1017/9781108612937

First published 2019

Printed and bound in Great Britain by Clays Ltd, Elcograf S.p.A.

A catalogue record for this publication is available from the British Library.

ISBN 978-1-108-42742-5 Hardback
ISBN 978-1-108-44618-1 Paperback

Library
Services

For my parents, Josette and Chris

Not always entirely rational, but perhaps that is why I love them.

Contents

Acknowledgments

Like every other academic in the world, I am sometimes asked at a dinner party, on a bus, or in the gym, by those not in this peculiar line of work, what I research. "What are you working on now?" they often inquire. The past few years I have told them about a book I am writing on rationality, and how we should not assume that foreign policy decision makers are rational. "Don't we already know that?" (Some book editors have said the same.)

We should. But perhaps more than in any field other than economics, political scientists and international relations scholars have been taken with the rational actor model. We could chalk this up to tractability and simplicity. It provides a useful starting point. But as people like myself question this "assumption," it becomes clear that is a deeply rooted conviction of not a few. As they admit the implausibility of rationality assumption and claim to use it only as an analytical convenience, they simultaneously resist conclusions resting on other, more substantiated bases of human decision making consistent with the evidence. Even those who don't believe in universal rationality have often been reluctant to offer nonrational alternatives, choosing instead to broaden the scope of what encompasses rational behavior, such as appropriate behavior in a particular context given a set of norms. This is likely a result of a desire not to depart too far from the international relations mainstream as well as a reflection of the difficulty of understanding just how to explain nonrational behavior. Surely we are not in the psychiatry business.

So I am just going to say it: human beings are not always very rational, even the most highly educated among us (and those considerably less so) to whom we entrust our foreign policy. See, that wasn't so bad.

But that is not even the central argument of this book. My claim is that human beings systematically vary in their rationality, even if highly rational decision makers are relatively rare given the cognitive demands and effort required by active deliberation and maintaining objectivity (which is how I define rational thinking). Just as it wrong to always assume pure rationality, so it is folly to assume that everyone is always irrational. While it is certainly true that rationality is a function of situation and that every individual displays both tendencies every day, I focus in this book on stable individual-level differences. It is best to think of more rational or less rational individuals rather than irrational or rational ones, and to judge this based not on the outcomes of their decisions and the substance of their beliefs but on the process by which they form their judgments. Nonrational individuals display more intuitive, even impulsive thinking styles with fewer concerns about seeing things as they are.

This is not a book just about leaders, as some have tried to make it. Too often those who study the psychology of decision making are dismissed as "merely" doing foreign policy analysis. Even though the case studies are of four key figures in history, the conclusions are meant to matter for international relations Theory with a capital "T." The fact that our most rational foreign policy makers (in this book, Bismarck and Richelieu) are realists, and realists are rare, tells us a lot about how to approach the universality of realism as a theory of foreign policy. It is more exception than rule.

Rationality is best judged in relative terms, which necessitates that we understand at least one type of nonrational leader. Here I seized on romantics, fulfilling a longstanding wish I have had to integrate insights from the humanities with those of the social sciences. The humanities tell us a lot about being human, and taking our humanity seriously is at the heart of the psychological approach to explaining decision making. Doing so allows us to understand how Churchill and Reagan tick, figures who seem larger than life and ill explained by existing theoretical frameworks. That's because they were not very rational.

This book is itself a mixture of romantic and rationalistic scholarship. It is rationalistic in the sense that it seeks to carefully consider concepts and demonstrate their causal role in human decision making. It is romantic in trying to make a bold argument that recasts our understanding of rationality even if it has little chance of succeeding. In other words, I hope it combines the best of two increasingly separate types of international relations theorizing: the more traditional approach focused on taking big swings and initiating grand debates, and the more modern positivistic turn toward making tangible progress on tractable research questions with a careful focus on research design. The former laments the narrowing of our research aims and claims and the increasing technicality of our research methods – the lack of romance, as it were, in our scholarship. The latter complains of the pointlessness of grand theory ill suited and uninterested in testing its hypotheses in a rigorous way since no one is going to change their mind anyway. Both are right.

Now for the delicate task of thanking co-authors. Two of the chapters in this book are the result of close partnerships. Joshua Kertzer and I together designed and implemented the bargaining experiment, previously published in *International Organization*, that forms the basis of Chapter 4. This was the first step in testing the hunch that formed this book, and there was no one else who could help me carry this out. Gold, Jerry! Gold! Therese Anders was my research assistant for a year and a half, the best I have ever had. She helped me construct and analyze a data set comprising Churchill's speeches and comparing them with those of government speakers, which is at the heart of Chapter 9. I thank both of them for teaching an old dog new tricks.

I have had many important conversations that have guided me along the way, and I cannot remember them all. Jon Mercer, Rose McDermott, Kathleen Powers, Teresa Capeloz, William Wohlforth, Vincent Pouliot, Nicolas Wheeler, Aaron Rapport, Keren Yarhi-Milo, and Marcus Holmes had a particular impact. A master class with Justin Grimmer gave me the idea for the textual analysis of Chapter 8 and Justin was always available for Python-related advice. I thank audiences at Cornell University, Oxford University, Brigham Young University, Dartmouth College, University of Birmingham, Brown University, University of Toronto, Northwestern University, Chinese University of Hong Kong, and University of Washington, where I presented parts of the book. I received indispensable research support from the Dornsife College of Arts and Sciences, the German Academic Exchange Service, and the Center for International Studies at the University of Southern California.

I dedicate this book to my parents, to whom I owe the particular left- and right-brain combination (rational and nonrational, perhaps) that enabled me to put this all together. My mom received her bachelor's degree only in her forties, earning a degree in theology and going on to a successful career in, of all things, finance. I remember my mom with papers splayed across the bed when she was taking a class on art history, and I kept the textbook, which I have been carrying around for years. I cite it in this book in my review of romanticism. My dad is a numbers guy, an accountant who derives his greatest pleasure from singing in choirs. In loving and deep partnership with my wife, Nina, I am trying to encourage the same broad understanding and love of the world in my sons, Luc and Max, as they become fine young men who appreciate both science and the arts. Combining the two makes for better scholarship and better people.

Introduction: Three Theoretical Arguments, Four "Great Men" of History, Multiple Methods and Disciplines

Rationality is one of the most central concepts in the field of international relations, yet we have little idea of what it means. Theorists, even those whose entire approach is premised on the construct, seem almost reluctant to grapple with the concept. Rational choice scholars typically define it in minimal terms, as the pursuit of a set of carefully and consistently ranked preferences. Rationality is simply having a goal and working toward it. This somewhat trivial conception of rationality makes it hard to argue with, since it merely means purposive behavior. What, exactly, would be the alternative? A foreign policy based on whim and fancy? Leaders with no sense of how to achieve their aims or interest in doing so? This conceptualization likely explains the absence of voices calling rational choice's foundation into question. It is completely unobjectionable.

When anyone else talks of rationality, they surely mean much more than that. However, just what we mean has been hard to pin down. I conceptualize rationality as a type of thinking that is marked by two important features: a commitment to *objectivity* and active *deliberation*. Rationality means trying to see the world as it is, free from bias. And it requires active work, a systematic engagement with information. This *process* of rationality has been systematically overlooked in most international relations scholarship. Rationality requires much more than just a set of stable preferences. Without an effort to see the world objectively and to deliberate before acting, rational behavior is impossible. Instrumentally rational choices, in which a set of political actors make calculating and utilitarian judgments to maximize their interests in light of structural constraints, presupposes a particular type of cognition that neither rationalists nor any other types of international relations theorists can either assume or ignore. Rational choice requires rational thinking, and not all thinking is rational. I call this the *psychology of rationality*.

This book makes the case that some foreign policy leaders are systematically more rational than others. They have greater "epistemic motivation," a commitment to rational thought. *Rationality is a variable,* one that systematically distinguishes the thinking style of some leaders from that of others. Those who demonstrate greater procedural rationality – that is, a commitment to deliberation and objectivity – are those who engage in instrumentally rational behavior: a careful consideration of the costs and benefits of different courses of actions, an understanding of the likely moves of others, the updating of beliefs based on new information, and an assessment of the relative risks of different choices, among other types of calculations.

Since it is to a large degree a dispositional trait of individuals, rational thinking is not something that we should take for granted or simply assume, even in an anarchic environment that should incentivize it. Highly rational thinking is the normative goal, not the descriptive norm. It is the exception, not the default. This is something that classical realists have long stressed. An analysis of historical realist texts reveals theorists making more prescriptive than explanatory claims, admonishing leaders to make careful choices based on an unvarnished look at the realities of the system but generally disappointed that they do not. *Raison d'état* requires reasoning of state. Yet this claim goes against much, perhaps even most, contemporary international relations thinking. There is no more common bedrock assumption in the field than that of rational leaders.

Practitioners of Realpolitik, realists in practice, are the most prominent rational thinkers in foreign affairs. However, this book shows that realists are a very rare breed in international relations, likely because rational thinking requires considerable effort and is not always our default option. Realists celebrate the great realist statesmen such as Bismarck and Richelieu, whose accomplishments are captured in this book. However, this very fact shows their relative rarity. Realists are so noteworthy because they are so uncommon. In this book, I show that the realism of these statesmen has psychological foundations and that their thinking style distinguished them from most others, including their allies at home who shared their foreign policy goals. Rather than being the norm in our foreign policy makers, realism is the exception. Otherwise, we would not even notice it at all.

Part of the reason that we have spent so little time coming to terms with what rationality means and entails is that we lack a clear concept of what nonrational, or less than rational, cognition looks like. Nonrational thinking is intuitive and preconscious. It is not deliberative and effortful, but rather automatic and fast. Conceptualizing and demonstrating nonrational cognition allows us to see procedural rational processes more clearly. This type of thinking is difficult to observe. Because it is preconscious, it does not leave the same trail as a deliberative rational thought process. Nevertheless, we should not ignore it. Most psychologists believe that this type of thinking guides the predominance of our actions, behaviors, and choices every day. It seems unlikely that even foreign policy statesmen can completely avoid it. International relations scholars, however, are just starting to come to terms with it.

I focus on a particular type of nonrational figure in international relations. *Romantics* often leave a mark as prominent as our great realists, although in most ways they are exact opposites. They are distinguished by a belief in agency. Romantics see themselves as capable of overcoming structural obstacles and remaking the world as we know it. They act on behalf of an idealistic cause that cannot be compromised, despite the (inevitably) daunting odds they inevitably face in their struggle with others. What they lack in power, romantics hope to make up for in resolve. Where there is a will, there is a way. Just as scholars differ in terms of the stress they place on structure or agency in their explanations of political and social events (Dessler 1989), real-world individuals differ in terms of the degree of control they believe that humans have in their lives.

Romanticism gives us a sense of what an emotional, impulsive, and intuitive decision-making process looks like in foreign affairs. It reveals that a lack of rationality does not imply incoherence, aimlessness, and insanity, as it might seem. Unlike realists, romantics are not instrumentally rational; they do not adapt efficiently to the obstacles around them, making the best choices in light of structural constraints. Instead, they simply push on while disregarding (and without contemplating) their slim chances. However, romantics are purposive; they have goals. They just do not pursue them in a highly deliberative fashion. As we will see, we cannot understand Winston Churchill and Ronald Reagan without a notion of romanticism and the nonrational thinking style that it entails.

Like realists, romantics seem to be a rare breed in international relations. However, they often leave the world in a very different state than that in which they found it. As with the rationalist, we know a romantic when we see one, but we lack the systematic understanding that this book tries to provide.

Studying realists and romantics and their thinking styles also shows us that a great level of rationality is not always the key to success. Romantics have achieved great things in history, perhaps because of – rather than despite – their less rational cognitive style. A central theme of this book is that rational thinking and nonrational thinking both have their own advantages and disadvantages. Rationalists, of which realists are one kind, are judicious and cautious and generally do not take risky decisions that will likely leave their countries worse off. However, their tendency to deliberate, constantly weighing the pros and cons of different paths, can leave them paralyzed in situations with no good choice, of which there are many in international relations. Romantics are impulsive and emotional and often charge into political (and military) battle without any real consideration. Even so, we admire them for their dedication to principles and their decisive leadership. Sometimes they are right; what everyone else see as insuperable obstacles that cannot be overcome dissolve in the face of resolute resistance (although sometimes this also needs a bit of luck).

This book makes three sweeping theoretical arguments based on engagement with other disciplines in both the social sciences and the humanities, and tests them with a diverse and novel variety of methods. I rely not only on psychology, but also on philosophy and art history. I undertake careful case studies based on archival sources, primary texts, and interviews with former high-ranking government officials, but also utilize quantitative textual analysis and bargaining experiments in a computer laboratory.

First, we can observe systematic individual-level variation in rational thought, both across college undergraduates and across kings and prime ministers. Rational choice theory assumes that rational choice is universal and/or argues that rational thinking is inconsequential to rational behavior. I demonstrate otherwise. I conceptualize rationality by working backward from the psychological literature that finds fault with rationalist assumptions about human behavior, what is often known as the heuristics and biases literature. Bias substitutes for objective understanding, heuristics for calm and collected deliberation. Rather than basing one's beliefs on evidence, one chooses what one wants to believe. Rather than changing one's beliefs based on new information, one engages in belief perseverance and assimilation. Heuristics are simplifying devices that ease the process of thinking, acting as "theories" that serve as one-size-fits-all decision-making rules in place of a careful contemplation of information regarding the specific instance at hand.

In the behavioral literature on rationality drawn from psychology and behavioral economics, authors tend to conclude that human judgment and decision-making generally fall short of the often admittedly normative (i.e., ideal) standards of rational choice. This conclusion has been used in the foreign policy analysis literature to question the rationality assumption in international relations. This point, while important, can be pushed too far and distract us from another important observation. While few individuals, either ordinary or extraordinary, might meet the rational ideal, some get closer to it than others. In making the justified claim about the inappropriateness of a universally assuming rationality, we lose sight of important individual-level differences in rationality. While heuristics and biases are indeed common, this observation masks substantial heterogeneity. Both scholars in psychology and those who apply their insights to foreign policy neglect this fact and its implications for the study of international relations.

Contrary to the untested claims made by many rational choice scholars, rational thinking is essential for rational choice. We need procedural rationality to engage in "instrumental rationality." The latter is what is familiar to international relations scholars – the most efficient pursuit of interests in light of structural constraints. When we conduct a cost–benefit analysis, for instance, we must make a mental list of all the pros and cons, asking ourselves if what we want is attainable at acceptable costs. We must separately estimate the desirability of an outcome and its likelihood, particularly when, as is often the case in foreign affairs, the latter depends on a strategic understanding of others' motives. This requires both objectivity and deliberation.

I first demonstrate this in a bargaining experiment, not involving state leaders (of course), but rather college undergraduates. The laboratory offers what historical cases do not: a controlled environment in which all individuals perform the same task, and subjects whose dispositional attributes (such as the need for cognition and closure) can be directly surveyed in the exact same manner. In an experiment conducted with Joshua Kertzer, we find that those "little Bismarcks" who combine epistemic motivation with an egoistic preference structure better adjust their behavior to reflect changes in the strategic situation – in this instance, changes in the distribution of power. In a scenario resembling a repeated ultimatum game, they make better offers to others when they are in a weaker position and worse offers when they are in a stronger position. Those egoists with low epistemic motivation do not vary their behavior as much across those conditions, undermining their own selfish interests in the long run. They even do worse than prosocials, those persons committed to joint gains for both parties. The conclusion is that only those with a particular psychology act in the way that rational choice theorists expect. Rationality is psychological and varies across individuals.

We also see this relationship between procedural and instrumental rationality in the empirical chapters that follow. Combining bargaining experiments with real-world cases assures both internal and external validity. It better establishes causation and indicates that we are observing something potentially universal in human decision-making.

The second theoretical argument made in the book is that the rational leaders who combine foreign policy egoism with epistemic motivation are predisposed to be foreign policy realists, and those realists are rare in foreign policy-making. This is a deeply subversive finding, in that modern-day realists typically assume either that rational decision-making is compelled by the imperatives of the anarchic system, or that the system selects out those who do not meet this standard. However, the rarity of Realpolitik does not come as a surprise to classical realists, whose work exhibits a deep psychological strain that differentiates them from their contemporary, systemic-oriented cousins. Classical realists consistently suggest that objectivity and deliberation are essential preconditions of Realpolitik, but also insist that this procedural rationality is a difficult standard to meet. Classical realism is more prescriptive than descriptive, admonishing decision-makers to act solely in the interest of their country and to think rationally. They offer such advice precisely because they need to: Rationality is hard, and Realpolitik is hardly the norm in international politics.

How can I make such a sweeping claim? As subjects of study, I choose the two most famous realists of all time – Bismarck and Richelieu. Their cognitive style was deeply rational, marked by a commitment to deliberation and objectivity. This epistemic motivation was put to work in favor of egoistic, statist interests, producing all of the instrumentally rational behaviors we would expect. That part is uncontroversial. More striking is how unique both statesmen were in their home countries, opposed at every moment not just by domestic rivals who wanted their jobs, but also by others who detested their foreign policy programs. Neither patriarch of Realpolitik had any significant following domestically, making their accomplishments all the more striking. Their opponents sometimes offered alternative foreign policies that contrasted with realist egoism, arguing their country was bound by obligations to others outside of their countries, such as the Catholic Church or other legitimist sovereigns. They also often demonstrated a remarkably different cognitive style that was considerably less rational.

If these two "great men," with all their great successes, were politically rare animals at home, how can we say that Realpolitik – and by association, rationality – is anything but an exception in foreign policy-making? We remember Bismarck and Richelieu precisely because of their extraordinary qualities. And if we do not find consistently rational thinking at the highest levels of thinking, where the situational incentives to think deliberately and objectively are so intense given the stakes, where can we expect to find such rationality?

What about all the death and destruction wrought by the pursuit of power historically? Surely this war of all against all speaks for the prevalence of Realpolitik. I take issue with this claim as well. The use of force is not synonymous with realism. Indeed, the record shows that rational foreign policy in many instances seeks to avoid armed conflict, not on a moral basis but for egoistic reasons. Richelieu and Bismarck both engaged in strategic restraint at times, even in the wake of success, based on a recognition that pushing too far could undermine the hard-gotten gains. Human begins are perfectly able to do horrible things to each other for reasons other than the cold calculation of egoistic interests. In fact, realism often limits such applications of power.

The third argument made in this book is that we must come to understand and take more seriously nonrational thinking styles. The corollary of the claim that some individuals are more rational is that others are less so. As yet, we have not yet come to terms with what this might look like in practice. Rationalists sometimes rightfully ask, If individuals are not rationally pursuing their interests, then what are they doing? Any criticism of rationality seems to incorrectly imply a rudderless, inconsistent, and incoherent political actor of whose behavior we can make little sense. This does not do justice to the varieties of ways in which people, foreign policy leaders included, might think.

I utilize a distinction commonly made in the psychological literature between two different systems of cognitive processing. On the one hand, System II is effortful, slow, and conscious and corresponds to the procedurally rational mode of thinking. On the other hand, System I is automatic, quick, and intuitive. The contrast is commonly captured in everyday analogies such as the struggle between the head and the heart. All human beings utilize both systems of thinking, with System I acting as the default and System II being drawn in to sometimes double check and correct the inclinations of System I. System II cannot operate alone; it requires inputs from System I. Most importantly, System II needs the emotions that tell us what we care about, without which we have little to deliberate about. I claim that those who are more epistemically motivated draw more on System II, while others who are less rational are guided automatically through intuition. They are less self-aware of the dangers of bias, make more use of heuristics, and do not update their beliefs in light of feedback from the environment.

Intuition and nonrational thinking are central to the behavior of the romantic. Theorizing about romantics requires me to go even further afield than the sister social sciences of psychology and economics. I delve into the humanities, deriving insights from the literature on romanticism in the arts, literature, music, and philosophy, so as to systematically identify the essence of the romantic sensibility. This literature reveals that romantics are in many ways the antithesis of realists in their style of foreign policy-making. Where realists adjust policy in the face of structural obstacles such as the distribution of power, romantics have a sense of agency and aim to remake the world through the application of will and resolve. Where realists make decisions based on a utilitarian moral logic, stressing the tradeoffs that must be made between competing ideals, romantics reject this approach, arguing in a deontological fashion that no exception can be made to the pursuit of their ideals regardless of the exigencies of situations.

Not surprisingly, romanticism as a movement celebrated emotion over cold cognition, impulse and spontaneity over deliberation, and subjective creativity over the accurate reflection of reality. Indeed, without nonrational thinking, a romantic could not be a romantic. He or she would bend to structural obstacles encountered in the path and compromise his or her ideals in light of what was possible instead of summoning the inner resolve to push forward in struggles with adversaries with no concern for the consequences.

This is not a fanciful contrast. It has important implications for some of the most important events in world history. My case chapters about Winston Churchill and Ronald Reagan show that without romanticism, the Cold War might not have ended as quickly as it did and World War II might have had a very different outcome in which the Nazis fared much better. The successes of these two "great men" are perhaps owed not so much to their rationality but rather to their lack of it. In May 1940, Churchill would not accept considering a settlement with the Germans, even as rationalists in his cabinet concluded that the fall of France required that Britain adjust its expectations downward. Reagan rejected the rationalist premises of mutually assured destruction and sought a world without nuclear weapons, a desire that drove him to directly engage the Soviets in talks to radically reduce arms.

My argument might appear as a takedown of rational choice theory. I would maintain the opposite: It is a necessary corrective that puts rationalism on a much stronger theoretical and empirical footing. Only by making more realistic assumptions about the universality of rationality can rational choice be of use to the social sciences. Seeking to maintain the beliefs that (1) rational choice need not adequately represent the cognitive processes of those under study and (2) their behavior can be universally explained by a few simple decision-making principles creates a perverse incentive to disregard the overwhelming findings in other disciplines that this strategy is not working. In other words, rational choice theory exhibits a stark disregard for rationality itself, whose hallmark is the objective assessment of evidence, incorporating it in an actively deliberative process. I do not argue in this book that rationality is of no use in our study of international politics, but rather suggest that it is of particular use in describing the behavior of some individuals more than others. It is only by showing that some people behave in decidedly nonrational ways that rationality becomes a useful concept. I take up this issue in the conclusion.

In Chapter 1, I articulate further the logic, theory, and existing evidence for my first theoretical argument. Chapter 2 exports these insights to the field of international relations theory, showing the crucial role that rational thinking plays in realist theory and introducing the concept of the romantic. Chapter 3 tests the first theoretical argument in a bargaining experiment. From there, I proceed to the historical case studies.

The book dedicates two chapters to Bismarck, with a particular focus on the question of German unification. In Chapter 4 we see how the future chancellor of a unified Germany owed his start in politics to reactionary conservatives. With them, he shared a hatred of the democratic revolutions shaking Europe that threatened to bring down the kings and emperors who ruled by divine right. However, he parted company with them on issues of foreign policy. His fellow conservatives raised issues with his aggressive pursuit of Prussia's egoistic interests at the expense of conservative solidarity, particularly vis-à-vis the Austrian Empire. Bismarck believed a split was necessary to expel the Austrians from the German Federation and unify the dozens of German city-states, duchies, and kingdoms under Prussian leadership. To reach his goals, Bismarck was even willing to consider an alliance with liberals, the strongest proponents of a unified Germany in which the German people could exercise their collective self-determination.

With much effort, Bismarck finally pushed the king toward a "fratricidal" showdown with Austria. After decisively winning the war, as discussed in Chapter 5, Bismarck then had to restrain King Wilhelm I from pushing Prussian gains too far through extensive annexation. As we would expect from a rationally thinking realist, Bismarck had the entire chessboard in mind – the reactions of the other great powers and the necessity of maintaining good relations with Austria in the future. The king's opposition was all emotion, impulse, and righteous indignation – that is, System I rather than System II thinking. The now Chancellor Bismarck engaged in two other acts of strategic restraint. Rather than using Prussia's newfound power to dominate a unified Germany, he designed a Northern German Federation that maintained the crowns of German sovereigns and gave them significant autonomy. Rather than crushing liberal forces, in Germany he gave them a federal parliament based on universal suffrage to act as a counterweight to the centrifugal forces of German royals. In Prussia, he made peace with the liberals, provoking a final split with his reactionary patrons. These choices helped to consolidate the German unification project and laid the foundation for an easier incorporation of the remaining southern German states following the Franco-Prussian war.

We see remarkably similar themes in Chapter 6 on Cardinal Richelieu. Like Bismarck, Richelieu was not a sovereign, but rather the most powerful civil servant advising the king. The parallels are uncanny. Where Bismarck had to contend with those who believed in the bonds of conservative legitimacy, Richelieu fought against those who would brook no violation of Catholic solidarity in the wake of the Thirty Years War. The great practitioner of raison d'état alienated the most important political force at home, *les dévots* (the devoted), who opposed any break with fellow Catholic powers Spain and Austria during the Catholic Counter-Reformation. The cardinal asserted French influence in Italy during the Valtelline and Mantuan crises, challenging the Spanish and even fighting papal forces. Whereas the Prussian politician countenanced allying with Napoleon III and eventually partnered with the forces of democracy to unify and consolidate Germany, the cardinal struck up alliances with Protestant countries in an effort to resist the expansion of Spanish and Austrian influence in Germany. Like Bismarck, Richelieu also practiced strategic restraint at home. After personally putting down the Huguenots' last major rebellion, he convinced the king to maintain their religious freedom in what became known as the Grace of Alais. This effort to consolidate peace at home, based on Realpolitik pragmatism rather than genuine religious tolerance, further alienated him from *les dévots*. Consistent with his rational thinking style, Richelieu continually made utilitarian moral judgments rather than deontological ones, pursuing the lesser evil.

We then turn to our two romantics. I devote Chapter 7 and Chapter 8 to the person of Winston Churchill, with a particular focus on his role as the key opponent of Britain's appeasement strategy of the 1930s. Recent historiography, picked up on by international relations scholars, has made the case that British appeasement of Nazi Germany was rational, structurally compelled by the poor position in which the British found themselves during the 1930s. If appeasement was rational, however, does this mean that Churchill was not? I argue that this is indeed the case. Whereas Prime Minister Chamberlain and Foreign Secretary Viscount Halifax were highly rational thinkers, Churchill was a romantic with an intuitive thinking style. Understanding this is necessary to account for his resistance to appeasement.

Churchill had a romantic view of history in which events turned on the decisive choices and resolve of important individuals, not impersonal structural forces. He had a romantic understanding of Britain's role in the world as the vehicle of civilization. He viewed the Nazis through this heuristic, as the barbaric threat to what Britain stood for, forming his judgment quickly with little reflection and acknowledging no possibility that he could be wrong. His colleagues and historians describe him as emotional, intuitive, and impulsive, lacking in "judgment" – in other words, as decidedly less than rational in cognitive style. Where the appeasers adjusted to unfortunate circumstances, Churchill wanted to boldly remake them, summoning the will and resolve of the British people for a final showdown with the Nazi Germans.

We see this both qualitatively and quantitatively in Chapter 8. A quantitative analysis of the speeches of Churchill and government spokespersons in parliament during the 1930s shows that Churchill's syntax indicates a decidedly less rational thinking style when compared to that of Chamberlain and other realist government representatives. Churchill relies heavily on romantic terminology, stressing the importance of summoning will and resolve in the face of arduous circumstances, a battle between good and evil in which there was no choice but to fight. Archival documents reveal that Churchill's romanticism was a necessary condition in Britain's decision to fight on in May 1940 as France was falling. In light of Britain's deteriorating circumstances, Halifax and Chamberlain (now demoted) advocated making diplomatic approaches to Germany and Italy to explore the potential of a negotiated settlement. Churchill, now bearing the heavy burden of responsibility as prime minister, still rejected these ideas, arguing that the country's deteriorating structural position actually made it all the more necessary for Britain to fight on. Churchill in office was no different than Churchill in the wilderness, consistently romantic. This position was strikingly noble and the world thanks him for it, as the course of the war might have been very different otherwise. But it was decidedly nonrational.

Ronald Reagan, the focus of Chapter 9 and Chapter 10, was also a romantic, one whose thinking style had profound effects. Reagan was not a deliberative thinker, instead relying heavily on intuition. His simple home-spun stories and anecdotes, often apocryphal, served as heuristics he used to make sense of politics and even foreign policy. Aides describe how he made no effort to understand the details of major policy questions and demonstrated little interest even in distinguishing truth from fiction.

Reagan was elected on a platform consistent with his romanticism – one based on restoring America's belief in itself, and seeking to regain its footing through force of will and agency. Even the Cold War, which appeared to so many as an intractable and irresolvable struggle, could be overcome. Although fiercely protective of America's national interest,

Reagan could not accept the pragmatic, utilitarian, and highly rationalist logic of mutually assured destruction upon which American postwar security was built – the notion that nuclear weapons were a lesser evil that provided peace given their immense destructive ability. This explains his pursuit and insistent belief in the Strategic Defensive Initiative (SDI), which persisted despite the fact that virtually no one believed it was possible. His faith in agency also helps us account for his strong desire to personally negotiate arms control agreements with Soviet leaders. This bore fruit in the conclusion of the Intermediate Nuclear Forces Treaty of 1987, marking the beginning of the end of the Cold War.

Reagan's romanticism made him completely unique. Conservatives in his administration disliked his engagement of the Soviets and pursuit of arms control and endorsed SDI only in the hopes it would derail talks. Pragmatists were aghast at Reagan's thoughts of upending the pragmatic strategy of mutually assured destruction through nuclear abolition and wanted to use SDI only as a bargaining chip. Understanding Reagan as a romantic helps resolve what has been called the Reagan "paradox" – that the most strident of Cold Warriors, who backed the greatest arms build-up in postwar American history, was the same figure who pursued the abolition of nuclear weapons and brought about a rapprochement with the Soviet Union.

Rather than summarizing already summarized conclusions, I end the book with a consideration of how to think about rational choice theory in light of what we have found about rationality. Rational choice, despite its contributions to international relations theorizing, has a number of long-diagnosed pathologies preventing it from moving forward. In light of what we know about rationally, both conceptually and empirically, I push this argument to its logical end. At its worst, rational choice is irrational, resistant to disconfirming information, willfully resistant to observing the very processes on which theories depend, and insistent on applying an all-purpose heuristic to explain all of politics.

1   The Psychology of Rationality: Cognitive Style in International Relations

Research premised on the assumption of rational choice has played an enormous role in international relations scholarship, particularly in recent decades. From rational deterrence theory, to bargaining models of war, to strategic choice frameworks more broadly, rational choice represents one of the most prominent approaches in the study of world politics today (Achen and Snidal 1988; Fearon 1994, 1995; Keohane 1984; Lake and Powell 1999; Milner 1998). While rationalism has never gained traction in international relations scholarship to the same degree that it has in economics, what Tetlock and Mellers (2002) write about its hold in that discipline could be said of a good many scholars in mine: "Many psychologists will find it difficult to appreciate the tenacious grip that rational-choice theory holds over economics. To many economists, rationality is a self-evident truth; anyone foolhardy enough to promote a counterhypothesis carries a deservedly heavy burden of proof" (94).

Central to the rational choice framework is the notion of instrumental rationality – actors making decisions that maximize their expected utility in light of structural constraints (Glaser 2010: 2, 24; Rescher 1988: 1–2; Snidal 2002: 74–5). Whether one calls it the environment, circumstances, or situation, constraints affect any cost–benefit calculation, with rational actors making judgments based on the likely consequences of their actions (Lake 1999: 31; Parsons 2007).

While rational choice work has been enormously influential in political science, critics both inside and outside the discipline claim that in practice, individuals generally do not live up to the standard of strategic, calculating, and purposive decision-making implied in the approach (Lane 2003; Levy 2013; Lupia, McCubbins, and Popkin 2000; MacDonald 2003: 552). We have known this for a long time. Herbert Simon wrote almost fifty years ago of the "complete lack of evidence that, in actual human choice situations of any complexity, these computations can be, or are in fact, performed" (1955: 104). "Pure rationality is something of a fiction when applied to human behavior," conclude Huddy, Sears, and Levy (2013: 6). This criticism has increased in volume in light of innovations in cognitive science. McCubbins and Turner write that "what we take for granted about human thought" in political science (and by implication, international relations "has proved in cognitive sciences to be unimaginably more complex than anyone had expected; to be profoundly misrepresented by our supposedly bedrock, commonsense, intuitive notions" (2012: 390; also Lupia, McCubbins, and Popkin 2000: 3). Rational choice expectations are therefore considered normative rather than descriptive of actual human behavior, with little hope of narrowing the gap between the two (Elster 1986: 1; Quattrone and Tversky 1988: 35; Stanovich 2011: 3; Stein 1999). We strive for rationality but do not reach it.

This basic insight has driven the "heuristics and biases" literature in psychology and behavioral economics, which shows how human beings systematically depart from the standards implied by the rational choice literature (Fiske and Taylor 1984; Kahneman and Tversky 1982; Nisbett and Ross 1980; Tversky and Kahneman 1973, 1983). The heuristics and biases literature has been so enormously influential because it explicitly tests the expectations of rational choice models on their own turf, such as choices between gambles, and finds them lacking (Stanovich 1999, 2011; Tetlock and Mellers 2002: 94). Demonstrating the role of heuristics and biases has loomed large in international relations scholarship, ranging from the fundamental attribution error, to reasoning by analogy, to the use of reference points in the assessment of risk (Khong 1992; Levy 2013; McDermott 1998; Mercer 1996; Tetlock 1998).

The rationalist response to this critique has been either indifference or a counter-assertion that even if individuals do not act as expected utility maximizers, the models based on these assumptions are nevertheless useful for understanding, explaining, and predicting international politics. In this view, it simply does not matter how decision-makers make their choices, which in turn gives rationalists an excuse not to come to terms with cognitive processes. In international relations scholarship, Achen and Snidal (1989) have made this case most forcefully: "[A] major reason for the various axiomatizations of expected-utility theory is to show that decision-makers need not calculate. If they simply respond to incentives in certain natural ways, their behavior will be describable by utility functions" (164). Rationalism in international relations is "implicitly misconstrued as a theory of how decision-makers think. Mental calculations are never mentioned ... the theory makes no reference to them" (164). In fact, "No sensible person pretends that it summarizes typical deterrence decision making well" (152).

These rationalists are drawing a distinction between instrumental rationality and what Simon (1978) calls "procedural" rationality.

Whereas instrumental rationality is making the best choice possible given the constraints (Bueno de Mesquita 2014: 8; Lake and Powell 1999), procedural rationality comprises all of those cognitive processes we associate with rational decision-making, most importantly the unbiased analysis of information and careful deliberation. Procedural rationality is rational thought or reason, as opposed to rational choice. Rationalists are essentially claiming that individuals or any other decision-making unit can act and choose rationally without thinking rationally. "The individual decision makers analyzed by rational choice theorists can be, at one and the same time, rational in the limited instrumental sense, and irrational in the sense of the proceduralist," explains Zagare (1990: 243).

The notion that we need to pay little attention to the process of decision-making, while still understanding it as rational, seems far-fetched for an approach with "choice" in its very moniker. Rationalists claim to offer a theory of choice without looking at all at the choosing. Consider the description of Bruce Bueno de Mesquita, perhaps one of the scholars most responsible for advancing rational choice theory in international relations, of instrumental rationality: "[E]ach decision maker and each individual or group looks ahead, contemplating what the likely responses are if they choose this action or that action. Then they choose the action that they believe, based on looking ahead and working back to the current situation, will give them to best result" (2014: 28). Similarly, Elster (1999) writes, "Rational choice involves three optimizing operations. The action that is chosen must be optimal, given the desires and beliefs of the agent. The beliefs must be optimal, given the information available to the agent. The amount of resources allocated to the acquisition of information must be optimal" (285). That is a lot of thinking for an approach that claims not to have a theory of decision-making process. The complexity of that task means none of this should be assumed.

Ultimately, however, this is an empirical question. This book makes the case, both theoretically and empirically, that rational choice is not possible without rational thought; instrumental rationality is not possible without procedural rationality. The latter is a necessary condition. I hope to establish the counterhypothesis with the heavy burden of proof to which Tetlock and Mellers (2002) referred. If I am right, the implication is that rational choice cannot ignore cognition and psychology. Indeed, rationalism is *inherently* psychological.

However, there are reasons to believe that the heuristics and biases critique is too severe as well, particularly as it applies to international relations. It is one thing to doubt the rationality of the choices made by your neighbor, whose garden gnomes have already raised questions about his or her decisions. It is another thing to question the decisions of a powerful state leader whose psychology might vary systematically from that of the layperson and who labors under heavy structural constraints that serve as powerful pressures to think more rationally. This external validity concern looms large in any application of psychological theory to foreign policy-making.

While it might be the case that many individuals struggle to meet the benchmarks of rational decision-making set by those who stress the necessity of procedural rationality for rational choice, this need not be the case for everyone. In their efforts to discredit and dismiss rational choice, its critics have precluded or occluded the possibility that there might be significant variation among individuals in their level of rationality, as Stanovich and his colleagues have repeatedly argued (Stanovich 1999, 2011; Stanovich and West 1998, 2000). They have shown that while the average respondent in psychological studies does indeed exhibit the cognitive failures documented so extensively by psychologists and behavioral economists, many with only modest cognitive abilities nonetheless give the response considered normatively rational in rationalist models. Empirically, we see that the same individuals who tend to make one kind of mistake highlighted in the heuristics and biases literature tend to make the others as well. Errors are not random, but rather systematic. This suggests "true individual differences in rational thought" (Stanovich and West 2000: 649). It also warns us to get rid of the bathwater, but not the baby.

If procedural rationality is necessary for instrumental rationality, and if procedural rationality varies by individual, then some individuals will inevitably make more instrumentally rational choices than others. Thus, there are times when it is more or less appropriate to expect the normative ideal of instrumentally rational behavior in international relations based on how who is doing the deciding. How rare or frequent this is, however, is again an empirical question. Based on the case studies in this book, we should have our doubts.

By developing a theory of who is more or less likely to behave in such a fashion, I seek instead to subsume rationality into psychology, establishing the unique psychology of *Homo economicus*. As Mercer (2005: 78) argues, rationality is not free of psychology. This lends a systematicity to the hodge-podge theorizing that often characterizes psychological approaches in international relations. What we might call the first generation of psychological critics of rationalism in international relations generally treat rational behavior as a normative baseline and use psychology to explain systematic departures from that benchmark (Lebow 1981; Lebow and Stein 1989; Mercer 2005; Stein 1988). Psychology then becomes a theory of mistakes on the part of decision-makers, which in turn points out the mistakes of rationalist theory. I think it can be (is) more than that. I move forward from this necessarily negative set of early findings to what I hope to be a new generation of positive psychological theorizing. We know now that many people are *not* rational in the ideal sense, but *who* is more or less rational? Psychological theory in international relations is to a large degree about both who acts and who does not act rationally and what this means.

Importantly, rational choice theory remains crucial for understanding international relations. Its application is simply bounded by, among other things, the cognitive styles of foreign policy decision-makers. Rather than unrealistic universalist assumptions about thinking, this book provides some guidance about where rationalism might apply and where it will not. It therefore contains an admonition to rationalism to be pragmatic, finding victories in some places while conceding in others.

Rationality as Objectivity and Deliberation: Avoiding Heuristics and Biases

I do not believe that we have as yet truly distilled the essence of procedural rationality. We can do so, however, by working backward from those who have done the most work in knocking down the universalistic rationalist assumption – that is, scholars in the heuristics and biases tradition. Rather than deliberating carefully, individuals rely on heuristics as cognitive shortcuts. Rather than objectively analyzing their constraints in an effort to maximize their interests, their information processing is biased. Therefore the key elements of rational thought are objective understanding and deliberation.

The rational thinker tries to develop the most accurate understanding possible of the world around him or her (Elster 2009: 11; Epstein et al 1996; Stanovich 2011: 88; Stanovich and West 1998). In other words, rational thinkers aim to be objective. Rationality involves the pursuit of the truth: not in its normative right or wrong sense – Truth with a capital "T", which can never be established – but rather what is truly real rather than imagined. Rational thinkers attempt to observe their environment impartially and without bias (Stanovich 2011: 105; Stanovich and West 1988). Stanovich (2011) writes that "rationality concerns how well beliefs map onto the actual structure of the world" (6). This does not guarantee success, but any approximation of rational thinking seems to be impossible without the self-conscious effort to see things as they are. The primary obstacle to objective understanding is bias.

Developing such an accurate understanding of the world, free from bias, requires the collection of information, a process that is often invoked in definitions of rationality (Baron 1985; Elster 2009: 11; Stanovich 2011: 36). Rational thinking requires an active approach to information gathering. This process is continuous; it does not end after settling on a particular conclusion. Thus, rational thinking is open-minded in nature. The rational thinker never closes himself or herself off from new evidence (Baron 1985; Lupia, McCubbins, and Popkin 2000; Stanovich 2011: 168; Stanovich and West 1998). Such a person is always willing to reconsider his or her beliefs, even if comfortable with previous conclusions. Rationalists call this "updating," the process by which incomplete information becomes more complete as more data are collected (Kydd 2005). Unlike rationalists, however, psychologists do not simply assume that this process occurs unproblematically and universally. Instead, they find much reason to believe this element of rationality is honored more in the breach than the observance.

Nevertheless, even as the goal is greater understanding, objectivity requires recognizing what one does not know. Lupia, McCubbins, and Popkin (2000) note, "The highest form of knowledge, Socrates famously observed is knowledge of one's own ignorance" (171). Rational thinkers must be comfortable with uncertainty. Rationality requires some degree of cognitive modesty, avoiding leaps to judgment. Rational thinkers only know what they have reason to believe, calibrating certainty to evidence (Baron 1982; Stanovich 2011: 35). There are no beliefs absent evidence.

At first blush, this seems uncontroversial, even trivial. However, such is not the case, for two reasons. First, fighting bias takes cognitive work. Simply by virtue of our need to make decisions quickly, we might have a tendency toward "unmotivated bias" – that is, bias generated by cognitive limitations. Perhaps more importantly for international relations, objectivity requires fighting the ever-present temptation to believe what we want to believe (Elster 1989: 37; Stanovich 2011: 34). Psychologists call this "motivated bias," with "motivated" being used to indicate that we are willing our lack of objectivity; it is not a problem of cognitive limitations. The truth, as we know, is often painful, and we often believe what we want to believe. Therefore, unsurprisingly, psychologists have consistently uncovered ways in which individuals choose to believe their own subjective truths despite evidence to the contrary, what is known as "belief perseverance" (Khong 1992; Nisbett and Ross 1980; Tetlock 1998). They interpret information in a twisted manner so as to leave their comfortable fundamental assumptions untouched, a phenomenon known as "belief assimilation." They also selectively seek out information that bolsters their preexisting attitudes while discarding evidence that contradicts those beliefs, what is called "confirmation bias." All of these tendencies have been documented at the level of foreign policy decision-making as well.

Human beings often do not recognize their own uncertainty either, demonstrating a consistent tendency toward overconfidence (Einhorn and Hogarth 1981; Fischhoff, Slovic, and Lichtenstein 1977). They are much more confident in their beliefs than information warrants (Baron 1985; Kruglanski and Webster 1996; Tetlock 2005). Mitzen and Schweller (2011) note that this "misplaced certainty" is much more of a problem in international relations than the uncertainty on which theorists generally focus: "Because the need for cognitive economy impairs rational and efficient information-processing, leaders' perceptions of others' intentions, resolve, trustworthiness and capabilities often persevere in the face of credible evidence and costly signals to the contrary" (20).

Rationality is also deliberative in nature (Baron 1985; Epstein et al. 1996; Stanovich 2011: 36). Rather than "reason" as a noun, in which we need to have a basis for believing something to be objectively true, this is "reason" as a verb. Instead of relying on intuitions, rational thinking requires analysis. Rather than impulsively and reflexively making quick choices, rational thinking necessitates considered and therefore more time-consuming scrutiny. Rational thinkers are "reflective," "engaged," and "active" (Kahnemann 2011: 46; Stanovich 2011: 14, 15; Stanovich and West 1988). They are constantly thinking (Bueno de Mesquita 2014: 28; Lake and Powell 1999; Lupia, McCubbins, and Popkin 2000: 8; MacDonald 2003: 552; Simon 1983: 13). However, rather than undertake a thorough consideration of the issue at hand, we often base our judgments on vivid, personal experiences that have high emotional but little informational content, even in foreign policy (Nisbett and Ross 1980; Yarhi-Milo 2014).

Heuristics help us avoid deliberation (Evans 2008; Kahnemann et al. 1982: ch. 1; Lupia, McCubbins, and Popkin 2000). As Nisbett and Ross (1980) explain:

Few, if any, stimuli are approached for the first time by the adult. Instead, they are processed through preexisting systems of schematized and abstracted knowledge – beliefs, theories, propositions, and schemas. These knowledge structures label and categorize objects and events quickly and, for the most part, accurately. They also define a set of expectations about objects and events and suggest appropriate responses to them (7).

Heuristics are, by definition, decision-making shortcuts, rules of thumb that serve as one-size-fits-all beliefs saving us from rationality's demand to carefully assessing every situation individually (Gigerenzer 2007: 18). They "extract only a few pieces of information from a complex environment" (39).

Heuristics allow us to engage in "top-down," "theory-driven" rather than "data-driven" analysis, in which we apply preexisting beliefs to make sense of the world, rather than allowing the world to reveal itself to us (Fiske and Taylor 1984: 98; Tetlock 2005). Theory-driven research sounds scientific and, by association, rational. However, the heuristics we use to make sense of the world are often derived from simplistic rules. Fiske and Taylor (1984) write, "As people's theories and concepts about the world, schemas are concerned with the general case ... the message of schema research has been that people simplify reality by storing knowledge at a molar, inclusive level, rather than squirreling away, one-by-one, all the original individual experiences in their raw forms, which would be pure data-driven processing" (98). For instance, if we reason by analogy, we are avoiding the deliberative process, instead looking for generally superficial similarities between a current situation and a previous one based on "availability" and "representative" heuristics, something that has been found to occur in international relations as well (Khong 1992). "Theory" is used by the layperson to think less systematically, not more.

There is a longstanding research program in international relations documenting the importance of foreign policy belief systems as heuristics that allow foreign policy-makers to quickly formulate positions on questions of international relations (and researchers to predict the latter) (George 1969; Hermann, Tetlock, and Visser 1999; Holsti and Rosenau 1988, 1990; Rathbun 2004, 2007; Wittkopf 1990). These belief systems act as subjective lenses that color the perceptions of decision-makers. For instance, foreign policy-makers frequently invoke the importance of credibility and resolve in dealing with other states in the international system (Fettweis 2013). This heuristic tells us that adversaries take advantage of any sign of weakness, the familiar refrain of "avoiding Munich" (Jervis 1976). This might be true in any particular situation, but it is unlikely that it always applies. Outside of international relations, in our everyday affairs, we call this stereotyping (Kruglanski and Webster 1996). This phenomenon affects even elites and academics. In his study of elites, Tetlock (1998) finds "a disturbing double standard in which judgments ... are driven ... by the consistency of the evidence with preconceptions, not by the rigor of the research procedures." He concludes, "The data initially look unpromising for defenders of human rationality" (357).

Objectivity and deliberation are, of course, closely intertwined. Heuristics "provide an interpretive framework for the lay scientist – one that resolves ambiguity and supplements the information 'given' with much 'assumed' information" (Nisbett and Ross 1980: 29). Heuristics do more than just make us cognitively lazy: we also use them to override our objectivity, making new data fit old beliefs (Nisbett and Ross 1980: 38). Once in place, the heuristics are applied to filter new information. However, to develop an accurate understanding of the world around us, we need to remain open to what it tells us, and then subsequently take those inputs and adjust our beliefs accordingly, which requires deliberation. Tetlock (2005) finds that the use of theory-driven thinking is associated with insufficient levels of updating in the face of disconfirming evidence.

Rationality Is a Variable: Individual Differences in Objectivity and Deliberation

Based on the findings in the heuristics and biases literature, most psychologists have generally drawn the conclusion that rational thinking is quite rare. However, this critique can be taken too far. While it might be the case that many individuals struggle to meet the benchmarks of procedural rationality, this need not be the case for everyone. In their efforts to discredit and dismiss rational choice, psychologists have precluded the possibility that there might be significant variations among individuals in their level of rationality, a point made in the psychological literature most consistently by Keith Stanovich (Stanovich 2011; Stanovich and West 2000). He points out that while the average respondent in psychological studies might exhibit the cognitive failures documented so extensively by psychologists and behavioral economists, many persons with only modest cognitive abilities (i.e., intelligence) nonetheless give the response considered normatively rational in rationalist models. Too much attention is paid to the modal response and not enough to individual-level differences. More importantly, empirically we see that the same individuals who tend to make one kind of mistake highlighted in the heuristics and biases literature tend to make the other kinds of mistakes as well. Errors are not random but rather systematic. This suggests "true individual differences in rational thought" (Stanovich 2000: 649). I follow Simon's (1978) longstanding advice that "a theory of rational behavior must be quite ... concerned with the characteristics of the rational actors – the means they use to cope with uncertainty and cognitive complexity" (8).

Stanovich and his collaborators note that psychologists and behavioral economists in the heuristics and biases tradition are largely dedicated to uncovering systematic patterns in human decision-making. This makes sense, given that the original purpose was to raise significant questions about the overall value of utilitarian assumptions drawn from economics. However, this does leave unexplored the possibility of significant individual-level differences that have been "long ignored" (Stanovich 2011: 10). The same can be said for much of the psychological literature on elite foreign policy decision-making. Its main contribution is often to disrupt rationalist models, showing the same heuristics and biases that are at play among the lay public. This is different, however, than offering a systematic account of individual differences in the propensity to exhibit those cognitive "failings."

An enormous body of work in cognitive psychology and related disciplines points to individual-level variation in what is known as "epistemic motivation." Epistemic motivation is a commitment to rational thought. According to Jost et al. (2003), "Epistemic motives, by definition, govern the ways in which people seek to acquire beliefs that are certain and that help to navigate social and physical worlds that are threateningly ambiguous, complex, novel, and chaotic. Thus, epistemic needs affect the style and manner by which individuals seek to overcome uncertainty and the fear of the unknown" (351). Those with epistemic motivation feel "the need to develop a rich and accurate understanding of the world" (De Dreu and Carnevale 2003: 236). In other words, they aim for objectivity. Many cognitive attributes fall under the rubric of epistemic motivation, the most important of which are "need for closure" (Kruglanski and Webster 1996; Webster and Kruglanski 1994) and "need for cognition" (Cacioppo and Petty 1982; Cacioppo et al. 1996). These attributes are utilized by others in their efforts to establish variation in rational thinking, although they do not always label it as such (Stanovich 1999, 2011; Tetlock 2005).

The "need for cognition" concept is based on the finding that individuals vary in the degree to which they engage in effortful cognitive activity. As Cacciopo et al. (1996) explain, "Some individuals tend to act as cognitive misers in circumstances that call forth effortful problem solving in most individuals, whereas others tend to be concentrated cognizers even in situations that lull most individuals into a cognitive repose" (197). Those with the need for cognition deliberate more and try harder to develop objective understandings. They "tend to seek, acquire, think about, and reflect back on information to make sense of stimuli, relationships and events in their world. ... [They] are characterized generally by active, exploring minds and, through their senses and intellect, reach and draw out information from their environment" (199). In other words, their thinking is more procedurally rational.

The "need for closure" is an inversely related construct based on the premise that some individuals have a demonstrated propensity toward "motivated closing of the mind" (Kruglanski and Webster 1996). Disliking ambiguity and uncertainty, they feel an urgency to make up their minds quickly and display a greater resistance to revising their beliefs in the light of disconfirming evidence. They "seize" and "freeze." Seizing is the expression of an "urgency tendency." Those with a high need for closure do not engage in the slow and effortful collection of information necessary to gain objective understanding. Freezing is the expression of a "permanence" tendency. Those with a high need for closure deliberate no further once they have settled on their beliefs. Those with a high need for closure are more likely to leap to judgments on the basis of inconclusive evidence and exhibit rigidity of thought and a reluctance to entertain views different from their own. They do not know what they do not know, nor do they want to. They aim instead for "decisiveness" (Webster and Kruglanski 1994). Those with a lower need for closure, in contrast, are reluctant to commit early to a definite opinion and are open to considering alternatives even after they form an initial judgment. Paradoxically, those with a greater need for closure feel more assured of their beliefs – demonstrating what we called overconfidence earlier – even though those beliefs were formed with far less deliberation. A low need for closure, in comparison, is a demonstration of cognitive humility.

Webster and Kruglanski (Kruglanski and Webster 1996; Webster and Kruglanski 1994) also note an association of closure-seeking with a desire for secure knowledge that can be relied upon on across circumstances. Beliefs that provide general rules allow individuals with a high need for closure to avoid reassessing their "priors" in every new instance. In other words, the need for closure predisposes individuals toward use of heuristics.

Those with high epistemic motivation put their mind where their mouth is: They demonstrate more procedural rationality. The need for cognition is empirically associated with a tendency to base judgments and beliefs on empirical information as well as a propensity to seek out and scrutinize relevant data when making decisions (Berzonsky and Sullivan 1992; Cacioppo et al. 1996; Leary et al. 1986). Such individuals are more responsive to arguments higher in quality than are those individuals who are lower in need for cognition, regardless of whether they confirmed or disconfirmed their initial expectations (Cacioppo, Petty, and Morris 1983; Priester and Petty 1995). High cognizers remain more committed to objectivity, keeping an open mind. They also have a reduced susceptibility to the fundamental attribution error (D'Agostino and Fincher-Kiefer 1992) of such importance in international relations (Mercer 1996), and engage in more intense information searches before forming judgments (Verplanken, Hazenberg, and Palenewen 1992). Need for closure is associated with the use of a reduced number of hypotheses to explain events, reduced information processing, and an enhanced reliance on early cues (Mayseless and Kruglanski 1987).

This is not just true at the mass level. Elites, even academics themselves, exhibit significant variation in their procedural rationality. Tetlock (2005) distinguishes between "foxes," equivalent to our rational thinkers, and "hedgehogs," who are distinguished largely through their responses to items from the need for cognition and need for closure scales. He writes, "High need for closure, integratively simple individuals are like Berlin's hedgehogs: they dislike ambiguity and dissonance in their personal and professional lives, place a premium on parsimony, and prefer speedy resolutions of uncertainty that keep prior opinions intact. Low need for closure, integratively complex individuals are like Berlin's foxes: they are tolerant of ambiguity and dissonance, curious about other points of view, and open to the possibility they are wrong" (75). Foxes are situationally minded and data driven, "content to improvise ad hoc solutions to keep pace with a rapidly changing world" (20–1). Hedgehogs are heuristic driven; they aim to "expand the explanatory power of that big thing to 'cover' new things" (20–1).

Not only are hedgehogs less likely to predict political phenomena in their area of expertise, but, paradoxically, they express more confidence in their initial incorrect judgments. Hedgehogs are also less likely to change their beliefs when they do not come to fruition, adjusting less even though their degree of failure is greater than that of foxes. "This latter pattern is not just contra-Bayesian," writes Tetlock (2005). "It is incompatible with all normative [read: rational] theories of belief adjustment" (128).

Rational thinking is dispositional, stylistic, and a matter of degree. Epistemic motivation is an individual-level difference that distinguishes some human beings from others across situations, even if some circumstances encourage it more than others. The term "motivation" is used advisedly. Epistemic motivation lies at the "intentional" level of analysis. In other words, it is under the control of individuals. Because it is hard work, epistemic motivation implies a commitment to rationality.

This distinguishes epistemic motivation from one's cognitive abilities, which act as a more structural barrier to behaving rationally by reducing one's capacity for making computations. Numerous studies, although finding a positive correlation between intelligence and epistemic motivation, demonstrate that the latter's effect remains robust to the inclusion of the former in various cognitive tasks (Cacioppo et al. 1996; Stanovich 2011: 34). Intelligence and epistemic motivation are not reducible to each other, and the former does not trump the latter.

Much work in political psychology and foreign policy-making – mine included (Rathbun 2004, 2007a) – has been preoccupied with ideological belief systems and the effects they have on foreign policy choice. Here the focus is instead on cognitive style (Baron 1985). As Tetlock's expert study concludes, "What experts think matters far less than how they think" in terms of their good judgment (2005: 2). The need for cognition is "process oriented" – based on "individuals' enjoyment and tendency to engage in effortful cognitive activity – rather than outcome oriented" (Webster and Kruglanski 1994). Similarly, those with a high need for closure are not motivated to draw any specific substantive conclusion; they merely seek an early end to their uncertainty. Any answer is desirable as long as it is definite. The need for closure aims at "nonspecific" closure (Webster and Kruglanski 1994).

A focus on dispositions allows us to use rational thinking as a variable without having to develop a test establishing once and for all a benchmark for rationality. By allowing rational thought to vary, we preserve the very concept. If everyone is simply presumed to be a rational utility maximizer, what use is there in the concept?

It is more useful to think of procedural rationality not as an absolute attribute that an individual either does or does not possess, but rather as something that varies along a continuum. As Baron (1994) writes, "Rationality is a matter of degree. It makes sense to say that one way of thinking is 'more rational' or 'less rational' than another" (36). Stanovich (2011) notes that it is difficult to measure whether thinking is optimally rational; it is easier to know "whether a person is committing a thinking error, rather than whether their thinking is as good as it can be" (6). As Tetlock (1998) writes, "There is no sharp dividing line between rationality and irrationality" (337). Therefore in this book I will refer to more or less rational individuals. However, if a particular individual exhibits very strong tendencies in one direction or another, I sometimes refer to rationalist and nonrationalist figures. This is nevertheless meant as a relative distinction, not as a final pronouncement on or diagnosis of any particular individual.

None of this precludes the possibility that situational factors, such as high stakes and group decision-making, can also induce procedural rationality. The argument here is that some individuals are more or less predisposed than others in that direction. Whether situation trumps disposition is ultimately an empirical question, one very relevant for international relations and partially explored in the next chapter. It might be that situation and disposition act independently of each other, with each contributing to procedural rationality. Or it might be that more rational thinkers are more inclined to react to structural circumstances. Structure and disposition could interact.

Rational Thought and Rational Behavior: Instrumental Rationality Requires Procedural Rationality

Having clarified what we mean by rational thought, I will make the case that procedural rationality of this kind is necessary for instrumentally rational behavior. As Stanovich (2011) writes, instrumental rationality is the "maximization of goal achievement via judicious decision-making" and the "thinking dispositions of the reflective mind are a means to these ends" (38). In the same vein, Rescher (1988) writes, "To behave rationality is to make use of one's intelligence to figure out the best thing to do in the circumstance." Most rationalists themselves deal little with procedural rationality, focusing instead on instrumental rationality in which agents are in pursuit of the most efficient means of reaching their goals (see, for instance, Elster 1989: 22–5).

These are not one and the same. Instrumental rationality lends itself to purposive, goal-seeking endeavors. However, we can use procedurally rational thinking for nonpurposive ends, such as puzzling about the nature of the universe and whether there is a God. Inquiring minds simply want to know, regardless of what it gets them.

There are two key elements of instrumental rationality: goals and constraints. Procedural rationality does not necessarily have an end in mind, whereas instrumental rationality does. Reason is an instrument in the pursuit of my aims (Simon 1983: 7). There are any number of things that I can think that do not require a choice between alternatives, which is the province of instrumental rationality. I can believe that Vladimir Putin is dangerous to American interests based on a set of beliefs drawn from Russian behavior. This is of no consequence for instrumental rationality until I am tasked with securing, for instance, American interests vis-à-vis Russia. Now I must wed the rational thought process to goal-seeking behavior. For instance, I might judge alternative paths of action based on my beliefs about the "type" of adversary I am facing. Those goals, of course, are completely up to the decision-maker in question; this is the "subjective" in subjective utility theory. Rationality makes no claim on the substance of our desires.

Instrumental rationality also assumes some kind of constraints. If we can simply have everything we want, we do not have to make choices at all; we are in the Garden of Eden. No instrumental thinking is really necessary, save perhaps directing our arm to casually lift our hand so that the luscious fruit (Not apples! Don't eat the apple!) drops effortlessly into our grasp. Once we introduce a limitation on the supply of food, such as seasons, and even worse, a food hoarder whose consumption endangers our well-being and maybe even our life, we have to start to think instrumentally. Now the environment has literally entered the equation.

Constraints beget restraint. We cannot have it all if there are constraints, or, if we do, it will require a very careful process to secure it. "Rationality is realistic; it does not require more than is possible" (Rescher 1988: 9). Instrumental rationality takes into account what we want but also what we need and makes choices between the two. The probabilities of different outcomes – that is, their feasibility – are part of any expected utility calculation.

Instrumental rationality is judged by its efficiency. Have I made the best choice, given my alternatives, my goals, my environmental constraints, and the information available? "Optimization in what one thinks, does, and values is the crux of rationality," writes Rescher (1988). Instrumental rationality has a "crucial economic dimension" even if decisions do not involve material or economic goals at all (Rescher 1988).

Instrumental rationality requires substantial objectivity and deliberation lest it result in significantly suboptimal behavior. If decision-makers are optimizing given constraints, then they are forced to consider the pluses and minuses of different courses of action in securing their goals. Cost–benefit analyses are at the very heart (perhaps, better said, "head") of the model of *Homo economicus* and his utilitarian judgments. These types of calculations are cognitively difficult and emotionally unpalatable. We can assume, for instance, that decision-makers will not want to believe that civilian casualties will accompany a military strike they believe to be in the national interest or that a new entitlement program will blow an enormous hole in the budget.

As rationalist theories remind us, political actors are often involved in situations of strategic interdependence since outcomes are a product of both their choices and those of others. Therefore they must also take into account their beliefs about what others will do. This requires trying to understand, as best as possible, what the other wants and perceives, often about oneself. This problem of understanding the other has been problematized by generations of psychologically minded international relations theorists (Jervis 1976; Rathbun 2012). It is cognitively difficult to put oneself in others' shoes, even if only for the instrumental reason of furthering one's own goals (Larson 2011: 24). Foreign policy-makers often substitute certainty for uncertainty (Mitzen and Schweller 2011). In security interactions with adversaries, decision-makers often proceed on the basis of the "inherent bad faith" model in which they "know" that the other means them harm (Holsti 1962).

A significant body of evidence suggests that those who have greater epistemic motivation are more likely to behave in an instrumentally rational fashion (Stanovich 2011: 24). In a series of laboratory experiments, Stanovich and colleagues have replicated many of the tasks from the heuristics and biases literature while also measuring individuals' epistemic motivation, captured largely with measures of cognitive closure and need for cognition (Stanovich 2000; Stanovich and West 1998). Importantly, epistemic motivation predicts what would be considered normatively correct behavior in all cases, even when controlling for individual variation in cognitive abilities (Bartels 2006; Chatterjee et al. 2000; Klacyznski and Lavallee 2005; Kokis et al. 2002; Ku and Ho 2010; McElroy and Seta 2003; Newstead et al. 2004; Pacini and Epstein 1999; Parker and Fischoff 2005; Perkins and Ritchhart 2004; Shiloh, Salton, and Sharabi 2002; Simon, Fagley, and Halleran 2004; Smith and Levin 1996; Stanovich and West 1998, 2000; Toplak and Stanovich 2003; Verplanken 1993). In short, more procedurally rational individuals are less guilty of those cognitive failings that have led many to question the usefulness of assuming rational behavior in politics. Tetlock (2005) has reached the same conclusions using experts.

The Head and the Heart: Dual-Process Models of Cognition

To this point we have devoted all of our time to understanding rationality but little to nonrationality. What does nondeliberative thinking look like? Indeed, can we even call it thinking at all?

It has become commonplace in psychology to differentiate broadly between two decision-making "systems" (Bargh and Chartrand 1999; Bazerman et al. 1998; Bickerton 1994; Chaiken 1980; Epstein et al. 1996; Evans 1984; Gawronski and Bodenhausen 2006; Johnson-Laird 1983; Kahnemann 2011; Metcalfe and Mischel 1999; Shiffrin and Schneider 1977; Sloman 1996; Smith and DeCoster 2000; Stanovich 2011: 18; Strack and Deutsch 2004; Toates 2006). In this "dual-processing" account of judgment, "System I" processing is described as automatic, intuitive, unconscious, reflexive, rapid, and impulsive. This is thought to be the system that guides most of our daily lives, only infrequently overridden by System II processing. The latter is deliberative, effortful, reflective, systematic, analytic, conscious, and explicit.

System I is a "hot" system, often emotional in character, which induces individuals to act quickly, without explicit thinking, based on their "gut feelings" (Gigerenzer 2007). System II is a "cold" system that proceeds slowly as individuals careful consider their beliefs and choices. As Kahnemann (2011) notes, System II is what we generally think of as rational in nature, although he himself avoids using the term in this way. Following other psychologists – most notably Stanovich, who himself originated the distinction – I embrace it.

Every individual utilizes both systems. They are both part of our neural architecture as human beings. System II processing is sometimes called in to check on and override our System I judgments (Kahenmann 2011). However, it is generally thought that most tasks in our lives involve little such conscious and deliberate thinking. System I suits us well when we continue to encounter the same situations over and over (Nisbett and Ross 1980: 38). Its presence is likely a function of our evolutionary past when rapid, quick judgments were superior, in a survival sense, to waiting and collecting more information. As Nisbett and Ross (1980) explain, we are attentive to vivid information for a reason: "During all but the most recent moments of our evolutionary history, dangers and opportunities have been relatively concrete and vivid. Saber-toothed tigers and food and water resources are highly palpable entities" (60).

The advantage of our preconscious cognition is its speed. System I processing is not procedurally rational but it has been ecologically rational. It is an efficient adaptation to the environment we once lived in and might still be valuable today, argue some (Gigerenzer 2007). Indeed, it is often stressed that heuristics – a key crutch of System I processing that are often utilized without conscious knowledge – likely perform very well in most instances, and without them our cognitive load would be crushing. I take up this issue again in later sections of this chapter (Nisbett and Ross 1980: 7, 34, 38).

System I is not procedurally rational, but this negative attribute does not give us a positive sense of what it is. System I is driven by *intuition,* "a general category of preanalytical nonreasoning based on knowing without knowing how you know. Intuitions are mental states that serve a belief-like function but are antecedent to beliefs. These are typically instantaneous responses to an environment or stimuli. Intuitions may be formed through affective processes or learned experience and play an important role in the decision-making process" (Holmes 2015: 713). Intuition is called "associative" in nature, in the sense that it guides us to behave based on a stimulus even before we recognize what the stimulus is. We instantly jump up when a bug crawls up our neck, for instance. Bugs are scary even before we think about what they can do.

Intuition has found a place in the "practice turn" in constructivist theorizing, which maintains that most forms of thinking hypothesized in international relations, despite the varying theoretical perspectives behind them, share something in common: They presume a conscious representation of reality on the part of the political actor. Practice theory maintains instead that much of human action is driven by a nonconscious "logic of practice" – hunches, feelings, and intuitions that cannot be articulated by those doing the acting. In politics, as in life, humans learn by doing rather than reflecting (Pouliot 2008). Practice theory explicitly acknowledges its debt to the System I/II distinction.

I use intuition differently, as a marker of a decidedly nonrational (or less than rational) cognitive style that characterizes some individuals more than others. While some use System I and II to describe the very different types of processing that all human beings engage in, others have noted that there are individual-level differences in the degree to which they use "intuitive–experiential" and "analytical–rational" thinking styles (Epstein et al. 1996). Therefore, while everyone uses System I most of the time and System II some of the time, we can still speak of meaningful differences among individuals in their relative reliance on these systems.

Emotions are thought to be the raw material of intuitions. After all, the latter are "gut *feelings*," and emotion provides us with our automatic urge to act in a particular way, even without deliberation or cognitive representation of the problem at hand. However, the relationship between emotion and rationality is still an area of significant contestation, with many making the case that there is no rationality without preconscious emotional input, thereby calling into question the System I/II conceptualization. The most important contribution in this field is the "somatic marker" hypothesis of Antonio Damasio and collaborators. Damasio (1994) hypothesizes that formative early experiences become marked with particular valences, and subsequent experiences that resemble previous ones then call forth emotions, which are physiological changes in the body. These function "as automated alarm signals which say: beware of danger ahead if you choose the option which leads to this outcome" (173). Damasio developed a novel experimental technique, called the Iowa Gambling Task, which showed that persons with damage to a particular part of the brain implicated in generating emotion (ventromedial prefrontal cortex [vmPFC]) were incapable of generating intuitions about which outcomes were better or worse (Bechara et al. 1997). These subjects performed more poorly in this task than those with unimpaired cognitive function; the latter individuals' bodies generated physiological responses to different choices even before they could articulate what they were doing.

I cannot presume to offer any resolution of this debate. Instead, I offer my understanding of how the outstanding question relates to my argument. Most importantly, the significance of these findings has often been wildly misinterpreted as implying that there is no difference between System I and System II thinking since rational judgment requires emotional outputs. Here Damasio and his collaborators make the conceptual mistake of judging rationality based on its outcome, rather than based on the process by which a decision is reached. In concluding that emotion is necessary for rational thinking, Bechara et al. (2005) argue that "knowledge and reasoning alone are usually not sufficient for making *advantageous* decisions" (337 [emphasis added]). It might indeed be that intuitive thinking makes for better judgments than deliberative thinking (something I consider later in this chapter), but that tells us little about the relationship between emotion and the *process* of System II thinking. Emotion might be necessary for making good choices, but that does not imply that it is necessary for making rational ones.

There is much evidence linking emotion to processing that is less calculating (Baumeister, DeWall, and Zhang 2007; Hsee and Rotten-streich 2004). Bechara et al. (2005) note that in the original Iowa Gambling Task, participants were never able to judge the probabilities of reward and punishment. In betting tasks developed subsequently in which respondents were given probabilities, skin conductance was not as high, perhaps because they could not rely on intuitive thinking styles (Rogers et al. 1999). Even Damasio fans recognize that emotional thinking is different from rational thinking, in that emotion does reduce deliberation and reflection (McDermott 2004; Mercer 2005), both of which are critical elements of rational thought. Those experiencing emotions such as fear, anger, and pride, common in international relations, feel an intense urgency to act, limiting their reflection (Hymans 2006). Mercer (2005) argues that trust is an "emotional belief," defined as one that goes beyond the evidence at hand, which would fail the test for procedural rationality. Emotion produces unreasonable degrees of certainty given the evidence (Mercer 2010: 2).

In the realm of moral judgment, scholars have found different neural bases for utilitarian and intuitive decisions as opposed to deontological and deliberative ones. This lends credence to the conceptual distinction between System I and II thinking (Greene et al. 2001, 2004; Kahane et al. 2011). More recently, research by Damasio and others has also shown that the vmPFC's function is not to judge the emotional response of outcomes (a function that is actually performed by the amygdala), but rather to link the amygdala with processing coming from other parts of the brain to make comprehensive judgments (Bechara et al. 1999).

It does appear that there are more emotional and more deliberative parts of the brain, with the vmPFC providing a crucial integrative link.

Emotion does seem necessary for rational processing, in the sense that it provides the good to maximize. This is an important point. As Bechara et al. (2005) note, the original utilitarian thinkers theorized in terms of maximizing pleasure and minimizing pain. It does seem that caring about outcomes is critical for rationality. If individuals cannot anticipate the emotional consequences of their actions or even feel pain and pleasure after the choice is made, rational thought is indeed impossible, as one of its key ingredients is missing (Greene et al. 2004; Mercer 2005). Those with vmPFC damage cannot associate an outcome with the feeling that will accompany it.

Our everyday experience tells us that our emotions often get the better of our deliberative functions. This observation has inspired the literature on "emotional regulation," which explores how individuals work to control "which emotions they have, when they have them, and how they experience and express these emotions" (Gross 1998: 275). In the dual process literature, System II is thought to oversee System I. Most of the time we are on auto-pilot. Sometimes, however, our rational faculties are implicated, drawn in to check whether our preconscious response was appropriate. While it is likely that System II processing cannot function without System I, which supplies important inputs, there is no rational thinking without the former.

For our purposes, since we cannot observe whether emotions are, in fact, physiological responses to stimuli providing inputs into the brains of our great men, I will rely on the phenomenology of emotion. In other words, I allow others to tell us whether they or others were acting emotionally. As we will see, they use the terms in ways that parallel the System I/II distinction.[1] Typically emotion goes hand-in-brain with other aspects of nonrational processing, such as a reliance on intuition and heuristics and a tendency toward belief assimilation and short-term thinking. While rational thinkers all have emotions, they are consciously aware of them and work to regulate them when they are detrimental to pursuit of their goals.

Is Rationality Just Bounded? Normatively Good?

What does my argument have to say about bounded rationality – the notion that decision-makers, limited in their cognitive capacity to cope

[1] I thank Jonathan Mercer for this suggestion.

with a very uncertain and complex environment, do not engage in the extensive calculations foreseen in formal rational choice models (Jolls, Sunstein, and Thaler 1998; Lupia, McCubbins, and Popkin, 2000; Simon 1983)? We use heuristics to instrumentally "adjust for limited computational capacity, discovering tolerable approximation procedures and heuristics that permit huge spaces to be searched very selectively," something that even the psychologically minded Simon (1978: 12) acknowledges to be rational. In bounded rationality, the costly acquisition of knowledge has been incorporated as another element in an expected-utility function. "We must require not only that beliefs be rational with respect to the available evidence but also that the amount of evidence collected be in some sense optimal" (Elster 1989: 25). After all, Stanovich (2011) notes, it is "difficult to call these instances of irrationality if we do not take into account resource-limited nature of the human cognitive apparatus" (9).

The notion of bounded rationality has done much to popularize the findings of behavioral economists and problematize the normative model of decision-making typically found in microeconomics. However, I have two significant reservations regarding its use. First, it is methodologically dangerous. Recourse to bounded rationality allows rational choice theorists a post hoc rationalization of any anomaly, thereby preserving the foundational stone of utility maximization. It is not that Prime Minister Smith did not think rationally; rather, she simply had too many things to do. Indeed, she acted like a good instrumentally rational individual, economizing on those parts of the job that were less important.

Rationalists are often the biggest fans of the bounded rationality assumption. Bounded rationality, while a critique of expected utility theory, can ironically exacerbate the falsifiability problems of rationalist scholarship. Stanovich (2011) notes that what he calls "Panglossians" – those who believe deeply in the universal application of the rationality assumption – have "reinterpreted the modal response in most of the classic heuristics and biases experiments as indicating an optimal information processing adaptation on the part of subjects" (9). Bounded rationality is paradoxically a life rope for rationalist theorists. This is something of a perversion of the original theoretical claim, as it implies a conscious choice on the part of cognitively impaired individuals to think less so as to conserve resources. However, the heuristics and biases literature has generally claimed that our use of cognitive shortcuts occurs automatically as part of our neural architecture. Heuristics might be rational in an ecological sense, but not in a conscious, instrumental sense.

Second, the concept of bounded rationality, while difficult to dispute, distracts from significant individual-level variation in thinking style, the subject of this book. I acknowledge, as a good cognitivist, that the demands on thinking, especially for foreign policy leaders, are great. This is a fundamental tenet of any psychologically minded argument about international relations (Rathbun 2007; Tetlock 1989). However, this is true of all individuals, and it does not explain variation among those in the same situation (Stanovich and West 1998). Conceptually, bounded rationality implies computational difficulties, which, as noted earlier, are not reducible to epistemic motivation, the commitment to rational thought. Bounded rationality might alert us to the ceiling we should not expect any decision-maker to exceed. However, I repeat that the focus is on relative differences in cognitive style rather than the establishment of an absolute standard of rational thinking. Again the dispositional differences in epistemic motivation allow us to say something about rational thinking in practice while avoiding the rationalization temptation to make everything rational after the fact.

The typical rational model of thinking microeconomics is often described as normative in character, indicating that even if humans do not think in this manner, this is the way that they *should* think. This same judgment is implicit in the typical focus of psychological scholars in the international relations literature on errors in foreign policy (Mercer 2005). Jervis's (1979) famous book is, of course, entitled *Perception and Misperception in International Politics*. We tend to celebrate System II thinking. Our instinct in Western societies and culture is to venerate rationality. No one likes to be called irrational.

At the same time we do not like obsessively rational individuals. Rational thinkers might be regarded as wishy-washy and unprincipled. They weigh everything, making them indecisive. In lining up the costs and benefits, they are willing to put a price on everything, even priceless things. Nonrational decision-makers, in contrast, while perhaps regarded as reckless, dogmatic, stubborn, and irresponsible, might also be understood as bold and courageous. They stick to their guns, often literally. At some point we need to just do it. In short, both thinking styles have their advantages and disadvantages in the normative sense (Tetlock, Peterson, and Berry 1993). As Tetlock (2005) cracks, "One observer's simpleton will be another's man of principle; one observer's groupthink, another's well-run meeting (6). The next chapter will bring this point home more forcefully when we consider romantics, largely intuitive individuals whom we typically admire.

We typically advocate rationality because deliberative and objective thinking is most likely to yield success. Indeed, rationality is the basis of scientific discovery, which is thought by many to be the precondition for societal progress. In this book, however, I make no such claims. Describing someone as more rational should not be understood as an endorsement of that cognitive style. The cases in this book focus on four very successful decision-makers who embraced very different cognitive styles, showing that rationality is not a precondition for political achievement.

It is an open empirical question whether procedurally rational decision-making leads to better outcomes than intuition, and one to which this book can offer no conclusive answer. While the heuristics and biases literature pioneered by Kahneman and Tversky sought to lament our cognitive limitations, a large strand of literature resists the normative implications of the work on rationality and the System I/II distinction. It does not dispute the empirical difference between these ways of thinking, but argues that heuristic-driven, intuitive, and nonconscious thought often yields results that are as good as, and sometimes superior to, the results of procedurally rational thought. Dijksterhuis et al. (2006) present significant evidence that in all but the simplest decisions, those who take time but do not deliberate actively – "sleeping on it," essentially – exhibit more normatively instrumentally rational outcomes and are more satisfied with their choices. The "gut" works. In an enormous body of work, Gigerenzer shows that simple heuristics can serve individuals as well as deliberative thought. He makes the normative case for bounded rationality (Gigerenzer and Goldstein 1996). If we accept the principles of evolution, the default way in which we make choices should be ecologically rational, efficiently adapted to our environment. Those who had the instinct to act without thinking were able to respond more quickly to danger and live another day to pass on their genes.

The bounded rationality literature reminds us that the primary weakness of careful and deliberative rational thinking is that it takes time (Gigerenzer 2007: 4). The work by Damasio draws our attention to the downsides of too much rationality. He famously describes "Elliot," who had suffered severe damage to a part of the brain involved in emotional processing. Elliot became unable to make a decision, constantly turning over different reasons for and against any particular path (McDermott 2004; Mercer 2005). The emotional part of our brains seems to act to induce more "rational" decision-making, in that it forces us to make decisions at all, rather than endlessly turning over pros and cons that we associate with deliberation. It stops us from being too rational for our own good. Similarly, Gigerenzer's (2007: 8, 36) work on gut feelings points out that relying on intuition is part of the evolved capacities of the brain and allows us to make decisions quickly, which has historically been necessary for human survival.

Over-deliberation can be crippling. If one of the hallmarks of emotion is a felt urgency to act (Hymans 2006), its absence has a downside as well. It is possible to overthink, resulting in suboptimal over-processing. Simon (1978) writes that "information may be an expensive luxury, for it may turn our attention from what is important to what is unimportant" (13). Tetlock (2005) notes the "danger of cognitive chaos, the mostly fox vice of excessive open-mindedness, of seeing too much merit in too many stories" (23). Gigerenzer (2007: 38) argues that human brains are designed to protect us from possessing too much information: The more options, the more possibility of difficult choices across multiple values. Intuition is ecologically rational in terms of its speed (Bechara et al. 2005).

Whether System I or II better serves us is likely contingent on the decision-making context. It is important to remember that our cognitive architecture reflects a natural environment dramatically different than the one that human beings currently face. The way human beings think could be efficiently adapted to – that is, *ecologically* rational for – a time where we lived in caves but not today, since our social systems change much more quickly than our biological systems. Heuristics still help us do basic physical tasks, such as catch a baseball, in an efficient manner. But catching a baseball is not the same as making a decision to go to war. The somatic marker theorists recognize this:

Evolutionarily, the amygdala has probably evolved to embrace one instantly for a "fight or flight" response, and it has evolved during a time when probably there was no harm in confusing false alarms and real ones: if the amygdala sent a person running away from what looked like a snake, the person was safe! Even if this turned out to be a false alarm, e.g., a wood stick that looked like a snake, the person was still safe, and there was no harm in responding to a false alarm. (Bechara et al. 2005: 353)

However, in international relations, it is the essence of the security dilemma to overstate the aggression of the adversary, something that leads to mutually detrimental outcomes. Our intuitions in this case might leave us worse off (Holmes 2015).

By comparison, intuition might provide for more successful outcomes in situations of profound uncertainty or novelty that paralyze procedurally rational thinkers. Bechara et al. (2005) write that when "information is so complex and the patterns are not so clear, our cognition may keep struggling explicitly to figure which strategy might be best, but our somatic signals are what implicitly or explicitly bias us towards the advantageous strategy" (359). In other words, in situations of uncertainty and ambiguity, logic and conscious deliberation may offer certain choices, but somatic states, in the form of "hunches" or "gut feelings," help us select the most advantageous response option. We see something like this in the case of British appeasement prior to World War II, when realist decision-makers in Britain waited for a costly signal from Germany that would reveal its character, whereas Churchill seemed to intuitively know that the Nazis were a special kind of threat. Similarly, Reagan seems to have seized on Gorbachev's "new thinking" in a way that other members of his Cabinet did not. Of course, Churchill badly misjudged the question of autonomy and independence for India, predicting disaster (Tetlock and Tyler 1996). Indeed, his career up until 1940 was filled with miscalculation. Therefore, I agree with Gigerenzer (2007) when he writes, of System I thinking, "A gut feeling is not good or bad. ... Its value is dependent on the context in which the rule of thumb is used" (48).

Identifying these situations, however, will have to be the subject of another book. For our purposes here, it will suffice to show that rational thinking does not always yield better outcomes – a conclusion that is profoundly at odds with the prevailing and historical tendencies of international relations theorizing. This observation is also important both conceptually and methodologically. We cannot and should not assess rationality based on the outcome of decision-making. Even in a world in which rational thinking is typically associated with better outcomes, there is always incomplete information and luck. Instead, we must identify rationality in the process of thinking.

2   The Three "R"s of International Relations: Realism, Romanticism, and Rationality

Rationality has psychological foundations. In the Introduction and Chapter 1, I argued that the highly deliberative and objective cognitive style that we characterize as procedurally rational is necessary for an instrumentally rational actor of the kind we see in formal models. However, the discussion was relatively silent on the implications of this claim for international relations theory. What does this finding tell us about international relations approaches that rely, implicitly or explicitly, on rationality assumptions? If many decision-makers are not as rational as others in thought and deed, what exactly are they doing?

Rational thinking is a necessary foundation for what we know as Realpolitik – instrumental rationality in the pursuit of exclusively statist goals. My argument implies, contrary to the implicit and sometimes explicit assumptions of modern realist theory, that Realpolitik has psychological foundations and, therefore, should not be something that we observe universally. Instead, it is the behavior we expect of leaders with a particular psychological make-up. In classical realist theory, we see the same emphasis on objectivity and deliberation as we do in the contemporary literature in psychology.

Despite its modern pretensions, realism is an intensely psychological theory and more prescriptive than descriptive. Realists admonish rationality but are pessimistic about being heeded. Indeed, Realpolitik is quite rare in practice, something that the case studies of Bismarck and Richelieu that follow demonstrate. This is a deeply subversive claim in the sense that realism has, despite its largely normative content, always simultaneously maintained that it offers a universal understanding of how international politics functions. If the political system does not select for highly rational individuals, then the international system will quickly teach less rational leaders a lesson, and ultimately dispose of them if they are bad students. If the realist practitioner is rare, how can this be? Were realism universal, realists would be plentiful, so much so that we would scarcely notice them. But we do, precisely because they are so uncommon. Along the way, I correct another misconception about realism, the belief that the realist is always bellicose. In fact, rational thought dictates an adjustment to structural circumstances, which may or may not always be tipped in the realist's favor.

If not Realpolitik, then what? Generally our answer is liberalism, typically set up as the antithesis of realism (Rathbun 2010). There are actually a multitude of nonrealist foreign policy strategies. In my previous work, I have showed the contrasts between nationalists, liberals, and realists in their diplomatic style (Rathbun 2014). However, in addition to being well-trod ground, the contrast between realism and liberalism revolves around different substantive beliefs about the way that international politics works, more so than the cognitive style and degree of rationality on the part of decision-makers. Liberals see more grounds for mutually beneficial cooperation (Rathbun 2012) and also define the national interest in a more prosocial way, as one that benefits not just one's own state but others as well (Rathbun 2014).

A more interesting comparison is that of romanticism, a completely unexplored concept in international relations theory. Romanticism, with its focus on agency, deontological decision-making, and intuitive cognitive style, is often defined in the humanities as the natural opposite to realism's structural and rational approach. This chapter introduces romantic thinking to the international relations audience, draws out its contrasts with Realpolitik, and demonstrates how it is predicated on a thinking style that is more intuitive than rational. Romantics in practice are often as egoistic in their foreign policy orientation as realists, allowing us in subsequent empirical chapters to indicate how the two approaches lead to fundamentally different behaviors on the part of leaders based largely on how (and the degree to which) leaders think.

I should be clear: not all rational thinkers are realists and not all intuitive thinkers are romantics, although I would claim that all realists are highly deliberative and all romantics are instinct- and gut-driven individuals. Realists are one kind of rational decision-maker; romantics are one kind of nonrational decision-maker. Many liberals, for instance, are highly rational, seeking joint gains in international affairs through the construction of international institutions in a manner consistent with neoliberal institutional theories (Keohane 1984). Other liberals might be nonrational. Liberal idealists whom realists accuse of allowing their desires to blind their perception come to mind (Carr 1964). We can also think of decidedly nonromantic, intuitively driven individuals. The current American president comes to mind. Trump's impulsiveness consistently undermines his ability to think strategically and to obtain his goals, yet we cannot identify any particular cause or vision he would fight and sacrifice for. Notwithstanding references to "making America great again," Trump is no Churchill – or even Reagan, for that matter.

This book therefore does not generate a comprehensive typology of all possible combinations of substance and style, nor does it explore whether certain substantive beliefs predispose those who hold them toward thinking in particular ways, although this does seem likely. Radicals of all types are likely to be romantic and nondeliberative. Nevertheless, the discussion here offers a template of how decision-making styles might be wedded to alternative conceptions of interest, even if the latter are purely self-serving.

The Real Realism: The Psychology of Raison d'État

The substantive essence of Realpolitik is the egoistic pursuit of national interest under the structural constraints of anarchy. From this simple premise – namely, that states think only themselves but must operate in a largely unregulated environment where others are doing the same – can be deduced all the other phenomena that have come to be identified with realism, such as the indispensability of power and the ultima ratio of military force (Donnelly 2000). While much was made for a time of the differences between "classical" realism and later "structural" realism, recent work has problematized this distinction, pointing out both that classical realism relies (implicitly and even sometimes explicitly) on the permissive cause of anarchy to generate power political dynamics and that structural realism relies (again often implicitly) on an egoistic theory of state motivation (Donnelly 2000; Parent and Baron 2011; Rathbun 2018; Welch 1995).

There is considerable debate among realists about what constitutes egoistic behavior. Do states seek to maximize power or security (Hamilton and Rathbun 2013)? Do they seek to become the dominant power of the system or merely preserve a modicum of peace? Are they driven by other goals such as honor and status (Lebow 2008)? Despite these differences, there is agreement that states are completely self-regarding, even if often by necessity (Donnelly 2000: 9). Niebuhr (1934) writes of the "natural egoistic impulse with which all life is endowed" (198; quoted in Donnelly 2000: 198). Mearsheimer (1994) claims that the "structure of the international system forces states to behave as egoists" (40). States cannot consider "cosmopolitan" (i.e., non-egoistic) interests, but must concern themselves only with "national" goals (Morgenthau 1946: 107; Murray 1996: 80, 84; also Carr 1964: 53; Haslam 2002: 15; Smith: 1986: 235). State interests in realism are self-interests; they are not other-regarding. Much can fall under that rubric, but much also falls outside it. Some see states as engaging in self-aggrandizement, whereas others see states as engaging only in self-preservation (Welch 1995: 12), but that behavior is self-centered in every case. Even motivations like domination and pride are all self-regarding (Donnelly 2000: 56). The preening prima donna is not thought of as selfless in character. However, selfish interests cannot include for the realist the internalization of moral norms whose purpose is to benefit the international community or some subset thereof, the kind to which constructivists often point (Kaufmann and Pape 1999; Krebs and Jackson 2007).

All realists, even the dead ones, note the importance of structural constraints. The classical realists use the language of "necessity" rather than "anarchy," but they are saying the same thing (Parent and Baron 2011). Meinecke (1957) writes, "[T]oo often ... a choice is out of the question. ... Raison d'état thus takes on the profound and serious character of national necessity" (2). He describes "the environment of the State. ... This is a situation of constraint in which the State finds itself, in the face of threats either from within or without, and which forces it to adopt defensive and offensive means of a quite specific kind. Today one usually says in such cases that its behavior is 'constrained'" (5–6). Similarly, according to Carr (1964), "The realist analyses a predetermined course of development which he is powerless to change" (12). Realism "tends to emphasize the irresistible strength of existing forces and the inevitable character of existing tendencies" (10). Of course, for many of the classical realists, the structural constraint was the egoism of other states, rather than the absence of a supranational coercive authority (Meinecke 1957: 15). However, egoism itself cannot logically lead to the power political outcomes they believe are ubiquitous without the permissive factor of anarchy (Donnelly 2000). A society composed of knaves with a really good police force might be completely peaceful.

The pursuit of egoistic interests in light of structural constraints is the very definition of instrumental rationality (Bueno de Mesquita 2014). States should behave as consequentialists that weigh costs against benefits, recognizing that one cannot have it all (Murray 1996: 84–6; Smith 1986: 45–7). As Morgenthau (1948) writes, "Political realism ... requires a sharp distinction between the desirable and the possible – between what is desirable everywhere and at all times and what is possible under the concrete circumstances of time and place" (7). He continues by noting that "prudence – the weighing of the consequences of alternative political actions" is "the supreme virtue in politics" (10). Raison d'état is defined by Meinecke (1957) as "the consideration of what is expedient, useful and beneficial, of what the State must do" (5; also Trachtenberg 2003: 179). The most important constraint in international relations is, of course, the distribution of power. For structural realists, power is called "capability." The term itself is etymologically derivative of "ability," which implies what *can* as opposed to what *should* be done. Parent and Baron (2011) observe that classical realists, just like their contemporary cousins, believed "structure ruled, that behavior was proportionate to power, and that interacting states had various appetites, but appetite was more a function of capability than taste" (201).

The Psychology of Realism: Prescribing Rational Thought

None of this happens automatically, however. In classical realist texts, we see a necessary condition: the distinctly psychological variable of rational thinking. Realists are not just telling us *what* to think, although they do this to some degree; they are also telling us *how* to think. Realist arguments are as much about cognitive style as empirical substance. Meinecke (1957) writes, "For raison d'état demands first and foremost a high degree of rationality and expediency in political conduct" (6). Morgenthau (1946) advises, "to eliminate from the political sphere not power politics – which is beyond the ability of any political philosophy or system – but the destructiveness of power politics, rational faculties are needed" (9; also Haslam 2002: 10).

We see emphasis on the same two core components of rational thinking reviewed in the previously cited sources – namely, objectivity and deliberation. "Political realism wants the photographic picture of the political world to resemble as much as possible its painted portrait," observes Morgenthau (1948: 8). Similarly, Carr (1964) suggests that the realist "will embark on that hard ruthless analysis of reality, which is the hallmark of science" (10). This is the "real" in "real-ism." Such rationality, however, is not unproblematic or a given, because it requires the admission of the painful truth that one is constrained from having it all. Motivated bias is tempting. According to Morgenthau (1948), realism

believes ... in the possibility of distinguishing in politics between truth and opinion – between what is true objectively and rationally, supported by evidence and illuminated by reason, and what is only a subjective judgment, divorced from the facts as they are and informed by prejudice and wishful thinking. (4)

Carr (1964) follows the same line:

The impact of thinking upon wishing ... is commonly called realism. Representing a reaction against the wish dreams ... realism is liable to assume a critical and somewhat cynical aspect. In the field of thought, it places its emphasis on the acceptance of facts [that one is] powerless to influence or alter. (10)

This objectivity is necessary for the hard choices of separating the vital interest wheat from the peripheral interest chaff, jettisoning some goals for other more important ones (Carr 1964: 53; Morgenthau 1946: 19, 1948: 3–4). Realism "aims at the realization of the lesser evil rather than of the absolute good" and one "must work with those forces, not against them" (Morgenthau 1948: 3–4). Alternative courses of action must be considered and judged according to an estimation of their consequences, which requires active and conscious deliberation.

Not surprisingly, realists caution against the passions, as they impede the cognition necessary for Realpolitik. In the terms of Chapter 1, they tell us to avoid System I processing. Meinecke (1957) writes that the realist "should rule himself strictly that he should suppress his emotions and his personal inclinations and aversions, and completely lose himself in the practical task of securing the common good. He should also seek, quite coolly and rationally, to ascertain the practical interest of the State, and to separate these from any emotional overtones – for hatred and revenge, as Bismarck says, are bad counsellors in politics" (6). He cautions that "raison d'état demands ... an ice-cold temperature (1957: 7; also Smith 1986: 47; Trachtenberg 2003: 159).

Thinking is therefore a core aspect of Realpolitik, as is evident from the very syntax of realist texts. "The *insight* and the *wisdom* of the statesman gauge accurately the distribution and relative strength of opposing forces and anticipate, however tentatively, the emerging pattern of new constellations," says Morgenthau (1946: 221 [emphasis added]). Carr (1964) distinguishes the "*imagination*" of the utopian from the realist who operates through "*intellectual effort*," what we have called epistemic motivation (63 [emphasis added]). The "function of *thinking* is to study a sequence of events which [one] is powerless to influence or to alter. ... The highest wisdom lies in accepting and adapting oneself to, these forces and these tendencies" (10 [emphasis added]; also Meinecke 1957: 1). These are all ways of describing rationality. According to Morgenthau (1948), "For realism, theory consists in ascertaining facts and giving them meaning through reason. It assumes that the character of a foreign policy can be ascertained only through the examination of the political acts performed and of the foreseeable consequences of these acts" (4–5 [emphasis added]). Carr's (1964) *The Twenty Years' Crisis*, perhaps most responsible for defining the realist and his antithesis in early international relations theory, was first and foremost a book about the cognitive failings of the utopians, in which the author claims "wishing prevails over thinking, generalization over observation, and in which little attempt is made at a critical analysis of existing facts or available means. ... Thought has been at a discount" (8–9).

As is clear in the previously cited passages, realism has a distinctly normative and prescriptive character (Haslam 2002: 17–18; Smith 1986: 221). Realpolitik requires rational thinking, but this cannot be taken for granted. Realists are advising such behavior as much as, perhaps more than, they are describing it (Jervis 1994: 859; Zarnett 2014: 3). Morgenthau (1948) admits this: "Political realism contains not only a theoretical but also a normative element" (7). He continues, "[P]olitical realism considers a rational foreign policy to be good for-eign policy; for only a rational foreign policy minimizes risks and maximizes benefits and hence, complies both with the moral precept of prudence and the political requirement of success" (8). Haslam (2002) concurs that rationality in realism "was thus an aim in and of itself, which was not infrequently breached, and not something one could confidently assume. ... Realists in the past have certainly not presupposed rationality; rationality was a goal, the idea towards which the statesman progressed" (10, 12).

This normative character of realism reveals that realists do not expect Realpolitik at all times. Rather, this will depend on the dispositional qualities of the state leader. Morgenthau (1948) explains:

We cannot conclude from the good intentions of a statesman that his foreign policy will be either morally praiseworthy or politically successful. ... It stands to reason that not all foreign policies have always followed so rational, objective and unemotional a course. The contingent elements of personality, prejudice and subjective preference, and of all the weaknesses of intellect and will which flesh is heir to, are bound to deflect foreign policies from their rational course. (6–7)

Thus, realism distinguishes between the good, rational statesman and the bad, irrational one (Smith 1986: 46–7).

Such rational thinking is not just normative; it might even be the exception, rather than the rule, if one believes Morgenthau (1948): "Political realism presents the theoretical construct of a rational foreign policy which experience can never completely achieve" (7). He is aware that "actual foreign policy does not or cannot live up to" realist demands (8). Indeed rational Realpolitik is exceptionally hard because of the intense psychological demands of rationality.

It is the nature of things that a theory of politics which is based upon such principles will not meet with unanimous approval. ... [T]he human mind in its day-by-day operations cannot bear to look the truth of politics straight in the face. It must disguise, distort, belittle, and embellish the truth – the more so, the more the individual is actively involved in the processes of politics, and particularly in those of international politics. ... Thus it is inevitable that a theory which tries to understand politics as it actually is and as it ought to be in view of its intrinsic nature, rather than as people would like to see it, must overcome a psychological resistance that most other branches of learning need not face. (Morgenthau 1948: 14 [emphasis added])

The gap between what is normatively required of statesmen and what they actually do empirically was "evidence of human irrationality" in Morgenthau's eyes (quoted in Jervis 1994: 859).

Does my claim – that rationality is central to realism – not contradict the very essence of realism as a reaction to liberals' misplaced faith in the power of reason? Here we must distinguish between a rationalist thinking style and the substantive belief that the power of reason is capable of solving social ills and remaking all politics for the better, both domestic and international. Morgenthau (1946) summarizes the latter: "As rationalism sees it, the world is governed by laws which are accessible to human reason in the last analysis" and "which enables man to understand the causes of events and ... to make himself the master of events" (11). It is the voluntarist belief in the ameliorating influence of reason that realists such as Carr and Morgenthau take issue with as being excessively optimistic, harmonious. and teleological (Carr 1964: 12; Morgenthau 1946: 47–9). Reason gives humans the ability to control, transform. and change their environment for the better. Morgenthau (1946) distinguishes between this type of rationality, which he characterizes as ideological in character, and his own (71–2). Liberals have faith in reason; realists believe that real rationality exposes the wishful thinking and cognitive failures of liberals (9). Liberals are "not unlike the sorcerers of primitive ages" in "the attempt to exorcise social evils by the indefatigable repetition of magic formulas" (40), he claims. They have only the "illusion of rationality" (209).

This is not to argue that the realist is, in fact, the true, impartial objective observer of political facts whose substantive take on international relations is accurate, but rather that it is an indispensable part of realism to think of itself in this way. On the one hand, the world may, in fact, be nasty, brutish, and short. On the other hand, perhaps the realist broadside of liberalism is a caricature. What is important is that realists place a great emphasis on self-conscious, rational thinking, giving realism a distinctive psychological quality that is often missed but that is critical for understanding the approach.

Pulling Punches: Realists Caution Restraint

Instrumentally rational statecraft guided by objective and deliberative thinking is, by nature, situational. One does what is best given the circumstances, which are constantly changing (Meinecke 1957: 2). This is another consistent theme in realist scholarship. The statesman "has a number of circumstances ... to take into consideration. Circumstances are infinite, are infinitely combined; are variable and transient; he who does not take them into consideration is not erroneous, but stark mad. ... A statesman ... is to be guided by circumstances; and judging contrary to the exigencies of the moment, he may ruin his country forever" (Morgenthau 1946: 221). Realists judge each problem on its own merits and eschew the formulation of universal principles or solutions (Carr 1964: 16).

Part of adapting to the particular environment is using the appropriate tools for the occasion. Realism is hardly all bellicose threats and power maximization. Coercion and force are not necessarily the most cost-effective way of reaching one's goals or the best strategy in the long run. Morgenthau (1946) recommends "not to advance by destroying the obstacles in one's way, but to retreat before them, to circumvent them, to maneuver around them, to soften and dissolve them slowly by means of persuasion, negotiation and pressure" (546; also, De Callières 2000: 12). He describes statecraft as "quick adaptation to new situations, clever use of a psychological opening, retreat and advance as the situation may require, persuasion, the quid pro quo of bargaining and the like" (Morgenthau 1948: 530).

This leads to the recognition that as important for state interests as the application of power is restraint in its use. Restraint – that is, the conscious and deliberate non-exercise of power, force, and violence – has been a central theme in both classical and modern structural realist scholarship. According to Meinecke (1957), "Power which gushes out blindly will end by destroying itself; it must follow certain purposive rules and standards, in order to preserve itself and to grow. Cunning and force must therefore unite in the exercise of power" (10). Restraint requires keeping emotions in check, preserving rational thinking. There is certainly a place for force and coercive bargaining, but there is no one-size-fits-all strategy. Restraint in foreign and military policy can have at least three distinctive and interrelated advantages, summed up nicely by Onea (2016): "Restraint proponents nearly always portray expansive national interests as self-defeating due to counterbalancing, imperial overstretch, and resentment" (113).

First, restraint lessens security dilemma dynamics, thereby avoiding unnecessary conflicts and tensions. In international relations, the pursuit of security by any state is often indistinguishable to outsiders from the pursuit of aggrandizement because military power is utilized toward both ends (Jervis 1978). What looks like territorial annexation to one state might be another state's security buffer. The security dilemma is often described as a "tragic" situation given that the structural nature of the dilemma makes it difficult to resolve. However, few realists would take a completely deterministic and fatalistic approach. Restraint, perhaps through cooperation with others, offers the ability to send signals of reassurance to other states. Realist scholars stress that leaders should "look at the political scene from the point of view of other nations" (Morgenthau 1948: 553). In other words, statecraft involves strategic thinking. Ken Booth and Nicholas Wheeler (2008) call this "security dilemma sensibility." Without it, one might falsely inflate the threat posed by others or clumsily convince another incorrectly that a state has malign intentions. This recalls Waltz's (1998) admonition that there is such a thing as too much power in international relations. Even offensive realists stress these pitfalls of power, at least in their normative interventions into American foreign policy-making (Mearsheimer 2005).

Second, fear is not the only source of conflict spirals; cycles of acrimony and indignation are possible as well. One also wants to avoid engendering hatred and anger on the part of others (Trachtenberg 2003: 164). Haslam (2002) notes that the realist "concern for utility meant that for Machiavelli, as indeed for all those committed to Reasons of State, calculation and self-control were mechanisms essential to effective rule. Whereas fear was useful, hatred was counter-productive" (30). Moreover, avoiding such an outcome holds open the possibility of using present adversaries as allies in future situations. Realists are particularly concerned about stoking nationalism in other countries (Mearsheimer 2005; Posen 2014: 52, 67). Sensitivity to identity politics requires strategic thinking – that is, seeing things as others do not out of a sense of genuine concern, but out of self-regard. It also necessitates a pragmatic realization that while when others might be physically subjugated, their hearts and minds are not.

Third, restraint helps statesmen avoid the problem of defining interests in such an expansive manner as to exceed one's own power to defend them. This can mean seizing territory that one cannot hold or govern, or taking on allies that one cannot defend. Defining interests in terms of power leads to moderation (Smith 1986: 221; Trachtenberg 2003: 167–8). The pursuit of interests with no sense of compromise is unrealistic; one's appetite exceeds one's ability to eat, with self-defeating consequences. We again see realism's normative element. "How difficult – often indeed how impossible it is, in the case of territorial annexation by a victor, to separate a pressing necessity of Realpolitik, from the pure pleasure of aggrandizement," writes Meinecke (1957: 7). Realism is hard – and rare. Meinecke (1957) notes:

Freely-released power shall (when raison d'état is properly exercised) really only constitute the means of implementing by force those vital necessities of the State. . . . But this means, once freed from legal fetters, threatens to set itself up as an end-in-itself, and to carry the State beyond that frontier of which it stands in real need. Then the excesses of power politics set in; the irrational outruns the rational. (14)

Realism cautions states to distinguish between vital and more peripheral interests, focusing on the former and jettisoning the latter (Onea 2006: 113). Having identified truly important state goals, Morgenthau (1948) cautions states to "promote the national interest with moderation and leave the door open for compromise in the form of a negotiated settlement" (534).

Thematically, classical realism overlaps considerably with recent rationalist models of reassurance like those offered by Glaser (2010) and Kydd (2005). Indeed, Glaser calls his approach "contingent" realism – contingent in the sense that the Realpolitik practitioner adjusts his behavior in light of prevailing circumstances. Truly rational actors will weigh the costs of potential conflict against the benefits of more conciliatory strategies. They will, in short, be pragmatic. Kydd (2005) talks of "Bayesian" realism, in which rational leaders remain open to new information, an open-minded objectivity central to Glaser (2010: 30) as well. Glaser and Kydd criticize Waltzian neorealism, in both its defensive and offensive variants, for neglecting the fact that the self-help nature of international relations dictated by the international system can lead states toward cooperative as well as competitive behaviors. There are significant risks in the latter (Glaser 2010: 7). These differences should not be overstated, however. As discussed earlier, the policy interventions, if not always the theoretical contributions, of structural realists almost always stress this same fact.

If the classical realists are empirically right – that rationality is a precondition of Realpolitik but is rare – then this is truly damaging for realism as an explanatory paradigm. Even as classical realists argue prescriptively and complain of the lack of rationality and realism in leaders, they simultaneously claim the universal applicability of their arguments, a tension that a number of scholars have noted. Jervis

(1994) and others believe this normative and explanatory combination is problematic and contradictory because realism, if an empirically accurate structural theory of international politics, should have no need to prescribe. These behaviors should occur naturally (Haslam 2002: 15; Jervis 1994: 859; Zarnett 2014: 4).

Structural realists might try to evade the implications of this finding, arguing that they make a systemic argument about constraints that is nondeterminative (Goddard and Nexon 2005; Rathbun 2008). After all, their argument is a third-image view, not a first-image one, and statesmen have every right to defy the system (Waltz 1959, 1979). Nevertheless, if there are in fact systemic constraints, then there will be consequences for nonrationality. Realist practitioners will be favored in an evolutionary sense. Any single departure from anarchy's dictates does not invalidate the theory. However, if very few statesmen can be identified as realists and these realists consistently face significant resistance at home, it becomes increasingly more difficult to claim that the system has any force at all.

Isn't It Romantic?: Agency, Will, and Nonrational Thinking

If realists are rationalists, marked by their cold and calculating System II processing, then are nonrationalists blathering fools tilting at windmills? System I processing is more poorly defined than System II processing. Indeed, it is generally defined with a grab bag of terms that stand in opposition to rational thinking – emotional, impulsive, automatic. This gives a potentially false impression that the nonrationalist is not purposive in nature, that he or she cannot act systematically in pursuit of goals. It appears as if the only consistent thing we can point out about a nonrational thinker is his or her inconsistency. There might indeed be individuals (and leaders) who match this description. The arbitrary dictator whose kingdom serves only his personal, constantly changing whims comes to mind. However, we are looking for a more general class of individuals with a certain set of somewhat predictable characteristics.

In considering this question, I turn to the construct of the romantic. Romanticism is of great use for international relations theory in that it articulates a way of decision-making and thinking about world politics that is fundamentally different than that of standard rational, realist conceptions. While seemingly obscure for international relations, romanticism is something of a natural fit. As an intellectual movement, romanticism arose in empirical and normative opposition to the Enlightenment's focus on reason and rationality (Barzun 1944: 15; Koch 1993: 125; Lovejoy 1924: 232). It formed the basis of the Counter-Enlightenment. Indeed, romanticism might be the major alternative to reason and rationality. Barzun (1944) notes that the romantic is generally juxtaposed with the "rationalist" and the "realist" (81). The very definition of romanticism is "fanciful," "impractical," and "unrealistic," imbued with "idealism," and "passionate." It deals with "heroic, fantastic, or supernatural events" (www.dictionary.com). In contrast, synonyms for "realistic" include "rational," "pragmatic," "sober," "unsentimental," and "utilitarian" (www.thesaurus.com).

Generally the antithesis of the realist in international relations theory is the liberal (Rathbun 2010). Liberals believe that progress in international relations is possible, and that the picture that realists paint of politics is too pessimistic and cynical. The expansion of democracy, growing inter-dependence, and increasing multilateralization of world politics are transforming international relations. While their perceptions differ sub-stantively, realists and liberals do not, however, necessarily differ in their thinking style. There are prosocially minded liberals who draw attention to the power of transnational norms, based on liberal ethical principles of the sanctity of individual rights that constrain egoistic behavior. And there are egoistic, rationalistic liberals who argue that states can adjust features of their institutional environment to allow for mutually benefi-cial cooperation (Keohane 1984). The realist–liberal divide does not serve our main purpose – to demonstrate the importance of different kinds of thinking styles, and degrees of rationality, in international rela-tions. Nevertheless, unlike for liberalism, which emerged from the Enlightenment tradition, it is not really possible to deduce a set of theoretical expectations about international relations from romanticism (Zacher and Matthew 1995). Rather, we see a set of emphases, both normative and ontological. Romanticism celebrates particular aspects of human life such as agency and emotion, thereby creating ontological room for them in our conceptions of social relations.

While one could trace the influence of this movement on the inter-national relations of its time, I focus instead on the romantic as a kind of individual, one with particular traits or dispositions both substantive and cognitive. Romantics have a thin ontology, a set of substantive beliefs about the social world, but also a particular way of thinking (or better said, feeling). The great theorist of romanticism, Jacques Barzun, refers to the romanticist "temper." Romantics "share certain broad predilec-tions in common such as the admiration for energy, moral enthusiasm and original genius" (1944: 23). Indeed, Barzun refers to the romantic as a "variety" of human being (23).

To better distill the essence of the romantic, we look for guidance from romanticism, a diverse intellectual and artistic movement of the eighteenth and nineteenth centuries. Barzun (1944) calls it a "literary or emotional complex," that to understand "takes us from political and social history to critical facts about poetry, the arts, and philosophy, and thence to matters of psychology, religion and common belief" (5). Just as we know what it means to be a rational thinker from the Enlightenment, so we can know what it means to be a romantic from the romantic period. This is not to say that before the romantic era there were no romantics, just as we cannot say that there were no rational thinkers before the Enlightenment. As Barzun (1944) argues, romantic can mean two things: "In one sense, it refers to human traits which may be exhibited at any time or place. In the second sense, it is a name given to a period in history because of the notable figures that gave it its peculiar character" (7). Romanticism is a "combination of human traits which for one reason or another happens to be stressed, valued, cultivated at a given historical moment," and by looking at that historical moment and its intellectual and artistic products we can better appreciate what a romantic is (14). This does not require that the romantic have any conscious knowledge of the romantic movement. We know whether someone is romantic by virtue of what he or she embodies, which is best read out of a broader intellectual tradition.

I have taken this track in previous research – for instance, on the effect of political ideology on foreign policy choices (Rathbun 2004, 2007a, 2012, 2014). If we want to understand what makes a particular conservative tick, for instance, we might read famous authors in a larger conservative movement. That helps us understand this individual, even if he or she has never read those authors. Ronald Reagan, for instance, was not a deep intellectual thinker with deep academic training, yet one cannot argue that he was not a conservative in many ways. Moreover, particular substantive views often have concomitant cognitive styles. What we think and how we think are often inextricably intertwined. For instance, it is a long-standing finding in psychology that conservative beliefs are associated with a particular cognitive style (Jost et al. 2007; Rathbun 2014).

I have distilled the essence of romanticism from works in philosophy, art history, and literature in an effort to operationalize it for social scientific use, coming up with a set of four interdependent elements. Particularly helpful in this quest, to utilize a highly romantic term, is Isaiah Berlin, who offers perhaps the most cogent explication of the romantic frame of mind.

First, romanticism stresses the importance of human agency in shaping the course of historical events, whether in the arts or in politics (Barzun 1944: 128; also Peckham 1951: 10). Berlin (2014) explains:

The necessities of which the universe is composed are no longer "given," no longer imposed upon us as an objectively necessary reality whose laws are either recognized for what they are or else ignored to our cost. Man is not ... a passive observer who can accept or reject a world which is what it is, whether he likes it or not. He is in virtue of being a "subject" wholly active. His "activity" consists not in contemplation but in imposing principles or rules of his own making upon the prima facie inert mass of nature. (236)

Romantics believe in the power of individuals, even when pitted against broad, impersonal structural forces. The exertion of human agency is the ultimate expression of human freedom, which "consists in the hewing of the dead lumps of reality according to any shape imposed by the spirit" (Berlin 2014: 227). Action is everything. The "goal of life is not happiness (in the sense of enjoyment) but activity" (Barzun 1944: 108). The "most salient feature of romantic life" is "its energy and the harnessing of its energy the production of large-scale achievements" (Barzun 1944: 130). Romantics celebrate those individuals who create something new, defying structural forces (Barzun 1944: 23; Berlin 2014: 223–5; Peckham 1951: 11; Rosenthal 2008: 38).

Agency is a creative process of making and shaping. Romantics prize imagination, the font of creativity. For romantics, "The painter, the poet, the composer do not hold up a mirror to nature, however ideal, but invent" (Dorra 1972). An early romantic in literature and philosophy, Friedrich Schiller likened art to play in which children "give full freedom to their imagination, and suspend those laws which may in fact hold in the ordinary world. ... They 'posit,' and thereby 'create', imaginary worlds in which all the freedom which is lacking in real life ... is restored" (Berlin 2014: 218). "The romantics defined imagination as an active power creating intuitive wholes," writes Garrison, continuing: "The romantic imagination invests life and politics with very different marvelous possibilities" and "puts forth extravagant dreams unaffected by what is actually known about human beings in history" (2013: 41). Just because it has not been done before does not mean it is not possible.

Romanticists celebrate genius, that quality of exceptional individuals whose imagination and creativity are used to make something completely new (Barzun 1944: 23; Peckham 1951: 11; Rosenthal 2008: 38). "[T]he world is conceived as the life and activity of a super-person, to which normal human beings ... stand as tongues of flame to the fire in which they play," asserts Berlin (2014: 225). Artists who battle against convention are especially revered (Berlin 2014: 244; Peckham 1951: 12). However, this admiration extends to those in public life as well. Berlin (2014) describes "the creative principle of the world, embodying itself ... in heroic individuals who transform society by violent revolutions, obedient to the creative impulse within them" (223). These might be "artists or generals or statesmen or thinkers" (225). Romanticists are fascinated by these "great men" of history, such as Napoleon (Barzun 1944: 136). "Their genius, the great men – their historical greatness – is in part defined by their ability to bend events to their will" (Berlin 2014: 225), that is, by their agency.

Romanticists believe in the power of human agency, but what do these great creators do? What are they driven by? What, in particular, do they create? Romanticism's geniuses always have a cause – not just artistic objects, but something much more meaningful. The romantic is not just purposive; he has a purpose.

For this reason, romanticism is often characterized as "idealist" in character, its second core feature (Berlin 2014: 219; Peckham 1951: 6). As Barzun (1944) notes, "the issues the romanticists fought for were larger than their personal selves" (118). The particular cause is not relevant. "On issues of the day, we can find Romantic spirits on opposing sides: progressive and conservative, democratic and monarchist, religious and agnostic," write De la Croix and Tansey (1986: 910). What is important is not the belief but the believing. "The truth or falsity of the ideal becomes comparatively irrelevant," says Berlin (2014: 244). In that sense, romanticism offers a thin, rather than a thick, ontology. It is idealistic but does not see politics or social relations progressing in any certain direction empirically, nor does it advocate for any particular path normatively. It is agentic, but not substantively teleological. This helps widen the possibilities for idealism in international relations. Idealists might be liberal, but they might not be – a useful corrective for a discipline that generally conflates the two (Carr 1964; Rathbun 2010).

Moreover, it is not so much a commitment to ideals that makes romanticism distinctive, but rather the particularly deontological way that romantics think about ethical principles. They cannot be compromised, no matter what. "[A] man must live for his ideal, whatever it may be, and if need be die for it, but above all never sell himself to the Philistines, never betray his cause, never permit himself any comfort which would make him depart an inch from that narrow path which the vision within directs him to follow," writes Berlin (2014: 244). The outcome is unimportant. "Romanticism could only admire an active greatness; it even admired failure if greatness had been shown, because it knew that it is by a succession of failures, by doggedness, that man can overcome both himself and the indifferent, or resistant, or simply mysterious universe" (Barzun 1944: 131). Romanticism does not judge action by its consequences, a theme I take up again later in this chapter. According to Berlin (2014), "What is admired is not the truth but the heroism, the dedication, the integrity of a life devoted to and, if need be, sacrificed on the altar of *an end pursued for its own sake*, for the sake of its beauty or sanctity to the individual whose ideal it is" (244 [emphasis added]).

Third, romanticists highlight and venerate struggle (Frye 1957: Lovejoy 1941: 274). History is made by exceptional individuals trying to create something completely new and different, and new ideas and ideals always encounter resistance. Koch (1993: 127) observes that for the *Sturm und Drang* movement, the first generation of German romanticists, staying true to one's ideals inevitably brought the genius into conflict with established institutions. According to Berlin (2014), among romantics, "A man is aware of himself properly only when he comes into collision with something not himself, another person or a thing which in some way obstructs, causes friction, perhaps altogether frustrates his activity" (226). Romantic art "is made of contrasts, oppositions, antitheses, strife and color," writes Barzun (1944: 98).

Romantics idealize these conflicts in the sense that they generally take on the cast of "light against darkness, of good against evil, of rights and laws and duties against blind force," suggests Berlin (2014: 226). Frye (1957) observes that in romanticism, "subtlety and complexity are not much favored. Characters tend to be either for or against the quest. If they assist it they are idealized as simply gallant or pure; if they obstruct it they are caricatured as simply villainous or cowardly. Hence every typical character in romance tends to have his moral opposite confronting him" (195). Romantics particularly love battles in which the hero or heroes are outnumbered and outgunned (Barzun 1944: 130). "What is most noble and deeply admired is the spectacle of a man alone, unsupported, with all the conventional values and forces against him, hurling himself into battle because he cannot do otherwise" (Berlin 2014: 244). Even though they are nonrationalist, romantics can hardly be said to lack a purpose. Indeed, they act in singular pursuit of a goal.

As romantic figures always face obstacles and seemingly insuperable odds, how can they hope to prevail when all is arrayed against them? This leads to romanticism's fourth element. Romanticists place great emphasis on the importance of will and resolve (Kertzer 2016). Although there is no guarantee of success, what heroes lack in objective power, they make up for in their intensity of commitment and their force of will. "Those with great will simply do not accept structural barriers to action." Instead, "the general or statesman or thinker ... knows how to will, that is, how to shape the less or more recalcitrant materials with which his life provides him to the pattern which is demanded by the real self whose presence he feels at his most exalted" (Berlin 2014: 225).

Central to romanticism is the concept of *Streben*, or "striving." As described by Barzun (1944), striving is "most salient feature of romantic ... life – its energy and the harnessing of its energy to the production of large-scale achievements" (122–3). In colloquial terms, where there is a will, there is a way. Those who continually strive are exhibiting their indomitable will. Lovejoy (1941) writes:

> This is the assumption of the primacy, in reality and in value, of process, striving, cumulative becoming, over any static consummation – the dislike of finality, *das Abgeschlossene*. ... *Streben* ... was one of the most sacred words of the German Romantics – and it was necessarily, for them, a *Streben ins Unendliche*, a striving without a terminus; and in spite of the various other senses and applications which this formula could and did receive, its vogue tended in the main towards that apotheosis of "the Will." (274)

We see all of these themes in the romantic genre of literature, which is marked by a special kind of narrative structure. Narratives set the scene, organize events into a causal sequence, identify protagonists, and describe their interactions (Krebs 2015). As Spencer (2016) explains, romantic stories feature three main characteristics: "exotic and emotional setting, a brave, heroic yet human character and an adventure emplotted as a struggle for an ideal in an asymmetrical conflict against a more powerful and unjust order" (44). Frye (1957: 186) explains that the essential element of plot in a romantic story is adventure, one which proceeds in three stages: (1) a perilous journey; (2) the crucial struggle, "usually some kind of battle in which either the hero or his foe, or both, must die"; and (3) the exaltation of the hero. Romantic stories feature "melodrama," in which the distinction between good and evil is clearly (perhaps hyperbolically) drawn (Anker 2005: 23–25; also Frye 1957). In a romantic story, a hero strives against structural obstacles that impede his just and good cause. As we will see, our romantic political figures all narrated the events of their time in this way.

The romantic individual, therefore, is one who stresses the potential for agency, emphasizes the importance of staying true to one's ideals, braces and yearns for the struggle inevitably entailed, and proposes to prevail by force of will. Not surprisingly, since romanticism is a tradition in the humanities, it cares little about the distinction between normative and empirical, but rather alights somewhere between the two extremes. The romantic movement thought, for instance, that agency was crucial for understanding the world, but also that it should be celebrated. Fighting on behalf of principles is something that romantics do in practice and also something to be admired.

"Feeling Is All": Romanticism, Emotion, and System I Processing

Focusing only on these four substantive elements of romanticism would neglect an indispensable part of romanticism, its emphasis on emotion (Appel and Daniel 1961; Berlin 2014: 234; De la Croix and Tansey 1986: 784, 809, 870; Dorra 1972; Janson 1991: 629; Peckham 1951: 6; Stokstad 2005: 899). Romanticism without emotion is not romanticism. Romanticism was "an aesthetic movement which praised feeling and passion and relied on the soul's intimate forces instead of asking for well thought out adhesion" (Rosenthal 2008: 28). This is evident in all the arts. As Appel and Daniel (1961) write, "Musical romanticism, there-fore, may be characterized as an art which emphasizes subjective and emotional elements, translating into music the feelings of the human soul – joy and sorrow, passion and tenderness, exuberance and despair" (253). Poetry, in the romantic point of view, has the "end of inciting the emotion against the reason" (Abrams 1971: 301). There is even a romantic style of chess, characterized by bold combinations and offensive action, either winning with style or losing gloriously.

Romanticism helped form the basis of the Counter-Enlightenment. It opposed the Enlightenment's focus on reason and rationality, both empirically and normatively (Barzun 1944, 15; Koch 1993, 125; Lovejoy 1924, 232). One cannot understand human events without emotion, and emotion should be esteemed and honored. Whereas one of the goals of the Enlightenment was to sweep away emotion as a barrier to objectivity and rational thought, "romantics expressed the fear that a 'rational-scientific' ontology negated the emotional character of life" (Koch 1993: 123). The "slogan," as De la Croix and Tansey put it, "is 'Trust your heart rather than your head,' or as Goethe puts it, 'Feeling is all!'" (1986: 785; also Lovejoy 1924: 232).

Consistent with this emphasis, romantics do not value objectivity. Romanticism marks a turning point in the conception of what art *is*. Art must be true, not in the sense that it corresponds to reality, but in the sense that it is a genuine and sincere expression of the feelings of the artist. With the romantics, art ceases to be conceived of and judged by how well it reflects nature, but rather by how it "yields ... insights into the mind and heart of the poet himself," Abrams (1971: 23) notes.

[F]or the representative eighteenth-century critic, the perceiving mind was a reflector of the external world; the inventive process consisted in a reassembly of "ideas" which were literally images, or replicas of sensations; and the resulting art work was itself comparable to a mirror presenting a selected and ordered image of life. By substituting a projective and creative mind and, consonantly, an expressive and creative theory of art, various romantic critics reversed the basic orientation of all aesthetic philosophy. (Abrams 1971: 69)

In fact, in romantic thought, effortful cognitive, rational thinking destroys the potential for agency. The more we simply observe, the more obstacles we see. "Mere contemplation yields only objects," writes Berlin (2014: 226) as he describes the romantic position. "The more successful and perfect the contemplation, the more frictionless the perception of the object, the more the contemplating self diminishes to a vanishing point" (226). Wordsworth, the great English romantic poet, asserts, "The ability to observe with accuracy things as they are in themselves ... supposes all the higher qualities of the mind to be passive, and in a state of subjection to external objects" (Abrams 1971: 53). Rather than accommodating one's vision to the prevailing objective reality, romanticism seeks to remake that world so that it reflects one's subjective vision. Berlin (2014) describes this process:

I begin by being inevitably faced with a world which in some sense hems me in: inanimate matter which limits my physical movements; the laws of physics or mathematics, which seem to be hard, immutable, objective realities not flexible to my will; everything, in short, whereby I distinguish the external world from the "free" world of my own imagination and fancy, my own unhampered thoughts and beliefs and likes and dislikes and ideals and emotions – the inner citadel. . . . The development of freedom, then consists in the gradual conquest of this outside world by assimilating it into the inner citadel. (228)

For the romantic, objectivity and structure are one.

In psychological terms, romantics are endorsing the value of the intuitive, preconscious, and emotional thought process of System I. In the romantic movement, we observe a "marked shift in emphasis from reason to feeling, from calculation to *intuition*, from objective nature to subjective emotion" (De la Croix and Tansey 1986: 785, 870; see also Koch 1993: 126; Lovejoy 1924: 238; Rosenthal 2008: 28). Romantics oppose rationalism in favor of "instinct" and "intuition" (Koch 1993: 126). The "imagination," so important for romantic creativity and agency, contrasts with "Reason and the Sense of Fact" (Lovejoy 1924: 232). "'Irrationalism' is one of the alleged symptoms of romantic temper," writes Barzun (1944: 15).

Romantics do not think hard and deliberately, instead celebrating "those expressions of human nature which are most spontaneous, unpremeditated, untouched by reflection or design" (Lovejoy 1924: 238). According to Berlin (2014), "The inspired artist at the moment of creation, the inspired statesmen or soldier or philosopher, is justified in acting as he does by his intuitive grasp. .... He cannot, perhaps, explain it by the kind of reasoning employed in everyday argument, or by calculation, which is but a stylized and deeply inadequate mechanical set of logical patterns invented for practical purposes" (249). That spontaneity is thought to be emotionally driven. "A work of art is essentially the internal made external, resulting from a creative process operating under the impulse of feeling," writes Abrams (1971: 22) of romanticism. "The experience of poetic inspiration is aid to differ from normal ideation" in that "composition is sudden, effortless and unanticipated. The poem or passage springs to completion all at once, without the prior intention of the poet, and without that process of considering, rejecting and selecting alternatives, which ordinarily intervenes between the intention and the achievement; the composition is involuntary and automatic; in the course of composition, the poet feels intense excitement" (189). The romantics juxtapose this type of action explicitly with the cold, scientific kind of thought that characterizes System II. "The eye of the scientist passively receives, while the eye of the poet receives what it has itself supplemented or modified; scientific discourse reflects data, but poetic discourse reflects data with emotional additions" (Abrams 1971: 315). In essence, the romantic movement represents a change in "popular epistemology" (57).

Thus, the romantic, while nevertheless consumed by a goal, will not exhibit the same reflective cognition as a more rational thinker. A romantic has a cause that he works toward: cajoling, aligning forces, and leading. However, his cognition is almost always nonrational in the sense that the romantic is less willing than the realist to call into question his goals in light of constraints. The romantic will be resistant to recognizing the cost side of the ledger. If we think of being strategic as rationalists generally do – that is, as objectively analyzing the situation based on conscious evaluation of information – then the romantic is not strategic. However, like the proverbial hedgehog, he is constantly working.

Ideal(ist) Types: Romantics versus Realists

In a way that would make romantics happy, the contrast with the instrumental rationality of realism is clear. Realists emphasize structural constraints, which frustrate the designs of even the most skillful and imaginative leaders. The contrast is between two mindsets:

one of empirical reality, where we obey laws willy-nilly and are frustrated by obstacles which we cannot remove, and at best can hope only to adjust ourselves to the inexorable pattern which we have neither created nor willed, and which we accept, but of necessity, not of choice ... and the other world, for which we are ourselves wholly responsible, in which we are totally free to create as we please, which embodies all that our intellects, imaginations, emotions and powers of creation are capable of achieving. (Berlin 2014: 219)

Therefore, just as we can distinguish between international relations theorists who emphasize structure versus agency (Dessler 1989; Wendt 1987), so the same might be possible at the level of individual leaders. This recalls the distinction made by Hermann et al. (2001) between crusading leaders, who pay little attention to constraints, and pragmatists, who pay heed to structural obstacles.

Romantics and realists also differ profoundly in terms of ideals. It is not that realists have no commitment to principles. On the contrary, navigating the ship of state through the choppy waters of international politics is a great, noble, and ethical responsibility one undertakes on behalf of one's citizens. Rather, the difference between realism and romanticism lies in the use or nonuse of instrumental rationality in making choices about ideals. Realist ethical judgments are utilitarian and pragmatic; romantic ethical judgments are deontological. Weber distinguishes the realist "ethic of responsibility" from a deontological "ethics of conviction" (Smith 1986). The former is judged by its consequences and outcomes, the latter by staying true to a set of principles regardless of the consequences. Smith (1986) writes pejoratively that those using the latter moral logic are "windbags who do not fully realize what they take upon themselves, but who instead intoxicate themselves with *romantic* sensations" (47 [emphasis added]). Utilitarianism is itself a distinct ethical decision-making postulate in moral philosophy based on the pursuit of the greater good and the lesser evil. The terms themselves indicate its moral character. Utilitarianism does not imply the absence of ethics; it is its own kind of idealism. One is generally pursuing multiple ideals at one time, making it necessary to trade some off against others. Romantics, in contrast, value "having ultimate issues – serving principles fanatically, without reckoning the cost" (Berlin 2014: 245).

We see this lack of consequentialism in the romantic tendency, mentioned earlier, to enter into battles without careful deliberation of the pros and cons, driven by the belief that one can will oneself to victory. As Berlin (2014) observes, "It made no difference whether the odds were great or small, whether the prospect was victory or death. Once the inner voice had spoken, there was no turning back; or rather any compromise, any evasion was the ultimate sin against the light, was ultimately the only contemptible and vicious act of which a man could be guilty in this world" (246).

It is not that romantics value the ends more than the realist – something that could be represented as cost inelasticity or risk acceptance in an expected utility function (Varshney 2003). If romantics are nonrational thinkers, then they will not make these kinds of calculations at all. Those who are willing to enter into such inevitably losing battles without thought (or without second thoughts) are the most esteemed in romanticism: "Those men, and only those, were good and admirable who, if need be, threw away all they had *without counting the costs*, spoke the truth, created beautiful objects, resisted injustice, or in any other way behaved in a disinterested, *uncalculating*, dedicated way" (Berlin 2014: 246 [emphasis added], also 188). Realists, in contrast, stress the need to be "realistic," to literally choose one's battles carefully. Instrumental rationality is the adjustment of behavior based on one's environmental constraints and doing the best one can given the circumstances, rather than obliterating structure through agency. The notion that one can will oneself to victory is a fantasy to realists. Struggle might be inevitable, but in their view it is best confined to favorable terrain.

The takeaway is that individuals can have the same set of morally sanctioned interests and yet make dramatically different decisions based on variation in how they make moral judgments. As we will see in the empirical chapters that follow, romantics and realists with the same set of goals for their country were often led by their different thinking styles toward radically different strategies. Romantics do, however, tend to idealize their interests in ways that realists do not. They often think of their country's interests as having a transcendent value beyond their material worth and an importance beyond their own country. Churchill and Reagan, as we will see, believed their countries stood for something special, so that an impingement on their security was a threat to moral values themselves. For realists, in contrast, no country's interests are any more morally superior to any others. They caution against these sorts of moralistic crusades, precisely because they threaten rational thinking (Trachtenberg 2003: 167). A sense of moral superiority is "politically pernicious, for it is liable to engender the distortion in judgment which, in the blindness of crusading frenzy, destroys nations and civilizations," writes Morgenthau (1948: 10).

To summarize, realists, owing to their rationalism, accommodate their policies to constraints; romantics try to overcome the same constraints. Realists concede to structure; romantics worship agency. Realists stress the role that objective outer reality must play in decision-making; romantics seek to make the world conform to their own subjective inner vision. Realists calmly think and plot; romantics boldly (and perhaps hastily) act. Most importantly, where the consequentialist runs away in retreat when the cause is lost and he or she is outnumbered, the romantic hero remains defiant. The realist is all System II, the romantic System I.

Not Very Romantic: Methodological Considerations

In Chapter 3, I provide evidence for a central claim of this book, that procedural rationality is necessary for instrumental rationality, using an experiment involving undergraduate students. In the chapters that follow, the argument leaves the laboratory. The advantage of careful case studies is their external validity. That is, we know if the causal argument we see in a laboratory matters in real life, even in actual life-and-death decisions. Focusing on foreign policy decisions, and on war and peace in particular, is the toughest case of all for an argument about variation in rationality. If there are individuals in this world who are under intense pressure to think deliberately and objectively, it is foreign policy leaders facing crisis situations involving national security. The uniquely anarchic nature of international politics is generally argued to cause or at least encourage egoistic, "self-help" behavior on the part of states, and the high stakes should induce careful deliberation on the part of decision-makers (Press 2005; Waltz 1979). In the four case studies that follow, I seek to establish the cognitive style of four major figures in world history.

How do we judge rational thought empirically when there is no recourse to the systematic survey instruments I utilize in the lab? The best way to establish whether (or better said, the degree to which) decision-making is rational is to focus on the process of thinking, rather than outcomes or the substantive content of beliefs.

Being rational is not the same as being right. We can get lucky and reach our preferred outcome based on nonrational decision-making. Because of incomplete information, we can make rational choices that do not realize our goals or efficiently optimize our choice set. If this were not the case, then we should consider those who bet black at a roulette wheel as being more rational than those who bet red when the ball lands on black. Even if we think rationally, we might "err," in the sense that we reach a suboptimal outcome, but with good reason. This point is often missed in international relations. In addition, it might not necessarily be the case that reason outperforms intuition all the time.

In theory, with omniscience, we can establish procedural reality and epistemic motivation based on the substantive content of one's beliefs and how well they track empirical reality. This is Tetlock's "correspondence" criteria of "good judgment," meaning rationality. Rational thinkers must have a reason to believe what they believe, a rationale and not a rationalization (Rescher 1988). Their beliefs must be "well calibrated" and "map onto the actual structure of the world" – in other words, reflect objective reality (Stanovich 2011: 38). Indeed, I have established objectivity as a constituent part of rational thinking. If someone believes that unicorns exist, that the possession of those unicorns is the ultimate weapon in international politics, and that all efforts should be made to find the horned beast, even at the risk of war, we have reasons to think that person is not terribly rational.

Such a standard, while perhaps useful in controlled laboratory settings or large expert studies of prediction like that carried out by Tetlock (2005), seems very difficult to apply as a measure of the rationality of decision-makers in complex environments in which it is impossible to determine just what it is that a rational person should substantively believe. There are not many who have such ostentatiously irrational beliefs as a belief in unicorns in this field (although experts on North Korea might disagree). Using the correspondence criteria requires accumulating all the information that a particular decision-maker knew (or should have known) at the time and judging whether his or her beliefs approximated objective knowledge. This is impossible with even the most careful historical work in the most information-rich research environments. In addition, it requires an act of tremendous intellectual arrogance, telling (often posthumously) people what they should have believed – easy for us to say. Moreover, there is always some set of plausible beliefs that make a behavior rational after the fact. This, however, is precisely the type of nonfalsifiability we should avoid in considering rationality.

In the case studies of this book, I try to avoid drawing any conclusion that a decision-maker was low or high in rationality based on a correspondence definition, even though this seems to be the case at several points, such as Churchill's belief that the United States would soon enter World War II and Reagan's conviction that the Strategic Defense Initiative (SDI) could yield an impenetrable nuclear umbrella.

I focus instead on the process of thinking. Does an individual make a self-conscious effort to be objective, even in the face of temptations not to do so, that they acknowledge? Do they make an effort to accumulate information relative to the decision? Do they recognize not only what they know, but also what they do not know and that they could be wrong? In other words, do they exhibit epistemic motivation? Tetlock (2005) calls this benchmark the "coherence" test of good judgment. The criteria are drawn from the discussion in Chapter 1 and are summarized in Table 2.1.

Table 2.1 *Ideal types of two cognitive styles*

		Less Rational	More Rational
Procedural Rationality	Processing System	System I	System II
	Perception	Subjective and self-serving (myside bias)	Objective and impartial
	Cognition	Simplifying heuristics	Deliberation
	Belief Change	Belief perseverance ("freezing") and assimilation	Evidential
	Approach to Uncertainty	Avoidance ("seizing") and denial ("overconfidence")	Acceptance, modesty
	Speed	Fast and urgent	Slow and effortful
	Consciousness	Unconscious, automatic, intuitive	Conscious, reflective, overrides default System I
	Decision-Making Rules	Top-down, theory-driven, one-size-fits-all	Bottom-up, information-driven, situational
	Need for...	Closure	Cognition
	Head or Heart?	Heart, emotional, "hot"	Head, dispassionate, "cold"
Instrumental Rationality	Updating	Heuristic-driven, closed-minded	Open-minded, costly signal-driven
	Cost–Benefit Analysis	Tradeoff avoidance, belief system overkill	Global maximization, cognitive and integrative complexity
	Interaction	Parametric	Strategic
	Expected Utility	Desirability leads to feasibility	Desirability and feasibility judged separately
	Time Horizons	"Two-selves" problem, short-sighted, "dynamic inconsistency"	Longer shadow of the future, short-term restraint
	Persistence	Resolve, "implemental" mindset	Cut losses, avoid sunk cost fallacy

Procedural rationality should be associated with a series of behaviors we characterize as instrumentally rational, most of which are familiar to international relations scholars. I have tried to make this list as comprehensive as possible, although there could conceivably be more entries. It is, of course, challenging to separate procedural from instrumentally rationality, risking tautology. This was one of the primary reasons that I undertake the laboratory experiment described in Chapter 3. Instrumental rationality, I argue, is the application of procedural rationality to the pursuit of goals in view of constraints. However, we can establish procedural rationality separately in assessments of how leaders think in general. Are they committed to objectivity? Do they actively prize deliberation? The line is not always entirely clear, but I do my to draw and not cross it. A summary can be found in Table 2.1.

Cost–Benefit Tradeoffs. In making the assumption that we can and will make such calculations, we are presuming what Tetlock and his collaborators have called "cognitive" and "integrative" complexity (Suedfeld and Tetlock 1977; Tetlock 1983, 1984). The former measures the number of dimensions along which we consider a decision (sometimes also called "differentiation"), the latter our ability to make compensating tradeoffs across them when they conflict. Cognitive and integrative complexity both require that we be good rational thinkers. We have to engage in an active process of information search in which we find all the important aspects of a dimension, doing our best to objectively represent the choice that faces us. We then have to deliberate conscientiously about how to resolve the tradeoffs we find (Rathbun 2004).

In System I processing, we do not see this. Larson (2011: 185), for instance, finds in her analysis of Truman's "intuitive" decision-making an absence of any discussion of pros and cons. Emotion, an attribute of System I thinking, has also been found to reduce cognitive complexity, something applied already to international relations (Hymans 2006; Welch 1993). Foreign policy calculations are cognitively difficult and emotionally unpalatable. We can assume, for instance, that decision-makers will not want to believe that civilian casualties will result from a military strike they believe to be in the national interest or that a new entitlement program will blow an enormous hole in the budget. Rather than a cognitively and integratively complex process, we often use simple evaluative rules – for instance, maximizing on one dimension rather than making tradeoffs across several dimensions (Luce et al. 1997). We might even deny any tradeoffs are necessary at all, engaging in what Jervis (1976) calls "belief system overkill." Our choice is the most cost-efficient, the most likely, and the most ethical – the best along every dimension. Doing this all the time, in Jervis's eyes (and mine, too), is irrational. It violates both the objective and deliberative requirements of rational thinking.

Global Maximization. Decision-makers are also often forced to make choices between goals themselves. While a particular decision might sacrifice one aim, it might nevertheless be the right choice in terms of overall benefits. Instrumental rationality requires seeing the whole picture. The reflective mind allows for "more global goals of personal well-being" (Stanovich 2011: 32). In chess, one often sacrifices the pawn to save (or capture) the king. Elster (1979) calls this "global maximization." In rationalist terms, one must be able to order one's preferences. Simon (1983) explains: "The SEU [Subjective Expected Utility] model assumes that the decision maker contemplates, in one comprehensive view, everything that lies before him. He understands the range of alternative choices open to him, not only at the moment but over the whole panorama of the future" (13). As we have seen (and will continue to see), this is a consistent theme of realist thinking historically, with the choice of the "necessary evil" being necessary precisely because one cannot have everything one desires given structural constraints. From the need to prioritize comes the construct of the "vital" as opposed to the "peripheral" interest.

Long-Term Thinking. Global maximization might occur cross-sectionally but also longitudinally over time. Rationality is "characterized by the capacity to relate to the future," Elster (1979: vii) notes. Humans are the most rational of animals because they are most capable of using "indirect strategies" for realizing their aims. They are capable of waiting, biding time, and taking a step back if it allows them to take two steps forward later. The very term "consequentialism" implies that we think forward to the consequences of our actions, rather than impulsively and automatically, envisioning the likely results of alternative paths of behavior. Rational thinking is marked by what rationalist international relations scholars call a longer "shadow of the future" (Axelrod 2006; Keohane 1984). Long-term thinking often requires restraint, short-term sacrifices for long-term gains (Elster 1989: 37). Monetary investments, for instance, require individuals to set aside the immediate pleasure of spending their earnings for the greater purpose of growing their nest egg so that they can purchase more later.

However, psychological research, as well as the fate of our New Year's resolutions, tells us that this type of optimal far-sightedness is not something we should assume, precisely because of the internal contest between our Systems I and II. We are frequently witness to a battle between our "multiple-selves," write Bazerman, Tenbrunsel, and Wade-Benzoni (1998: 226). They maintain that individuals have two different types of "wants": one long-term and rational, the other short-term and emotional.

One type may be characterized as "impulsive wants" and the other as "reasoned wants." ... [W]e use the term "want" as a proxy for the former. The latter type of want is what drives that which we refer to as "should." Operationally, want refers to the emotional or affective preference of the decision maker, whereas should refers to the cognitive or reasoned preference of the decision maker. (Bazerman et al. 1998: 226)

In their definition, the rational choice is that which takes into account our long-term interests, but this is a normative ideal rather than an empirical expectation.

It might be tempting to simply attribute short-term satisfactions to our real underlying utility function, thereby preserving our instrumental rationality in a post hoc (and nonfalsifiable manner). In fact, we have not maximized our utility globally, over time, when we give in to our impulses, demonstrating what economists call "dynamic inconsistency" by our "hyperbolic discounting" of the future (Laibson 1997). Stanovich (2011: 84) distinguishes between "wants" and "wantons," with the latter being the impulsive and unthinking pursuit of that which gives us pleasure without reflection or consideration of future consequences. We have to, quite literally, stop and think. While we all struggle to make it to the gym as often as we would like, we can still expect that more epistemically motivated actors will engage in more cross-sectional and longitudinal maximization than those less committed to rational thought.

Strategic Thinking. Good strategic thinking requires understanding the point of view of one's partners or adversaries, anticipating their actions, and realizing how they perceive and what they infer from one's own behavior. It requires objectivity and deliberation. Foreign policy-makers often mistakenly believe that their motives and the reasons for their actions are as clear to others as they are to themselves (Jervis 1976). Rationality requires that foreign policy-makers think hard and honestly about how others actually view them, rather than how they want to be viewed. It necessitates that they recognize that others' behavior might be a product of a situation and not an inherent disposition, though the latter is the cognitively easier and emotionally more comforting conclusion (Mercer 1994; Tetlock 1989). Behavioral game theorists have used the concept of "level k" reasoning to specify a "cognitive hierarchy" of those who think more or less rationally (Arad and Rubinstein 2012). More rational thinkers have more considered "higher-order" beliefs – that is, beliefs about the beliefs of others.

Rational choice scholars do not consider such calculations particularly problematic. However, this is a highly complex process in which multiple variables must be taken into account, all of which are marked by considerable uncertainty. Political actors often fail to understand that their situation is partly of their making. This distinguishes strategic decisions from parametric ones, as Elster (1986) explains:

In a parametric decision the agent faces external constraints that are in some sense given or parametric. First he estimates them as well as he can, and then he decides what to do. A strategic situation is characterized by interdependence of decisions. Before making up his mind, each agent has to anticipate what others are likely to do, which may require an estimate of what they anticipate that he will do. (7; also 1979: 18)

Security dilemmas frequently take on this parametric dynamic. When adversaries react hostilely to one's own hostile behavior, actions on their part are thought to confirm their hostile "type" rather than reflect one's own aggressive actions. In psychological terms, dispositional rather than situational attributions are more common because they are cognitively easier and more pleasant than realizing our role in the process. In Booth and Wheeler's (2008) terms, "security dilemma sensibility" – the understanding that one might be in a structural situation that drives behavior and the opponent might be as scared of me as I am of him – is rare in international politics. This makes the security dilemma even more tragic and pernicious than it might naturally be given the structural constraints of uncertainty and anarchy. Deliberative thinkers are more likely to have this sensibility than are intuitive thinkers.

Updating. In any strategic interaction, one gleans information from the behavior of others that should be used to update one's beliefs about the situation, the other's type, and other variables in an instrumentally rational calculation. This new information might make us more confident of our beliefs and our course of action. However, it also might make us less so.

Rationalists argue that in situations in which there are "incentives to dissemble" (in English, "lie"), only costly signals should lead to updating. Following Schelling (1966), the focus has primarily been on the signaling of resolve in crisis bargaining situations (Fearon 1994; Schultz 1999, 2001). How do states indicate to other states the importance they place on prevailing on some issue when they have incentives to overstate what they would be satisfied with (that is, their "reservation price") and the other state knows this (Fearon 1995)? Before the recent surge of interest in crisis bargaining, international relations scholars were more preoccupied with questions of cooperation, such as sending signals of reassurance so as to escape mutually detrimental security dilemma dynamics (Axelrod 2006; Glaser 1994, 2010; Keohane 1984; Kydd 2005). This vein of research has led scholars to hypothesize a number of ways by which states might demonstrate costly signals, such as by tying their own hands or sinking costs.

Rationalists assume that this process occurs automatically. However, as we have seen, much of the research on biases focuses on how individuals resist changing their beliefs, instead engaging in confirmation bias or belief perseverance. Rational updating requires constant open-mindedness based on a desire to objectively understand one's environment. We expect that only those who demonstrate epistemic motivation, a preexisting and conscious commitment to objectivity and deliberation, will parse information in the way that rationalists generally assume.

More intuitive thinkers, in contrast, will pay attention to different types of information. Research shows that observers are often more attentive to vivid information that is emotionally interesting and concrete, compared to other bits of data that might be more informative but are abstract and colorless. Pictures, for instance, are worth a thousand words for a reason. Powerful sensory experiences have a greater impact on us than bland ones, even if they are not as informative. This can lead us astray because "the vividness of information is normally related only obliquely at best to its true value as evidence" (Nisbett and Ross 1980: 8). Rather than a thorough search of relevant information, we seize on specific things that happen directly to us or others close to us and, therefore, are more available cognitively (Nisbett and Ross 1980; Yarhi-Milo 2014). For instance, we are likely to make choices about whether to buy a specific type of car based on our brother-in-law's experience than its rating in *Consumer Reports*; the latter, of course, gives a much better sample to draw from and is more informative of the chances of buying a lemon. Yarhi-Milo (2014) and Holmes (2018) have demonstrated, in this vein, that quick impressions gained from face-to-face diplomacy have a greater effect on foreign policy leaders' assessments than more considered deliberation.

This tendency is likely true of all individuals to one degree or another. However, I think it is particularly likely to be true of intuitive thinkers, those who are less procedurally rational.

Feasibility, Desirability, and Risk. In a typical expected utility function, there are two primary variables: the actor's goals and his valuation of them on the one hand, and his estimate of the probability of attaining them on the other hand. The latter term is likely a function of structural constraints, such as the expected response of others in an arms race or the number of black slots on a roulette wheel. A rational person separates these two processes. We might want something very badly, but that has nothing to do with whether we can obtain it. "Within an analytic view of judgment and decision-making, risk and benefit are distinct concepts. The nature of the gains attained from pursuit of a hazardous activity or technology is qualitatively different from the nature of the risks," assert Finucane et al. (2000). Particularly in strategic contexts, our most favored outcomes are probably the least likely. Indeed, there is usually some "risk–reward" tradeoff in any substantively interesting and meaningful political judgment. A rational actor, if he or she values some goal enough, might nevertheless make a risky bet but with the knowledge that the odds are not in his or her favor.

In fact, our estimates of feasibility are closely tied to our assessments of desirability (Fischoff et al. 1978; Mc Daniels et al. 1997; Slovic et al. 1991). The more we want something, the better we think our odds are of getting it. Our feasibility estimates are subjective rather than objective in nature, a function of motivated bias. In essence, we often refuse to admit the risk–reward tradeoff that is commonplace in our lives. Thus, risky choices are not regarded as risky at all by the intrepid gamblers who take them. These gamblers are not counting cards; they are relying on their overconfidence, their false belief that they are on a hot streak. Heightened emotion, an attribute of System I processing, is associated with greater tendencies to conflate desirability and feasibility (Finucane et al. 2000).

What this means is that we are systematically underestimating the constraints in the achievement of our goals. Our desires are making us overconfident, giving us an "illusion of control" (Frank and Brandstätter 2002; Gollwitzer and Kinney 1989; Langer 1975). They interfere with our careful deliberation of risks. Intense preferences give us a feeling of agency and cause us to overlook structure. I think that this tendency is likely to be particularly true of those low in epistemic motivation, whereas more procedurally rational thinkers will be more cognizant of the conceptual distinction between feasibility and desirability.

Persistence and Sunk Costs. Even the most rational thinkers do not always get it right given incomplete information. Instrumental rationality is about decision-making under constraints, with one of those constraints being knowledge. The question then becomes, what do they do about it? The behavioral economics literature refers frequently to the "sunk cost fallacy," the tendency to throw good money after bad, to double down on failing enterprises (Arkes and Ayton 1999). This is an error of instrumental rationality because in doing so, decision-makers are incorporating the previous costs into their evaluation of the benefits, thereby violating expected utility maxims. In other words, we want to succeed more when we have spent resources in trying to do so. Our estimation of the worth of various outcomes should remain unchanged in a normative model of rational choice.

Those who think rationally should have an easier time pulling the plug on goals that have proved unexpectedly costly. Psychologists sometimes distinguish between "deliberative" and "implemental" mindsets (Gollwitzer and Kinney 1989), a distinction that has been applied to foreign policy as well (Johnson and Tierney 2011). When we are deciding what to do, we behave in an instrumentally rational fashion, weighing the costs and benefits of different paths. When we decide what to do, we cross a decision-making Rubicon, shifting to an implemental mindset in which our only concern is the achievement of the goal, come what may. Implemental mindsets are empirically associated with greater persistence as costs rise – in other words, a sunk cost fallacy (Frank and Brandstätter 2002). More epistemically motivated thinkers should remain in a deliberative mindset at all times, always able to cut their losses.

For each historical figure, we witness a variety of these behaviors, but some are more the focus than others in each chapter depending on the particular problems each leader faced. For Bismarck, for instance, there is a considerable focus on strategic restraint and time horizons. For Churchill, the question of persistence comes into play given Britain's initial failings in World War II. I do not consider every major decision these leaders ever made, as each figure deserves several books of his own. Instead, I focus on what they are known best for – Richelieu's battles with Spain and Austria during the Counter-Reformation. Bismarck's unification of Germany, Churchill's leadership of Britain during the darkest days of World War II, and Reagan's diplomatic rapprochement with the Soviet Union. Certain events prior to these momentous turning points are also illustrative of cognitive style; they are used to establish a consistency that is important because my argument claims that individual-level dispositions are relatively robust to situational dynamics.

As mentioned earlier, it is difficult to disentangle procedural rationality from instrumental rationality empirically. Is not a cost–benefit analysis an instrumentally rational behavior – an example of deliberation, a procedurally rational one? In some sense, this lends credence to my argument about how instrumental rationality does not occur magically; it has a psychological foundation. However, I claim in this book that one needs a prior commitment to rational thought and procedural rationality – epistemic motivation – before one can begin to calculate the best course of action to realize one's interests in light of constraints. Empirically I need to establish procedural rationality and epistemic motivation separate from instrumentally rational choices so as to avoid tautology. In qualitative case studies, besides being conceptually clear, one strategy is to establish cognitive style in an individual chronologically prior to his foreign policy choices.

In judging the effect of cognitive style, it is important to control for as much as possible, as well as to take into account alternative explanations for the same behaviors – in particular those that could make sense of nonrational thinking in a rational manner, but also those that question the rationality of our rational decision-makers. Importantly, all of the foreign policy leaders examined in this book are national egoists primarily interested in the security and prosperity of their own states, not the promotion of broader collective interests that extend beyond the nation-state or the creation of some regional or global order thought to benefit all. As seen in the laboratory experiment, epistemically motivated prosocial individuals make different choices than epistemically motivated proself individuals. This is another reason not to include liberal leaders in the sample, since they typically have very different substantive foreign policy goals. As will be seen, variation in egoism does explain some of the differences between both Richelieu and Bismarck and their domestic allies, but not all.

Since rationality is not an either/or proposition but rather a relative quantity, it is best seen in relief. I compare leaders not to those in other countries, but rather to their compatriots, particularly their political allies. For Bismarck, it is the reactionary conservatives who promoted his career early on as well as the king he served. For Reagan, it is the factions of his administration, both pragmatist and hardline conservative. For Richelieu, it is "the devoted," the ardent Catholics buoyed by the Catholic Counter-Reformation sweeping France in his time.

In every case I also consider counterhypotheses that seek to make sense of the behavior of our research subjects in a different way. This is more relevant in the chapters on Churchill and Reagan, whom I characterize as romantics with an intuitive thinking style. It is possible, of course, to make their behavior understandable through a rationalist lens after the fact. (This, though, is part of the problem of rationalism.) I find these accounts lacking. The best evidence for my claims is the process of thinking itself, or in these cases, the lack thereof.

Sources

I use four main sources to establish cognitive style: (1) these individuals' own self-understandings, if available; (2) the judgments of those historians who have studied these individuals most closely; (3) the perceptions of those who knew them personally, both friend and foe; and (4) my own careful examination of primary documents drawn from published collections as well as original archival research. Only through a combination of all four sources can we make a judgment about cognitive style. No individual is likely to exhibit all of the phenomena in one column. Indeed, as mentioned earlier, it is possible that System I is composed of a number of different systems whose commonality is only their distinction from System II. Nor will any leader's behavior be completely confined to one side or another. Everyone uses both System I and II thinking at some point. We are looking, however, for significant differences among individuals.

We must be aware of "naïve realism," the finding that many individuals regard themselves as objective, deliberative, and rational thinkers while others are not (Ross and Ward 1996). Accusations of irrationality also serve as a normative and political cudgel given the privileged position rationality occupies in Western society. Thus, I am particularly interested when I find agreement about the cognitive style of our leaders in the assessments of their domestic allies and adversaries and their admonishing and fawning biographers. As will be seen, for instance, Churchill and Reagan are understood by both their detractors and their fans as intuitive thinkers. For the former, this is a vice; for the latter, a virtue. The conclusion is nevertheless the same. As discussed earlier, rational and nonrational thinking both have their strengths.

Case Selection

To anchor the study of rationality in international relations, I have identified two archetypes of foreign policy, the realist and the romantic. Why focus only on four individuals? In a way, that part of the book asserted itself. The great realists of all time, as has been and will be argued, are relatively rare. By definition, the romantic leader is extraordinary and singular. They might not all have "genius," but they act as if they do, loyal only to their cause. Nevertheless, I would argue that this focus on a set of extreme individuals is of great importance. These are four of the most consequential individuals in world history. Even so, I would bridle at any reduction of this book to the simple claim that "individuals matter." Saying something about the right four individuals tells us something about international relations as a whole, and rationality's role in it.

In considering potential cases, I looked for the biggest, baddest realists I could find. Two names come to the top of any list of famous practitioners of raison d'état: Bismarck and Richelieu. As argued earlier, if we can show that these two found little political backing for their foreign policy among otherwise like-minded domestic counterparts, we can say a lot about the prevalence of realism, and by implication, instrumental rationality, at the highest levels of government. My focus on romantics emerged more organically and inductively in an effort to understand the cognitive style of Reagan and Churchill. Both have defied categorization through the theoretical lenses typical in our field. As I came to term with them as romantics, I realized that this served as an important juxtaposition to a rational thinker, one that was necessary if for no other reason than to offer a contrast allowing us to see the former in greater relief. Considering the historical importance of our two romantics, however, an account of their behavior is valuable in and of itself. Plus, romanticism is fun.

3   Little Bismarcks: A Laboratory Experiment on Variation in Rational Thinking and Rational Behavior (with Joshua D. Kertzer)

In the quest to discover whether there is variation in individual-level rationality at the highest levels of government and whether that matters for state behavior, we begin in what might seem like an unlikely place – a university. Yet this makes perfect sense if the goal is to say something universal about human decision-making. If rational thought is a necessary condition for instrumentally rational behavior, as this book argues, then this should not be true just for state leaders, but for everyone.

We hypothesize that egoism and epistemic motivation – the commitment to procedurally rational thought – combine to produce the instrumentally rational, strategic behavior generally expected in rationalist models. When one is concerned with one's own utility but is procedurally rational enough to recognize that this depends on situational constraints and the actions of others, one acts in a strategic manner predicted by international relations rationalists. We are looking for the psychology of rationality, the cognitive preconditions for *Homo economicus*. Note that this is not a royal "we": Joshua Kertzer and I worked together on this experiment.

A laboratory offers what the world can almost never provide – a controlled setting in which the experimenters provide the same decision-making task to all subjects. In international politics, we can almost never recreate the decision-making environment in the same way for different individuals. With the captive audience in the laboratory, we can also measure directly and systematically our independent variables of interest – that is, epistemic motivation and egoism. In our bargaining game, we also have an actual normative benchmark in terms of instrumentally rational behavior against which we can compare the actions of our subjects, something that is difficult to define in actual instances of foreign policy given the complexity of the issues and our inability to faithfully recreate the decision-making environments that we study. In a laboratory experiment, subjects interact through a computer with anonymous opponents on the basis of information that we provide to them. The experimental setup also allows us to measure procedural rationality, self-reports of one's own thinking style, separately from instrumentally rational (or less than rational) behavior, the choices that participants make in the game. This approach circumvents concerns about tautology. The combination of original experimental economics-style laboratory work and the archival-based case studies that follow in subsequent chapters is unique, and in my mind necessary to establish the unique psychology of rationality in international relations.

Strategic, rational decision-making in international relations and in daily life requires that decision-makers adjust to changes in their own and others' power. It is captured in what might be the oldest international relations dictum: the strong do as they will and the weak as they must. Whether individual actors, however, respond to these structural differences is ultimately an empirical question, not a theoretical one. We identify which parties are most responsive to their strategic situation. Egoistic, rational-thinking actors who think strategically should be highly attuned to the relative distribution of power that prevails at any particular time. Those who combine an egoistic "social value orientation" and epistemic motivation should be most responsive to variation in situations; this is our *Homo economicus*. I call them "Little Bismarcks" because they exhibit the same behavior as the realists we will learn about later, based on the same set of dispositional attributes.

To preview the results, we find that those individuals with an egoistic value orientation and a higher degree of epistemic motivation are more likely to restrict their demands of others in situations in which they are weak and to raise those demands when they are strong. Indeed, in situations in which they are not favored by the distribution of power, their behavior tends to converge with prosocials, who prefer to maximize joint gains and share them more equally. Egoists with lower epistemic motivation, even though they share the same goals as their more cognitively engaged brethren, do not adapt to situational constraints to the same degree. As a consequence, we can claim that the egoists with higher epistemic motivation are more instrumentally rational than those who engage in less cognitive effort and activity, a difference manifested even in the relatively simple strategic situations of our bargaining game.

Showing that individual variation in rational thought is a necessary (if not sufficient) condition for instrumentally rational behavior calls into question the epistemological and ontological premise of those rationalists who argue that rational behavior can be expected even if individuals do not approach the normative ideal of rational thought. The results of the bargaining experiment offer an empirical test of this claim and offer support for the alternative epistemological idea, that the assumptions in our theoretical models should be empirically plausible and validated.

Bargaining Game

We modified an incentivized bargaining game created by Tingley (2011), one of the few experimental protocols suited to testing predictions from the bargaining model of war (Fearon 1995). In the game, participants are tasked with dividing a resource worth 10 experimental points: one of the players proposes a division of the resource to the other player, who can then choose to accept or reject the offer. Unlike in a typical ultimatum game in behavioral economics, if the recipient rejects the offer, the resource is then allocated to one of the players by a costly lottery that assigns the 8 remaining points to one of the players with a known probability. Both the 2-point lottery cost and the shift in bargaining power are common knowledge.

Tingley's (2011) game is ideal for our purposes because subjects play a repeated game in which the distribution of power, captured by the likelihood of winning the entire resource, shifts from the first round to subsequent rounds. While the subject tasked with making an offer has only a 30 percent chance in the first round of winning the costly lottery if the recipient rejects the offer, that probability increases to 70 percent in subsequent rounds. In other words, we have variation in the strategic situation, the set of constraints that rational actors should adjust to so as to realize their goals.

Tingley's (2011) original purpose was to test how players' offer size and probability of acceptance shift with the length of the shadow of the future, operationalized with a probabilistic stopping rule that terminates the game at the end of any given round with a known probability. We are less interested in that variation here, so in our version of the game we fixed this probability at 50 percent. As with most bargaining games operating out of the experimental economics tradition, Tingley (2011) focuses on average treatment effects rather than individual-level heterogeneity, finding that, on average, offers by players in the weaker position were indeed higher than those made by participants in the stronger position. Building on his work, we look for individual-level variation in behavior based on psychological attributes captured in survey questionnaires measuring social value orientation and epistemic motivation.

After an instructional period in which participants were taught the rules of the game and completed two practice rounds, participants played a series of matches against one another. The instructional period was based on the protocol developed by Tingley (2011). Participants were given an oral presentation, a slide presentation, and written instructions. The game was programmed in *Multistage* (http://casselweb .ssel.caltech.edu). At the beginning of each match, players were randomly assigned a role as either the proposer who makes the offer or the recipient who decides whether to accept or reject it. Each player occupied that role for the remainder of that particular match. The chance of occupying either position was 50 percent. After every round, the probability that a subject would continue to be matched with the same player for an additional round was 50 percent, so participants played from 1–7 rounds in each match, depending on luck (the 50 percent stopping rule at the end of each round). When a match concluded, each subject was paired with another player for a new match, for 15 matches in total. All matches were anonymous, such that players were not aware of the identity of their opponent.

The game was incentivized for egoistic behavior. First, the game was distributive rather than mixed motive in nature. Second, subjects were paid a certain amount based on the number of points they accrued in seven randomly chosen matches plus a show-up fee of $10. Third, even though bargaining ended in each match once the costly lottery began, players who won the costly lottery were awarded the full resource of 10 points for all remaining rounds, modeling the extent to which actors can profit off the spoils of war in the future. There were therefore strong incentives to exploit bargaining leverage.

An example might help. Suppose Player A is randomly assigned in the first match to play Player F and makes the offer in the first round. She offers 6 points of the total 10-point resource and Player F decides to accept the offer. Player A receives the remaining 4 points. The computer then chooses with 50 percent probability whether they will face each other again for a second round. Player A now perhaps offers 3 points. Play F might reject this lower offer. If so, the computer decides who receives the 10 points for that round on the basis of a known probability (70/30) that in the second round and after favors Player A, who is in a position of strength after the first round. However, each player is charged 2 points for failing to reach an agreement. Suppose Player A wins this costly lottery. She receives 8 points for that round as well as 10 points for every remaining round. The computer decides again with 50 percent probability whether Players A and F will face each other for a third round. If there is another round after any failure to agree, the two do not actually make choices. Player A gets the full 10 points, and the computer decides again whether there will be a fourth round (or fifth, or sixth, and so on) until this coin flip eventually ends the game.

Note the strategic incentives of the game. The player making the offer in the first round is in a position of weakness because if her offer is not accepted, she will likely lose the lottery (she has a 70 percent chance of losing and a 30 percent chance of winning). Her incentive is to make an offer good enough to keep her partner in the game until the second round (provided they make it past the stopping rule), when she can bargain more forcefully, since any rejection will induce a lottery that will favor her. The incentives for the player receiving the offer, of course, is the opposite. She has reason to reject weak offers in the first round because the costly lottery favors her. This changes if the players go into the second round (and beyond). The game requires that players take into account the likely moves of their partners, the probability of prevailing in any round, and how the present round affects the prospects for future rounds. These are three elements of instrumentally rational thinking identified in Chapter 2.

Because of the extensive instructional period and the game's relatively straightforward setup, the game can hardly be said to be cognitively taxing. Thus it creates a harder test for our argument that a commitment to procedural rationality and cognitive effort captured by epistemic motivation is necessary to play it more optimally. Nor should differences in cognitive capacity matter much, although we test for these differences explicitly later in the chapter. In addition, participants completed a quiz on the main features of the game, and could not proceed until they had answered all of the questions correctly. This should be something of an easy win for the rationalist case that participants will adjust their behavior "in natural ways" as Achen and Snidal (1989: 64) put it, independently of cognitive style.

Measures

In addition to engaging in the bargaining game, participants completed a dispositional questionnaire measuring their social value orientation, epistemic motivation, and demographic characteristics. To avoid order effects, participants randomly received one of two different survey orderings. In each case, the survey was split in half and administered in two parts, one at the beginning of the session, and the other after the bargaining game had concluded. We were therefore able to use this order manipulation to ensure that our measures of participants' social value orientations and epistemic motivations were not affected by the bargaining game, and vice versa. (They were not.) In total, 204 subjects participated. Each session (in groups of 10, 12, or 14) lasted a little less than an hour, and the average payout was approximately 15.

To measure epistemic motivation, we employ a 13-item scale, modified from Cacioppo's (1984) short-form Need for Cognition scale. Subjects were asked, for each of the following items, "whether the statement is characteristic of your or what you believe," with a 5-item Likert scale. Items denoted with an asterisk were reverse-coded.

1. I would prefer complex to simple problems.
2. I would rather do something that requires little thought than something that is sure to challenge my thinking abilities.*
3. I only think as hard as I have to.*
4. I like tasks that require little thought once I've learned them.*
5. The idea of relying on thought to make my way to the top appeals to me.
6. I really enjoy a task that involves coming up with new solutions to problems.
7. Learning new ways to think doesn't excite me very much.*
8. I prefer my life to be filled with puzzles that I must solve.
9. The notion of thinking abstractly is appealing to me.
10. I would prefer a task that is intellectual, difficult, and important to one that is somewhat important but does not require much thought.
11. I feel relief rather than satisfaction after completing a task that required a lot of mental effort.*
12. It's enough for me that something gets the job done; I don't care how or why it works.*
13. I usually end up deliberating about issues even when they do not affect me personally.

We can judge the effect of epistemic motivation on behavior in a bargaining situation only if we have some sense of the preexisting preferences of the players. We cannot assume, as rationalists often do, that all individuals prefer to maximize their own payoffs. Social psychologists point out that individuals frequently make choices that do not maximize their own personal utility. The literature on social value orientation tries to make sense of the great empirical variation in individual behavior in the same structural circumstances, particularly the high level of cooperation in one-shot prisoner's dilemma experiments, in which the optimal strategy is to defect. Social psychologists theorize that individuals transform objective decision matrices given by researchers into "effective" decision matrices that reflect their own subjective weights of particular outcomes (Kelley and Stahleski 1970; McClintock 1972). In other words, egoism, like rational thought, is a variable.

Researchers separate subjects into different types. Individuals are often classified as being "proself" or "prosocial" in nature. While the former look out only for themselves, the latter seek joint gains. Proselfs are sometimes divided into "competitors" and "individualists," with the former seeking to maximize the difference in payoffs between themselves and others, and the latter making choices that maximize their own personal take irrespective of how others do. Empirically, however, proselfs often demonstrate very similar behavior and are often aggregated into a single category (Kuhlman and Marshello 1975; Kuhlman and Wimberley 1976; McClintock and Liebrand 1988). Proselfs are the kind of actors typically assumed to be operating in rationalist models.

Prosocials are not altruistic or self-abnegating, expecting reciprocity from others. They will stop cooperating when faced with a partner who consistently defects. However, they do prefer joint gains to individual gains, such that they typically opt for mutual cooperation even when they have the opportunity to defect for greater payoffs (Kuhlman and Marshello 1975; Kuhlman and Wimberley 1976; McClintock and Liebrand 1988). They seek gain for both themselves and for others.

We measure social value orientations using the Triple-Dominance Measure developed by Van Lange et al. (1997). Respondents were given the following prompt:

In this part of the survey we ask you to imagine that you have been randomly paired with another person, whom we will refer to simply as the "Other." This other person is someone you do not know and who you will not knowingly meet in the future. Both you and the "Other" person will be making choices by circling either the letter A, B, or C. Your own choices will produce points for both yourself and the "Other" person. Likewise, the other's choice will produce points for him/her and for you. Every point has value: the more points you receive, the better for you, and the more points the "Other" receives, the better for him/her.

Here's an example of how this task works.

	A	B	C
You get	500	500	550
Other gets	100	500	300

Subjects were then given nine choice situations in which they would choose from three distributions of points. For each situation, one of these response options represents a *prosocial* choice (for instance, option B in the example), an *individualistic* choice (option C), and a *competitive* choice (option A). Both individualistic and competitive orientations are forms of proself orientations, but individualistic orientations maximize what political scientists would call "absolute gains," whereas competitive orientations maximize "relative gains" (Grieco 1988): subjects with a competitive social value orientation would rather receive a smaller payoff (e.g., 500 rather than 550) if it meant their opponent received even less (e.g., 100 rather than 300). Social value researchers classify participants' social value orientations based on whether at least six of their responses are of the same type.

We deviate from this approach in two respects. First, following Kuhlman and Marshello (1975), Kuhlman and Wimberley (1976), and McClintock and Liebrand (1988), we lump together competitive and individualistic responses into one proself category, since these two types of proselfs tend to display very similar behavior in distributive games, and we have little theoretical value riding on the distinction between absolute and relative gains. Second, to avoid missing data, we classify a participant as prosocial or proself if a simple majority of that person's response options fall into one of these camps. Concerns might be raised about our adopting a dichotomous measure of social value orientation rather than employing continuous scores (since such an approach treats strong prosocials, for example, as equivalent to moderately strong prosocials), but we note two rationales for this choice. First, the distributions of these social value orientation scores in our sample were highly bimodal: most respondents either provided nine proself responses, or zero. Second, when we replicated our analyses using continuous measures of prosocial value orientation, we found the results continued to hold.

Hypotheses

Our argument has a number of observable implications that we can formulate into hypotheses:

> H1: In the first round, when the subject making the offer is in a position of weakness, proselfs with greater epistemic motivation should make larger offers than those with lower epistemic motivation.

> H2: In the second and subsequent rounds, when the subject making the offer is in a position of strength, proselfs with greater epistemic motivation should make less generous offers than those with lower epistemic motivation.

> H3. The difference in the offer size between rounds one and two should be most pronounced for proselfs with high epistemic motivation.

> H4: In the first round, when the subject receiving the offer is in a position of strength, proselfs with greater epistemic motivation should be less likely to accept an offer, controlling for offer size, than those with lower epistemic motivation.

> H5: In the second and subsequent rounds, when the subject receiving the offer is in a position of weakness, proselfs with

greater epistemic motivation should be more likely to accept an offer, controlling for offer size.

H6: In positions of weakness, proselfs with high epistemic motivation should demonstrate convergence with prosocials who are likely to make more generous offers in general.

H7: High–epistemic motivation proselfs should play more consistently over time than low–epistemic motivation proselfs, as they will more quickly grasp the strategic situation given their higher level of deliberation.

Results

In the fall of 2013, we recruited 204 undergraduates from a large private American research university in southern California with a very good football team to play our game. Participants ranged in age from 18 to 30 years (mean: 20 years) and were predominantly (65.5 percent) female; 39.4 percent of participants self-defined as White and 47.8 percent as Asian American; and 63.4 percent of participants had taken an economics class before. In this section, we present the laboratory results in two phases. First, we simply look at the average effect of the change in bargaining power on offer size and the probabilities of acceptance. Second, we examine players' epistemic motivation and social value orientations to show how different types of players responded to changing incentives differently.

On average, our participants responded to the shift in bargaining power as bargaining models would predict: situational factors mattered. First, proposers made less generous offers when their probability of winning the lottery was higher: on average, first-round offers were 2.94 points higher (95 percent clustered bootstrapped confidence interval (CI): 2.63, 3.27)[1] than offers in later rounds. Similarly, recipients were 16.5 percent more likely to accept offers in the second and later rounds (when their bargaining position was weaker) than in the first round (95 percent clustered bootstrapped CI: 10.5 percent, 22.2 percent). In the aggregate, then, the strong did as they wished, while the weak did as they must. Importantly, offer size was not affected by the order manipulation; it did not matter when the subjects completed the survey.

However, simply focusing on the strategic situation leaves much individual-level variation to explain. We therefore turn to a series of

---

[1] We cluster the data at the individual level to take into account the multiple offers per player, which, as Tingley (2011) notes, produces a more conservative test.

multivariate models to explain this variation theoretically, exploring the extent to which social value orientation and epistemic motivation predict how our participants play the game. Two points are important to note here. First, we measured participants' preexisting levels of epistemic motivation and social value orientation, rather than trying to induce them through random assignment. This allows us to explore how participants with certain dispositions responded differently to the situational features of the game, but it also means that we are not studying their effects experimentally. Second, our measures of epistemic motivation and social value orientation were not correlated with one another. If we measure epistemic motivation using need for cognition, 34.5 percent of our sample were low–epistemic motivation proselfs, 17.0 percent were low–epistemic motivation prosocials, 29.5 percent were high–epistemic motivation proselfs, and 19.0 percent were high–epistemic motivation prosocials. We obtain similar distributions if we measure epistemic motivation using need for cognitive closure. Because we have multiple observations for each participant, we employ a linear mixed effects model with a random effect on each participant, as well as a random effect on each session to control for potential session effects.

Since we expect that the impact of social value orientation depends on epistemic motivation, we include an interaction term between the two variables. Tingley (2011) shows that how players play the game changes as their familiarity with it increases, such that he conducts separate analyses for the first and second half of the matches. We have our own expectations about how dispositions interact with time. To model this longitudinal effect, we include a dichotomous variable ("Matches 1–7") indicating whether the offer was given in the first half of the matches. However, since this learning dynamic likely manifests itself differently in participants with differing social and epistemic orientations – in particular, we expect in H7 that high–epistemic motivation proselfs will play more strategically from the beginning, and thus display more consistent behavior across matches – we interact this longitudinal variable with these two dispositional characteristics, producing a three-way interaction model.

Take It or Leave It: Variation in Offer Size

We begin by exploring how social value orientation and epistemic motivation, operationalized as need for cognition, affect offer size when the proposer is in a position of strength, controlling for demographic characteristics such as age, race, gender, and previous enrollment in any economics classes.

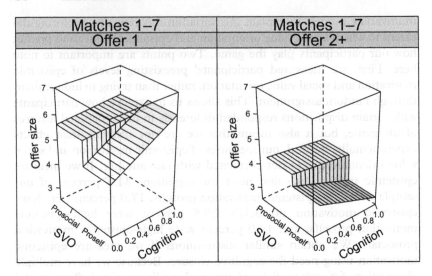

Figure 3.1 The joint impact of social value orientation and epistemic motivation on offer size.

For ease of interpretation, we plot the results visually with wireframe plots in Figure 3.1 and present the complete regression tables in an appendix at the end of this chapter. We separate subjects into two categories – proself or prosocial, represented by the two planes – and plot their offer size on the vertical axis by a continuous measure of the need for cognition. Following traditional practices in the social preferences literature, we employ a dichotomous measure of social value orientation separating prosocials from proselfs. The farthest left-hand panel shows that, as predicted by H1, when in the first round and thus in a position of weakness, proselfs with greater epistemic motivation make better offers than proselfs with lower epistemic motivation ($p < 0.004$). High-cognition proselfs in this situation act more strategically than low-cognition proselfs do, behaving more generously to avoid a costly lottery not in their favor. They give offers indistinguishable from those extended by high-cognition prosocial players (as predicted by H6). In contrast, low-cognition proselfs fail to appreciate their position of weakness and make stingier offers. This is consistent with impulsive, unreflective thinking of the System I variety. Low-cognition proselfs want more for themselves but do not deliberate enough to recognize that this requires short-term sacrifices. They simply claim more.

However, as the third box from the left shows, by the second half of the matches, the low-cognition proselfs have caught on and now play indistinguishably from low-cognition prosocials; high-cognition proselfs still give

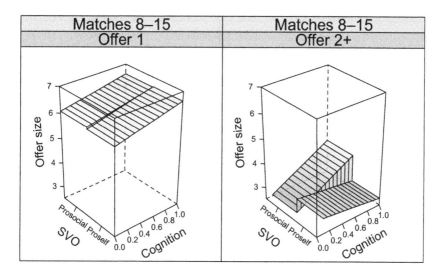

slightly more generous offers than their low-cognition counterparts, but the difference just escapes statistical significance ($p < 0.128$). Low-cognition proselfs need the experience and reinforcement provided by the game to induce their strategic behavior, whereas high-cognition proselfs adjust to strategic circumstances immediately, consistent with H7.

The second panel shows the converse effect when proposers are in a position of strength, and offers considerable support for H2: high-cognition proselfs exploit their position of bargaining strength compared to their high-cognition prosocial counterparts ($p < 0.06$ for both the first and second half). Importantly, the slope of the proself plane shifts entirely. When players are in a position of weakness, the plane slopes upward toward the back of the plot, with offer size increasing as need for cognition increases. Conversely, when players are in a position of strength, the proself plane slopes downward toward the back of the plot. High-cognition proselfs also give offers closest in size to the game's equilibria as solved by Tingley (2011) – another finding that supports our claim that proselfs with high epistemic motivation are the approximation of *Homo economicus*.[2] Prosocials also sometimes exhibit different behaviors based on their levels of epistemic motivation and demonstrate unique over-time effects consistent with prior research (Kertzer and Rathbun 2016). The fourth panel shows that as time goes by, the behavior of low-cognition proselfs converges with that of high-cognition proselfs, as was the case when they were in a position of weakness.

---

[2] See the appendix in Tingley (2011) for a discussion of the solutions to the game.

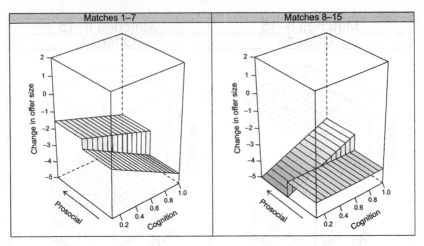

Figure 3.2 Changes in offer size in response to bargaining power.

We combine the previous two sets of analyses by examining the within-subject changes in offer size between the first and later rounds of each match. Figure 3.2 shows that especially early in the game, the high-cognition proselfs most fully take advantage of their increased bargaining power, and display larger decreases in offer size (4.4 points) compared to both their low-cognition (2.1 points: a difference significant at $p < 0.02$) and prosocial (2.8 points: significant at $p < 0.05$) counterparts, in a manner consistent with H3. By the end of the game, however, the approaches of low-cognition proselfs have converged with those of high-cognition proselfs.

What a Deal!: Variation in the Probability of Acceptance

So far, we have seen that high-cognition proselfs propose offers in the manner that rational choice theory would predict: unlike low-cognition proselfs, they know not to overplay their hand when they are in a position of weakness; but unlike prosocials, they are more inclined to take advantage of their position of strength. What happens when they are the recipient rather than the proposer? To address this question, we estimate a series of logistic mixed-effect models (the regression tables are presented in the appendix at the end of the chapter) examining the extent to which these dispositional characteristics predict whether players accept the offer. Since the probability of accepting an offer depends on what the offer is, we control for offer size. For ease of interpretation, the substantive effects are illustrated in Figure 3.3, in which the probability of accepting an offer, controlling for offer size, is scaled on the vertical axis.

The farthest left-hand panel, depicting the results for the first half of the matches, offers support for H4: in first-round offers when the recipient has a higher probability of winning the costly lottery (and is thus in a position of bargaining strength), high-cognition proselfs are more likely to exploit their bargaining position and reject an offer ($p < 0.046$) than are low-cognition proselfs, who play more similarly to their low-cognition prosocial counterparts. The second panel shows that by the second half of the matches, the high-cognition proselfs play as they did in the first half, but the low-cognition proselfs attempt to compensate for their generous acceptance rate in the first half of the matches by being far less likely to accept, overshooting the high-cognition proselfs. As with the offers, we find support for H7: high-cognition proselfs adjust to the change in bargaining power from the very beginning of play, whereas low-cognition proselfs tend to display greater variation between their strategies in the first and second half of the game.

The third panel displays the probability of offer acceptance when the recipient is in a position of weakness. Here, we find support for H5: when in a position of weakness, high-cognition proselfs are more likely to accept the offer than are low-cognition proselfs ($p < 0.12$ in the first half of the matches; $p < 0.06$ in the second half). Note that the slope of the proself plane again shifts direction in the fourth panel as the distribution of power shifts. Among proselfs, need for cognition leads to a greater likelihood of acceptance when they are in a position of weakness and a lower likelihood acceptance of acceptance when they are in a position of strength.

Thus, as both the proposer and the recipient, high-cognition proselfs play as *Homo economicus* would expect: they drive hard bargains when in positions of strength, but behave generously when in positions of weakness. In contrast, in these situations low-cognition proselfs display what Keohane (1984) calls "myopic self-interest": they attempt to maximize gains, but in a manner that ultimately leaves them worse off. Their behavior is egoistic, constantly claiming more of the pie than prosocials, but is not strategic. Low-cognition proselfs simply demand more with less consideration of their strategic position and with less appreciation of how this affects their likelihood of success.

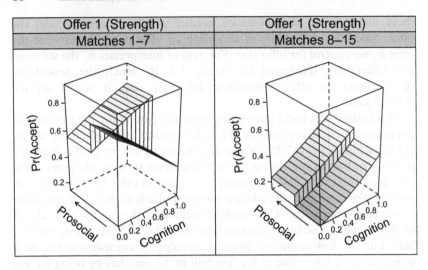

Figure 3.3 The joint impact of social value orientation and epistemic motivation on the probability of acceptance.

Overall Performance

As a final test of how social orientation and epistemic motivation predict players' behavior in the bargaining game, we explore how participants with these clusters of orientations ultimately fare in the game. If procedural rationality truly promotes instrumental rationality, we would expect that high-cognition proselfs would accrue more points in the game than their low-cognition counterparts. We thus regress the logged number of points each player received in the game on epistemic motivation, social value orientation, their interaction, and the various demographic characteristics included in the previous analyses. We then bootstrap the model to produce measures of uncertainty around the predicted number of points for low-cognition proselfs, high-cognition proselfs, low-cognition prosocials, and high-cognition prosocials. We use a one-unit change in need for cognition, which represents the difference from the minimum to the maximum value.

In general, high-cognition players outperform low-cognition ones, but high-cognition proselfs do the best, receiving the highest expected number of logged points: 4.27, which is higher than the expected score for low-cognition proselfs (3.76; bootstrapped p-value for difference: $p < 0.01$) and high-cognition prosocials (4.04; bootstrapped p-value for difference: $p < 0.08$). Importantly, the high–epistemic motivation proselfs outperform the low–epistemic motivation proselfs in both the first and

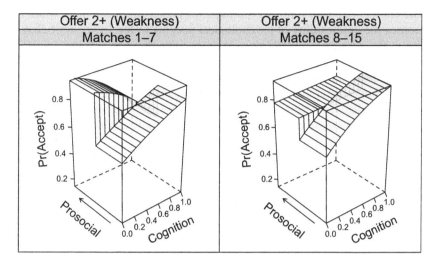

second half of the matches, showing that they maintain their advantage even after controlling for learning dynamics. These results offer further evidence that the low-cognition proselfs play suboptimally, failing to respond to the changing incentive structure.

Rathbun, Kertzer, and Paradis (2017) demonstrate that these results hold with a continuous measure of social value orientation, an alternative measure of epistemic motivation (the need for cognitive closure), and with the inclusion of intelligence metrics (measured with self-reported SAT scores).

From Little Bismarcks to Big Bismarck?

Our bargaining experiment provides evidence for the microfoundations of the argument made in this book. There is significant variation in rational thought across individuals, which when coupled with egoistic orientations leads to more optimally instrumentally rational behavior. We believe that our laboratory study is the first empirical test of the epistemological position adopted by many rational choice scholars – namely, that they need not take into account cognitive processes or the plausibility of their assumptions because their models will in any case still have predictive power. Our results do not bear this position out.

There are, of course, important questions of external validity in laboratory studies, both because of the difficulty in generalizing from non-elite samples to the target population of interest, and because of the stakes of the choice. External validity is perhaps the biggest question mark when it comes the applicability of psychological insights to foreign policy behavior at the elite level. In addition, we recognize that social value orientation and epistemic motivation will vary by situation. Experimentalists have found that increasing incentives can induce more proself behavior and that accountability for decision-making raises epistemic motivation, for example (De Dreu et al. 2006; Lerner and Tetlock 1999). Our interest is whether, even in those instances, individuals might exhibit differences in behavior.

Ultimately, the external validity of this argument is an empirical question – one that I tackle in subsequent chapters, now that I have established its internal validity. Those who combine egoism and high epistemic motivation are not just the formal modeler's ideal, of course. They are also the epitome of realist prescriptions, albeit at an individual level of analysis in which strategic adversaries are other individuals rather than states. What we have shown is the microfoundations of Realpolitik. These rational actors are "lay realists" – Little Bismarcks. The strong might do as they will and the weak as they must, but more so if they are egoistic and think rationally.

In Chapter 4, we turn to Bismarck to see whether his rational thought was necessary for his rational behavior and whether his realism was commonplace or unique in nineteenth-century Prussian politics. A high-stakes foreign policy environment poses perhaps the most difficult test for an argument about variation in rational thinking and egoism. One could argue that if there was a situation that would induce or select for both, this would be the one.

Appendix

Table 3.1 *High-cognition proselfs give the most strategic offers.*

	Offer 1 (Weakness) (1)	Offer 2+ (Strength) (2)	Δ Offer (3)
Cognition	0.646	−0.386	−0.026
	(0.566)	(0.897)	(1.166)
Prosocial	0.076	−0.771	−1.157
	(0.595)	(0.993)	(1.279)
Male	0.346**	−0.457*	−0.645**
	(0.175)	(0.250)	(0.321)
Age	−0.039	0.026	0.032
	(0.045)	(0.066)	(0.087)
White	−0.035	0.043	0.228
	(0.181)	(0.262)	(0.345)
Taken economics	0.230	0.308	0.388
	(0.177)	(0.255)	(0.329)
Matches 1–7	−1.386**	0.589	2.242***
	(0.259)	(0.525)	(0.712)
Cognition × Prosocial	−0.096	1.875	2.152
	(0.965)	(1.599)	(2.058)
Cognition × Matches 1–7	0.898**	−0.567	−2.509**
	(0.431)	(0.872)	(1.176)
Prosocial × Matches 1–7	0.930**	1.189	1.624
	(0.464)	(0.993)	(1.329)
Cognition × Prosocial × Matches 1–7	−1.213	−1.182	−1.081
	(0.750)	(1.611)	(2.136)
Constant	6.541***	2.341*	−5.123***
	(0.909)	(1.333)	(1.769)
N	1,492	540	371
Log likelihood	−2,674.62	−985.31	−767.98
AIC	5,379.24	2,000.63	1,565.95
BIC	5,458.86	2,065.00	1,624.69

Note: Linear mixed-effect models with random effects on participant and session, not shown here. To substantively interpret interactions, see Figure 3.1. * $p < 0.1$; ** $p < 0.05$; *** $p < 0.01$.

Table 3.2 *High-cognition proselfs are the most strategic about which offers to accept.*

	Accept Offer 1 (Strength)		Accept Offer 2+ (Weakness)	
	(1)	(2)	(3)	(4)
Cognition	0.732	1.631*	2.234**	1.922
	(0.624)	(0.985)	(1.045)	(1.246)
Prosocial	0.250	0.541	1.069	0.679
	(0.682)	(1.054)	(1.037)	(1.220)
Male	−0.559***	−0.911***	0.009	−0.073
	(0.178)	(0.289)	(0.264)	(0.314)
Age	−0.007	−0.009	0.075	0.099
	(0.046)	(0.077)	(0.069)	(0.079)
White	0.111	0.276	−0.368	−0.612**
	(0.181)	(0.301)	(0.263)	(0.307)
Taken economics	−0.167	−0.173	0.393	0.294
	(0.180)	(0.296)	(0.252)	(0.295)
Matches 1–7	0.593	3.014***	0.242	−0.390
	(0.417)	(0.598)	(0.757)	(0.939)
Offer size		1.665***		0.954***
		(0.099)		(0.099)
Cognition × Prosocial	−0.076	−0.137	−2.244	−1.731
	(1.102)	(1.715)	(1.690)	(1.977)
Cognition × Matches 1–7	−1.683**	−3.403***	−0.889	−0.415
	(0.700)	(0.986)	(1.312)	(1.604)
Prosocial × Matches 1–7	−0.776	−1.559	1.135	2.075
	(0.779)	(1.085)	(1.414)	(1.686)
Cognition × Prosocial × Matches 1–7	1.917	3.046*	−0.932	−2.383
	(1.250)	(1.757)	(2.271)	(2.696)
Constant	−0.058	−11.465***	−2.083	−4.633***
	(0.922)	(1.705)	(1.418)	(1.668)
Observations	1,478	1,478	534	534
Log likelihood	−968.37	−688.17	−328.78	−256.68
AIC	1,964.73	1,406.34	685.56	543.36
BIC	2,038.91	1,485.81	745.49	607.56

Note: Logistic mixed-effect models with random effects on participant and session, not shown here. To substantively interpret interactions, see Figure 3.2. * $p < 0.1$; ** $p < 0.05$; *** $p < 0.01$.

4   The "Prince" among Men: Bismarck's Realpolitik in Prussian Politics

What is Realpolitik and how common is it? We might assume that Realpolitik simply amounts to following the dictates of the international system, the inevitable fighting of the war of all against all. Under this structural understanding, Realpolitik will be everywhere, the norm rather than the exception. After all, what choice is there?

I argue that Realpolitik is the pursuit of egoistic interests under structural constraints in international politics, most importantly anarchy and the distribution of power. In other words, it is instrumental rationality in foreign policy. Even so, Realpolitik cannot be taken for granted. Foreign policy-makers have all kind of interests that are not exclusively egoistic in nature. More importantly for the purposes of this book, Realpolitik rests on a particular psychological foundation. Instrumentally rational behavior requires rational thought, what we call procedural rationality. Realistic statesmen must see the world objectively and dispassionately. To make cost–benefit calculations based on an assessment of the constraints posed by the environment, they must be committed to deliberate thinking. Realpolitik is as much cognitive as it is substantive. Even as realism stresses the importance of structural constraints in international politics, these constraints need to be recognized by a rational statesman of Realpolitik. This is the "real" in realism.

Rational thought varies across state decision-makers based on their individual psychology. As psychologists frequently maintain, procedural rationality is an imposing cognitive standard, threatened by the over-reliance on heuristics and biases that facilitate the decision-making process but often reduce its efficiency. Moreover, some decision-makers are simply more epistemically motivated than others – putting in more cognitive effort, self-consciously reminding themselves of the need to see the situation objectively, avoiding the temptation to make short-sighted and emotional decisions that do not take into account the whole picture, and sacrificing smaller interests to secure more important ones.

All of these points become evident in a close examination of the policies of Otto von Bismarck. Bismarck is distinguished from his peers, even fellow conservatives who shared his foreign policy goals, by his Realpolitik. Virtually no one in Prussian – or, after unification, German – politics shared the foreign policy views of the man whose successes would eventually make him a prince. Bismarck was both an egoistic Prussian and a thinker with a high level of epistemic motivation, which in turn made him highly consequentialist in his foreign policy preferences.

The man who would become known as the Iron Chancellor explicitly stressed the importance of seeing things as they are, real-istically, rather than how one wanted things to be. Bismarck had a structural understanding of politics in which the statesman makes the best of circumstances rather than trying to change what is unchangeable. As a consequence, foreign policy is full of tradeoffs, lesser evils that one must accept. There are no general principles of politics, only rare windows of opportunity that must be recognized and exploited. The Prussian politician was aware of uncertainty, highly cognizant that there was more that he did not know than that he knew. Bismarck was cold-blooded, consciously repressing his natural passions to make the best choices possible. Both Goddard (2009) and Hall (in press) have recently shown the strategic nature of Bismarck's foreign policy thinking: the former by showing the Minister President's shrewd use of rhetoric, and the latter his ability to manipulate emotions to achieve his goals. I aim to ground these elements of Bismarck's Realpolitik in his highly rational thinking style and demonstrate the importance of doing so for international relations theory.

Bismarck sought to establish Prussian primacy in German affairs, which meant pushing the Austrian Empire out of the German Bund and minimizing the influence of smaller German kingdoms such as Bavaria, Hanover, Saxony, and Baden Württemberg. His Machiavellian realism pitted him against what he called "romantic" conservatives, who instead argued for legitimist solidarity among monarchies given the continued ideological threat posed by the kind of democratic revolutions that gripped Europe in 1848.[1] Romantic conservatives protested against Bismarck's insistent advice to take advantage of Austrian weakness in the 1850s when the Habsburgs were bogged down by the Crimean conflict and fighting a war with France. Their objections reflected both substantive differences about the degree to which egoistic interests alone should govern Prussian policy and cognitive differences about whether to make distasteful tradeoffs in the service of goals. Bismarck was a moral utilitarian, willing to accept certain lesser evils – in particular, distasteful alliances with ideological foes such as revolutionary France and liberal

---

[1] Haas (2005) has pointed out the importance of this ideological cleavage, albeit between (rather than within) European states.

German nationalists – that other conservatives would simply not contemplate. With no like-minded peers on either the nationalist and liberal left or the conservative, monarchical, and aristocratic right, as a *Homo economicus* in foreign policy Bismarck was an extremely rare breed. He was the Machiavellian "prince" among men.

The empirical evidence cited in this chapter relies heavily on primary sources, captured in Bismarck's private letters and memoranda (compiled in his *Gesammelte Werke*, or "collected works"), to reveal his cognitive style. It is not meant to offer new historical interpretations of specific episodes, but rather to highlight the internal contestation over the direction of Prussian foreign policy and the implications of this conflict for international relations theory. The conclusion raises some potential objections to my characterization of Bismarck as a rational thinker and finds them lacking.

"Riding the Wave": Bismarck's Procedural and Instrumental Rationality

Bismarck is one of the great realist statesmen, perhaps the most famous practitioner of Realpolitik in the history of international politics. He embraced many of the substantive views associated with the realist theoretical tradition: that force was the ultima ratio in international politics, and that the great questions of his time would be settled through military might. Looking back at German unification, he complained in his memoirs, "The fundamental error of the Prussian policy of those days was that people fancied they could attain through publicist, parliamentary, or diplomacy hypocrisies results which could be had only by war or readiness for it, by fighting or by readiness to fight" (Bismarck I: 84). As will be seen, Bismarck believed that wars with Austria and France were somewhat inevitable in his quest to unify Germany. Consistent with realist theory, he believed that power was the most decisive factor in international politics: "Whichever finds itself in the combination that is weaker in the event of war is inclined to be more yielding; whichever completely isolates itself renounces influence, especially if it be the weakest among the Great Powers" (Bismarck I: 173–4; also Pflanze 1955: 493). He expressed at times a belief in classical realist tenets, such as the inherently self-interested quality of human nature (Feuchtwanger 2002: 2). At certain points, his views came close to those of social Darwinism (Pflanze 1955: 495; 1990: 81–2). Perhaps most famously, Bismarck prognosticated in his very first speech as the Prussian Minister-President that German unification "will not be settled by speeches and majority decisions – that was the great mistake of 1848 and 1849 – but by blood and iron" (Ludwig 2013: 207).

Yet these traditional realist views fail to do justice to the sophisticated character of Bismarck's Realpolitik. Likewise, they do not distinguish him from those who opposed his foreign and domestic policies. Most importantly, they miss the highly rational quality of his cognitive style, a function of his epistemic motivation. Bismarck was highly deliberative and calculating in a way that many of his contemporaries were not. Combined with his nationally egoistic orientation, in which the promotion of the Prussian interest was the first goal, Bismarck was naturally led toward Realpolitik.

"The Only Sound Basis": Bismarck's Egoism

Everything that Bismarck did, he did for Prussia (Feuchtwanger 2002: 32; Gall 1986: 61; Ludwig 2013: 151). Bismarck was a Prussian, not a German egoist (Pflanze 1955: 549). He declared, "My country is Prussia, and I have never left my country and I shall never leave it" (Pflanze 1990: 69). At another point, he asserted, "I am a disciplined statesman who subordinates himself to the total needs and requirements of the state in the interest of peace and the welfare of my country" (Pflanze 1990: 56). Bismarck felt no identification with other countries: "I do not borrow the standard of my conduct towards foreign governments from stagnating antipathies, but only from the harm or good that I judge them capable of doing to Prussia" (Bismarck I: 173). He contrasted this with what he called romanticism, which he defined as a foreign policy based on sentiments that extended beyond Prussian boundaries. In one of his most famous speeches, Bismarck proclaimed, "The only sound basis for a large state is egoism and not romanticism" (Steinberg 2012: 108).

It would be sloppy, however, to call Bismarck a Prussian "nationalist," since his loyalty was to the Prussian state and its monarchy, which were one and the same to him. He wrote, "My loyalty to my *sovereign* is of Vendeean completeness, but as regards all others, not in one drop of my blood do I feel a trace of an obligation to lift a finger on their behalf" (Gall 1986: 282 [emphasis added]). Nationalists at the time identified with the self-determination claims of the German people; they were liberal proponents of democracy. Bismarck, in contrast, embraced strong conservative political principles. Prussian conservatives had an organic and corporatist understanding of Prussian society in which there was a natural hierarchy: each class performed its task and knew its place. They viewed society as a partnership not between contemporaries, but rather spanning the generations. This order was based not on rational norms, but on historical development; it was an organic product of God's will rather than a social contract between free and autonomous men. The

Enlightenment had emphasized the rights of the individual and the power of man to construct a better society through the application of reason, a faculty of which all humans were capable. Conservatives, however, believed that liberals were attempting to replace a historically developed form of life with an arbitrary system of man-made institutions, unnatural and unsanctioned by God (Gall 1986: 30–1; Holborn 1960: 89–90; Pflanze1990: 16, 57).

Bismarck was a genuine believer in what he believed to be a God-given hierarchical order of divine right monarchical rule and aristocratic privilege (Gall 1986: 92, 195; Holborn 1960: 90). He wrote, "How people who do not believe in a revealed religion, in a God of goodwill, in a higher judge and in a life to come can live together in an ordered manner is something I fail to understand" (Gall 1986: 29). Bismarck asked rhetorically: "For why, if not by divine decree – why should I bow down to these Hohenzollerns? They are a Swabian family no better than my own and absolutely no concern of mine" (Gall 1986: 29–30). Bismarck is generally recognized by historians as more loyal servant than personal opportunist (Gall 1986: 195; Holborn 1960: 90, 95–6; Pflanze 1990: 55, 77). For Bismarck, the pursuit of the reason of state was "a matter of moral duty," a "responsibility imposed upon him by the deity," writes Pflanze (1955: 495).

As was true of other conservatives, Bismarck was a fierce critic of the democratic revolutions that rocked Europe in 1848, beginning in France but spreading to the Austro-Hungarian Empire and Prussia. At one point, this movement even threatened to topple the Prussian king, Friedrich Wilhelm IV. A speech before the Prussian Landtag, in which Bismarck served as deputy in the early stages of his career, clearly expressed his views on the revolutionary fever:

What preserved us [during revolution] was that which constitutes the real Prussia ... that is, the Prussian army, the Prussian treasury, the fruits of an intelligent Prussian administration of many years' standing, and that vigorous spirit of cooperation between king and people that exists in Prussia. It was the loyalty of the Prussian people to their hereditary dynasty. It was the old Prussian virtues of honor, fidelity, obedience, and bravery, which permeate the army from its nucleus, the officer corps, outward to the youngest recruit. This army harbors no revolutionary enthusiasm. You will not find in the army, any more than in the rest of the Prussian people, any need for a national rebirth. They are satisfied with the name Prussia and proud of the name Prussia. ... Prussian we are and Prussian we wish to remain. (Pflanze 1990: 68)

Pflanze (1990) notes, "In this passage appear all the elements that composed Bismarck's conception of the nation: dynastic loyalty, autocratic paternalism, military discipline, and patriotic sacrifice" (69).

Saying that Bismarck rejected a liberal faith in reason does not mean that he was not a highly rational thinker, as will be seen later in this chapter. The Prussian was opposed to the idea that through the application of reason one could discover universal principles of natural laws in society like those in nature – a common belief of liberals at the time. In the eyes of those liberals, the recognition of these laws would lead to steady progress in the direction of individual rights and freedom (Pflanze 1955: 499). Bismarck opposed both the substance of those teleological views and the cognitive style of those who believed them. Ridiculing the liberals, he said, "What we chatter and resolve about it has no more value than the moonlight reveries of a sentimental youth, who builds castles in the air" (Pflanze 1990: 70). They were threatening to social order, perhaps, but also hopelessly idealistic and naïve. Liberals, he asserted, were distracted from the application of reason by the principle of reason. Bismarck would use his rationality in the service of the Prussian national interest, not the liberation of individuals from the shackles of the traditional order.

"A Child in the Darkness": Bismarck's Epistemic Motivation

All observers of Bismarck comment on his high level of procedural rationality (Feuchtwanger 2002: 4; Pflanze 1990: 77). Bismarck was committed to seeing things as they were – objectively and *realist*-ically. Bismarck compared himself to a "natural scientist" (GW III: 190; Pflanze 1955: 495). He wrote a colleague: "I take great care in all my official tasks to see them with the greatest possible objectivity and correctness" (GW III: 148). Bismarck was highly deliberative: "After his scientific manner," he took "action only after extensive analyses and experiments" and would "proceed carefully" (Ludwig 2013: 204). While Pflanze (1990) correctly observes that it "is doubtful ... whether the kind of objectivity Bismarck claimed for himself as a statesman is actually possible" (56), the point is that he consciously tried in a way that others did not. Whether Bismarck succeeded in always seeing the environment exactly as it was, or always made the right decision, is not our criterion for procedural rationality. Instead, the key point is that he was more rational than this peers.

Another indication of Bismarck's highly rational cognitive style was his explicit commitment to not allowing passion and emotion to influence his judgment and ability to draw utilitarian conclusions (Gall 1986: 83; Ludwig 2013: 146; Pflanze 1955: 554). Bismarck proclaimed, "Not even the king himself has the right to subordinate the interests of the fatherland to personal feelings of love or hatred toward foreigners" (Pflanze 1990: 77). Revenge and punishment were not a part of his foreign policy calculations (Pflanze 1990: 77). As Pflanze (1955) notes, "The wizard of the Wilhelmstrasse has long been celebrated as a complete realist, guided in his conduct of public affairs entirely by the head rather than the heart" (562).

Bismarck had a structuralist view of history, politics and foreign affairs (Gall 1986: xiii; Holborn 1960: 95). He believed that history moved glacially: "Political developments proceed as slowly as geological ones. Plates move on top of one another and produce new banks and mountains" (GW XIII: 557–8). He thought the potential for human agency was extremely limited. Bismarck's favorite Latin proverb was "unda fert nec regiture" ("One cannot make a wave, only ride it") (Feuchtwanger 2002: 4, 149). He used other metaphors as well. Bismarck liked to say "that one could not hurry the pace of history, that one might put the clocks on but time would not move any faster, that one could not harvest fruit that was not ripe for plucking" (Feuchtwanger 2002: 163). Later in his career, he reminisced to a group of students: "Man can neither create nor direct the stream of time. He can only travel upon it and steer with more or less skill and experience; he can suffer shipwreck and go aground, and he can also arrive in safe harbors" (GW XIII: 557–8).[2] In 1892, when his position as perhaps the most influential German in history was safely secured, he flatly declared: "One cannot possibly make history" (Pflanze 1955: 498; 1990: 2). This was no different than his view in 1851, when he wrote, "The stream of time flows inexorably along. By plunging my hand into it, I am merely doing my duty. I do not expect thereby to change its course" (Pflanze 1990: 3). Pflanze (1990) notes the irony: "His political career was one of the most effective of all time. Yet he felt to the end comparatively helpless before the push of historical forces" (3).

Bismarck was also constantly aware of another structural limitation, that of uncertainty – what he might have called "incomplete information," had he lived long enough to have been a student of contemporary international relations theory. Highly epistemically motivated, he avoided premature judgments and cognitive closure. As a consequence, he was acutely aware of what he did not know. Bismarck wrote:

I could never foresee with certainty whether my plans would succeed. . . . Politics is a thankless job, chiefly because everything depends on chance and conjecture.

---

[2] Navigation was a favorite metaphor. At other times, he said, "World history cannot be made. One can steer the ship of state on the currents if one carefully watches the compass of the public well-being and knows how to correctly judge it" (GW XIII: 304). At another, he wrote: "I am not so presumptuous to believe, that we can make our own history. My task is to observe the currents and steer my ship the best I can in them. I do not have the power to lead the currents, much less produce them" (GW XIIV: 751–2). See also GW XIV: 879–80.

Man is required to calculate with an array of possibilities and unknowns and base his plans on this calculation. If one correctly evaluations these uncertain factors, things go well and one has success; if one errs, things go badly and one is not only blamed, but also harms the Fatherland. (GW IX: 397ff)

This was true regardless of how clever one was: "None of us can see the future and even the most powerful monarch and the most clever states-man cannot command or lead it" (GW XIII: 304). There were limits to agency. In the thick of his career, Bismarck wrote his wife, 'It is a lesson one learns well in this business, that one can be as wise as the wise ones of this world and yet at any point find oneself the next moment walking like a child into the darkness" (GW XIV: 672; see also GW IX: 49; GW XIII: 557–8).

Grasping the Hem of the Garment: Bismarck's Instrumentally Rational Approach to Politics

Foreign affairs egoism and procedural rationality lead naturally to a calculating, utilitarian, and consequentialist approach to politics. Bis-marck was a highly epistemically motivated individual whose foreign policy choices were, therefore, instrumentally rational. Prussia, he believed, must do its best in light of the structural circumstances it faced. He wrote: "I am not so presumptuous to believe that we can make our own history. My task is to observe the currents and steer my ship the best I can in them. I do not have the power to lead the currents, much less produce them" (GW XIV: 751–2; see also GW XIV: 879–80; GW XIII: 304). He cautioned, "Even after the greatest success one cannot say with certainty: 'Now I have succeeded, I am finished' and look back at what was achieved with satisfaction" (GW IX: 397). Bismarck felt this uncer-tainty and the high stakes acutely (GW IX: 397ff).

Bismarck thought like a utilitarian: "One has to reckon with a series of probabilities and improbabilities and base one's plans upon this reckoning," he said (Pflanze 1990: 81). Bismarck's mode of thinking was observed both by his contemporaries and by those who have stud-ied him most closely since then (Gall 1986: 330, also 179). Albrecht von Roon, who served as Prussian Minister of War during the 1860s and worked with Bismarck closely, described the latter's decision-making process: "To construct the parallelogram of forces correctly and from the diagonal, that is to say, that which has already happened, then assess the nature and weight of the effective forces, which one cannot know precisely, that is the work of the historic genius who confirms that by combining it all" (Steinberg 2012: 6). Clemens Theodor Perthes, a prominent professor of law of the period, wrote how Bismarck "calculates so coldly" and "prepares so cunningly" (Steinberg 2012: 6).

Clearly, in the views of his peers, Bismarck's rationality set him apart. His Realpolitik was rare – a view with which historians concur (Holborn 1960: 96). According to Pflanze (1955), Bismarck's "patience and careful timing[,] ... accurate evaluation of one's opponents" and other manifestations of his highly deliberative cognitive style were part of his "political virtuosity" and were "qualities of individual judgment and personality" (501). The "final secret of his success certainly lay in the sheer facility of his intellect to judge the implications and impossibilities of each political solution more clearly and quickly than his contemporaries" (Pflanze 1955: 493). Feuchtwanger (2002) argues, "His strength was that he could gauge the immensely complex web of forces that were operating at any given moment and that he had ... the enormous mental energy to manipulate them in his own interest" (4).

Bismarck was so instrumentally rational that it was literally unhealthy. According to Bismarck's doctor:

[He] examined every question and every event from every possible angle ... with the help of his rich political experience and comprehensive historical knowledge he thought through all possible constellations with all their conceivable consequences, tracing out the details in such a way that not a gap remained, nor for that matter could remain. Through this intensive kind of reflection, to which he was especially addicted at night in bed, his brain developed naturally such a lively phosphorescence that but seldom was there any chance for sleep. (Holborn 1960: 513)

As politics (and life in general) are full of obstacles and constraints, politicians must often be content with what was possible and not overplay their hand in the pursuit of the ideal. Thus, Bismarck's realism was realistic. According to Steinberg (2012), "As Bismarck said, a statesman does not create the stream of time, he floats on it and tries to steer. Bismarck operated within the limits of the politically realistic and he frequently defined politics as 'the art of the possible'" (8; see also Holborn 1960; 95). Bismarck said after his retirement: "Positive undertakings in politics are extraordinarily difficult, and when they succeed, one should thank God that they led to a boon and not find fault with trivialities ... but rather accept the situation" (GW XIII: 557–9).

As we will see, this view made Bismarck an advocate of restraint at several times in his career when he believed that Prussia should not push its luck. He would advise others, "When we have arrived at a safe harbor we should be satisfied and care for and maintain what we have won." This was a general rule of politics for him "in confessional as well as in social relations. ... We want to carefully hold on to what we have, also with the concern that we will lose it if we do not value it" (GW XIII: 557–8).

Another indication of Bismarck's instrumentally rational political approach is his emphasis on the importance of adapting to each situation (Gall 1986: 146; Pflanze 1955: 554). There was no one-size-fits-all answer, he believed; circumstances mattered. A statesman must be given "the freedom to decide based on the changing requirements of states, the changed situation abroad. ... He must always be directed by the prevailing circumstances at the time" (GW IX: 397ff). Bismarck situated his situational approach against one in which there were general, inviolable *principles* of conduct: "One can only recognize a principle as generally applicable if it applies to all circumstances and all times." In his eyes, "this was continually refuted by the requirements of practice" (GW II: 227ff). He complained of those who "believe that every land at every time can governed by the same formula" (GW IX: 397ff). Later in his career, Bismarck lampooned his fellow Germans, "Because they have as yet scarcely outgrown the political nursery, the Germans cannot accustom themselves to regard political affairs as a study of the possible" (GW IX: 93).

As an egoist pursuing only Prussia's interests, Bismarck saw his country as engaged in strategic interaction with others. He stressed: "[M]y belief is that no one does anything for us, unless he can at the same time serve his own interests" (GW I: 202; also Pflanze 1955: 495; 1990: 77). The goals and strategies of opponents were key elements of the situation with which one had to contend. It was instrumentally important to understand their motivations, to see things as they saw them. "Correct evaluation of the opponent is ... indispensable to success," he observed (Pflanze 1990: 82). Others would do the same.

Steinberg (2012: 130) notes that the metaphors that Bismarck used to explain his views of politics came from strategic games of cards, dice, and chess (the last being a particular fondness). Sizing up the opposing player was difficult, however, given the uncertainty inherent in the situation:

In chess one should never base a move on the positive assumption that the other player will in turn make a certain move. For it may be that this won't happen, and then the game is easily lost. One must always reckon with the possibility that the opponent will at the last moment make another move than that expected and act accordingly. (GW IX: 397ff)

In this passage, Bismarck articulates the notion of "strategic interdependence" and "incomplete information" of later rationalist international relations theorists: "In politics one realizes that one is crucially dependent on the decisions of others that one has counted on. ... One never acts completely independently. And when the friends on whose support you have relied change their position ... the whole plan fails (GW XIII: 557–8).

Bismarck's structural understanding of politics and foreign policy led him to stress the importance of seizing opportunities when the particular circumstances were favorable, since these situations could not easily be recreated (Gall 1986: 264; Steinberg 2012: 128):

History with its great events ... does not roll on like a railway train at an even speed. No, it advances by fits and starts, but with irresistible force when it does. One must just be permanently on the look-out and, when one sees God striding through history, leap in and catch hold of his coat-tail and be dragged along as far as may be. (Gall 1986: 28)

This was a favorite metaphor for the statesman: "By himself the individual can create nothing; he can only wait until he hears God's footsteps resounding through events and then spring forward to grasp the hem of his mantle – that is all" (Pflanze 1990: 80). The statesman "must observe or seek out every favorable opportunity to implement what seems to him correct and appropriate for the fatherland's interests" (GW IX: 397ff).

Seizing opportunities, he suggested, required far-sightedness and the acceptance of short-term costs for long-term gains (Holborn 1960: 95). Bismarck wrote:

The statesman must see things coming ahead of time and be prepared for them. ... An indispensable prerequisite is patience. He must be able to wait until the right moment has come and must precipitate nothing, no matter how great the temptation. From childhood I have been a hunter and fisher. In both cases waiting for the right moment has been the rule which I have applied to politics. I have often had to stand for long periods in the hunting blind and let myself be covered and stung by insects before the moment came to shoot. (GW XIII: 468)

This was not necessarily easy. Bismarck likened it to waiting to eat a tasty treat until it had fully cooked. The statesman "must be able to wait until the correct moment has arrived and not rush, even when the incentive is so great. If man takes the most beautiful pastry out of the fire too early, it collapses" (GW IX: 397ff; also Ludwig 2013: 303).

Tortured Romance: Bismarck and the Prussian Conservatives

Bismarck made a name for himself in Prussian politics as a strident conservative opponent of the liberal opposition in the late 1840s. In his maiden speech before the Prussian Landtag, he castigated and ridiculed liberals, arguing that resistance to Napoleonic rule earlier in the century was not indicative of a latent German nationalism and commitment to national self-determination, but rather a natural reaction to an oppressive foreign occupation (Feuchtwanger 2002: 27; Steinberg 2012: 77–8). Bismarck accused the revolutionary Frankfurt parliament, which convened in 1848 to draft a constitution for a unified German nation, of seeking to "undermine and demolish that house of state constructed by centuries of glory and patriotism and cemented throughout by the blood of our ancestors" (Pflanze 1986: 68). He opposed "every ignominious association with democracy" (Gall 1986: 81) and insisted that a parliament should "never have the power to force the crown to act against the king's will or to coerce the king's minister" (Pflanze 1990; 65). More menacingly, he threatened that in the event of a new breakout of revolutionary violence, the "true Prussian people" would "bring the big cities to heel, even if it means obliterating them from the face of the earth" (Gall 1986: 110). In addition, Bismarck lauded Friedrich Wilhelm IV's refusal to accept the parliament's offer of an imperial crown to rule over a constitutionally governed Germany. Bismarck proclaimed, "The Frankfurt crown may glitter but the gold that gives its reality is to be obtained by first melting down the Prussian crown" (Gall 1986: 62). The Prussian king instead unilaterally promulgated a new Prussian constitution with limited parliamentary rights.

Bismarck's interventions attracted the attention of reactionaries – most notably the Gerlach brothers, Leopold and Ludwig, who formed the "Christian-Germanic circle" to resist liberal ideas in post-1848 Prussia (Pflanze 1990: 59). The Gerlachs brought Bismarck into the "camarilla," a shadow group of conservative advisers to the king. Bismarck became active within the "Kreuzzeitung" party, named after the newspaper that served as a mouthpiece for opponents of democratization (Gall 1986: 49–51). Owing to these activities, in 1852 Bismarck somewhat shockingly secured a major appointment for a political novice: he became the Prussian envoy to the German Bund ("Diet"), putting him at the center of German affairs and interaction with Prussia's rival – Austria (Ludwig 2013: 113). The Bund was a federation of dozens of German states established in the wake of the Napoleonic Wars, and was dominated by Austria and Prussia.

Bismarck owed his early political opportunities to his domestic views. Foreign policy, however, would drive a wedge between him and his conservative friends. Stationed in Frankfurt, the home of the Bund, Bismarck came to believe that Austria was Prussia's primary competitor and main obstacle to becoming a great power (Bismarck I: 319, 322; Gall 1986: 95). In his memoirs, Bismarck complained that at the time, "Prussia was nominally a Great Power, at any rate the fifth" (Bismarck I: 320). He described his primary vocation in Frankfurt: "My period of office here ... has ... been one continuous struggle against encroachments of all kinds, against the incessant attempts that have been made to exploit the Confederation as an instrument for the exaltation of Austria and the diminution of Prussia" (Gall 1986: 113). He wrote to Ludwig Gerlach in late 1853: "In the long run we cannot coexist with each other. We breathe the air out of each other's mouths; one must yield or must be 'yielded' to the other. Until then we must be enemies" (Steinberg 2012: 122). War was not necessarily foreordained. Bismarck envisioned, however, that the only other possibility was an agreement on zones of influence; that is, there could be a "political or geographical line of demarcation," like the Main River (Pflanze 1990: 97).

The other obstacle to Prussia's aims of greater influence in Germany was the smaller German states – particularly the medium-sized monarchies of Saxony, Baden, Württemberg, and Bavaria, which feared diluted influence in a unified Germany under Prussian leadership that might even cost their sovereigns their crowns. This "particularism" had long stymied efforts to unify the German states. According to Bismarck, the "key to German politics was to be found in princes and dynasties, not in publicists, whether in parliament and the press or on the barricades. ... [W]ith the promotion of German unity there was a prospect of the diminution of their independence in favour of the central authority or the popular representative body" (Bismarck I: 318). The smaller monarchies were also anxious that any efforts toward unification would empower German nationalist movements in their own states demanding greater democracy.

The medium-sized German states considered Prussia a greater threat than Austria given the geographic realities and the fact that the latter was preoccupied with maintaining its multinational empire. The Habsburgs could not incorporate any other unit into their empire, particularly Protestant states that would lead to confessional fractures. "[N]o angel can talk the distrust out of them so long as there exist maps at which they can cast a glance," Bismarck recognized (Bismarck I: 175). As sovereign states in the Bund, the medium-sized German states could play Austria and Prussia against each other (Ludwig 2013: 134); in Bismarck's words, they could exploit "our federal relationship as a pedestal to play the European power" (Gall 1986: 282). With the Habsburgs leading the recalcitrant states, they could always outvote Prussia in the Federal Diet.

Bismarck's views on Austria and the German question caused severe frictions with his conservative patrons, ultimately ruining his relationship with many of them. Both Austria and Russia were fellow members of the Holy Alliance, a "league against revolution" (Gall 1986: xv) dedicated to the preservation of monarchical rule and the repression of democracy and liberalism since the end of the Napoleonic Wars. The governments of all three powers believed in the legitimacy of absolutist rule and shared contempt for government by the masses. This view even extended to dictatorships such as that of Napoleon III, whose right to rule was conferred by the "general will" of the French people rather than by divine right or aristocratic lineage. Bismarck's political allies were "romantic conservatives" who felt a conservative solidarity with Austria and other monarchies that limited their foreign policy egoism (Gall 1986: xv; Pflanze 1955: 555). Their fear of liberal revolution persisted well past 1848 given the monarchical troubles in France and Italy, among other states.

Bismarck explicitly denigrated romanticism as a guide for foreign policy, a term in which he "lumped everything that did not directly serve to uphold and extent the power of the [Prussian] state" (Gall 1986: 83). He wrote to a colleague in 1860:

In regards to domestic Prussian policy I am, not merely out of custom, but rather out of conviction and utilitarian grounds so conservative, and will be loyal even to a king, whose policies do not appeal to me; but only to my king. In regards to the circumstances of all other lands, I recognize no kind of principled commitment for the policy of a Prussian. I regard policy solely by the measure of its usefulness for Prussian goals. In my view, the duty of a Prussian monarchy is limited to the borders of the Prussian empire drawn by god. (GW III: 148)

Whereas the romantic conservatives were reluctant to interfere with the legitimate rule of German kings and princes as fellow monarchical powers, feeling a bond with them that extended past Prussia's borders, Bismarck had no such compunction (Holborn 1960: 91; Pflanze 1990: 71). He wrote a close friend in 1861, before his appointment as Minister-President:

The system of solidarity of the conservative interests of all countries is a dangerous fiction. ... We arrive at a point where we make the whole unhistorical, godless and lawless sovereignty swindle of the German princes into the darling of the Prussian Conservative Party. ... Our government is in fact liberal domestically and legitimist in foreign policy. We protect foreign monarchical rights with greater tenacity than our own. (Steinberg 2012: 169)[3]

---

[3] To the extent that Prussia had an interest in the outcomes of revolutions in Italy, France, or Austria, Bismarck thought it was merely a case of "what shape of events abroad would be the most favorable for the power position and security of the Prussian crown" (GW III: 148). A letter to von Roon contained the same themes: "No one will thank us for our life in the princely houses from Naples to Hanover, and we practice towards them real evangelical peaceful love at the cost of the security of our own throne. I am loyal to my king to the end, but towards others I feel ... not a trace of commitment to lift a finger for them" (GW XIV: 570–1). He expected no good results in Prussian foreign policy until it was made more "independent from dynastic sympathies" (GW XIV: 570–1).

He lamented that this put him at odds with the camarilla and the Kreuzzeitung set (GW III: 148).

Bismarck's issues with his colleagues were not just substantive in character; they cannot simply be reduced to different degrees of foreign policy egoism. Instead, they were also cognitive in nature, owing to a different and more rational way of thinking. The romantic conservatives viewed their alliance against democracy and liberalism as a matter of principle that could not be compromised. This was deontological, not utilitarian judgment. Pflanze (1990) observes: "To romantic conservatives the conflicting forces in European politics were opposed principles, not interests. As a matter of dogma they believed that the three great eastern monarchies had but a single cause: the maintenance of conservative order against France, the home of Jacobinism and Bonapartism, and against the forces of liberal and national subversion everywhere" (28). Bismarck complained that the "Gerlachs and others" drew their "political consequences from dogmatic fundamentals, which I believe to be a fallacy. They expand the duties of the Prussian king's scepter in unnatural ways to include the protection of each and every Carolingian policy in Europe and come to the practical result that they become better Austrians than Prussians" (GW III: 148).

In other words, both constitutive aspects of Bismarck's Realpolitik – egoism and procedural rationality – separated him from his friends. One fed into the other. By refusing to make painful tradeoffs, Bismarck's friends undermined Prussian interests in his eyes. He complained to a colleague in 1861:

We have among our best friends so many *doctrinaires*, who demand the same obligation to the protection of the sovereignty of foreign princes and countries as they do ours. ... [I]t becomes Don Quixoterie, which only distracts our king and our government from the implementation of our own tasks. ... up to the point of blindness to all dangers that threaten Prussian and German independence in the future. (GW XIV: 578 [emphasis added])

The "Foliage and Not the Root": Thinking Styles and the Gerlach Letter Exchange

Relations between Bismarck and the camarilla deteriorated as he began, while still the German delegate at the Bund, to advocate that Prussia establish better relations with Napoleon III of France, the nephew of the first Napoleon, who had come to power in 1852. Bismarck hoped the newest Bonaparte would be invited to Berlin for a state visit, and he had himself visited Paris earlier to make Napoleon's acquaintance without any permission from his government (Ludwig 2013: 145). Napoleon was a dictator, not a democrat, but could and did not ground his claims in divine right and monarchical inheritance. Instead, he based his rule on the will of the people. This stance made him illegitimate and persona non grata to Prussian conservatives (Feuchtwanger 2002: 45). The Prussian king would not receive him. "The tradition of Austrian leadership and conservative solidarity were too deeply embedded in his thinking," Bismarck remembered later. "The displeasure felt at my intercourse with Napoleon sprang from the idea of 'Legitimacy'" (Bismarck I: 170). Steinberg (2012) notes, "To think such thoughts, let alone to express them to either of the Gerlach brothers, amounted to an attack on their fundamental principles. Napoleon III embodied 'revolution' and must be quarantined, not accepted" (130).

These thoughts led to a heated and now famous exchange of letters between the Prussian envoy to the Diet and his mentor, Leopold von Gerlach, "famous for their illustration of the differences between the romantic and realistic views on foreign policy" (Pflanze 1990: 95). This was the first time that Bismarck openly broke with conservatives.

For the first time ... the great realist stands up against the Potsdam romanticists, the man without principles stands up against the legitimists. ... In lengthy correspondence with Gerlach, he now parts company from his master, on utilitarian grounds; sacrifices the fundamental principle of legitimacy to which he was supposed to be devoted. The party man has become a statesman who is willing to abandon his own obsolete judgments. (Ludwig 2013: 148)

In this exchange we see particularly clearly how Bismarck's realism set him apart from his domestic allies.

Bismarck sought better relations with Napoleon because Prussia's traditional alliance with Austria and hostility toward revolutionary France denied it the flexibility necessary to pursue egoistic Prussian interests.

Alliances are the expression of common interests and purposes. ... Yet up to the present we have the probability of an alliance only with those interests who traverse and contradict ours – that is, with the German states and Austria. If we desire to regard our foreign policy as being limited to that, then we must also become accustomed to the idea of seeing our European influence reduced in time of peace to a seventeenth part of the voices of the smaller council in the Bund. (Bismarck I: 174)

Bismarck used one of his favorite metaphors for the instrumentally rational and strategic nature of international politics: "As long as each of us is convinced that a portion of the European chess-board will remain closed against us by our own choice, or that we must tie up one arm on principle while everyone else employs both his to our disadvantage, this sentimentality of ours will be turned to account without fear and without thanks" (Bismarck I: 177).

Bismarck was not advocating a formal alliance of any type, however. He merely wanted to use the perception of this possibility to create leverage by showing that Prussian support and solidarity could not be taken for granted. "To me France would be the most dubious of all allies," he wrote his friend, "although I must hold open the possibility of such an alliance because one cannot play chess if 16 out of 64 squares are excluded from the game" (GW XIV: 558ff). He explained: "All I want to do is to rid other people of the belief that *they* may adopt whomsoever they wish as brothers, but that *we* would rather have our skin cut into strips than defend it with French aid" (Bismarck I: 177).

Bismarck's approach was based on Prussia's egoistic interests first and foremost. He wrote, "I cannot feel it right, either in myself in others, that sympathies and antipathies with regard to foreign Powers and persons should take precedence over my sense of duty in the foreign service of my country; such an idea contains the embryo of disloyalty to the ruler or to the country which we serve" (Bismarck I: 171–2). Bismarck contested Gerlach's assertions of conservative solidarity and moral principle on egoistic grounds, as a constitutive part of his Realpolitik. "I rise and fall with my own lord, even when he in my view foolishly runs [Prussia] into the ground, but France remains for me France, whether Louis Napoleon or Louis governs there, and Austria remains for me abroad" (GW XIV: 548ff). France was merely a tool for the pursuit of Prussian interests. "France," he declared "interests me only in so far as she reacts upon the condition of my country, and we can only deal politically with the France which exists, and this France we cannot exclude from the combinations" (Bismarck I: 171). Bismarck remarked "as a romanticist, I may shed a tear over" the deposed French monarch's fate,

and as a diplomatist I would be his servant if I were a Frenchman; but as I am, France counts for me, without regard to the person at its head for the time being, merely as a piece, though an unavoidable one, in the game of political chess – a game in which I am called upon to serve only my own king and my own country. (Bismarck I: 171–2)

He told Gerlach, "Regard me not as a Bonapartist but rather as an ambitious Prussian" (GW XIV: 377).

To some degree, then, Bismarck's differences with Gerlach stem from the former's greater degree of egoism in his foreign policy thinking. However, the differences were also cognitive in nature, owing to the two men's distinct thinking styles. Gerlach also valued Prussian interests first and foremost, writing to Bismarck that in terms of "Prussian patriotism," basing judgments on "hurtfulness or utility to Prussia" and being in the "exclusive service of the King and of the country," there was no difference between them as "these are things which are matters of course" (Bismarck I: 181–2). Gerlach was also convinced of the egoism of Austria and the smaller states in Germany. "That Austria and the German middle states will do nothing for us, of that I am as convinced as you are" (Bismarck I: 184). He had the same goals as his protégé: "With regard now to our German policy I believe that it is still our vocation to show the small states the superiority of Prussia ... in Germany is also the place where, as it seems to me, we have to oppose Austria" (Bismarck I: 186).

However, Gerlach considered the question of improving ties with the French in deontological, not utilitarian, terms, reflecting an underlying cognitive difference in thinking style than that employed by Bismarck. As a result, even as both put Prussia first, the two men came to different conclusions. Gerlach made the principled case against even a dalliance with France. "My political principle is, and remains, the struggle against the Revolution. ... You will not convince Napoleon that he is not on the side of the Revolution." The French dictator, although an authoritarian, was to Gerlach an illegitimate affront to the principle of divine right. His was "an absolutism based on the sovereignty of the people – and that he feels this as much as the old one did" (Bismarck I: 190). Napoleon was "l'élu des sept millions" (the chosen of seven million) (Bismarck I: 191). Cavorting with the French was therefore a taboo that could not be countenanced, regardless of what benefits it might bring. Gerlach expressed his disappointment with Bismarck's stance: "[I]t depresses me that ... you have allowed yourself to be diverted from the simple choice between Right and Revolution. You play with the idea of an alliance with France and Piedmont, a possibility, a thought, that for me lies far away as it should be, dear Bismarck, for you" (Steinberg 2012: 133). No pragmatic compromises could be made. "[I]f a principle like that of opposition to the Revolution is correct ... then we must also constantly stick to it in practice" (Bismarck I: 186). Gerlach had before cautioned Bismarck, on an entirely different matter, "of the apostle's warning against doing evil that good may come" (Ludwig 2013: 140). Gerlach lamented Bismarck's turn to "Machiavellianism" (Ludwig 2013: 156).

For Bismarck, however, this was not a simple choice at all. He opposed the deontological thinking of Gerlach and the other conservatives, in which only one consideration dictated policy:

[I]f my views diverge from yours you must seek the reason in the foliage and not in the root, for I claim that at bottom my convictions are in unison with yours. The principle of the battle against the Revolution I acknowledge to be mine also, but I do not consider it ... possible to carry out principle in politics as something whose remotest consequences break through every other consideration and which forms to a certain extent the only trump suit in the game, the lowest card of which still beats the highest of every other suit. (Bismarck I: 192–3).

Similarly he wrote to Edwin Freiherr Manteuffel, the prominent German military officer, "I also recognize as my own the principle of struggle against revolution, but ... in politics I do not believe it possible to follow principle in such a way that its most extreme implications always take precedence over every thither consideration" (Pflanze 1990: 78). Bismarck maintained, "I do not see how, before the French Revolution, a statesman, even were he the most Christian and conscientious, could have conceived the idea of subordinating his entire political aims, his conduct both in foreign and home politics, to the principle of fighting against the Revolution and of testing the relations of his country to others solely by that touchstone" (Bismarck I: 195).

Bismarck saw the difference in thinking styles and said as much to Gerlach: "You want to have nothing to do with Bonaparte or [the Italian revolutionary leader] Cavour as a matter of principle. I want to avoid France and Sardinia, not because I think it wrong, but because in the interests of our security I consider them very dubious allies" (GW XIV: 548ff). The very notion of universal principles was distasteful to a realist like Bismarck, as they made no allowances for situations – a key point for Bismarck, as described earlier in this chapter. "If, however, I acknowledge a principle to be supreme and universally pervading I can only do so in so far as it is verified under all circumstances and at all times" (Bismarck I: 193).

Using France as a tool was indeed distasteful for ideological reasons, Bismarck argued, but something Prussia must be nevertheless willing to do given its other interests. As a realist, he was a pragmatist. Bismarck wrote Gerlach: "I am convinced that it would be a great misfortune for Prussia if her government should enter into an alliance with France, but, even if we make no use of it, we ought never to remove from the consideration of our allies the possibility that under certain conditions we might *choose this evil as the lesser of the two*" (Steinberg 2012: 123 [emphasis added]). A categorical resistance to improved ties with France would inhibit Prussia's ability to adapt to new situations. Bismarck explained:

[I have] no desire to make an apology for persons and conditions in France; I have no predilection for the former and regard the latter as a misfortune for that country; I only desire to explain ... that it is neither sinful nor dishonourable to enter into closer connexion, should the course of politics render it necessary. ... That this connexion is in itself desirable I do not say, but only that all other chances are worse, and that we must, in order to improve them, go through with the reality or the appearance of closer relations with France. (Bismarck I: 200)

Gerlach could not understand how Bismarck, being a good conservative, could take this position. He did not regard Bismarck as a closet liberal: "The manner in which you regarded the Opposition in the last Diet would alone free you from the reproach. . . . But that is just the reason why the view which you take of our foreign policy is inexplicable to me" (Bismarck I: 189). Bismarck regarded it as a "mistaken Conservatism" to avoid relations with countries simply "because their substance is distasteful" (GW XIV: 548ff). Gerlach seemed to acknowledge the cognitive nature of their disagreement when he penned, "I want to acknowledge willingly the practical side of your view" (Bismarck I: 204). Bismarck told Gerlach, "Much as I agree with you in regard to internal policy, I can enter but little into your conception of foreign policy, with which I find fault in general, because it ignores the reality of things" (Bismarck I: 171).

Might this dispute simply reflect differing beliefs about the threat posed by France, one based in substantive considerations? "Revolutionary absolutism is by its nature given to conquest," Gerlach argued (Bismarck I: 191). And Bonapartism was the worst: Bonapartes "have not only an unlawful revolutionary origin . . . they are themselves the Revolution incarnate . . . no Bonaparte can disown the sovereignty of the people, nor does he do so" (Bismarck I: 207). However, as Bismarck pointed out, Gerlach was forming his beliefs based on a general heuristic that all Bonapartes were similar; in Bismarck's view, this misplaced analogy overlooked important differences between Napoleon III and Napoleon I. Gerlach's type of top-down, theory-driven processing is more characteristic of nondeliberative, less rational thinking. Bismarck cautioned: "I believe, you overestimate the current Napoleon because you identify him too much with he whose forceful appearance in 1800 pushed state development out of its present direction" (GW XIV: 548ff). Bismarck continually pointed out all the differences between the two men as well as the limited evidence that Napoleon III had any revolutionary ambitions. He wrote Gerlach: "I do not consider it right to set up Louis Napoleon as the sole . . . representative of the Revolution" (Bismarck I: 192–3).

Turning to the Devil: An Alliance with the National Liberals as Lesser Evil

Consorting with the French was not the only taboo Bismarck would consider breaking. In his quest for German unification under Prussian leadership, Bismarck's most important ally would become the liberal nationalist movement. In describing his strategy he liked to quote the Latin: *"flectere si nequeo superos, acheronta movebo* – "If I cannot move the gods, I will turn to the devil" (Feuchtwanger 2002: 5). They were, quite literally, a lesser evil.

Bismarck began considering this option as early as his first years in Frankfurt at the Bund. In his reports, he frequently noted that mobilizing nationalist public opinion could neutralize the Austrians, since the Habsburgs were regarded as the most repressive and reactionary great power, as well as the princes and kings of the smaller German states, who also feared democratization. The German nationalists' interests ran in parallel to those of Prussia, not Austria, he argued. Just as fear of an alliance with France would make the medium-sized states (which Bismarck referred to contemptuously as Würzburgers) and Austria more solicitous of Prussia, the same would be true of flirtation with liberal forces. He wrote, "In order to fill the Federal states with sufficient fear, as they have of Austria, we have to show ourselves capable, if others make us desperate, to join with France and even Liberalism. As long as we behave well, nobody takes us seriously" (Steinberg 2012: 126).

Bismarck also recognized the economic and "material interests" (GW XIV: 578) of the German middle class, among whom support for liberalism was the strongest. The growing commercial bourgeoisie sought an expanded marketplace that a unified German state would provide (Pflanze 1990: 127). Its interests coincided with that of the Prussian state. Bismarck hoped to separate the more pragmatic liberals, who were driven largely by material considerations, from the more ideological and radical believers in democratic freedom, who might consider association with a conservative such as him to be a betrayal of liberal values.

The alliance would, of course, be completely instrumental. In a letter to Manteuffel in 1854, Bismarck stated:

Prussia has not become great on account of Liberalism ... but rather on account of a series of powerful, determined and wise regents, who held together the self-determining military hand, so that they could throw themselves onto the scales of European politics with wanton courage when an auspicious moment arose. We must maintain this system into the future. ... Parliamentary liberalism can serve as a temporary means to this end, but cannot be itself the goal of state policy. (GW I: 375)

He wrote Gerlach, "at home we have no use for them, but in the small states they are the only elements that want anything to do with us" (Pflanze 1990: 129). Bismarck later wrote in his memoirs, "I was ready to pay the opposition blackmail as needed in order to be in a position to throw our full power into the scale" (Pflanze 1990: 410). This was a simple alliance of convenience, a Baptist–bootlegger coalition. Bismarck was as contemptuous of liberal nationalists as he was of the German princes and small monarchies, even using the same term to describe them – that of the "national" or the "German *swindle* " (Feuchtwanger 2002: 39, 145). "The shift was one of strategy rather than conviction," writes Pflanze (1990: 145), one that "from the outset [was] conceived as a means to an end" (Steinberg 2012: 115). Yet Bismarck would not let this ideological distaste deny him the option of working with them, provided such a partnership proved useful (Holborn 1960: 92).

This was another expression of the "art of the possible" in light of the existing structural constraints. Bismarck increasingly realized that the bourgeoisie, liberalism, and nationalism were unpleasant political facts that could not be changed, so it was best to make use of them (Gall 1986: 202, 217; Holborn 1960: 92; Ludwig 2013: 152). This was a painful admission, but he did not resist it. When he revealed his intentions to von Unruh, a prominent moderate liberal, Bismarck stressed the structural constraints Prussia was under: "Prussia is completely isolated. There is but one ally for Prussia if she knows how to win and handle them ... the German people!" He invoked implicitly his commitment to seeing things objectively, one of the key elements of epistemic motivation. "I am the same Junker of ten years ago ... but I would have no perception and no understanding if I could not recognize clearly the *reality of the situation* " (Gall 1986: 147; GW VII: 38).

At the same, Bismarck insisted that Prussia would lead the nationalist liberals, and not the reverse (Feuchtwanger 2002: 122). He wrote in 1861, "I cannot see why we should shrink so fastidiously from the idea of popular representation. ... One can create a truly conservative national assembly and nevertheless earn thanks from the liberals" (GW XIV: 578). He refused to be instrumentalized; he would do the instrumentalizing, an idea captured in the famous Bismarckian aphorism: "If we do not prepare for ourselves the role of the hammer, there will be nothing left but that of the anvil" (Pflanze 1990: 77). Later on, he would proclaim, "If there was to be a revolution, it is better to make it than to suffer it" (Feuchtwanger 2012: 145; Pflanze 1955: 553). He wrote to Auerswald, one of the moderate liberals whose support he sought, "In the long run we have only one reliable mainstay ... and that is the national strength of the German people, as long as it sees the Prussian army as its champion and its hope for the future and as long as it does not see us waging wars to please and promote other dynasties than that of the Hohenzollern" (Gall 1986: 147).

Nevertheless, Bismarck's realism made him revolutionary. Indeed, he remarked later, "They accuse me of being reactionary ... but I would march if need be even with revolution" to achieve the goal of unification. Bismarck encountered significant resistance to his ideas from conservatives, who regarded the Minister-President as betraying conservative principles: "In every case my hearers became very agitated and upset about it. They fear such a possibility more than cholera" (GW I: 505–6). Indeed, the Gerlachs described the policy as "revolutionary," "godless," and "wholly de-Christianized" (Gall 1986: 40).

"Favorable Weather": Opportunism against Austria?

Bismarck's realist views both distinguished and estranged him from his arch-conservative friends and allies consistently throughout the 1850s. He continually urged that Prussia take advantage of Austrian difficulties, first in the Crimean War of 1854 and subsequently in the Franco-Austrian War of 1859, fought largely over Italy.

The Crimean War marked the beginning of the end of the Holy Alliance and the conservative solidarity that had prevailed since 1815. Beginning as a conflict between the crumbling Ottoman Empire and Russia, it drew in all the other major powers, becoming the first major European conflict since the Napoleonic Wars. Russia demanded a protectorate for the Christian population in the Ottoman Empire. When Russia occupied the Danubian principalities, the Turks declared war, backed by Britain and France. Alarmed by Russian incursion into its sphere of influence, Austria demanded that the Russians withdraw and appealed to the Bund for help.

The war saw Bismarck again in a no man's land between nationalist liberals and romantic conservatives. The former, particularly a group of moderate liberals known as the *Wochenblattpartei* (named, like the *Kreuzzeitung* group, after the newspaper that expressed their views), wanted to ally with the Western powers on behalf of the Turks. This sought-after partnership reflected an ideological alignment: Britain was the model for the moderate constitutional monarchy they desired. It also promised to promote Prussian interests at the expense of Austria, and weakening the influence of the Habsburgs was a necessary condition for the group's *Kleindeutschland* (smaller Germany) plan for national unification (Feuchtwanger 2002: 51). The conservatives were bereft about the split in the Holy Alliance but also wanted to preserve close Prussian ties with Austria. In April 1854, the Prussian government renewed its defensive alliance with the Habsburgs and agreed that if Austria became involved in hostilities with Russia, the Prussians would mobilize 100,000 troops on the country's eastern frontier to protect the Austro-Hungarian empire (Pflanze 1990: 89–90).

Consistent with his egoistic approach, Bismarck opposed helping Austria simply out of a legitimist bond: "That at the sound of the first shot against the Russians we shall turn ourselves into the whipping boy for the Western Powers and let them dictate to us the terms of peace while we carry the main burden of war is as clear as a school arithmetic exercise" (Steinberg 2012: 125). He did not want "to couple our smart and seaworthy frigate to Austria's worm-eaten battleship" (Ludwig 2013: 145). In Bismarck's instrumentally rationalist calculus, there were only costs and no benefits from this position. He called this "our Prussian and egotistical policy" (Feuchtwanger 2002: 53). Overruled, he complained later in his memoirs that Prussia "sacrificed all our own policy and every independent view" (Bismarck I: 105). Bismarck, however, did not side with the liberals either. He castigated the idea that England, grateful for any help, would later exert itself on behalf of German unification as "childish Utopias" (Bismarck I: 121).

Instead of an alliance with the Western powers, Bismarck advised the king to opportunistically use Austria's preoccupation with Russia to Prussia's advantage: "Great crises make the weather favourable to Prussia's expansion, if we exploit them fearlessly and perhaps ruthlessly; if we want to go on growing, then we must not be afraid to stand alone with 400,000 soldiers, especially as long as the others are fighting" (Feuchtwanger 2002: 51; also Steinberg 2012: 123–4). Bismarck had a particular plan in mind:

I proposed to the King to utilize this occasion for raising Prussian policy out of a secondary, and in my opinion unworthy, position; and for assuming an attitude which would have won for us the sympathy of and the lead among those German states which desired, with and through us, to preserve an independent neutrality. I considered this practicable if, when Austria should call upon us to bring up our troops, we should at once acquiesce in a friendly and willing manner; but should station 66,000 and in point of fact more men, and not at Lissa, but in Upper Silesia, so that our troops should be in a position whence they could with equal facility step over the frontier of either Russia or Austria. . . . With 200,000 men his Majesty would instantly become the master of the entire European situation, would be able to dictate peace, and to gain in Germany a place worthy of Prussia. (Bismarck I: 106–7)

Once Austria was involved on the Balkan front, it would hold Austria hostage, withholding support and evening threatening to attack in Bohemia unless the Austrians signed a treaty establishing separate spheres of influence (Pflanze 1990: 89). Ultimately, the king could not countenance such a move against a fellow monarchical power, contrasting his approach with that of the illegitimate Bonaparte: "[A] man of Napoleon's sort can commit such acts of violence, but not I" (Pflanze 1990: 90; Steinberg 2012: 123–4; also Bismarck I: 108). Bismarck's plans went nowhere.

The same cleavage between Bismarck and his fellow conservatives reemerged during the Franco-Austrian war. The French had signed an alliance with Piedmont to come to its aid in the event of Austrian aggression and promised Cavour help in establishing a new Italian state (Steinberg 2012: 148). Bismarck again advised the king to take advantage of Austria while it was tied down in Italy: "The current situation yet again holds the jackpot for us if we just let Austria's war with France really bite and then move south with all our armies, carrying the border posts with us in our knapsacks and banging them in again either at the Lake of Constance or wherever the Protestant confession ceases to predominate" (Gall 1986: 99; also Feuchtwanger 2002: 63). The crown prince, Wilhelm, now a regent given Friedrich Wilhelm IV's deteriorating health, could not bring himself to break with the Habsburgs any more than his brother had done (Steinberg 2012: 155). Bismarck complained about the pro-Austrian press in the conservative Kreuzzeitung, again revealing how he was out of step with his allies (Feuchtwanger 2002: 64).

Crazy Like a "Fox"?: Misconceptions about Bismarck

Bismarck's willingness to maintain maximum flexibility meant that he would consider many things deemed taboo by others, which gave (and gives) Bismarck an undeserved reputation for lacking political principles and ethical guidelines to which he was true. As seen earlier, he was scornful of the concept. Even his friend Perthes wrote that he "has no scruples about methods" (Steinberg 2012: 6). Bismarck, he contended, was "cynical and believed in nothing, a cold, calculating rationalist" (Steinberg 2012: 236). The famous German academic, Treitschke, caustically remarked, "Of the moral powers in the world he has not the slightest notion" (Steinberg 2012: 247). Bismarck did not help matters when he made observations such as "If I had to go through my life with principles, I would feel as though I had to walk a narrow path in the woods and had to carry a long pole in my mouth" (Holborn 1960). At another point, he cynically wrote to his wife: "One clings to principles only for as long as they are not put to the test; when that happens one throws them away as the peasant does his slippers and walks after the fashion that nature intended" (Gall 1986: 83). This suggests that what made Bismarck so special was his amoralism, a lack of an ethical center.

Yet such a conclusion would mistake moral consequentialism for moral nihilism. As mentioned earlier, Bismarck had a distinct moral compass predicted on conservative values and allegiance to the Prussian monarch and state. The key point to realize is not that Bismarck had no ethical commitments, but rather that he pursued them in a utilitarian fashion. By "principles," Bismarck meant standards of behavior or practice that applied in every instance. He complained that a colleague regarded "insistence on doctrinaire fundamentals as political consistency. This silliness goes so far that you overlook factual relations and compelling circumstances" (GW IX: 90). Precisely so as to pursue his political principles, centered on service to the Prussian state, Bismarck felt the need to constantly adjust. As has been seen, this cognitive style differentiated him from those whose conservative values and goals he shared.

Many historians maintain that Bismarck was an emotional hothead who struggled to keep his feelings in check. He was indeed prone to anger and depression (Feuchtwanger 2002: 91; Gall 1986: xvi, 86; Ludwig 2013: v; Steinberg 2012: 173, 183, 266). According to Feuchtwanger (2002), Bismarck was a "man of extraordinary passion, which he had to struggle to keep under control. He lay awake at night hating his enemies" (2). His contemporary Perthes wrote, "he can be easily stirred by sympathies and antipathies. . . . By nature he has an unforgiving, vengeful tendency" (Steinberg 2012: 173). Feuchtwanger (2002) claims that "for his adversaries he had nothing but contempt and his attacks were unrestrained by any feeling of respect for them" (27). Ludwig (2013) contends that he was a "character filled with pride, courage and hatred" (v).

However, Bismarck recognized this fact and self-consciously worked to control it (Ludwig 2012: 203). As argued in Chapter 1, all human beings have emotions. The essence of System II is not that one has no feelings at all, which might actually incapacitate the individual by denying purpose. Instead, the more rational thinker does not let emotions interfere with objective perception and careful deliberation, thereby exhibiting conscious emotional regulation. System II processing acts as a check on the emotional, intuitive, and impulsive System I (Kahneman 2011). Bismarck subjected his impulses to conscious scrutiny. His contemporary, the British diplomat Morier, captured this tension, stating that Bismarck was "made up of two individuals": the rational diplomatic calculator and the vituperative and vindictive political operator. Yet Morier noted that the politician would "sacrifice everything, even his personal hatreds, to the success of his game" (Steinberg 2012: 128). Bismarck deliberately cooled his hot blood during the pursuit of his domestic and foreign policy goals. In any case, the argument offered in this book is not that Bismarck was perfectly rational, a concept for which we do not have any standard to judge in absolute terms, but that he was more procedurally rational than those around him. Indeed, Bismarck's struggles with his emotions indicate how even the greatest realist struggles with rationality.

Bismarck also liked to say, "Politics is less science than art" (GW IX: 397FF; see also GW IX: 90). The evocation of the term "art" implies that his decision-making style was not actually deliberative and methodical, but rather intuitive in nature – System I as opposed to System II. Bismarck asserted that politics "is not a subject which can be taught. One must have the talent for it" (Pflanze 1955: 499; 1990: 82). In other words, it either came automatically or did not come at all. At another point, he wrote, "More than anything else politics demands the capacity to recognize intuitively in each new situation where the correct path lies" (Pflanze 1990: 83). Some biographers of the Iron Chancellor use this language as well (Gall 1986: xviii; Holborn 1960: 38; Pflanze 1955: 514).

Yet it would be incorrect to describe Bismarck's decision-making style as intuitive. When Bismarck writes of the "art" as opposed to the "science" of statecraft, he is simultaneously making the case for adaptation and the futility of one-size-fits-all strategies that work for every situation. His understanding of "science" in this instance is not equivalent to rationality, but rather refers to the discovery of laws that apply universally: "Politics is not in itself an exact and logical science, but the capacity to choose in each fleeting moment of the situation that which is least harmful or most opportune," he explained (GW XIII: 468). Mathematical formulas are always true. Two plus two will forever equal four. But there was no such truism in international politics, thought Bismarck. It was not always the case that force would succeed, for instance. "Politics is neither arithmetic nor mathematics. To be sure, one has to reckon with given and unknown factors, but there are no rules and formulas with which to sum up the results in advance" (GW IX: 93). For Bismarck, to think that something as complicated as politics could easily be reduced to a formula would be irrational, something clearly contradicted by objective observation.

When Bismarck wrote that someone must have the "talent" for Realpolitik, he was making implicitly the same claim of this book: that epistemic motivation is a dispositional trait, a way of making decision-making, that is more characteristic of some individuals than others. He was also expressing the view of the classical realist theorists, that rationality is not something that comes easily to everyone. Thinking rationally had a natural and intuitive appeal to Bismarck. He was particularly good at it. If Bismarck's thinking style were actually intuitive and automatic, he would not have been self-aware and reflective enough to describe it. Yet he did this consistently throughout his entire career.

Get Real: Bismarck's Exceptionalism

Focusing on the period before Bismarck became the most powerful civil servant in Prussia, this chapter has laid out in some detail Bismarck's realism, a combination of foreign policy egoism and rational thinking.

Although Bismarck continued at the time to count the conservatives as his political allies, his realism left him without a true political home. His anti-revolutionary ideals angered liberals; his foreign policy views were anathema to conservatives. History reveals the striking fact that the great foreign policy realist, perhaps the greatest of all time, had no real consistent political allies. Bismarck's realism was rare, indeed.

All historians seem to agree on this point.

[T]he anti-idealist sobriety and the often cynical skepticism that Bismarck exhibited in his politics very early on and continued to profess more and more outspokenly constituted an extraordinary challenge to his time. They cut him off from the various political groups and their respective ideals and convictions. . . . It turned him, in other words, even in the years of his greatest success, into a lone wolf. (Gall 1986: xix).

Of Bismarck, Steinberg (2012) writes, "No crowds followed him and no party acknowledged him as leader" (84). Bismarck cared little for their disdain: "I am also as indifferent to 'revolutionary' or "Conservative" as I am to all phrases" (Bismarck II: 6). Feuchtwanger (2002: 150) argues that Bismarck was "far too intelligent" to be a typical reactionary Junker, that aristocratic class of which he was a member, but he was not a liberal either. "Neither liberals nor conservatives could regard him as one of theirs" (163). He "rebundled all the prevailing tendencies and forces into a new package" (150). His unique way of thinking made Bismarck a "man between the fronts in 'no man's land'" (Gall 1986: 138). "[H]ardly anyone had occasion to identify with him personally or see him as symbolizing a specific political direction and a set of convictions (Gall 1986: 33). "[A]mong all these Hohenzollern there is not one who supported him," writes Ludwig (2013: 217). "There is no real confidence between Bismarck and any of the ministers, generals, courtiers, or leaders of parties. Fundamentally he has no party" (Ludwig 2013: 219). "He was not tied to either [liberals or conservatives] – a lone hunter who followed no rules but his own," observes Taylor (1955: 90).

Realpolitik, rather than being the natural approach of any statesman in the highest circles of Prussian foreign policy, actually separated Bismarck from almost everyone else. This contrast, largely a product of different individual levels of rationality, remains evident as we continue to recount Bismarck's struggles with his conservative political allies over the direction of foreign policy in Chapter 5.

5   Cold Blood and Iron: Bismarck, the Struggle with Austria, and German Unification

Chapter 4 demonstrated that Bismarck was a different animal when compared to his Prussian peers, not just liberals but even conservatives. This chapter shows that those differences continued as Bismarck rose to become the highest-ranking civil servant in Prussian politics, the Minister-President. Brought in as a "conflict minister" in 1862 to crack down on a legislature asserting its democratic rights, Bismarck simultaneously pushed his pro-Prussian and anti-Austrian agenda in the face of both external and internal resistance. In this chapter, I focus primarily on Prussia's relationship with Austria, because Austria, rather than France, was the main obstacle to a unified Germany dominated by Prussia. There were still those at the time who favored a *grossdeutsch* consolidation of German states under the Austrian Habsburgs rather than the Prussian Hohenzollerns.[1]

Bismarck's position as Minister-President put him in charge of foreign affairs, where he pursued his goal of German unification under Prussian leadership. We see all of the same themes of the previous chapter: his desire to undermine the power of German princes and small monarchs and his indifference to their claims of legitimacy; his insistence that liberal forces work for him, and not vice versa; and conservative opposition to his policies that generally left him as the lone voice of Realpolitik.

Opposition to Bismarck was partially driven by a desire to preserve the legitimate rights to rule on the part of other sovereigns. For a time, conservative solidarity trumped egoistic interests for the king and his advisors. Bismarck had to convince the new sovereign, Wilhelm I, to resist an Austrian plan to unify Germany under Habsburg domination. He then pushed for Prussian annexation of Schleswig and Holstein during a crisis precipitated by the Danish king, but was opposed by both Prussian liberals and conservatives. The latter were concerned that

---

[1] Excellent work in political science has recently been done on the other decisive points in the unification process – namely, the Schleswig–Holstein crisis and the Franco-Prussian War (Goddard 2009; Sambanis et al. 2015).

Prussia had no dynastic right to rule over the provinces. For similar reasons, conservatives resisted going to war against the Austrians, necessary for decisively excising the Habsburgs from the Germanic sphere.

However, Bismarck and conservatives differed not only in preferences, but also in cognitive style. Prussian conservatives had problems with both the egoistic and rational elements of Bismarck's realism. Following Prussia's early victories over the Austrians, the Minister-President struggled to contain their desire for territorial aggrandizement, which Bismarck believed would ultimately weaken, rather than strengthen, Prussia. He advocated a policy of strategic restraint, pragmatically accepting the more limited gains of a Northern German Federation excluding Austria, which would set Prussia up for an eventual unification of all the smaller German states. Bismarck's efforts to restrain the Prussian King Wilhelm I from a much more extensive annexation demonstrate a contrast between a deliberate, careful, and sober statesmen and (at least at the time) an impulsive and emotional sovereign. Where previous differences reflected competing conceptions of foreign policy, egoistic versus solidaristic, this was a conflict between different processing styles – System I and System II. The Minister-President was concerned that pushing the Prussian victory too far would frighten Napoleon III and induce French intervention, poison future relations with Austria, and create new territories that could not be easily digested by the new Northern German federation, the formation of which was Bismarck's primary aim for fighting the war. The war had turned the king into a rabid egoistic, and Bismarck had to constrain him. As he would later say, his challenge was first getting the king into Austria and then getting him out again.

Bismarck also advised strategic restraint in his constitutional plans for the new Northern German federation, in which smaller German states would retain significant autonomy, and in his rapprochement with Prussian liberals. His federation, which laid the legal foundation for the German Reich, retained significant prerogatives for German princes. It also created a new German legislature, the Bundestag, elected on the basis of a universal franchise. Rather than exploiting the Prussian position of strength, Bismarck killed his enemies with kindness. This model made it much easier to incorporate the remaining southern German states into the empire following the Franco-Prussian War five years later. Closer to home, he ended the protracted constitutional struggle in Prussia, making allies of pragmatic liberals who were willing to drop their demands for democratic rights in exchange for the realization of their longstanding goal of a unified Germany. Splitting from their colleagues, they formed the National Liberal party, the most powerful party in the new unified Germany. Bismarck would rely on its support for a decade. Now known as Germany's chancellor, he had made good on his long-standing idea to form a Baptist–bootlegger coalition with the National Liberals. With these two acts of restraint vis-à-vis the forces of democracy, Bismarck broke once and for all with his old conservative patrons.

A central lesson of this chapter is that when statesmen combine national egoism with a rational cognitive style, the Realpolitik they practice resists the crude characterization of bellicose, trigger-happy warmongers we sometimes find in the literature, even by some realists. The epistemically motivated and egoistic decision-maker, coldly conscious of others' interests, often has reason to practice conciliatory policies of restraint so as to mitigate the concerns of others. Realism is as much about *not* using power as it is about using it. Being weak and being strong can both pose problems for the state. Cold blood is not the same as iron.

"A King as Courier!": Bismarck's Opposition to the Congress of Princes

In 1862 Bismarck became the Minister-President of Prussia, the most important political position in the country other than the crown itself. It was a surprising appointment, one that King Wilhelm I resorted to only in light of his intense and intractable conflict with the Prussian parliament, called the *Landtag*. Unable to secure approval of a budget and in the face of a disagreement on a military reform bill, the crown proceeded on dubious legal grounds, arguing that it had the right to collect and spend taxes in the event that the Landtag and the king could not agree because the constitution did not specify otherwise (what became known as the *Lücketheorie*, the "gap" or "hole theory") (Steinberg 2012: 208). Bismarck was brought in as a "Konfliktminister" because of his reputation as a heavy-hitting arch-conservative in domestic affairs. To most observers, this seemed to portend (correctly) a no-holds-barred approach on the part of the monarchy. Under the new Minister-President, the government muzzled the press and banned civil servants and soldiers from engaging in any political activities, among other anti-democratic measures (Feuchtwanger 2002: 90–5; Steinberg 2012: 190–208). Bismarck had told the king before his appointment, "The question now at issue is not between conservative and liberal, but whether the regime Prussia shall be monarchical or parliamentary. If needs must, parliamentarianism should be withstood by a period of dictatorship" (Ludwig 2013: 199).

Bismarck's ability to deal forcefully with the Landtag was deemed more important than his unorthodox foreign policy views, which had previously put him on ice (Ludwig 2013: 196; Pflanze 1990: 175). He was regarded as a Bonapartist, to which he responded: "If am to be falsely described as a devil, at least let it be as a Teutonic and not as a Gallic one!" (Ludwig 2013: 180). Bismarck had been passed over in 1860 for the position of foreign minister when, in his interview with the king, he made the case for a drastic reform of the German Bund so as to restrict Habsburg influence. His competitor, who ultimately received the job, identified France as Prussia's primary threat, like a good conservative for his time.

Newly empowered, Bismarck first had to play defense. He sank an effort by the Habsburgs to unify Germany on Austrian terms. In summer 1863, the Emperor Franz Josef II proposed a reform of the Bund as a preparatory stage to a voluntary union that would privilege Austria over Prussia. The Bund would create a new executive organ, a federal directorate in which the Prussians might be outvoted, and a chamber of deputies whose deputies were chosen by parliaments of member states (rather than through direct elections) (Feuchtwanger 2002: 97; Ludwig 2013: 232–4; Pflanze 1990: 197; Steinberg 2012: 196–7).

The Austrians invited the German monarchs to a "Congress of Princes" to discuss the issue. All quickly accepted his offer, and Wilhelm I felt an obligation to go as well. The Saxon king had visited him personally to urge him to attend. "Thirty reigning princes, and a King to take their messages!" he famously said (Bismarck I: 376). This was another case of the attachment felt by Wilhelm I to other sovereigns, a sentiment that in Bismarck's eyes distracted the king from Prussia's egoistic interests. Wilhelm "favoured the Austrian proposal because it contained an element of royal solidarity in the struggle against parliamentary Liberalism, by which he himself was just then hard pressed at Berlin" (Bismarck I: 375). Wilhelm did not have romantic dreams of a new Holy Roman Empire like his brother, Friedrich Wilhelm IV. He did not want Prussia "merged into Germany," and believed that Prussia must dislodge Austria from German affairs (Aronson 1971: 17). Nevertheless, the new king was "a legitimist both for himself and for others" and initially loathe to break with the Habsburgs (Ludwig 2013: 165).

Bismarck was immediately opposed, later writing, "[T]he reform in the Bund that Austria endeavoured to obtain with the aid of the 'Diet of Princes' would have secured the pre-eminence of Austria, on the basis of the apprehension of Prussia and of parliamentary conflicts felt by the ruling houses, by means of a permanent and systematically founded majority in the Diet" (Bismarck I: 369). Bismarck wanted a *kleindeutsch* solution to the German problem – that is, one that excluded the Austrians and maximized Prussian influence. The Minister-President's effort to convince the king not to participate in the congress led to a severe fight. Bismarck had to threaten to resign so that he could prevail – a tactic to which he frequently resorted (Ludwig 2013: 211; Steinberg 2012: 197). The Minister-President believed rejecting the congress was tremendously important for the direction of German unification. Bismarck later argued: "Had I dropped my resistance to the King's efforts to go to Frankfort, and, according to his wish, accompanied him thither in order, during the congress, to convert the rivalry of Austria and Prussia into a common warfare against revolution and constitutionalism, [it] would have closed the road to German nationality" (Bismarck I: 376). Historians agree. Steinberg (2012) even calls it the "most important achievement of Bismarck's entire career" (197).

"No Right to Schleswig–Holstein": Conservative Resistance to Prussian Annexation

The Schleswig–Holstein crisis erupted in March 1863 when the Danish king, Frederick VII, in violation of the London Protocols of 1854, attempted to impose a new constitution on the two duchies, which had German majorities. Although the territories were bound in a "personal union" with Denmark, recognizing Frederick VII as their sovereign but maintaining separate laws and administration, the king was bound by treaties not to seek any closer incorporation of the territories without prior consultation. The Danish action elicited nationalist outrage, especially in the smaller German states, on behalf of the embattled and oppressed Germans who they believed deserved the right of national self-determination. Almost immediately after the promulgation of this "March Patent," as it was known, Frederick VII died.

Despite the fact that the London Treaty specified the king's son, Christian IX, as the rightful heir, another claimant, the Duke of Augustenburg emerged. For symbolic reasons he announced his claim in Coburg, a bastion of liberal and German nationalist support. Given the intense pressure of nationalist public opinion, the smaller German states argued that the Bund should take action against the Danish kingdom on behalf of their German brethren. Holstein was a part of the Bund and the Danish king was therefore represented in the body, although Schleswig was not (Feuchtwanger 2002: 101–3). The duke was an enlightened, liberal aristocrat, with democratic sympathies.

As Minister-President, Bismarck most wanted to avoid an outcome in which the duke, riding a wave of German nationalist sentiment, succeeded in wresting the two duchies (regarded historically as inseparable – "forever undivided") from Denmark with Prussia paying the costs.

He identified this as the one option that "must absolutely be avoided – that is to say, to fight out Prussia's struggle and war for the erection of a new grand duchy" (Bismarck II: 11). Bismarck repeatedly expressed the view that Prussia had "no interest in fighting a war ... to install a new Grand Duke, who will vote against us at the Bund because he fears our lust for annexation and whose government will become a willing object of Austrian intrigues, forgetful of any gratitude which he owes Prussia for his election" (Steinberg 2012: 210; also Bismarck II: 5; Feuchtwanger 2002: 106). Again Bismarck's only concern was Prussian interest. "We have greater concerns and dangers to face than the misdemeanours of Danish overlords in Schleswig," he had commented derisively back in 1861 (Feuchtwanger 2002: 101). As Bismarck told a Danish minister in Frankfurt, "he was no friend of a sentimental or national policy and much too Prussian to make any distinctions in his feelings between Spaniards, Bavarians, or Danes. His only concern was whether Prussia had an interest in quarreling with Denmark" (Pflanze 1990: 241).

According to Bismarck, Prussia might use, but should not be used by, the nationalists (Feuchtwanger 2002: 101–2). At the time of the crisis, he advised that "to throw ourselves in to the arms of the policy of the minor states – enmeshed as it is in the net of club-democracy – that would be the most wretched position, either at home or abroad, to which the monarchy could be brought. We should be pushed instead of pushing; we should not lean for support upon elements which we do not control" (Bismarck II: 4–5; also Feuchtwanger 2002: 103).

Bismarck was also concerned that any bold Prussian action at this time would lead to British intervention, as the English were supporters of the Danish king and would regard Prussian military action as hostile to their vital interests given Denmark's location in the North Sea. He asked sarcastically, "[A]re we now, at the side of [famous liberal figures] Pfordten, Coburg, and Augustenburg, supported by all the chatterboxes and humbugs of the party of movement, suddenly to be strong enough to take an off-hand tone towards all four of the Great Powers?" (Bismarck II: 5). Instead Prussia "must attach more weight to our relations with the other major powers than to any agreement with the present trend of public opinion and I further believe that we must prepare for an open fight against rather than an alliance with the incipient national and revolutionary movement" (Feuchtwanger 2002: 102; also Bismarck II: 11). This was an example of his higher-order beliefs, strategic thinking, and global maximization, in which Schleswig–Holstein was perceived as just one theater among many.

To avoid great power intervention and to squash the push of the middle-sized German states to create yet another German state,

Bismarck recruited the Austrians, who also opposed the duke's candidacy. "Austria once with us ... the possibility of a coalition of the other Powers against us disappeared," he recalled later (Bismarck II: 12). Together the two powers were formidable, and Austria provided cover against the suspicion that Prussia sought to annex the duchies. Despite the Bund's official veto, the two countries jointly marched into Schleswig with the goal of forcing the Danish king to abide by the London protocols and restore the status quo. These limited aims, to reestablish the existing legal order, were meant to reassure the British, in particular, of their limited intentions. Bismarck was also careful to frame his country's actions rhetorically as upholding the Treaty of London and maintaining European equilibrium (Goddard 2009). A conference was convened in London for Britain and other powers to mediate the crisis. However, when the Danish king still refused to return the two provinces to their former status, the Prussians and Austrians declared the London treaties null and void (Ludwig 2013: 249).

While the Schleswig–Holstein issue was not worth a war if the primary beneficiary was to be a liberal duke, a Prussian annexation of the duchies was a very different matter for Bismarck. This was his preferred outcome at the time, although he was mindful of the potential costs. "[F]or me annexation by Prussia is not the highest and most necessary aim but it would be the most agreeable result" (Steinberg 2012: 218; also Feuchtwanger 2002: 106). Bismarck was also aware of the need to adjust to situations and seek other paths: "From the very beginning, I kept annexation steadily before my eyes, without losing sight of the other gradations," he wrote later (Bismarck II: 11). The Minister-President was willing to take another bird in the hand if it came to that.

His conservative colleagues, however, were again opposed to his policies on grounds of legitimist solidarity. In a crown council meeting in February 1864, Bismarck made the case for the first time for taking Schleswig–Holstein for Prussia (Bismarck II: 10; also Pflanze 1990: 251). According to Bismarck, everyone else in the crown council remained silent except the crown prince, who "raised his hands to heaven as if he doubted my sanity" (Bismarck II: 10). The king's commitment to the principle of legitimacy led him to rebuff Bismarck; he had no rightful claim to the duchies (Ludwig 2013: 248; Steinberg 2012: 225). Bismarck's suggestions were so controversial that the king had them stricken from the minutes of the meeting, believing that Bismarck would not want them recorded. The Minister-President, however, was not embarrassed. He had them reinserted (Bismarck II: 10; also Feuchtwanger 2002: 108; Ludwig 2013: 249).

The king's reluctance was reinforced by the liberal sensitivities of his wife and some other moderate aristocrats, who supported Augustenburg. German liberals opposed any Prussian annexation on the grounds that it violated the principle of national self-determination. King Wilhelm instead decided to support the duke's candidature (Pflanze 1990: 241). Bismarck later complained, "it certainly cost us much trouble to loosen the threats by which the King, with the co-operation of the Liberalising influence of his consort, remained attached to that camp ... he stuck to his motto: 'I have no right to Holstein'" (Bismarck II: 13). Both liberals and conservatives opposed the Minister-President.

Bismarck's realism made him again, at least for the time, a minority of one. It is striking that, as Pflanze notes, Bismarck was "almost alone in nourishing the ambition to annex the Duchies to Prussia," both at home and abroad.

Not one of the many important interests involved in the controversy desired this end. The Copenhagen government was attempting to incorporate the Duchies into Denmark; the British Cabinet desired to maintain the integrity of the Danish monarchy; Austria wanted a return to the status quo before the crisis arose; the lesser German states wished the creation of a new Confederate state ruled by the Prince of Augustenburg; the liberal majority in the Prussian parliament and the German liberal–national movement as a whole desired a similar solution; the Prussian King and Crown Prince were also sympathetic to the Augustenburg cause. (Pflanze 1955: 504)

Yet despite this, Bismarck achieved all of his aims in a process color-fully captured by Goddard (2009). Concerned about the prospect of Prussian annexation, the Austrians eventually changed their mind and embraced the Duke of Augustenburg's right to rule Schleswig–Holstein as a separate state, increasing the prospects of Bismarck's least preferred option – the formation of a new German middle-sized power. Bismarck adjusted to the new situation, identifying a set of Prussian conditions for agreeing to the duke's claim that Augustenburg could never accept; they amounted to a de facto annexation of Schleswig–Holstein.[2] Bismarck painted the duke's refusal to Wilhelm in the most unflattering terms, turning the king against him. When an armistice in Denmark negotiated at the London peace conference expired, Austro-Prussian forces occupied the rest of Denmark, compelling the Danish king to forever

---

[2] Bismarck insisted on the incorporation of the duchies' armed forces into the Prussian army (which would proclaim an oath of allegiance to the Prussian king), a canal under Prussian control across the peninsula connecting the North Sea and the Baltic, a Prussian garrison in a Bund-owned fortress, the inclusion of the duchies in the Customs Union (from which Austria was excluded), a naval base in Kiel, and guarantees of a conservative form of government (Feuchtwanger 2002: 124; Ludwig 2013: 253; Pflanze 1990: 253).

renounce the duchies. In Bad Gastein, the two monarchs agreed to joint administration and divided the territories, with Austria controlling Holstein, Prussia controlling Schleswig, and a smaller area called Lauenberg to be sold to Prussia.[3] Liberal nationalists deeply resented the outcome, seeing it as a blow to the principle of self-determination.

A Fratricidal War?: Starting the Conflict with the Austrian Empire

Frictions over the disposition of Schleswig and Holstein provided Bismarck with the spark he needed to incite a final showdown with Austria that would expel the Habsburgs from German affairs forever. Bismarck continued to press the king and others in the crown council for annexation of both provinces, with little initial success. A military officer recounted a meeting in February 1866: "Bismarck gave hints that the war must decisively achieve the rounding off of Prussian territory. ... The King answered angrily, that there is no question of war yet and still less of deposing German princes" (Steinberg 2012: 245; also Feuchtwanger 2002: 133). Bismarck again faced opposition from the queen, the queen dowager, and the crown prince (GW VII: 123).

The problem for Bismarck was the king's disdain for Realpolitik. Bismarck later stated, "One of the greatest difficulties was the punctilious conscientiousness and the hesitation of the old King William, who never wanted to agree to anything that seemed in the slightest bit unconstitutional or that was not consonant with the most stringent estimation of righteousness and truth and faith" (GW VII: 234–5; also Pflanze 1990: 293). Bismarck, it was said in Berlin, acted as a clockmaker every morning, winding up the monarch (GW VII: 123). The king's son complained:

The King wants no war but for months now Bismarck has twisted things so that the old Gentleman has become more and more irritable and finally Bismarck will have ridden him so far that he will not be able to do anything but commit us to war. ... Bismarck's talent to manipulate things for the King is great and worthy of admiration. (Steinberg 2012: 240)

The Minister-President described himself at the time as "exasperatingly using spurs, so that the old, noble racer" would act. He had to overcome the "conservative disposition of the king" (GW VII: 234–5).

---

[3] The Austrians also conceded many of the February conditions to Prussia, including the canal, naval base, and garrison (Feuchtwanger 2002: 127; Pflanze 1990: 264).

Members of the conservative camarilla supported Wilhelm I's position. Ludwig von Gerlach wrote against war with Austria in the Kreuzzeitung on legitimist grounds. He accused Bismarck of pursuing a raison d'état divorced from morality and the divine principles that should govern foreign policy (Feuchtwanger 2002: 137). Conservatives like Gerlach warned against a "civil" or a "fratricidal" war, terms that indicate how they saw Prussia's egoistic interests as constrained by a broader social solidarity: "Let us take care not to fall into the dreadfully false belief that God's commandments stop at the field of politics. ... The justified calling on Prussia to expand its power in Germany matches the equally justified Austrian claim to maintain its power in Germany. Germany is no longer Germany if Prussia is not there or when Austria is not there" (Feuchtwanger 2002: 125).

Matters came to a head in June 1866 when the Austrians allowed the Holstein estates to meet, thereby violating the terms of the Gastein Convention. Prussian troops invaded the duchy to stop the convocation. The Bund voted to mobilize forces against Prussia in response. This was the emotional spark that Bismarck needed to convince the king. Wilhelm responded wrathfully: "Austria follows up perfidy with falsehood, and falsehood with a breach of faith" (Ludwig 2013: 274). He was ready to fight for Prussian honor. Wilhelm was particularly keen to avoid a humiliation such as Prussia had experienced at Olmütz in 1850 (Ludwig 2013: 270; Taylor 1955: 71). He declared, very romantically, "I know that they are all against me. Everyone one of them! But I shall myself draw my sword at the head of my army, and would rather perish than that Prussia should give way this time!" (Ludwig 2013: 270). As will be seen later in this chapter, Wilhelm approached the conflict in a very non-consequentialist manner.

Prussia declared the Bund to be dissolved. All of the larger states – Saxony, Württemberg, Hanover, Electoral Hesse, Baden, and Bavaria – allied with the Habsburgs. Only the states geographically isolated and most susceptible to Prussian pressure – such as the small Mecklenburg territories and Anhalt – sided with Prussia (Feuchtwanger 2002: 143; Ludwig 2013: 275; Pflanze 1990: 304). Bismarck, demonstrating his realist flexibility again, had meanwhile arranged a secret treaty of alliance with nationalist Italians so that Austria would have to fight on two fronts (Ludwig 2013: 266; Pflanze 1990: 295). For this support, the Italians were promised Venetia (Feuchtwanger 2002: 141). The Minister-President also conspired with Hungarians to foment an internal rebellion in the Austrian empire (Pflanze 1990: 309).

The "Sour Apple": Ending the Conflict with the Austrian Empire

The Austro-Prussian War of 1866 is interesting less for how it began, and more for how it ended. The conflict was not much of a contest. Indeed, the "Fraternal War" is also known as the "Seven Weeks War." The Prussians decisively defeated the Austrians at the Battle of Königgratz, ending any chance of Austrian victory. The question was how far the Prussians would push their mastery of the Habsburgs. Bismarck's Realpolitik guided him not to exploit Prussian success, as a crude understanding of realism might expect, but rather to engage in strategic restraint. This looked like "retreat in the very moment of victory," writes Ziblatt (2006: 122). However, Realpolitik, as we have seen, is marked by a global understanding of one's position. It involves a consideration of not just the short term but also the long term. Realpolitik, as a rational approach, takes into account not just the particular adversary one is facing at the time, but also how one's actions are viewed in the broader environment.

Both of these considerations led Bismarck to conclude that the Prussians should seek a negotiated peace that left the Austrian Empire intact, with no loss in territory. He advised "His Majesty to make peace on the basis of the territorial integrity of Austria" (Bismarck II: 41). Ludwig (2013) writes:

As a liegemen of the king of Prussia ... his only concern was with the expansion of Prussia; and he would much rather, after the manner of earlier centuries, have conquered German princes in order to enlarge Prussia, than have troubled himself about the problems of the German Federation. ... But his sinister intelligence ... and his clear view of reality, overpowered these wishes. ... He kept his eyes fixed on what was attainable, ignored what was merely desirable. (262–3).

We expect more epistemically motivated thinkers to distinguish between what is desirable and what is feasible.

Bismarck wanted to limit war aims to the expulsion of the Austrians from northern German affairs and the creation of new but small unified German state in northern Germany that could be added to gradually. This had been Bismarck's position even before the war began. He wrote von Moltke, the head of the Prussian army, in March 1866: "The goal ... is the agreement of Austria to the new German constitution we are striving for. Limiting our ambitions to northern Germany also offers the ... possibility of an understanding with Bavaria" (GW V: 396). He cautioned against the "occupation of Elbe duchies" because this would led to a "new range of continuous conflicts and unabated burdens" (GW V: 396). He would later recount that "a quick peace was very surprising for some" but that he pragmatically "thought it the best that could be done" (GW VII: 234–5). It was a "mistake to place the entire result in question in order to win a few more square miles of territorial concessions or a few million more reparations from Austria," he wrote the king (GW VI: 78–81). At another point Bismarck wrote a colleague, "As far as I am concerned the difference between a successful reform of the German federation and the direct acquisition of some countries is not practically high enough to risk the future of the monarchy. Our political requirements are limited to the disposition of the powers of northern Germany in some form" (GW VI: 40–5). Prussia should not go south of the Main River, a limit to which the French indicated their acquiescence and support (Bismarck II: 47). As Bismarck later put it, "In positions such as ours was then, it is a political maxim after a victory not to enquire how much you can squeeze out of your opponent, but only to consider what is politically necessary" (Bismarck II: 43).

The king and the military, however, had different plans. They wanted to continue the fight, seizing Vienna and even moving on to Hungary, as well as demanding significant territorial concessions (Feuchtwanger 2002: 144). Wilhelm proposed a striking list of desired territorial annexations from Austria and its allies: Bohemia, Austrian Silesia, Ansbach–Bayreuth, East Friesland, Hanover, and part of Saxony, in addition to Schleswig–Holstein (Bismarck II: 45; Steinberg 2012: 255). These land grabs would have meant an expansion of Prussia past the Main River. In their arguments about how and when to end the war, Bismarck was all sober and deliberative thinking, the king all deontological indignation and impulse. The Minister-President wrote to his wife, "If we do not exaggerate our claims and do not believe that we have conquered the world, we can arrive at a peace worth the effort. But we are as quickly intoxicated as discouraged, and I have the thankless task of pouring water into the effervescent wine" (Feuchtwanger 2002: 144; Steinberg 2012: 254).

The divide separating Bismarck and his political allies was not simply substantive, but also cognitive. The Austrian question was not marked by a cleavage between reluctant romantics and a revisionist realist, but rather reduced to fundamentally different styles of thinking. Bismarck could be both expansionist and forgiving, depending on what he believed a cold, objective analysis of the strategic situation dictated. The king, however, had by all accounts been emotionally aroused by the conflict, leading him to violate a central tenet of even the most restricted definitions of rationalism – consistent preferences. The Minister-President had needed to push Wilhelm I into the conflict; now he had to restrain him. "My greatest difficulty was first to get the king into Bohemia and then to get him out again," was Bismarck's pithy memory of the divide (Feuchtwanger 2002: 145). Ludwig (2013) describes the situation: "Hardly was the war he had so reluctantly entered upon brought to a successful issue, when the king was seized with a lust for conquest" (286).

Bismarck's plans were marked by instrumental rationality, combining strategic understanding and long-term thinking. Pushing further might feel good, but would ultimately undermine Prussian interests.

It was my object, in view of our subsequent relations with Austria, as far as possible to avoid cause for mortifying reminiscences, as it could be managed without prejudice to our German policy. A triumphant entry of the Prussian army into the hostile capital would naturally have been a gratifying recollection for our soldiers, but it was not necessary to our policy. It would have left behind it, as also any surrender of ancient possessions to us must have done, a wound to the pride of Austria, without being a pressing necessity for us, would have unnecessarily increased the difficulty of our future mutual relations. … [I]t would be of great importance whether the feelings we left behind in our opponents were implacable or the wounds we had inflicted upon them and their self-respect were incurable. … Moved by this consideration, I had a political motive for avoiding, rather than bringing about, a triumphal entry into Vienna in the Napoleonic style. (Bismarck II: 43)

Bismarck put himself in the shoes of the Austrians, a difficult task that required an objective and dispassionate thinking style (GW VII: 137, 234–5). Austria "must be made into a friend, and as a friend it could not be completely powerless" (GW VII: 234–5).

Thinking about the future, Bismarck concluded that alienating Austria would reduce Prussian options in the future. He again used his chess metaphor:

We had to avoid wounding Austria too severely; we had to avoid leaving behind in her any unnecessary bitterness of feeling or desire for revenge; we ought rather to reserve the possibility of becoming friends again with our adversary of the moment, and in any case to regard the Austrian state as a piece on the European chessboard and the renewal of friendly relations with her as a move open to us. If Austria were severely injured, she would become the ally of France and of every other opponent of ours; she would even sacrifice her anti-Russian interests for the sake of revenge on Prussia. (Bismarck II: 50)

Bismarck was also concerned about the broader European environment, demonstrating the security dilemma sensibility of the rationally thinking realist and the cognitive complexity to maximize benefits across multiple dimensions. Disturbing the equilibrium any further would create fear in London, Paris, and Moscow and invite outside intervention, particularly if Prussia pushed the fight into Hungary and left itself exposed on that flank (Bismarck II: 51). Bismarck was particularly worried about Napoleon and therefore pushed for a quick peace. After Königgratz, he believed "we could not lose a fortnight without bringing at least the danger of *French* interference very much nearer than it otherwise would be" (Bismarck II: 41; also Bismarck II: 45; VI: 78–81, VII: 234–5). He wrote to the king that Napoleon had consented to adding four million northern German inhabitants, "but one could not count on support of anything more far-reaching or calculate even how these Prussian demands would be received by the other great powers" (GW VI: 78–81). The Minister-President complained to his wife that he had the responsibility of "reminding people that we do not live alone in Europe but with three other powers, who hate and envy us" (Steinberg 2012: 254). His preoccupation with the appearance of Prussian motives was also evident before the war. Bismarck argued, "we cannot allow to be seen, in conflict with Europe, as committed in advance to a wanton war of aggression (GW V: 396). Instead, the Austrians had to be seen in Europe to be hindering natural German national aspirations (GW V: 396).

Bismarck was also worried about biting off more than Germany could chew. Some new territories would be more difficult to integrate than others, making them more cost than benefit. The Minister-President wanted to pass on conquering those states whose particularism was strongest, particularly the Catholic, southern states. He commented at the time: "I believe it is impossible to incorporate the Bavarian south German Catholic element. ... [T]he effort to violently conquer it would create for us the same element of weakness that southern Italy has created for that state" (GW VI: 40–45; also Pflanze 1990: 369; Ziblatt 2006: 126). More colorfully, he said to a Hungarian aristocrat, "We cannot use these ultramontagnes. We should also not swallow more than we can digest" (GW VII: 140). He said the same of Austrian provinces; their acquisition would not "strengthen but rather weaken" (GW VII: 234–5). Given their geographical location on France's borders, Bismarck was also keenly aware that incorporation of those same states would be perceived as the most threatening to Napoleon's interests (Bismarck II: 45; Pflanze 1990: 367). The Minister-President, of course, had ultimate aims on the southern German states. However, only a patient, long-term, stepwise process would allow for success. In a meeting with the crown prince, he described his limited aims in northern Germany as a "step towards greater unification" (GW VII: 137).

Wilhelm's thinking was by all accounts less rational – more short-term oriented and less instrumental and utilitarian. The king was emotional and impulsive, rather than calculating and deliberative. According to Bismarck, the king, in the midst of a stormy session, "said that the chief culprit could not be allowed to escape unpunished, and that justice once satisfied, we could let the misguided partners off more easily, and he insisted on the cessions of territory from Austria" (Bismarck II: 51; also Ludwig 2013: 287–88). His position was the same in regard to the smaller German powers (Bismarck II: 52). A senior military officer wrote, "The peace negotiations are going well and the peace would have been signed if the King had not made difficulties. He insists that Austria surrender territory to us. ... It looks as if this point of honour is the stumbling block" (Steinberg 2012: 254). Bismarck summarized the situation: the "king and the military party ... were very proud of the great victory of Prussian weapons and believed that such a great success demanded a greater reward" (GW VII: 234–5).

This was not a case of a leader adjusting his aims in light of military successes, as a rationalist model would suggest (Fearon 1995; Goemans 2000). As seen earlier, the king's initial resistance to fighting Austria had never been based on power considerations; it was principled in character. The king would not countenance a break in conservative solidarity. Now, however, after the conflict had started, he wanted retribution. Taylor writes that is was not a matter of consequentialist judgment for Wilhelm: "The king ... had been dragged reluctantly into war. ... Now he regarded them as wicked and insisted that they be punished. For him, as for many lesser mortals, war was a matter of moral judgement, not an instrument of power" (Taylor 1955: 86).

This makes sense given Wilhelm's lower level of rational thought. The king was highly emotional during this period. Bismarck describes his interactions with the king at this time: "The resistance which I was obliged, in accordance with my convictions, to offer to the King's views with regard to following up the military successes, and to his inclination to continue the victorious advance, excited him to such a degree that a prolongation of the discussion became impossible" (Bismarck II: 52). Pflanze (1990) suggests that "Wilhelm, whom he had dragged into the conflict, became most immoderate in his rage against Austria and in the demands to be made on her" (314). At one point the king threw himself weeping onto the sofa, saying, "My first minister will be a deserter in the face of the enemy and imposes his shameful peace to me" (Steinberg 2012: 255). Bismarck believed Wilhelm was at least partially intoxicated by military success (Bismarck II: 54; also Taylor 1955: 84). This was a longstanding dynamic between the two. Ludwig (2013) observes,

"The king had, as a rule, the equable pulses of an heir; but he would become excited at critical moments, and give way to furious passion" (166). This was the exact opposite of Bismarck, who "in moments of crisis ... was ice-cold and clear-sighted" (166). Bismarck treated Wilhelm as a father "whose fits of temper and caprices must be accepted" (214). The king did not exhibit the same degree of emotional regulation that would indicate a highly active System II.

Bismarck described his efforts to get the king to listen to reason. The Minister-President explained that Prussia must be dispassionate at this moment. He "regarded the principle of retaliation as no sound basis for our policy, since even where our *feelings* had been injured, it ought to be guided, not by our own irritation, but by consideration of its object" (Bismarck II: 82 [emphasis added]). He also demonstrated objectivity: "Austria's conflict in rivalry with us was no more culpable than ours with her" (Bismarck II: 51). This shows Bismarck's ability to avoid the temptation of "myside bias," in which Prussian interests were held to be more ethically justified than those of Austria. His position was based explicitly on instrumental rationality, one that weighed costs and benefits and focused on securing vital interests first. Bismarck told the king: "[W]e were not there to sit in judgment, but to pursue the German policy. ... [O]ur task was the establishment or initiation of a German national unity under the leadership of the King of Prussia (Bismarck II: 51). He stressed that punishment was counterproductive and short-sighted, telling the king "we were there not to administer retributive justice, but to pursue a policy" (Bismarck II: 52). Retribution is, of course, punishment without regard to the future consequences.

The military was another obstacle to Bismarck's realism. To their desire to take the fight all the way to Vienna, Bismarck reacted sarcastically: "If the hostile army surrenders Vienna and withdraws into Hungary we must follow them ... then it will be best to march on Constantinople, found a new Byzantine empire, and leave Prussia to her fate" (Feuchtwanger 2002: 145). He thought the military had undue influence over the king: "What seemed to me to be paramount with his Majesty was the aversion of the military party to interrupt the victorious course of the army. ... All the generals shared the disinclination to break off the uninterrupted course of victory; and during these days the King was more often and more readily accessible to military influences than mine" (Bismarck II: 47).

With Bismarck threatening to resign, the king relented after an intervention by his son, the crown prince. Wilhelm sent a note to the Minister-President. Bismarck paraphrased it as reading, "Inasmuch as my Minister-President has left me in the lurch in the face of the enemy, and here I am not in a position to supply his place, I have discussed the question with my son; and as he as associated himself with the Minister-President's opinion, I find myself reluctantly compelled, after such brilliant victories on the part of the army, to bite this sour apple and accept so disgraceful a peace" (Bismarck II: 53). Bismarck had convinced the king to be a realist, accepting the lesser evil. Apples cannot always be sweet. Feuchtwanger (2002) writes, "The trial of wills Bismarck had over this with his master were among the most serious of their long relationship" (145).

In the end, Prussia confined its annexation to the area north of the Main River, in northern Germany, gaining the significant territories of Hanover, Saxony, and Schleswig–Holstein. The Hanoverian king lost his crown, although at French insistence, the Saxon king kept his (Steinberg 2012: 125). The incorporation of part of Hesse–Kassel made Prussia contiguous but was "only so reduced was as to allow the [territorial] binding of east and west Prussia" (GW VII: 137). Bismarck used the same pragmatic reasoning: "I was against taking half of Saxony and half of Hannover. A despoiled commonwealth remains unsatisfied forever. One must leave the commonwealth untouched, then everyone gets used to the new regime" (GW VII: 137). The three large southern states – Bavaria, Baden, and Württemberg – retained their independence but were made to sign treaties of alliance. Upon hearing the generous terms, the Bavarian negotiator embraced Bismarck and wept (Ludwig 2013: 292–3). However, even with Bismarck's strategic restraint, Prussia had added 4 million habitants and now was a truly great power with a population of 30 million.

This rational, realist strategy was hardly structurally determined. Bismarck, as has been stressed, was unique in his views, making the outcome all the more incredible. There is universal recognition of this fact in the historical literature (Ludwig 2013: 282; Ziblatt 2006: 14). The "scale of Bismarck's triumph cannot be exaggerated" writes Steinberg (2012). "He achieved this incredible feat without commanding an army . . . without control of a large party, without public support, indeed, in the face of almost universal hostility, without a majority in parliament, without control of his cabinet and without a loyal following in the bureaucracy. He no longer had the support of the powerful conservative interest groups who had helped him to achieve power" (257). Apropos of this fact, when the conflict ended, Bismarck is said to have pounded on his desk and proclaimed, "I have beaten them all!" By this, he surely meant both domestic *and* foreign opponents, both liberals *and* conservatives (Feuchtwanger 2002: 148; Pflanze 1990: 316; Steinberg 2012: 257). "They took me for a Junker, a reactionary . . . with the king they denounced me as a secret democrat," he crowed (Feuchtwanger 2002: 148). At its core, though, Bismarck's approach was cognitively driven. He wrote, "It is about leading a government based on the views of the *thinking* in the nation" (GW VII: 147 [emphasis added]), deliberately contrasting this with the approach taken by his former Kreuzzeitung allies.

The Reich's Restraint: The Northern German Federation and the Prussian Indemnity Bill

While Bismarck's success in holding back Prussia during the Austro-Prussian war has received the most attention by historians, less noticed are the Minister-President's actions in regard to the new Germany created in the war's aftermath as well as his management of the domestic political situation in Prussia after he returned home victorious. These were also instances of historically important strategic restraint. Bismarck largely drafted the proposed constitution for the North German federation himself based on longstanding plans that predated his assumption of the Minister-President role (Ludwig 2013: 182; Steinberg 2012: 267). "Seldom in history has a constitution been so clearly the product of the thought and will of a single individual," writes Pflanze (1990: 341).

At the time of Prussia's triumph and within days of its victory at Königgratz, Bismarck summoned a new federal parliament, to be selected based on direct and universal male suffrage. This was the same formula that had been included in the Frankfurt parliament's radical 1848 constitution (Pflanze 1990: 306). The new assembly would negotiate a new constitution for a new federation including Prussia and all the other German states that had not been annexed, with the exception of the three larger southern states (but including Saxony). This was another example of Bismarck's strategic restraint. He made the greatest concession to liberals and nationalists – the one for which they had fought since 1848 with withering resistance from Bismarck – precisely at Prussia's pinnacle of strength. Chapter 4 explored how this possibility had been on the Prussian's mind for a considerable time and grew out of a pragmatic recognition that Prussia could not resist democracy forever, so the best course was to make use of and manage it.

The Minister-President had made his plans for such a parliament clear before the war in an effort to court liberal nationalists to Prussia's side in the showdown with Austria. Bismarck boasted of how he would "rub some black-red-gold," the colors of the Frankfurt parliament's flag, "under [the Austrian foreign minister's] nose" (Feuchtwanger 2002: 128; Ludwig 2013: 264). The Austrians could not make such a proposal themselves, boxing them into an untenable position in the battle for German public opinion (Feuchtwanger 1990: 307).

The initial proposal was met with ridicule by liberals. A liberal paper in Cologne asked derisively, "If Mephistopheles climbed up in the pulpit and read the Gospel, could anyone be inspired by this prayer?" (Steinberg 2012: 242). The Austrian ambassador to Saxony was not cowed: "The Prussian motion for a German parliament has caused laughter because they see it as ludicrous to accept such a move from the hand of a Count Bismarck" (Steinberg 2012: 241). The Prussian comedic journal *Kladderdatsch* announced facetiously that it was ceasing publication as it could no longer keep up with the Minister-President (Feuchtwanger 2002: 136; Pflanze 1990: 321).

The plan also caused resentment on the part of conservatives in Prussia. The crown prince described Bismarck's support for a parliament "an expression of his bottomless frivolity and piratical politics," all the more outrageous "in the light of our domestic parliamentary conflict! With such a man everything is possible" (Steinberg 2012: 240). Gerlach complained, "In the midst of the clanging of weapons Prussia introduces at the Bund a demand for universal suffrage. Universal suffrage means political bankruptcy – in place of living relations of law and political thought, instead of concrete personalities, we get numbers and exercises in addition" (Steinberg 2012: 243). Another conservative complained of Bismarck's inconsistency at home and abroad: "To treat the [Landtag] chambers at home with a riding crop ... and then to hurl the parliament idea into Germany!" (Steinberg 2012: 243). Count Adolf von Kleist wrote Ludwig von Gerlach, "Our allies are now the revolution in all its nuances. We are absolutely stunned. I am in despair" (Steinberg 2002: 242). King Wilhelm was also nonplussed. "Why, that is revolution you're proposing to me," he said when Bismarck first broached the subject (Pflanze 1990: 309).

Bismarck was not joking. This was not a principled conversion, of course. In his instructions to his colleagues, Bismarck described the "principle of direct elections and general suffrage" as "the only one possible" (GW V: 432–4). Bismarck was accepting the facts on the ground. He recognized the limitations of the monarchy's power and was careful not to let his goals overtake his capacities Years before he had written, "As soon as popular representation ... exists in every German State, it becomes impossible to regard a similar institution for Germany as a whole as essentially revolutionary" (Ludwig 2013: 182). Pacification of German national wishes "through ordered means" was "in the interest of the monarchical principle in Germany," lest the people "take matters into their own hands with force" (GW V: 514–5). To his colleagues he still spoke of the "national swindle," but it was one he would use to Prussia's advantage (Feuchtwanger 2002: 145). Bismarck noted: "The goal requires sacrifices, not just from some but from all" (GW V: 514–5).

Bismarck's constitutional design also exhibited strategic restraint vis-à-vis the power of newly incorporated states, many of which still were governed by monarchs. Mindful of nationalist resistance, he did not push centralization too far. Bismarck sought to balance the forces of national centralization against those of particularism, particularly the German sovereigns who would be incorporated into the new federation. Just as Bismarck had restrained Prussian power vis-à-vis the defeated powers, he did so vis-à-vis the new members of his federation. Indeed, years before he had written of the need "to tranquilise the German princes concerning the scope of our designs, so that they may realise that we are not aiming at their mediatisation but at a voluntary understanding among them all" (Ludwig 2013: 183).

Two features of the draft, which was adopted with few changes, were key to appease particularist interests that might resist the new German state. First, the federation was to be partly governed by a Bundesrat, or Federal Council, whose members were to be directly appointed by the German states. This council would share legislative power with the new federal parliament (Feuchtwanger 2002: 152). The Northern German federation was a "compact among princes" (Steinberg 2012: 267). So as to minimize the loss in sovereignty and to "preserve the fiction that the new confederation was simply a reformed version of the old" (Pflanze 1990: 343), rather than an entirely new country, the Bundesrat was largely modeled on the now-disbanded Bund, even using the same voting rules (Feuchtwanger 2002: 152–3; Pflanze 1990: 343–5; Steinberg 2012: 267). Delegates to the Bundesrat were even given "diplomatic protection" and the members of the federation sent diplomatic envoys to Berlin (Pflanze 1990: 347). Bismarck wrote of a "viable creation on the basis and within the framework of the old federation" (GW V: 432–4).

Second, significant powers of administration and legislation were delegated to the states, something Bismarck had also long had in mind (Ludwig 2013: 183). The Northern German federation had legislative authority over customs and commerce, transportation and communication, banking and coinage, and had the right to levy tariffs and some consumption taxes. States retained the right to legislate on all other matters, including how to implement laws passed by the central government. Judicial matters were left to state courts (Pflanze 1990: 347–52). Bismarck explained that instead of the "the integration and complete merger with Prussia itself even in the face of popular resistance . . . by civil

servants and officers who feel duty-bound to the previous governments,"
the "Prussian government intends to overcome the difficulties of these
[groups] in a German way, through indulgence for particularities and
through gradual habituation" (Ziblatt 2006: 126). In other words, Bismarck was mindful of the likely resistance that would result if Prussia
pushed too hard toward creating a unified state; for strategic reasons, he
decided to proceed slowly. Bismarck successfully predicted that this
delegation of powers and federal structure would make it easier to
incorporate the southern German states, something accomplished just
five years later with the Franco-Prussian War (Feuchtwanger 2002: 152;
Pflanze 1990: 342).

By restraining Prussia from pursuing overly ambitious goals, Bismarck
could avoid much worse outcomes, such as the advent of true democracy
in Germany and Prussia. Unlike in a true parliamentary system, the
executive branch was not constituted by parliament and could not be
dissolved by it. The king's ministers would have to appear and justify
policies before the Reichstag, but only the king could dismiss them. In
the event of an inability to agree on taxation, the government would rely
on the "gap theory," maintaining the status quo until an accord could be
reached (Feuchtwanger 2002: 153–5; Ludwig 2013: 297; Pflanze 1990:
343–5; Steinberg 2012: 267). The power of the federal parliament was
also limited by the need for Bundesrat approval over legislation. The
Prussian king could summon or adjourn both the Bundesrat and Bundestag, and with the former dissolve the latter indefinitely. If there were
to be steps toward democracy, they would be managed. Treitschke
famously stated of this period, "The revolution in which we stand comes
from above" (Steinberg 2012: 259; also Ludwig 2013: 296). The constitution amounted to the "perpetuation, by the use of revolutionary means,
of the Prussian aristocratic-monarchical order in a century of increasingly
dynamic economic and social change" (Pflanze 1990: 342).

Bismarck's strategic restraint was also in Prussia's interest. The Prussians had special prerogatives in the Bundesrat. In his initial memorandum on the subject years before, Bismarck had written, "Prussia cannot
accept in Germany the role of a subordinate minority" (Ludwig 2013:
182). The chair of the Bundesrat was the Bundeskanzler (federal chancellor), appointed by the king. The chancellor was also to be the
Minister-President of Prussia, a position that of course Bismarck was to
fill. The king had complete control over foreign policy with the sole
right to negotiate treaties, supreme military authority, and the power
to declare war and martial law. The Northern German federation's
army was composed of state "contingents" headed by princes, who
could use them for police purposes within their borders. However, the

highest-ranking officers of the contingents were appointed by the Prussion king and swore allegiance to him (Feuchtwanger 2002: 152–3; Pflanze 1990: 343–5; Steinberg 2012: 267).

Bismarck's constitutional plan "provided a place within the new governmental structure for all the important political forces of the country: the German nation, the various political parties, the Hohenzollern crown, the Prussian government, and the dynasties and governments of the lesser states" (Pflanze 1955: 506). Historians comment on the realist quality of the constitution, "entirely guided by pragmatic considerations" (Feuchtwanger 2002: 152). It was a "masterpiece of realism." (Pflanze 1990: 342). The constitution "mirrored [Bismarck's] thoughts of statecraft and it may be called an image of his soul" (Ludwig 2013: 296). It carefully balanced nationalist and particularist forces, and put the Prussian monarchy at the crux. Years before, Bismarck had written that "a national representation of the German people in the federal central authority is perhaps the only means of connexion whereby a counterpoise can be established to the centrifugal tendencies of the separatist policies of the dynasties" (Ludwig 2013: 182).

Even the process was carefully designed to be led from above. Elections would take place while the states negotiated the main contours of the new constitution. After the new members of the federal diet were seated, they would advise on a document whose main features were more or less set. In Bismarck's words at the time, the Prussian government "recommends that responsibility for the federal reform" be taken by the states in the meantime. "The time between the convocation and the meeting [of the assembly] will suffice to allow the governments to establish the outlines of the proposals through negotiations, which will be presented before the assembly in the name of all the German governments" (GW V: 432–4; also V: 514–5). These proposals would be "limited to the most essential points of practical significance" (GW V: 432–4; also V: 514–5). Bismarck wrote of a "timely reform from above" (GW V: 514–5; also V: 447–9). The assembly would "receive and advise on" the proposals on which the governments had already reached "understanding" (GW V: 447–9).

Bismarck's final act of strategic restraint during this immediate postwar period occurred in Prussia itself. The Austro-Prussian war fundamentally reoriented Prussian politics. Landtag elections held on the same day as the Battle of Königgratz, before the battlefield results were even known, resulted in a decisive conservative victory. Reactionary forces increased their representation from 28 to 123. Progressives, the radical democrats, found that their number fell from 143 to 83. Moderate liberals' representation declined from 110 to 65 (Feuchtwanger 2002: 149;

Pflanze 1990: 327–8). The decisive turn in the public mood led many arch-conservatives to urge and expect Bismarck to undo the gains of 1848, perhaps even to lead a coup d'état (Ludwig 2013: 289; Pflanze 1990: 328). These were the "exertions of the Extreme Right" that Bismarck describes in his memoirs (Bismarck II: 70). Ludwig (2013) sets the scene: "The king has not been allowed to take vengeance on the enemy abroad; at least he will take vengeance on the enemy at home. All the extreme reactionaries whom Bismarck has been fighting for so long have now flocked to headquarters, declaring that the moment has now come to overthrow the constitution" (289).

Bismarck had exactly the opposite idea. The Minister-President instead proposed an end to the constitutional conflict with the Prussian parliament through the passage of an "indemnity bill," which would essentially admit the illegality of the crown's spending without authorization but legally forgive it at the same time (Ludwig 2013: 291).

Romantic conservatives again virulently objected (GW VII: 147). Hans von Kleist wrote Bismarck to complain:

How is it remotely conceivable, all old Prussian institutions, all elements of its power, are to be surrendered through this one declaration in the Speech from the Throne and that through it – its finances, its army, its House of Lords, the Monarchy, Prussia itself – is to be given over to the temporary majority of a second chamber which will emerge from its new provisions? It would in the short or long run hopelessly go under. ... Prussia without the spirit which made it is as good as dead ...without an independent Monarchy. (Steinberg 2012: 260)

In the cabinet, only one minister supported Bismarck; the others sought to block his plan. Bismarck was again isolated among his (now former) political allies.

The differences were again not over principle. Instead, they revealed a difference in thinking style. Bismarck did not argue that conservative desires were undesirable. Rather they were self-defeating; they would turn over a powerful weapon to Prussia's adversaries in the new federation:

By the suspension and revision of the Constitution, by the humiliation of the Opposition in the [Prussian] Diet, an effectual weapon against Prussia in the struggles looming in the future would have been placed in the hands of all those who were discontented with the events of 1866 in Germany and Austria. One would have had to be prepared meanwhile to carry out, in opposition to the parliament and the press, a system of government in Prussia which would be combated by all the rest of Germany. (Bismarck II: 76–77)

In a cost–benefit analysis, it was not worth it. "We could, indeed, have constitutionally gained an increase of strength for the monarchy within the amended boundaries of Prussia, but it would have been in the presence of fiercely dissentient domestic elements, to which the Opposition in the new provinces would have united itself" (Bismarck II: 76–7).

Instead, Bismarck believed, it was necessary to build a "golden bridge, either in policy or in words, in order to restore the internal peace of Prussia, and from this solid Prussian basis to continue the German policy of the King" (Bismarck II: 78; also Pflanze 1990: 329). He told the king that if liberal gains were rewound in Prussia, "All of those in Germany who are dissatisfied with the victory would, in that case, draw away from an absolutist Prussia; the new provinces would join the opposition; we should have waged a Prussian war of conquest, but Prussia's national policy would have been hamstrung" (Ludwig 2013: 289).

Bismarck scolded conservatives for their short-sighted, nonrational, thinking: "The little people don't have enough to do; they see no further than their own noses and like to swim on the storm sea of phrases. With the enemy one can cope, but the friends!" (Pflanze 1990: 338; also Feuchtwanger 2002: 149). His friends lacked the global awareness characteristic of the rational realist: "They all wear blinkers and only see a patch of the world," he declared (Steinberg 2012: 260).

Given Prussia's victory, it was now in a safe position to grant such concessions. "Before the victory I would never have mentioned the word 'indemnity'; but after the victory the King was in a position to make the concession magnanimously, and to conclude peace, not with his people … but the section of the Opposition which had got out of harm with the government" (Bismarck II: 77). He explained: "Concessions on the constitutional issue now had the appearance of a royal benevolence rather than of a government defeat" (Pflanze 1990: 329).

Bismarck sought out the crown prince, his frequent nemesis, for support for this plan. His contemporaries were somewhat astounded. General von Hartmann, who was privy to some early conversations, wrote his wife: "I have something interesting to tell you. The *crown prince* and Bismarck have reconciled" over the issue of the indemnity bill (GW VII: 147). The crown prince's aide wrote of Bismarck's far-seeing, deliberate thinking in the minutes of a meeting, remarking on "the clarity and the expansiveness of his views. … [E]very thought encompassed the entire world" (GW VII: 137).

The king, however, was originally opposed, again on the basis of a different cognitive style. "I tried to combat the difficulties which his own views, but still more external influences, and especially the influence of the Conservative deputation, had left on the King's mind. To this was added a view of political affairs which made his Majesty regard a request for a bill of indemnity as an admission of a wrong committed" (Bismarck

II: 78). The king understood the issue in emotional and deontological, rather than pragmatic and utilitarian, terms. "I cannot admit for a moment that I have done anything wrong!" he told Bismarck (Ludwig 2013: 290). Only at the last minute did Wilhelm reluctantly succumb to Bismarck's argumentation and agree to submit the indemnity bill.

Bismarck's victory over Austria and his indemnity bill won him the support of moderate liberals, leading to a fundamental realignment in the Prussian Landtag and soon after the new Reichstag (Ludwig 2013: 300). Pragmatic in nature, moderates recognized that Bismarck had done through force what they had long failed to do – namely, erect the foundations of a national German state. They traded these gains for domestic freedoms. One of the moderate liberal leaders, Twesten, spoke in parliament: "No one may be criticized for giving precedence to the issue of power at this time and maintaining that issues of freedom can wait, provided that nothing happens that can permanently prejudice them" (Pflanze 1990: 334). In contrast, radicals in the Progressive party refused to support the indemnity bill, which legitimized unconstitutionality in their view. The moderates then broke off to form a new party, the National Liberals, opening up a divide between "opportunists" and "men of principle" or "practical statesmen" and "naïve idealists," depending on which side they were on (Pflanze 1990: 336). The National Liberals were the largest party in the new federal parliament (Feuchtwanger 2002: 154). Bismarck relied on their support for the next decade, abandoning his old conservative allies. This abandonment of democracy by the bourgeoisie is thought to have been a decisive turn in the evolution of German democracy, denying liberalism the foundation on which democracy in other European nation-states was built.

Bismarck himself had no political party. A Free Conservative Party also formed in the new federal parliament, supporting the chancellor wholly and completely – "sans phrase," it was said. There were only 15 of them, however, hardly enough to govern with (Feuchtwanger 2002: 154; Pflanze 1990: 338; Steinberg 2012: 1, 259–61). Bismarck was still the lonely realist.

Conclusion: What Can One Man Tell Us about Universalist International Relations Theory?

I have demonstrated that Bismarck was in many ways *sui generis*. Despite his successes, he never had a true following of those who thought like him. Many basked in his triumphs after the fact, but they were not likeminded souls. Seeing as Bismarck comes as close to the realist as perhaps anyone else in world history, what does this mean for realism as a theory of international politics? Structural realists tell us that they cannot explain any particular instance of foreign policy-making, perhaps even anything about any particular statesman. But what if someone who does most things right in their estimation is profoundly rare, as Bismarck's case suggests? What can one man tell us about realist theory?

Quite a lot, when that man is Bismarck. It is precisely his status in foreign affairs that makes his uniqueness so momentous for realist theory, particularly of the structural variant. If there are indeed constraints of anarchy and power pushing and shoving foreign policy-makers in particular directions, rewarding them for successes and punishing them for failures, then Bismarck should not be the exception; he should be the rule. In other words, we should not really think much of him. Bismarck was just another man.

We know this is not true, of course. In advocating their understanding of how politics works, realists often make reference to the great realists and their successes. However, by doing so they inadvertently show us the relative infrequency of Realpolitik. The "great men" (which, of course, could just as easily include women) are great because of their exceptionality. The findings of this chapter offer more support for classical realist claims that procedural rationality is a prescriptive standard that statesmen should aspire to, but rarely reach, and that the difference is one of individual-level psychology. If readers are not satisfied, I offer the case of another realist, Cardinal Richelieu, in Chapter 6.

One might dispute the findings of the case, casting doubt on Bismarck's rationality. After all, he did not demonstrate much strategic restraint after the defeat of Napoleonic France that brought about the final step in German unification. He annexed Alsace and Lorraine and pushed for King Wilhelm to be crowned emperor of the new Reich in France's own Hall of Mirrors at the Versailles Palace, symbol of French greatness, thereby setting the stage in 1914 for a war of revenge that would kill more people than any war in history to that date. This, however, is completely consistent with the argument offered here – that rational thinking is hard, that is therefore a matter of degree, and that it should not be assumed to be the standard in international relations. Even Bismarck was not always driven by reason. And if Bismarck was not rational, then who is? We are led to the same conclusion. Bismarck was a relatively more rational prince among relatively less rational men, and it is unreasonable to assume Realpolitik and rationality are standard behavior among foreign policy leaders.

Following German unification, Bismarck did again engage in strategic restraint. He formed first a Dual Alliance (with Austria) and later a Triple Alliance (adding in Russia), with the aim of preserving the status quo in Europe that was so favorable for Germany. It was only with Bismarck's dismissal by a decidedly less rational thinker, Wilhelm II, that German foreign policy became increasingly reckless, provoking numerous great powers simultaneously (Byman and Pollock 2001; Snyder 1991). Bismarck focused instead on creating cohesion in Germany, something made more difficult now that significant confessional differences existed with the inclusion of the Catholic south. He relied on the support of the National Liberals in pushing his *Kulturkampf*. When this went poorly, he reversed course and abandoned the liberals in favor of a coalition with conservative economic interests.

During the last years of Bismarck's career, the main threat to cohesion in the Reich became socialism. As he had done with liberals, he persecuted this new movement mercilessly, banning the Social Democratic Party. At the same time, recognizing that industrialization had created massive structural changes in the domestic and international economy that could and should not be turned back, he sought to buy off the workers through the most generous welfare system in Europe, again enraging the conservatives. This calls to mind the Minister-President's willingness decades before to offer nationalists universal suffrage in a new German parliament. Bismarck was a realist to the end, adapting to new environments, in both domestic and international politics.

It is important to recognize that Bismarck's rationality and epistemic motivation did not guarantee success. His foreign policy achievements were matched by domestic difficulties, even though he utilized the same thinking style in both. Rationality should not be measured by outcome but rather by process, and even the greatest realists sometimes misjudge or make decisions based on incomplete information that turn out poorly. This theme repeats itself when we transition to our romantics, who often had spectacular successes despite – or perhaps because of – their intuitive, nonrational cognitive styles.

Before Bismarck, there was Richelieu. The parallels are striking. Like the German chancellor who appeared more than 300 years later, the man who would become a cardinal and the "first minister" of the king owed his rise to others who did not think like him. To earn his place, Richelieu curried favor with *les dévots* ("the devoted"), those defenders of the Catholic faith eager both to rescind the privileges of the French Huguenots that had been hard won during the French Wars of Religion and to improve relations with fellow Catholic powers Spain and Austria. Richelieu, in contrast, saw France as surrounded by hostile powers, Catholic or not, whose interests did not always coincide with those of his king. Sometimes difficult tradeoffs had to be made.

Just like the Iron Chancellor, the then Bishop of Luçon was initially viewed skeptically by the sovereign. When he did join the close advisory circle of Louis XIII, he pushed him to beat back Spanish influence in the Valtelline, a key transit point between Spain and its holdings in the Netherlands. He succeeded over the objections of the dévots, who were aghast at the French seizure of forts manned by papal forces in the valley. The cardinal's policies were so controversial they almost cost him his life. A plot by the king's mother and the dévots, enraged by armed French intervention in the Mantuan secession crisis (again against the Spanish), failed on the Day of the Dupes. French historian Victor Tapié (1967) concludes, "Richelieu spent his life in a continual battle with his enemies" (133). His realism, like Bismarck's, was a rarity.

In domestic affairs, Richelieu also advocated different policies than the deontologically minded Catholic devoted. Having finally personally put down the last of the Huguenot rebellions in 1629 at La Rochelle, the cardinal convinced Louis XIII to promulgate the Grace of Alais, in which the Protestants maintained their religious freedom but not their political prerogatives. Richelieu understood this as a pragmatic decision in light of structural constraints. Fighting with the Huguenots sapped the strength of the French state and was unlikely to yield any converts. Like Bismarck,

Richelieu had a unification project, an absolutist consolidation of the French central state that required strategic restraint.

Richelieu was a foreign policy egoist. It is tempting to explain the difference between Richelieu and his domestic opponents on the basis of foreign policy preferences or religious and ethical commitment. In noting Richelieu's role in formulating the doctrine of reason of state, Kissinger (1994) writes: "Raison d'état asserted that the well-being of the state justified whatever means were employed to further it; the national interest supplanted the medieval notion of a universal morality" (58). Such a narrow interpretation, however, misses the important cognitive aspect of realism, the rational style of Richelieu's decision-making. Richelieu shared the religiosity of many of his opponents. All else equal, he preferred Catholic solidarity and believed that the Church should, indeed, be the ultimate arbiter in religious matters. However, the cardinal's epistemic motivation led him to make moral judgments in a utilitarian as opposed to a deontological fashion. In matters of politics, this meant that France must sometimes assert its egoistic interests at the expense of Catholic unity. Blanchard writes, "Richelieu was to statesmanship what Machiavelli was to political theory, Gallileo to science, or Descartes to philosophy," but "with the caveat that his greater aim still remained the triumph of Catholicism" (2). The cardinal had faith, but not blind faith. Just as Bismarck and Wilhelm I had very different cognitive styles, Richelieu's deliberative and objective decision-making contrasted strongly with his more impetuous master, Louis XIII, and indeed with most of those he encountered in high political circles, a point to which I return in the conclusion.

With domestic peace secured and court opposition minimized after 1629, Richelieu believed France was in a better position to resist Spanish hegemony and the growing threat of the Austrian-based Holy Roman Empire, which had seized much of Germany during the early campaigns of the Thirty Years' War. The two French adversaries were ruled by the same Habsburg house. Like Bismarck, Richelieu feared Habsburg dominance; also like the chancellor, he sought unlikely allies deemed by others in France to be out of bounds. Centuries before Bismarck made an alliance with liberal democratic nationalists, Richelieu struck a deal to support the Protestant Swedes as they beat back the forces of the Austrian emperor, Ferdinand II. These instrumentally rational decisions, made to avoid direct and costly conflict, proved insufficient, however, and finally Richelieu advocated full-scale intervention in the bloodiest conflict in European history. The Catholic French declared war against the Catholic Spanish and also fought the Holy Roman Empire on France's eastern borders. The outcome is seen as decisive for checking the

Spanish bid for hegemony in Europe and laying the foundation for French preeminence under Louis XIV. This chapter tells an abridged version of Richelieu's story, noting the consistent similarities between the policies of the cardinal and the Prussian realist who came centuries later.

Over the Mountain?: French Divisions over Religion and Foreign Policy

The France in which the future cardinal grew up was a shattered country. For almost forty years, beginning in 1562, the Wars of Religion divided France between the Catholic majority and a Calvinist minority called the Huguenots who counted powerful noble families among their adherents. This was a time of destructive military campaigns and mob massacres in which "fanaticisms dissolved all social bonds and left the country ravaged" (Blanchard 2011: 11). The most famous incident was the Bartholomew Day's massacre. Catherine de Medici, the recent widow of Henry II, allowed a Parisian crowd to murder thousands of Protestants celebrating the wedding of Henry of Navarre to her own daughter, Marguerite (Blanchard 2011: 12). The powerful Guise family backed the creation of the Catholic League to more vigorously persecute the Calvinists, even seizing control of Paris from the Catholic king (Blanchard 2011: 12; Treasure 1972: 7; Wright 2011: 9). During this period, loyalties were regional or religious, rarely national (Levi 2000: 3).

The domestic religious conflict become an international one when the Catholic League invited in Spanish support to prevent Henry of Navarre, a Huguenot and next in line to the throne, from becoming king upon the death of Henry III. Had it been successful, it is likely that France would have become a mere dominion of Spain, the most powerful country in the world at the time, with imperial possessions in the Americas, Italy, and the Netherlands. The Catholic League essentially acted as an agent for the Pope and the Spanish and was backed in France by powerful religious orders such as the Jesuits (Blanchard 2011: 12; Erlanger 1968: 9ff; Levi 2000: 15; Treasure 1972: 38ff).

The French Wars of Religion ended with a truce in 1598, when Henry of Navarre converted to Catholicism and concluded a peace treaty with Spain. He subsequently promulgated the Edict of Nantes, which granted extensive autonomy to the Huguenots in their strongholds, making the Calvinist minority, in Richelieu's famous words, a "state within a state." The Huguenots had their own heavily fortified towns where they enjoyed religious freedom and self-government. They even had military forces paid for by the French state. In the rest of France, Calvinist nobles could worship privately at court, and religious discrimination in the professions, hospitals, and educational institutions was prohibited (Blanchard 2011: 18; Erlanger 1968: 53; Knecht 1991: 65ff; Treasure 1972: 94ff). As Treasure (1972: 7) puts it, this was a "necessary surrender to an armed minority."

In the years following the conclusion of the conflict, France experienced a deep religious reawakening, part of a Counterreformation occurring in Europe at large. Church (1972) describes the "almost complete fusion of religion and politics in the period," in which the "functions, ideology and objectives of the French state were shaped to a great extent by its Christian traditions, values and purposes" (9). Louis XIII himself was the most scrupulously religious king of France in generations, and the pressure to subordinate French state interests to religious considerations and Catholic solidarity was enormous (Church 1972: 41). As Erlanger (1968) notes, "During this period, religion permeated every gesture and thought of Christians; for most Frenchmen, it superseded the concept of patriotism" (33).

This contributed to the political ascendance of *les dévots*, the most fervent of Catholic believers. The dévots were *ultramontagne* (literally in French, "across the mountains" – in this case, across the Alps to Rome) in their understanding of papal authority. The pope, they believed, had the final say on all religious and temporal matters and, therefore, political matters between states (Church 1972: 93; Knecht 1991: 31, 35; Levi 2000: 80; Tapié 1967: 120; Treasure 1972: 89, 113; Wright 2011: 11).

The dévots were strong adherents of absolutist rule and loyal to the French king (provided he was a Catholic) (Church 1972: 42ff; Wright 2011: 10–1). They were "interested in protecting the interests, secular and religious, of the French state" (Church 1972: 95). Nevertheless, they also believed that religious principles were inviolable (Church 1972: 42–4). In deontological fashion, they would countenance no deviation from or compromise of religious principles, including allegiance to the pope and the religious duty to end heresy in France and abroad (Church 1972: 120ff). In their view, religious principles and France's state interests were identical (Church 1972: 43). This meant no painful tradeoff was necessary. The dévots, in Church's words, had a "simpler intellectual position, the unqualified supremacy of theological values over all human activity" (1972: 129). He continues: "Those who held to a more rigorous religious posture and insisted upon the subordination of all temporal matters, political as well as personal, to a single standard of religious morality ruled out any special ethic of public policy and regarded reason of state as no more than good government according to the universal principles of justice" (92). The devoted did not exhibit the same cognitive complexity that is the hallmark of epistemic motivation. This faction "desired the king and his council, no matter what the circumstances, to adopt a policy both at home and abroad which was in conformity with the interests of the Catholic Church. In advocating this policy they had no intention of sacrificing French interests; they simply refused to admit that there could be any incompatibility between the interests of France and the admonitions of the papacy," concludes Tapié (1967: 139). They "fit the preponderant pattern of French political life which combined royalism, Catholicism and statism" (Church 1972: 95).

The influence of ultramontagne ideas was particularly pronounced at the French court (Church 1972: 93). Louis XIII's mother, Marie de Medici, who governed France as a regent until the king reached his "majority," had deep Catholic sensibilities (although it is difficult to establish where her religious beliefs ended and her personal interests began) (Knecht 1991: 6, 31; Levi 2000: 80, 88; Tapié 1967: 143). At this time in French history, mystic clergymen such as Cardinal Bérulle, who had a vision of the "seamless robe of Christendom" (Treasure 1972: 112), mixed freely with nobles and attendants of the royal family in the French court (Treasure 1972: 113). Anne of Austria, the queen, also had dévot tendencies.

Richelieu owed his start in politics to his cultivation of leading ecclesiastic figures of the French Counter-Reformation such as Bérulle, who thought the young bishop would be an ally (Blanchard 2011: 65; Elliot 1984: 11; Levi 2000: 4; Treasure 1972: 18, 107, 112). A memorable performance speaking on behalf of the Church in the Estates-General of 1614 won Richelieu the attention of Marie de Medici, who took him on and gave him increasingly important roles. On her behalf, Richelieu negotiated a peace with her son, when he asserted his kingly authority by killing the Queen Regent's main adviser and head of the king's council, the Italian aristocrat Concini, forcing Marie into temporary exile at Blois.

Richelieu's Realism

Richelieu had the same rational cognitive style as Bismarck. Church (1972) writes of the "reliance upon reason which was to be his guide through his entire career" (83), Elliot (1984) of the "profound conviction in the overriding importance of reason, and of applying the principles of rational statecraft to the world of affairs" (25; also Tziampiris 2009: 79). Richelieu's epistemic motivation is seen most clearly in his *Political Testament*, a collection – given to Louis XIII and the *dauphin* (his son, the future "Sun King" Louis XIV) – of "thoughts on what I consider most important for the proper governing of his kingdom" (TP: 4). Although Richelieu did not write the Testament word-for-word, it is nevertheless believed that he supervised its composition and that it accurately reflects his point of view (Church 1972: 481; Stankiewicz 1960: 135; TP: ix; Treasure 1972: 246). According to Church (1972), there is "no doubt among ranking authorities that the work is an accurate guide to Richelieu's broader and more fundamental political concepts" (482), which are particularly important for the purpose of this book. The collection is a "highly personalized document" that "occupies a unique place in that it alone presents within the covers of a single work the essentials of his social and political ideology" and is "invaluable because it sets forth in specific terms many of his fundamental assumptions that are merely implicit in other documents" (Church 1972: 485). The Testament was not designed for public consumption, making it a particularly useful window into Richelieu's cognitive style. It is brutally honest. At one point Richelieu proclaims, "While everyone knows there has never been a king who has advanced the prestige of his state as much as Your Majesty has, it also cannot be denied that no one has ever allowed the reputation of his household to sink so low" (TP: 49).

The Testament devotes an entire chapter to how "reason should guide the governing of the state," beginning with the statement, "If man is sovereignly reasonable he ought to make reason sovereign, which requires not only that he do nothing not in conformity with it, but also that he make all those who are under his authority reverence it and follow it religiously" (TP: 71). The Testament reveals high levels of epistemic motivation and its hallmarks, objectivity and deliberation. The cardinal writes of the importance of open-mindedness as opposed to premature cognitive closure: "It is necessary ... to avoid self-deception"; leaders have "the obligation ... of opening wide their eyes to take more adequate measures, after having weighted every consideration of which the human mind is capable" (TP: 83). Richelieu complains;

Presumption is one of the greatest vices a man in public office can have and if humility is not required of those charged with the direction of state certainly modesty is. ... Without modesty ... men are so enamored of their own opinions that they condemn all others. ... While it is the essence of wisdom on the part of a minister of state to speak little, it is also wise to listen a great deal. One can draw profit from all kinds of suggestions. (TP: 58–9)

Richelieu also expresses a belief in deliberation, arguing "it is more difficult to make a mistake when something has been thought through" (TP: 81). He worries about those who "covering their eyes ... do blindly whatever pleases them" (TP: 45).

Richelieu explicitly contrasts his preferred cognitive style with its alternative, a short-sighted and impulsive one driven by emotion (Knecht 1991: 43; Tziampiris 2009: 80). In the 1600s, the cardinal drew a distinction between System I and System II processing. The Testament states, "Although it is common enough with many men to act only when driven by some emotion ... I cannot help reminding Your Majesty that such a character trait is dangerous in any kind of person, and it is particularly so in kings, who more than all others should be motivated by reason" (TP: 39). Richelieu is universally described by historians as cool in his calculations (Elliot 1984: 29, 75; Levi 2000: 26; Treasure 1972: 11).

Emotion, he argues, causes individuals to make decisions rashly, rather than slowly and deliberately: "One often has to repent at leisure what emotion has hastily engendered, but such results never occur when action springs from reasonable consideration" (TP: 72). Even when situations demanded a rapid response, Richelieu urges the king to literally sleep on it: "There are occasions, to be sure, when it is not possible to deliberate at length because the nature of the matter does not permit it. But in affairs of this kind it is best to sleep on them, making up with the speed of final execution for any delay created during their thorough consideration" (TP: 81). Advising reason as the primary guide, he notes, "Often indeed have evils befallen princes and their countries when they have been more inclined to follow their emotions than their minds" (TP: 39).

As was the case for Bismarck, it took effort to think in this way. Richelieu had to "conquer an excessive emotional instability" (Levi 2000: 26). He was prone to tempers and tears and would collapse during moments of depression. Like Bismarck, this reaction was likely due to the exhaustion brought about by his superhuman work habits (Elliot 1984: 16). Early in his career, Richelieu wrote himself a memo entitled "instructions to myself on how to appear at Court," which included the admonition: "Keep constant control over yourself; never give in to a spontaneous urge" (Erlanger 1968: 43). Historians consistently note his degree of self-control (Elliot 1984: 29; Levi 2000: 77, 118). Some even surmise that any emotional displays the cardinal did let out were strategic in nature. Richelieu told a fellow bishop, "My rages are all inspired by reason" (Elliot 1984: 17). His mentor and later adversary, Marie de Medici, noted that "he cries when he wants something" (Elliot 1984: 17). Like Bismarck, the cardinal frequently threatened to resign in a huff to get his policies through.

Richelieu was a foreign policy egoist, firmly dedicated to the promotion of French interests in Europe. The Political Testament describes the goals he set for himself at the beginning of his service to the king: "to ruin the Huguenot party, to abase the pride of the nobles, to bring all your subjects back to their duty, and to restore your reputation among foreign nations to the station it ought to occupy" (TP: 11). Like Bismarck, the cardinal is regarded as a faithful servant, not a mere opportunist. He was "thoroughly imbued with a sense of honor and felt it to be both his obligation and his mission to serve his king and his state" (Church 1972: 82). While Richelieu certainly profited personally from his close proximity to power, no one makes the argument that he was not a loyal French patriot.

Richelieu's procedural rationality, combined with an egoistic orientation in foreign affairs, led naturally to an instrumentally rational approach to decision-making in the affairs of state. In other words, his psychology and his foreign policy goals made him a realist (Erlanger 1968: 44; Stankiewicz 1960: 108). The cardinal believed that decisions had to be made in light of structural constraints. The statesman "skillfully practices the art of the possible" (TP: vi). Constraints meant that "everything could not be changed at once without violating the laws of prudence, which do not permit the passing from one extreme to another without preparation" (TP: 10). Richelieu frequently put an "emphasis on necessity," a "major raison d'état concept" (Tziampiris 2009: 80). Flexibly adapting to circumstances "was dignified in the seventeenth century with the name of 'prudence'" (Elliot 1984: 25). In the Political Testament, Richelieu compares two kinds of architects: one who tears down an ancient building and starts fresh, and one who corrects defects to make a tolerable structure. He endorsed the second approach, working around existing constraints (Elliot 1984: 66).

Interests must be carefully ranked, with statesmen focusing on what is of vital interest. Richelieu writes in the Testament, "I cannot help repeating again a plea I have made many times before to Your Majesty, begging you to apply yourself to the matters of greatest importance to your country. . . . If you preoccupy yourself with the small matters . . . you will even bring misfortune upon yourself" (TP: 37). As will be seen, in his memos to the king, even as he expressed a preference, the cardinal laid out the pros and cons of each option (Knecht 1991: 43).

Richelieu's epistemic motivation led him to think about the long-term (Elliot 1984: 28; Stankiewicz 1960: 92; TP: vi):

Nothing is more necessary in governing than foresight, since by its use one can easily prevent many evils which can be corrected only with great difficulty if allowed to transpire. . . . [Men] who see far ahead do nothing precipitously since they consider things well in advance. . . . It is necessary to see as far in advance as possible what will be the outcome of one's acts. (TP: 81)

Like Bismarck, Richelieu stressed the importance of patience, waiting for the most favorable opportunity to act (Levi 2000: 9, 118; TP: vi; Tziampiris 2009: 80). He once wrote, "[I]f one foresees from far away the designs to be undertaken, one can act with speed when the moment comes to execute them" (Papiers II: 392). This might require denying an impulse to act in the short term and waiting for a more propitious circumstance to arise in the future. He noted the importance of "swallowing offenses which will be avenged on the morrow" (Erlanger 1968: 43). Even revenge must be served cold. Such far-sighted thinking would require conscious effort: "[I]t is quite usual for ordinary men to content themselves with little effort, preferring to enjoy the pleasures of a month rather than demand of themselves a few days of effort which could guarantee many trouble-free years, a matter they ignore, for they see only the present and cannot mold the future by a wise foresight" (TP: 81).

Richelieu was data rather than theory driven, an "empiricist" (Stankiewicz 1960: 92) who avoided heuristics. As such, he expressed the same skepticism that Bismarck did about general rules of policy-making: "There is nothing more dangerous for the state than men who want to govern kingdoms on the basis of maxims which they cull from books. When they do this they often destroy them, because the past is not the same as the present, and times, places and persons change. The councilors require only goodness and firmness of mind [and] stable judgment" (Elliot 1984: 27; TP: 58).

Even with the most careful deliberation, there would always be unintended consequences (Elliot 1984: 27). Richelieu recognized that politics were marked by uncertainty. The Testament reads: "The experience of governing that Your Majesty has acquired ... makes you well aware of the fact that the outcome of large undertakings rarely conforms directly with the orders initially given" (TP: 38). There were "definite limits beyond which they can see nothing" (TP: 82).

As was the case with Bismarck, Richelieu's realism made him think twice, literally, about the use of force. Even though Richelieu argued sometimes that stiff and unyielding punishment was necessary to establish order, he also believed that restraint was oftentimes the most instrumentally rational action, even when one's interests were solely egoistic. He wrote, "A government cannot survive where no one is satisfied and everyone is treated violently. ... It is far preferable that men should return to their duty by themselves than by force" (Knecht 1991: 44). In the Political Testament, he tells the king, "I believe it would be committing a crime if I did not beseech you to avoid war in the future in as far as it is possible" (TP: 38). Richelieu backed the use of force, but on the basis of a consequentialist and pragmatic calculus, not enthusiasm.

"[W]ar is one the scourges with which it pleases God to afflict men," he wrote, while simultaneously recognizing it as a necessary evil:

The aversion that populations have to war is not reason enough to bring about such peace, seeing that they often feel and complain both about necessary evils as well as about those that could be avoided; and that they are just as ignorant in knowing what is useful to a State as in being sensitive and quick to complain about evils that must be put up with to avoid greater ones. (Lettres III: 665)

The Four Square Feet of the King's Study: The Decision-Making Style of Louis the Just

Richelieu's political fortunes depended on his ability to influence the king yet also remain in his good standing. The king's cognitive style made this job particularly challenging. In Richelieu's own words, "the four square feet of the king's study were more difficult to conquer than all the battlefields of Europe" (Elliot 1984: 46; Knecht 1991: 41). Given their very different dispositions, the king's "partnership with Richelieu makes one of the more unlikely combinations of political history," writes Treasure (1972: 29). This again calls to mind the Bismarck comparison: the Iron Chancellor formed an implausible partnership with Wilhelm I.

Louis XIII had a complicated personality to which this chapter cannot do justice. However, there is a clear consensus among historians that the king did not demonstrate much epistemic motivation and procedural rationality (Elliot 1984: 38; Erlanger 1968: 240). Treasure (1972) writes of how the king "seemed to invite emotional scenes"; Levi (2000) describes him as "highly strung, impetuous and willful and in consequence moody, ill-tempered, imperious and sometimes violent" (59); Blanchard (2011) calls him "dark and enigmatic" (4) and describes the "fierce tantrums" he had as a boy that brought him close to seizures (23); Erlanger (1968) writes of his "violent tempers" (218). To Elliot (1984), Louis XIII is a "moody and unhappy man" (46). The eminent French historian of this period, Tapié (1967: 91), concurs.

Richelieu thought the same. He famously ran down the king's character defects in front of the sovereign's own mother, mentioning "his congenital suspiciousness, his jealousy, his quickness of temper, and his tendency to lose himself in trivial detail to the neglect of great matters of state" (Elliot 1984: 42). A famous memorandum written in 1629 dwells much less on policy substance and much more on how the king should improve his decision-making (Lettres III: 179–213). Richelieu instructed his king:

It is necessary to be strong with reason and not with passion. Many of those who have a fever, while the heat of their illness shakes and overheats them, act with violence against all their brain suggests, but no sooner does the heat of the fever pass that they are left weak, languid without words or action. ... Those who act more by ... their natural impetuousness than by reason will make great mistakes that often cannot be repaired neither by time nor by prudence. (Lettres III: 197–8)

While cautioning reason and equanimity, the Political Testament notes "the great emotional outbursts to which you have been subject on several occasions" (TP: 37). It describes Louis XIII as having a "restless, impatient disposition" (TP: 38). Richelieu writes that "it is difficult for you not to act impulsively, and sudden waves of emotion occasionally overtake you when you least expect them" (TP: 42), although he hoped that "the first ebullience of your ardent youth having passed, the stability of a greater maturity will help you protect yourself by forethought in the future" (TP: 36–37). In the memo, Richelieu cautions the king, among other things, against responding to small slights and speaking without first considering his words.

The Narrow Pass: The Valtelline, *les Dévots*, and les bons Français

After a brief period as foreign minister several years earlier, Richelieu returned to the king's service as his first minister in 1624, a position he maintained until his death in 1642. The cardinal was thrust immediately into a dispute over the Valtelline, a mountain pass through the Alps that links Tyrol with northern Lombardy, thereby connecting the Po and Danube river basins. Under Louis XIII's predecessor, Henry IV, the French had negotiated exclusive access with the *Grisons* (the Grey Leagues), virulently Protestant mountain dwellers who controlled this otherwise Catholic area. Access to the pass was particularly vital for the Spanish, as it was the only route between the Spanish Habsburg holdings in Italy and the Netherlands that did not traverse Venetian territory and violate its sovereignty. In 1620, the Spanish took advantage of a Catholic revolt against the Grisons to seize control of the valley, quickly establishing a series of forts. French protests led to papal intervention, and a compromise was reached in which papal troops would man the forts. Given the close ties between Rome and Madrid, however, the valley was now Spanish in all but name (Blanchard 2011: 52; Church 1972: 104ff; Levi 2000: 88).

The Valtelline issue must be seen in its larger European context. The Spanish surrounded the French. Besides sharing France's southern border, the Spanish held extensive territories in Italy and the Spanish

Netherlands (present-day Belgium). Spain was also one of the two branches of the Habsburg dynasty, which had split into two in 1555. The Holy Roman Empire was left to the Austrian branch, which held sway over Hungary, Bohemia, Germany, and Lorraine. The powers in Vienna and Madrid closely coordinated their foreign policies. The Habsburg presence in Germany, including the Alsace region, therefore added to the French sense of encirclement and generated concerns that the Spanish aspired to a universal monarchy (Blanchard 2011: 17ff; Elliot 1984: 99; Levi 2000: 2–3). There had not been such a hegemony in Europe since the Romans.

The issue of growing Spanish power was especially acute in these years. In 1618, the defenestration of Prague rekindled religious conflicts in Germany, as Protestants in Bohemia revolted against Catholic rule, triggering the intervention of the Austrian empire. In 1621, the truce between the Dutch United Provinces and their former rulers, the Spanish, expired, leading again to armed conflict. This made control of the Valtelline particularly important for the Spanish, as it offered the best way to send materials and troops to fight the Dutch. The English would disrupt sea supply on behalf of their fellow Protestants. With the Austrian Habsburgs moving into Germany to fight Protestant forces such as Frederick, ruler of the Palatinate, and the Spanish Habsburgs renewing their fight with France's northern neighbors, France might be encircled (Treasure 1972: 73ff).

Since the end of the Wars of Religion, France had pursued a largely pro-Spanish and pro-papal foreign policy, due in large part to the influence of the dévots and the strong Catholic feeling in France during the Counter-Reformation. The country cooperated with the Habsburgs, recognizing them as the leaders of international Catholicism (Church 1972: 5, 41). Louis XIII was married to the daughter of the Spanish King Philip III, Anne of Austria, and his sister was married to the Spanish heir to the throne. The issue, as Church (1972) explains, was now: "Should the prevailing policy be continued, largely for the benefit of European Catholicism, or should the anti-Habsburg interests of the French state prevail?" (92). Richelieu decided to take action, expelling papal forces through armed French intervention in 1624 and 1625 and pushing farther into Italy. He also began financially subsidizing the Dutch in their struggle against the Spanish.

Bismarck felt a tension between his support for the monarchical system of government on the one hand and his concern for promoting Prussian interests on the other hand, ultimately admitting and resolving the trade-off in favor of the latter. The same was true of Richelieu, who had to weigh his religious loyalties and interest in promoting the unity of the Catholic Church against France's national interests. He ultimately thought the latter more important (Tziampiris 2009: 81). While the cardinal believed that the pope was the ultimate authority on religious matters, he considered the temporal concerns of interstate relations to be a separate sphere beyond papal purview (Church 1972: 90–1; Levi 2000: 68–9). For instance, Richelieu thought the pope had no authority to depose a sovereign leader. Levi (2000) reminds us, "however unremarkable that distinction may seem to us, Richelieu took it to an extent virtually unconceived of by most of his contemporaries, of whatever religious commitment" (104). Richelieu had his own narrow pass to protect.

This stance led to a profound break with the dévots to whom he owed his start in politics. The dévots advocated for an alliance with Spain that would preserve the unity of the Catholic states and opposed any alliance with Protestant powers such as England, the Dutch, and Sweden (Church 1972: 93; Knecht 1991: 31, 35; Levi 2000: 80; Treasure 1972: 89, 113; Wright 2011: 114). France's primary interest was to fight against their heresy. The dévots felt betrayed by Richelieu's actions since they had backed his promotions and had assumed his religiosity would ensure a policy of Catholic solidarity (Blanchard 2011: 66; Treasure 1972: 89, 112). Like Bismarck later, in arguing for a foreign policy that put France's egoistic interests first, the cardinal was seen as abandoning his principles. The most powerful dévot, Michel de Marillac, the Keeper of the Seals, who also held a position in the king's council of state, informed Louis XIII that "the pope asks the Valtelline to be delivered from the subjection of the Grisons and demands that the Catholic religion is assured that so that he no longer fears the power of heretics over them." By not doing so, Louis XIII would "render himself blameworthy if the aid he gives [the Grisons] deprives Catholics of their states and detracts from their obedience to the provinces to which they are subject" (Mémoires V, Appendix VI). In the eyes of the dévots, Louis XIII owed his allegiance to more than France. "It is even less just because, God having given to the king the force and authority over a Catholic People, he abandons them to the fury and cruelty of heretics," wrote Marillac (Mémoires V, Appendix VI). The dévot leader accused the French king of "having found a province delivered from heresy ... it takes this province with weapons away from Jesus Christ and renders it to Satan. ... If his Majesty is advised to undertake this action, I fear greatly divine punishment, causing him to lose his own provinces" (Mémoires V, Appendix VI).

The cardinal's preferences on Italian policy made him an ally of *les bons Français*. The term, meaning "good Frenchmen," showed where their interests lay – in the promotion of France's egoistic interests against the expansion of Spanish power and the ecclesiastical reach of the pope into French affairs (Church 1972: 93; Treasure 1972: 45–6). Treasure (1972) argues that the bons Français were "inspired by nothing other than the good of the crown, as against the dévots, who put the first the international interests of Catholicism" (43). The bons Français were hostile to Spain, which they saw as the primary threat to French interests, perhaps threatening France's very survival. They accused the Spanish of using the unity of the Catholic Church as a pretext for pursuing designs on their own country, as the Spanish had done during the latter years of the Wars of Religion.

In a revealing episode in his first turn as a minister, which had lasted just a few months in 1617, Richelieu had instructed Schomberg, his envoy to Germany, to inform the Protestant princes that "to say that we are so Roman and Spanish that we would embrace those interests of Rome, or Spain, with prejudice to our former alliances and to ourselves, meaning also the French Protestants and anyone else who hates Spain and thus professes to be a *good Frenchman*, is pure defamation" (Lettres I: 210). In the same memo, he wrote:

Diverse beliefs do not make us into diverse states; divided by religion, we find ourselves united in the service of a prince ... in matters of state no Catholic can believe that a Spaniard would be better than a Huguenot. One will find true divisions between us, not in this world but the other, not produced by the marriage of France and Spain but by the diversity of our religions. (Lettres I: 224)

Richelieu himself, however, never openly identified openly with the group.

Richelieu's actions now put him in a politically and personally perilous position. Most "good Frenchmen" were jurists and administrators, part of the absolutist apparatus but deprived of the most obvious source of power in seventeenth-century France – the ears of the king. The dévots were stronger in court and had an ally in Marie de Medici, the king's mother. Louis XIII's religious dévotion also made him sympathetic to arguments stressing Catholic solidarity (Treasure 1972: 111). Richelieu's memoirs read, "*The greatest difficulty that the Cardinal had to overcome was in the King's council* where the principals, by a too ardent and precipitous desire to ruin the Huguenots ... or by too good and false opinion that they had of Spain, wanted ... to accommodate itself to her" (Mémoires V: 206 [emphasis added]). Just as Bismarck broke with his ideological fellow travelers over how to balance his country's egoistic interests against those of a broader transnational solidarity with the Habsburgs, so did Richelieu. And just as would be the case for the Prussian politician to come, Richelieu's Realpolitik orientation was not shared by his peers.

At the time, French foreign policy was contested to a large degree through the publication of pamphlets, often authored under pseudonyms or by ghost writers so as to allow for deniability. Richelieu was the first French minister to appeal to public opinion, which he did through a massive publishing campaign on behalf of his policies (Church 1972: 114; Elliot 1984: 98). Richelieu made frequent use of an ardent bon Français named François Langlois de Fançan to support his Valtelline policy. Fançan drew a distinction between a fait d'état (action of state) and a fait de religion (action of religion), drawing on Richelieu's distinction between temporal and religious affairs. Action against the Spanish was an "evident necessity" to preempt aspirations toward a universal monarchy in which religion was only a pretext (Church 1972: 118ff). The dévot rejoinder was the *Admonitio ad Ludovicum XIII Regem*, likely authored by Jesuits outside of France (Stankiewicz 1955: 149; Tapié 1967: 145). Alliances with Protestant powers were heretical, that pamphlet declared, as they promoted the interests of those who would damage the Catholic Church, something that no circumstances could justify. While war with the Spanish would be justifiable if it involved merely riches and power, the Valtelline issue concerned souls, so Catholic states were bound to enter the war on the Catholic side (Church 1972: 118ff; Stankiewicz 1955: 149).

These differences were as much about cognitive style as ideological substance (Church 1972: 95). The dévots took a deontological position, arguing that there could be no alliance under any circumstances with Protestant forces. Only one aspect of the problem need be considered. Marillac asked the king for "peace at any price" (Mémoires V, Appendix VI), something noted in Richelieu's memoirs: "The keeper of the seals Marillac ... maintained in the king's council that it was necessary to terminate the dispute in the Valtelline in whatever manner possible" as gains could not "justify the price of destroying heresy that could be exterminated in France if we made peace" (Mémoires V: 206–7). Marillac was not a utilitarian. Church (1972) notes the difference between the Admonitio and another pamphlet that Richelieu supervised and edited. "The *Catholique d'estat* is a more complex work than the *Admonitio* because Richelieu's ultramontane critics adhered to a simpler intellectual position, the unqualified supremacy of theological values over all human activity" (129).

Ultimately, Richelieu was forced to back down on the Valtelline issue given a combination of pressures from the dévots and a simultaneous Huguenot rebellion (Blanchard 2011: 79; Church 1972: 107–8; Elliot 1984: 78; Levi 2000: 89; Treasure 1972: 112; Wright 2011: 116). The Treaty of Monzon restored the Valtelline to the Grisons but permitted only the exercise of Catholicism in the valley. The Spanish and the French were to have equal access to the region, but all forts were to be raised. The dispute nevertheless revealed deep domestic divisions between the realist Richelieu and others involved in French foreign affairs.

Grace under Pressure: The Huguenots, the Siege of La Rochelle, and Strategic Restraint

In the years before Richelieu took office as first minister, there had been a number of Huguenot rebellions, often backed by Protestant members of the French court. As the cardinal himself later recalled to the king, "When Your Majesty resolved to admit me both to your council and to an important place in your confidence for the direction of your affairs, I may say that the Huguenots shared the state with you" (TP: 9).

Richelieu had long argued adherence to the Edict of Nantes, which guaranteed freedom of religion. When installed as a bishop in Luçon in 1609, he said, "I know that there are some here who are separated from us in faith. I hope in return that we may be united in love ... which will benefit them as well as ourselves and be agreeable to the king whom we must all seek to satisfy" (Knecht 1991: 68). Richelieu argued that the king cherished both Calvinists and Catholics equally (Church 1972: 88). He sponsored a pamphlet, *Response au Manifeste du Sieur de Soubise*, which argued that both factions shared an allegiance to the king.

As a religious Catholic, the cardinal very much wanted to convert the Huguenots (Tapié 1967: 138–9). The Protestant faith, he wrote, "must be abhorred by everyone" (Knecht 1991: 69). Upon taking office he promised the king that he would "ruin the Huguenot party" (TP: 11). However, he had peaceful rather than forceful measures in mind. Richelieu urged toleration in the speech before the Estates-General in 1614 that had attracted the attention of Marie de Medici: "We desire only their conversion and we wish to promote it by our example, teaching and prayers. These are the only weapons with which we want to fight them" (Elliot 1984: 11; Knecht 1991: 69; see Mémoires I: 353–56).

Richelieu's tolerance, however, was purely pragmatic, due to the strength of the Protestants in France (Church 1972: 88; Stankiewicz 1960: 92; Tapié 1967: 139). Using force to ensure religious conformity would prove costly and ultimately unsuccessful – a losing combination for a realist. The cardinal wrote in the Political Testament:

There is not a single sovereign in the world who is not obliged ... to procure the conversion of those who, living within his kingdom, have deviated from the path to salvation. But ... prudence does not permit anything so hazardous as to risk uprooting the train while pulling out the tares, for it would be difficult to purge the state in any but a gentle way without a shock capable of bringing down ruin upon it, or at the very least greatly weakening it. (TP: 68)

Instead, Richelieu suggested, the Huguenots should be "ruined by peace" (Mémoires V: 187–8). A pamphleteer made Richelieu's case in 1626 for the Treaty of Paris, which had ended the most recent Protestant revolt. War for religious purposes was self-defeating, as it provoked the Huguenots without destroying them (Church 1972: 193ff).

The dévots were dissatisfied with his efforts, labeling him the "Cardinal of la Rochelle," after the Huguenot stronghold on the west coast of France (Church 1972: 149; Stankiewicz 1960: 93; Tapié 1967: 152). Richelieu was isolated again. The "spirit of appeasement that Richelieu showed ... were the result of theories which suited his character and which he found expedient in political realities. Apparently only a few people thought the same," writes Stankiewicz (1960: 98). He had drawn their ire by recommending a settlement during a recent Huguenot rebellion, so as to allow France to devote all its energies to its Valtelline struggle (Lettres II: 83). "Prudence does not permit the undertaking of two wars at the same time," he observed (Mémoires V: 187), another example of realist thinking driven by constraints. This position enraged the dévots, who accused him of having heretical sympathies (Knecht 1991: 32).

Richelieu distinguished between political sedition and religious nonconformity (Church 1972: 88; Knecht 1991: 69). In a 1618 work that predates his appointment as first minister, entitled *Les principaux points de la foi d l'église catholique*, he identified the main failing of Huguenots as their lack of allegiance to the crown and argued that toleration should end when dissent led to political action (Richelieu 1618). During his first stint in the king's council, he wrote, "this is not a question of religion, but of pure rebellion; not just that the king wishes to treat his subjects of any religion equally, but also, as reason requires of him, that they all hold themselves to their duties; that for nothing in the world would he wish to assist any rebel" (Lettres I: 226).

Therefore, when the Huguenots rose again at La Rochelle, this time with English assistance, Richelieu advocated a vigorous response. With no competing claim for resources in Italy, the French could act decisively. Stankiewicz (1960) writes, "His approach to tolerance was practical. The same political moves which later induced Richelieu to launch an all-out offensive against the Huguenots at first urged him to show good will" (93). He told Louis XIII, "The goal we had to have was to take La Rochelle and ruin the Huguenot party in France" (Stankiewicz 1960: 92).

The port of La Rochelle was the most fortified town in the entire French kingdom, situated in a salt marsh that made approach very difficult. A member of the prominent Calvinist Rohan family, the Duke of Soubise, attempted to seize the city with the help of a fleet of 100 English ships that he had recruited during his exile in England. The Duke of Buckingham commanded the English troops, who appeared off the coast of the Île de Ré in July 1627. Soubise sought to enlist the population of the city, which had not been informed of the invaders' arrival prior to the landing. Louis XIII and Richelieu personally began preparations for a siege of La Rochelle. The duke's brother, Henri de Rohan, launched a rebellion in another Huguenot stronghold, Languedoc, in the south of France (Blanchard 2011: 92ff; Levi 2000: 90ff; Treasure 1972: 105ff). The French forces fought off the English fleet not once but twice and starved out the city, whose population fell from 28,000 to 5,400 over the course of the next year and a half. After the English failed to break through the blockade, the town surrendered. Languedoc followed suit several months afterward.

In prior instances of this sort, there was a "robust tradition that fallen cities should be sacked" (Treasure 1972: 105). Even massacres of defeated foes were common during France's earlier religious wars. The king had done as much personally when putting down another revolt led by Henri de Rohan in Mountauban a few years before Richelieu had taken up his post (Levi 2000: 65). Richelieu, however, proceeded with the same strategic restraint that Bismarck later demonstrated after Prussia had conquered the Austrians. He ordered his troops not to molest the townspeople, but instead brought in food to feed the starving population, although an enormous number died from eating too quickly in their weakened state (Knecht 1991: 78). Entry into La Rochelle was marked by a simple procession with no pomp and circumstance.

More significantly, despite pressure from the dévots to use the occasion to stamp out the Calvinist problem once and for all, Richelieu convinced the king to maintain the Huguenots' religious freedom (Blanchard 2011: 223; Church 1972: 201; Knecht 1991: 78; Levi 2000: 110; Tapié 1967 191–2; Treasure 1972: 106). The king declared a general amnesty so as to facilitate the reintegration of the Huguenots into France. Only a dozen leaders were exiled, and for only a short period of time. Indeed, Rohan would eventually be summoned back to lead a military campaign on behalf of the king abroad. No property was confiscated.

The peace was granted, not negotiated – an important indication of strategic restraint. Richelieu wrote the king, "I am sure that your majesty will have extreme joy, not only because the king gave peace to his subjects but because of the way in which he did so. The king did not make peace with his subjects, as he had done in the past, but instead he gave them his grace" (Lettres III: 359). The Peace of Alais also became known as the Grace of Alais. Richelieu had convinced the king to pass up an opportunity to strike the Huguenots when he was in the position of greatest power. Richelieu said after La Rochelle, "The rest is work in which it is necessary to wait for the heavens, undertaking no violence except that of the good life and of example" (Treasure 1972: 215). He wrote, it is "now a question of winning the heart of their spirit through good treatment" (Lettres III: 364). Historians often compare Richelieu's strategy to the almost simultaneously promulgated Edict of Restitution, in which the Holy Roman Emperor called for the restoration of all lands seized from the Catholic Church during the first round of religious conflicts in the early 1500s. The more dogmatic Ferdinand II, by comparison, did not exhibit the same restraint in victory.

Richelieu's failure to exact vengeance reflected a recognition of structural restraints consistent with realism, not a genuine religious tolerance. Richelieu (1651) had authored a pamphlet during the siege entitled *Traité qui contient la méthode la plus facile et la plus asseurée pour convertir ceux qui se sont separez de l'église*. The title, translated as "treatise on the easiest and most assured method to convert those who have separated themselves from the church," indicates his pragmatic approach. France would "recover from heresy by reason those whom the king had recovered from rebellion by force" (Elliot 1984: 30). Richelieu was "careful not to make the terms too hard, because that might have brought a dangerous reaction. . . . He would not have troubled about such niceties if he had not been afraid that the Huguenots, if goaded to desperation, might attempt to regain some of the power they had once enjoyed" (Stankiewicz 1960: 114).

Richelieu instead focused on literally dismantling the Huguenots' political prerogatives. The Protestants were forced to surrender many special privileges granted in the Edict of Nantes, such as governmental autonomy, as well as others they had enjoyed for centuries, including exemption from duties on imports and exports. Local *intendants* were installed to control courts and finances and to establish order. The walls of all the Protestant towns were razed and garrisons disbanded (Blanchard 2011: 115–6; Levi 2000: 112ff; Treasure 1972: 105). Richelieu saw to it that future rebellion would become impossible, prioritizing this over conversion.

This again caused frictions with the dévots, who had been so pleased with Richelieu's vigorous prosecution of the siege (Knecht 1991: 35; Tapié 1967: 182). However, Richelieu's strategy worked. The Grace of Alais marked the end of Huguenot uprisings and established a stable status quo until Louis XIV revoked the Edict of Nantes (Blanchard 2011: 223).

Reputation or Repose?: The Mantuan Succession Crisis and the Day of the Dupes

The victory over the Huguenots in 1629 put the French crown in a position to more vigorously defend its interests vis-à-vis the Spanish in a way that had not been possible in previous years (Blanchard 2011: 223; Weber 1992: 55). Richelieu had written the king in 1625:

> As for the Huguenots, they are accustomed to advance their cause at the expense of the State, and to seize their opportunity when they see us occupied against those who are our declared enemies. ... We must fear that they will do the same on this occasion. ... As long as the Huguenots have a foothold in France, the King will never be master at home and will never be able to undertake any glorious action abroad. (Church 1972: 189; see also Holt 205)

Richelieu argued pragmatically at the time that France must solve its internal problems before engaging in any extensive action abroad:

> [I]t is too much work serving two masters at the same time, of which only one can be handled. ... It is an old aphorism of doctors that an internal sickness, although small in itself, should be feared more than an external one that is larger and more painful. This leads to the realization that it is necessary to forego the external in order to take care of the internal. If it is possible to use simple remedies and light purges that do not disturb or corrupt the body, we do not need to have recourse to others. But if the illness is so great that such a remedy only aggravates the problem, rather than curing it, we should use those remedies which are able to attack it at the roots, providing not just for the present but also for the future, which must be taken into account. (Lettres II: 83)

Richelieu was advising Louis XIII to prioritize French interests, focusing on problems one by one so as to lay the foundations for longer-term goals.

Having vanquished the Huguenots, the situation was now different, and the realist adviser thought that France should take advantage of the opportunity. In January 1629, Richelieu wrote to the king: "Now that La Rochelle is taken if the king wishes to become the most powerful monarch in the world and the most esteemed of princes, he should consider before God and carefully and secretly examine with his faithful servants what personal qualities are required of him and what should be reformed in his state" (Lettres III: 179–80).

The cardinal had the Spanish in mind. Richelieu believed that Spanish power was a threat to the very existence of France; the country could deal a "mortal blow" (Tziampiris 2009: 71). In 1629, he wrote: "One's constant aim must be to check the advance of Spain" (Lettres III: 181). Richelieu complained that the policy of Catholic solidarity promoted by the dévots would make France "at best play some role as a Spanish satellite" (Levi 2000: 80). After initial Spanish successes in what would become known as the Thirty Years' War, Richelieu warned through a pamphleteer: "The passage of the Rhine is now in the power and dispos- ition of the Marquis Spinola. ... In a night he can be at the gates of Strasbourg. ... On the other side Spain has seized the passes of the Val Telline ... the realm of France will be entirely blockaded" (Treasure 1972: 33).

Richelieu argued that France should devote its attention to northern Italy, which had again become a flashpoint of conflict with the Spanish as well as the Austrians. The Duke of Manuta had died in December 1627, to be rightfully succeeded by the French Duke of Nevers. Mantua abutted Milan, which was held by the Spanish, and contained the stra- tegically important citadel of Casale, which overlooked the Po Valley. The Spanish opposed the Duke's rightful claim and laid siege to Casale. The pope and the Austrians sent troops to fight alongside them. After the fall of La Rochelle, the king and Richelieu personally traveled to Italy, passing through the Alps in winter, to end the siege, taking Savoy in the process. Under Richelieu's command, the French took another strategic- ally important town, Pinerolo (Blanchard 2011: 113ff; Knecht 1991: 90ff; Levi 2000: 118ff). Louis XIII had to decide whether to keep it.

The dévots were incensed that France was again at war with fellow Catholic powers (Tapié 1967: 194). Marillac, Keeper of the Seals, made the case in the king's council against further intervention, citing the need to focus on domestic issues (Blanchard 2011: 110; Treasure 1972: 112–13). Marillac opposed conflict with other Catholic powers, natural allies in the struggle against heresy still raging in Germany and the Netherlands (Church 1972: 202; Elliot 1984: 97; Knecht 1991: 36; Levi 2000: 118, 125). He and other dévots enlisted the support of Marie de Medici, whose relationship with Richelieu had deteriorated due to a combination of petty jealousies and Catholic allegiance (Blanchard 2011: 110; Knecht 1991: 35). They made the case against a narrowly egoistic conception of French interests.

Richelieu laid out his case for continued intervention in Italy in a utilitarian fashion reflective of his rational cognitive style, honestly describing the pros and cons (Knecht 1991: 36). "He rehearsed the arguments for and against with scrupulous fairness but left the king in little doubt as to which course he favored," writes Treasure (1972: 112). Holding Pinerolo would amount to the "greatest conquest imaginable," making France the "arbiter and master of Italy." However, this meant indefinite war with Spain and Savoy. "If the king decides on war, it will be necessary to abandon all thoughts of tranquility, of economies and reorganization within the realm," he admitted (Elliot 1984: 106). "It is difficult for a prince to have great reputation and great repos, since frequently the esteem of the world is gained only by great actions, and ordinarily those which engender esteem excite the envy and hatred of neighbors" (Elliot 1984: 105). In the royal council session, Richelieu responded to Marillac's arguments: "The arguments presented by the Keeper of the Seals make it clear that one cannot wage war without great inconvenience. This is true not only of this particular occasion but all others" (Lettres III: 665ff). The king backed Richelieu's position.

However, the conflict with the dévots continued for months. When the king suffered an acute illness that incapacitated and almost killed him, Marie de Medici and Marillac plotted the cardinal's demise. Richelieu would be dismissed if the king died since he was to be succeeded by Louis XIII's brother, Gaston, the Duke of Orleans, who hated Richelieu. After the king recovered unexpectedly, Marie de Medici continued to lobby her son. In November 1630, in something out of a Dumas novel, Richelieu entered through a secret door and interrupted a harangue against the cardinal by the queen mother to the king. Louis XIII did not defend the cardinal, who left the room. Thinking that this snub meant she had won, Marie de Medici celebrated with Marillac. Although he contemplated escaping into exile, Richelieu instead went to see the king, who backed him and his policies resolutely. Expecting to be summoned to take Richelieu's place as first minister, Marillac was instead arrested and put in prison, where he subsequently died. The event became known as the Day of the Dupes (Blanchard 2011: 127ff; Levi 2000: 126ff; Treasure 1972: 114–5). Other dévot allies were imprisoned, fired, and even executed, including Marillac's brother.

While the court intrigue certainly involved petty jealousies, historians agree that what Pagès later called the "great storm" in French politics also had a significant policy dimension (Elliot 1984: 108; Knecht 1991: 35; Pagès 1937: 85; Treasure 1972: 107). When Marillac and Marie de Medici met to draw up an indictment of Richelieu, they focused on his conduct in regard to the Manutan crisis (Treasure 1972: 114). Essentially those who would do Richelieu harm for the sake of their own ambitions found allies who opposed Richelieu's foreign policy agenda on substantive grounds. Louis XIII's choice to support Richelieu rather than his mother was fundamentally a decision about French foreign policy, amounting to a victory of the bons Français over the pro-Spanish faction (Church 1972: 206; Knecht 1991: 40; Tapié 1967: 207).

The Day of the Dupes was Richelieu's last major struggle with the dévots. "With Marillac gone," writes Elliot (1984), "there remained no one in a position of influence to contest the Cardinal's reading of events – a reading which made the defeat of the House of Austria the first priority" (112; also Sturdy 2004: 51: Weber 1992: 51). In the wake of the botched attempt to oust and perhaps even kill Richelieu, both Marie de Medici and her son Gaston, the heir to throne, fled France for sanctuary in Spanish lands. The queen mother never returned home, dying in poverty abroad.

After 1630, Richelieu was in firm control over both internal and external French policy, with some historians arguing that he was the real ruler of France during this period. He installed his "creatures" into high positions, including the council of state (Church 1972: 283). Like Bismarck, the cardinal's realism had isolated him at court, so much so that his personal safety was at risk. However, just as the Iron Chancellor would later do, Richelieu won over an erratic king in the face of opposition by those who favored a less egoistic foreign policy approach.

Deals with the Devil: France Enters the Thirty Years' War

Richelieu's consolidation of power at home was likely necessary to take the next steps toward checking the rise of Spain and the House of Habsburg more generally. In 1630, Austrian Emperor Ferdinand II was at the zenith of his power. After fighting off the intervention of the Protestant Danes into Germany so as protect Denmark and its faith, Austrian control reached up to the Baltic. At this point Ferdinand II felt empowered to issue his Edict of Restitution.

In realist fashion, Richelieu proceeded carefully, slowly, and with limited aims that reflected France's relative weakness, particularly militarily (Church 1972: 98; Treasure 1972: 169). On several occasions he stated that France could not survive a prolonged war in which it fought Spain on its own (Weber 1992: 50). On France's eastern borders, the French should wait for fear of provoking the Habsburgs. "We may think of Navarre and the Franche-Comté as belonging to us, since they are contiguous to France and easy to conquer whenever we have nothing else to do. This, however, should not be bruited about since ... it could not be done without causing open war with Spain, which must be avoided as far as possible" (Church 1972: 297). The cardinal sought to avoid a direct conflict with the Spanish for as long as possible (Tapié 1967: 278). He advised his king that France should avoid the "kindling of an open war against Spain in so far as lies in our power. We should consider the possibility of edging forward cautiously and covertly. ... But we should only engage in these operations gradually over a long period of time, unobtrusively and with great circumspection" (Lettres III: 180–1).

Richelieu instead preferred indirect action through subsidies to and alliances with other powers opposed to Habsburg expansionism, particularly in Germany (Sturdy 2004: 57). Richelieu wrote the king:

As for the grand design that [the Habsburgs] have for Germany, the king can compete with good effect ... without entering overtly into an actual league with Holland to that end. It is also just as necessary if at the expense of our security the loss of Germany is assured thereby Spain becomes the master, she will have already advanced far in her goal for a universal monarchy. (Papiers V: no. 196)

After the Day of the Dupes, Richelieu concluded financial agreements with the Dutch, still fighting the Spanish, and the Swedish, whose Protestant king, Gustavus Adolphus, had invaded Germany. The Swedish, feeling threatened by imperial advances up to the Baltic, took over from the Danes the role of savior of the smaller Protestant states of Germany. Under the Treaty of Bärwalde, Sweden would maintain an army of 30,000 soldiers and 6,000 cavalry in Germany, which France would pay for at the cost of 1 million livres per year for the next five years. The plan worked, as the formidable Swedish army won the first major Protestant victory since the war had broken out in 1618, routing imperial forces at the Battle of Breitenfeld in Saxony in 1631.

In this way, like Bismarck, Richelieu made distasteful alliances with forces whose ideological goals he did not share in utilitarian service of French interests. The Prussian great had recruited the liberals in his aim to unify Germany; the cardinal dealt with heretics. This move was extremely controversial in France (Church 1972: 340, 372). "The inclusion of Protestant powers in Richelieu's coalition – the Swedes and the Dutch and two German principalities – has conventionally been regarded as a landmark in Europe" that marked the triumph of raison d'état over confessional diplomacy (Elliot 1984: 121). Treasure (1972) writes, "France's reputation in Germany, her natural role of patron of the Catholic princes as against the Emperor, the security which depended upon the equilibrium in Germany – all were jeopardized" (130). Kissinger (1994) agrees: "That a prince of the Church was subsidizing the Protestant King of Sweden ... to make war against the Holy Roman Emperor had revolutionary implications as profound as the upheavals of the French Revolution 150 years later" (61). Richelieu tried to neutralize some of this opposition by also concluding a neutrality agreement with the Catholic Bavarians (Sturdy 2004: 55) and by insisting on provisions in the Swedish treaty that any Catholic lands conquered by Gustavus Adolphus would enjoy freedom of religion, a "sop to the dévots" (Treasure 1972: 130).

In 1634, Richelieu beat back a faction of advisers at court, including the king himself, who wanted to intervene directly in the conflict straight away. Just as the realist Bismarck would be forced to restrain his sovereign, so was the cardinal. The king was "straining at the leash for war, while Richelieu holds him back" (Elliot 1984: 117). Richelieu instead preferred trying "all sorts of reasonable means to bring the Spanish to a just peace" (Weber 1992: 65). According to Tapié (1967):

In this critical situation Richelieu's greatest strength lay in his remarkable poise. In his case ambition and daring did not degenerate into megalomania. ... The prestige enjoyed by France was due to his own achievements, but it did not dazzle him and he would have no truck with rash ventures which might impair it. If we analyze the cautious way in which the cardinal made his preparations, we are almost tempted to take his caution for timidity. Yet it is here that his greatness as a statesman is revealed, rather than in sensational exploits such as others would have hastened to attempt had they been in his place. (307)

Richelieu's approach to the Thirty Years' War illustrates his Realpolitik in action.

France only entered the war when absolutely necessary. The defeat of Swedish forces at Nördlingen in 1634 by a combination of Austrian and Spanish forces created a power vacuum that Richelieu felt was necessary to fill, lest the House of Habsburg consolidate its hegemonic position. After the Catholic victory, Saxony and other protestant states dropped out of the alliance, suing for peace with Ferdinand II. Richelieu complimented Louis XIII for embracing the cardinal's approach up to that point: "It is a sign of singular prudence to have held down the forces opposed to your state for a period of ten years with the forces of your allies, by putting your hand in your pocket and not on your sword, then to engage in open warfare when your allies can no longer exist without you." He went on to compare the king to "economists" (Kissinger 1994: 62–3). Milton Friedman would be proud.

The entry into open armed conflict against co-religionists caused great controversy in France. Although France officially declared war only against the Spanish, it ended up fighting Austrian forces as well. Again the opposing sides attempted to mobilize supporters through the publication of pamphlets (Church 1972: 372). The most damaging to Richelieu was *Mars Gallicus*, written by a prominent Catholic bishop in Flanders named Jansenius, whose views "closely parallel those of the dévot faction in France," and was similar to the *Admonitio* (Church 1972: 387–9). Jansenius argued that any alliance with heretical, Protestant powers damaged the Church by promoting the efforts of those who would do it harm. Even if Catholic interests were protected in occupied territories, Protestant gains still allowed the practice of non-Catholic faiths, which could not be tolerated. The French king had only religious obligations: "Should not the Most Christian King believe that in the guidance and administration of his realm there is nothing that obliges him to extend and protect that of Jesus Christ, his Lord? ... Would he dare say to God: Let your power and glory and the religion which teaches men to adore You be lost and destroyed, provided my state is protected and free of risks?" (Kissinger 1994: 63–4). The bishop argued that the war must not be fought for political goals, only for religious ones.

Like the *Admonitio*, *Mars Gallicus* was based on deontological moral reasoning. Religious considerations trumped all others, with no effort made to weigh them against one another in a utilitarian fashion. One was either on the side of good or the side of evil. Jansenius wrote, "One needs but a small ray of God's grace to distinguish what is just from what is not ... what is pious from that which is mere irreligion and hypocrisy" (Church 1972: 387). France's "dastardly perfidy ... can no more be sanctioned by Catholic kings and soldiers than theft, sacrilege or adultery" (Church 1972: 388). Church (1972) calls the argumentation "simple and uncompromising – much more so than that of Richelieu and his supporters" (387). Jansenius "quite ignored such practical, mundane problems as the nature of the interstate relations that confronted Louis XIII and Richelieu. ... He simply asserted that Catholic kings should seek first and always the Kingdom of God by supporting the cause of international Catholicism" (Church 1972: 389).

France's entry into the Thirty Years' War was extremely costly, fought in theaters in the Spanish Netherlands, on the southern border with Spain, in the Valtelline in Italy, and in eastern regions such as Lorraine, the Rhineland, and the Franche-Comté. The king's brother, Gaston d'Orléans, in league with the Spanish, used the misery it wrought as a pretext for conspiratorial assassination attempts on Richelieu in an effort to force the abandonment of war efforts. However, the decision also had major consequences for France and Europe. Willing to go to war against fellow Catholics, France put itself in a much stronger position, by securing French borders: "Perpignan in the Roussillon, Pinerolo and Susa in Savoy, Lorraine and Franche-Comté, Brisach in the Rhineland, Arras and Hesdin in Flanders – all these contested territories and outposts constituted a defensive belt from which the French king threatened the possessions of Habsburg monarchs Philip IV and Ferdinand III," writes Blanchard (2011: 223). France was more secure at the end of the wars than it had been in decades (Sturdy 2004: 64; Knecht 1991: 117). Richelieu's efforts set the stage for the emergence of French greatness under Louis XIV and forestalled Habsburg hegemony in Europe. Kissinger (1994: 65) argues that Richelieu helped delay German unification by 200 years. Moreover, the protracted conflict led to internal rebellions in Portugal and Catalonia, severely wounding the Spanish.

Richelieu the Rarity

As was true of Bismarck, Richelieu's realism made him a unique figure in the French politics of his time. Most significantly, his cognitive style – in particular, his moral utilitarianism – attracted the ire of the dévots, the most important faction in French politics at the time. Church (1972) writes:

> Because of the intensity of religious rivalry in the developing Thirty Years' War and the crucial role of religion in the factionalism at the French court, any foreign policy that he might pursue was certain to be subjected to the sharpest scrutiny and criticism. As his moves unfolded and his method of strengthening the position of the French state in Europe became clear, his policies gave rise to a violent polemic. (103)

The dévots' confessional tendencies led them to support Habsburg hegemony in a manner that contradicted what a realist would expect and advise. Richelieu had his work cut out for him, given their power and the religious sensibilities of his king (Treasure 1972: 111). Tziampiris (2009) notes that while structural forces seemed to propel France toward confrontation with the Habsburgs, this was not the case "because the Habsburgs were also the leading military and political force behind the Counter-Reformation" (70).

Might we locate the source of differences between Richelieu and the dévots in varying levels of religiosity, which in turn might have influenced the degree to which they placed Catholic interests before exclusively French ones? In other words, did the two sides simply have different substantive preferences? The problem with such a counterargument is that Richelieu was, by all accounts, highly religious, even at one point soliciting special dispensations from the pope excusing him from his daily obligation to recite his prayers (Church 1972: 86; Levi 2000: 4, 79; Knecht 1991: 4; Treasure 1972: 17) as well as to participate in state measures that involved the shedding of blood (Knecht 1991: 44; also Blanchard 2011: 16). This *homme d'état* (man of state) was also an *homme d'église* (man of the church) (Orcibal 1948). Indeed, Tapié (1967) admonishes us that "it would be a serious error to imagine that he was lukewarm in his religious convictions and that he only valued his position as bishop or cardinal as a means of achieving his ambitions or as a cover for his policy" (131).

Unlike Machiavelli, who simply dismissed the relevance of morality in these instances in a purely secular manner (Church 1972: 47;

Tziampiris 2009: 79), Richelieu took this value conflict seriously. Treasure (1972) writes of the cardinal:

The central problems of his life arose from political decisions which he knew to be necessary, but which ran counter to the principles of dévots of one sort or another, which either complicated or contradicted the promptings of faith and morality. He was not, as is sometimes suggested, insensitive to the problem, even though hardened by experience. He was, and remained in his own way, a dévot. (16)

Thus a strong case can be made that Richelieu exhibited a unique cognitive style, one that distinguished him from the Catholic zealots.

As was the case with Bismarck more than 300 years later, Richelieu's realism often left him politically isolated, particularly before he consolidated power. The cardinal's unique approach meant his "existence ... was a constant fight for survival" (Blanchard 2011: 5). In fact, Richelieu's realism made him the object of so many intrigues at court that he was subsequently featured in the romantic stories of Alexandre Dumas. Richelieu knew "that he stood on shifting ground at home and that he could be sure of little: not of the king not of the army, not even of his own health" (Treasure 1972: 85). He was "faced with the hatred of [his] enemies, whether covert or open, and the hostility of a public opinion which seemed incapable of appreciating the ideals for which [he] struggled" (Elliot 1984: 59). Richelieu felt this isolation, complaining that he was living in an age when men were unwilling to listen to reason (Elliot 1984: 31). Kissinger (1994) observes, "In an age still dominated by religious zeal and ideological fanaticism, a dispassionate foreign policy free of moral imperatives stood out like a snow-covered Alp in the desert" (62). This is, of course, another self-identified realist noting that realism in practice is rare.

7 "Blood, Toil, Tears, and Sweat": Churchill, Romanticism, and the Rational Appeasement Debate

Forgive Chamberlain. He had little choice. This is the conclusion drawn from recent work on Britain's appeasement of Nazi Germany in the 1930s. Drawing from the revisionist historiography that emerged in the 1970s, when the full documentary record became available, a number of international relations scholars have made the argument that Britain's behavior vis-à-vis the Nazi regime was highly instrumentally rational given the structural constraints the country faced – too many adversaries, an overstretched empire, and limited financial reserves. Appeasement was the realist strategy par excellence considering Britain's material weakness in the mid-1930s. Given the disastrous consequences expected from even a victory in a new world war and a balance of power that heavily favored the Germans, Chamberlain appeased Hitler in hopes of avoiding war or, if war came, fighting only when that imbalance was rectified in Britain's favor.

This revisionist account upends the traditional narrative that appeasement was an irrational strategy based on biased, wishful thinking. Chamberlain and his colleagues did not admit the hard truths that only robust deterrence could stop Hitler. While this new thinking was highly controversial when first introduced by historians, most now accept that Chamberlain was operated under heavy constraints.

If appeasement was a rational strategy in light of structural limitations, what does that imply about Winston Churchill, whose heroic status in the history of international relations stems from his resistance to this policy? Churchill is curiously absent from most recent accounts of the rational appeasement argument (Layne 2008; Ripsman and Levy 2008). Was he not as rational as the appeasers? I argue that he was not. Churchill was a *romantic* who made decisions in a highly emotional, intuitive, and often impulsive manner. This distinguished him from the highly deliberative and objective rational thinkers who dominated Conservative governments while he was in the "wilderness," the term that Churchill used to describe the period in the 1930s when he was kept out of the cabinet and the party leadership. Churchill embodied all the four key elements of

176

romanticism: a sense of agency, deontological idealism, belief in resolve, and veneration of struggle.

Churchill's romanticism and cognitive style are necessary to account for his attitude toward the rise of Nazi Germany in the 1930s. Romantics fight for their ideals, even in the face of daunting odds. They do not pragmatically adjust to the circumstances. Taking up the reins of government just as the Germans entered France, Churchill told the British he had nothing to offer them but "blood, toil, tears, and sweat." The obverse of the instrumentally rational, realist appeasement approach of the Chamberlain government, Churchill's whole political philosophy was premised on battling on when in a position of weakness and letting up when in a position of strength. In the first pages of the volume of his autobiography dedicated to the 1930s, we find the "moral of the work": "In War: Resolution; In Defeat: Defiance; In Victory: Magnanimity; In Peace: Good Will" (Churchill 1948). *Defiance* is a deeply romantic word, which captures the emotion and the resolve of the romantic. One defies only when one is weak. As a romantic, Churchill believed that great leaders make international history; their job is to push past structural obstacles through force of will.

In this chapter, following a review of Churchill's romanticism, I consider the appeasement policy of Neville Chamberlain and his government, buttressing the rational appeasement thesis that it was highly instrumentally rational. However, my argument differs in an important way. The rational appeasement argument is structural; it implies that had Churchill been in power during the 1930s, facing the responsibility of government and living daily with the limitations imposed on the Chamberlain government, he would have made the same decisions. I argue instead that appeasers appeased because they were more procedurally (and therefore instrumentally) rational than Churchill. Consequently, they were attuned to structure in ways that Churchill was not. This cognitive style was a necessary condition for appeasement. Like the high-cognition egoists in our laboratory experiment in Chapter 3, appeasers adjusted British policy to structural constraints, appeasing in a situation of weakness, but simultaneously investing in rearmament so as change the distribution of power and negotiate in the future from a position of strength.

Given the intense mythology surrounding Churchill, I am careful to rely heavily on those historical works that have sought to skewer the Churchill myth as the savior of Britain in addition to the hagiography that emerged in the early postwar years and persists in popular histories. The latter accounts are themselves highly romantic (Ball 2001: 317). "The notion of the prophet in the wilderness, the lone voice of truth, crying out the dangers of Hitler and the Third Reich is a romantic one, and it is the view of Churchill that prevails in the popular imagination," writes Catherwood (2009: 11). Precisely because he was a romantic, Churchill wanted to be remembered as a great man. The valorization of Churchill is largely a function of his romanticism, even if we do not consciously realize it. Yet the more we read about Churchill, the more we realize that almost everyone saw him in the same way; they simply disagreed about whether his romanticism and intuitive, nonrational thinking was a good or bad thing. In the discussion that follows, I do not attempt to reconcile the alternative historiographical interpretations based on some new "smoking gun" piece of evidence, but rather through a conceptual advance that shows that critics and detractors empirically agree.

"Here Firm Though All Be Drifting": Churchill as Romantic

I am not the first to describe Churchill as a romantic. Indeed, this has been one of the most common descriptions of him by biographers and contemporaries – both admirers *and* critics – as early as the turn of the twentieth century (Charmley 1993: 282; James 1970: 205; Keegan 2002: 8; Scott 1905: 87). Isaiah Berlin (1949), one of our foremost experts on romanticism, sees Churchill as the quintessential example of the "romantic conception of life" with a "vision in foreign affairs" that "has always been consistently romantic" (1949). Shelden (2003) notes the "romantic temperament that flowered in his youth and never entirely disappeared"; a "romantic vision" guided his career (5). In addition, he describes Churchill as "strong-willed, idealistic, romantic, intense" (153). Ball (2003) refers to his "romantic imagination" (92). Jock Colville (1996), a British civil servant, remembers, "Churchill was essentially a romantic, and although he only once wrote a poem – as a boy of fifteen – he was a poet at heart" (121). James (1970) refers to the "essentially romantic nature of Churchill's character" that was "constant throughout his life" (383).

While Churchill is commonly described as romantic, the term is undefined. What exactly does this mean? Guided by the preceding review, I show that Churchill embodies every element of romanticism – a belief in human agency, a veneration of will and resolve, a desire for struggle, and a morally deontological approach to ideals. By establishing his romanticism, we have a way of understanding why and how Churchill opposed the rationalist, realist, and pragmatic foreign policy pursued by the British during the 1930s. He had the same substantive goal as his colleagues in the Conservative government – to safeguard the British Empire – but his cognitive style led him to take radically different positions.

Churchill believed deeply in the power of human agency. In *My Early Life*, the first volume of his autobiography, he admonished the youth:

Twenty to twenty-five! These are the years! Don't be content with things as they are. "The earth is yours and the fullness thereof." ... Raise the glorious flags again, advance them upon the new enemies, who constantly gather upon the front of the human army, and have only to be assaulted to be overthrown. Don't take No for an answer. Never submit to failure. Do not be fobbed off with mere personal success or acceptance. You will make all kinds of mistakes; but as long as you are generous and true, and also fierce, you cannot hurt the world or even seriously distress her. She was made to be wooed and won by youth. She has lived and thrived only by repeated subjugation. (Quoted in James 1970: 364).

Churchill also wrote, "I believe in personality. ... We live in an age of great events and little men ... and if we are not to become the slaves of our own system ... it will only be by the bold efforts of originality" (Shelden 2003: 5).

Lady Bonham-Carter, one of Churchill's closest friends, remembers meeting him when he was only thirty-two years old. The young politician "burst forth on the immensity of possible human accomplishment – a theme so well exploited by the poets, prophets and philosophers of all ages" (Bonham Carter 1965: 4). His great admirer, Berlin (1949), writes, "he does not *reflect* a social or moral world in an intense and concentrated fashion; rather he *creates* one of such power and coherence that it becomes a reality and alters the external world by being imposed upon it with irresistible force." Even if we should be more circumspect about Churchill's ability to successfully exercise agency than Berlin – luck, for instance, was a key component of Churchill's ultimate triumphs – it seems indisputable that personal belief in such a power was a central part of his motivation and self-understanding.

As a romantic, Churchill had a great cause and ideal: the maintenance of the glory and power of the British Empire (Gilbert 1977: 886; Rubin 2003: 158). That goal explains why he joined the Conservative Party in the first place (CHAR: 2/576A-C). In a private letter, Churchill wrote: "Of course my ideal is narrow and limited. I want to see the British Empire preserved for a few more generations in its strength and splendor" (CHAR: 2/301; also CHAR: 2/332).

Churchill romanticized Britain's role in the world above all. Historians consistently describe his conception of England as romantic (Baxter 1983; 10; Charmley 1993: 282; James 1970: 344, 383; Keegan 2003: 8).

Consider the following quote from Churchill's history of the Duke of Marlborough, one of his ancestors:

No dreamer, however romantic, however remote his dreams from reason, could have foreseen a surely approaching day when, by the formation of mighty coalitions and across the struggles of a generation, the noble colossus of France would lie prostrate in the dust, while the small island, beginning to gather to itself the empires of India and America ... would emerge victorious, mistress of the Narrow Seas, and the oceans. Aye, and carry forward with her, intact and enshrined, all that peculiar structure of law and liberty, all their own inheritance of learning and letters, which are to-day the treasure of the most powerful family in the human race. (Alkon 2006: 205)

James (1970) describes Churchill's *History of the English-Speaking Peoples* as reflecting his "idealized and over-romanticized concepts," citing in particular his embrace of the myth of the "small island" (222).

Of course, Churchill's colleagues were equally committed to protecting the interests of the British Empire. For Churchill, more than for others, Britain represented something larger. It was the manifestation of a set of ideals, which can be seen in the previous quote. In his romantic view of England's past and her future destiny, Churchill upheld his country as the main vehicle for "civilization" in the world (Addison 1980: 40; Best 2001: 10). This was one of his central concepts (Kemper 1996). Churchill fully accepted the "Whig view of history," that image of Britain's past as a gradual and steady progression toward enlightenment, the fruits of which Britain subsequently bequeathed to its colonies (Addison 1980: 46; Alkon 2006: 205). "We have built up a kind of civilization here," he once wrote, "which contains within itself ... all the means of almost limitless improvement" (CHAR: 2/282). In a letter to the English author George Bernard Shaw, he stated, "I think the English constitution and Parliamentary system expressing the English character has produced results superior to those now existing in any other country, and I hope I shall die before it is overturned" (CHAR: 2/576A-C).

According to Churchill, British imperialism was therefore good for its colonies, a triumph of "civilization" over its opposite – "barbarism" (Addison 1980: 32; Rubin 2003: 188). He declared, "[O]ver all this, uniting each Dominion with the other and uniting us all with our majestic past, was the golden circle of the Crown. What was within that circle? Not only the glory of an ancient unconquered people, but the hope, the sure hope, of a broadening life for hundreds of millions of men" (CC: 1423). He had a highly paternalistic and self-righteous conception of Britain's role in the world (Addison 1980: 41; Kemper 1996: 3). Consistent with this, Churchill fervently believed that British colonies were not capable of self-government because they were not yet civilized enough (Colville 1996: 124–5). Even though Churchill was not a racist in a biological sense, he believed in the "White Man's Burden." Churchill was similarly paternalistic and elitist when it came to class relations at home (Charmley 1993: 282; Quinault 2001; 202).

Churchill saw civilization breaking down in the twentieth century. He wrote in 1922:

What a disappointment the Twentieth Century has been. ... We have seen in every country a dissolution, a weakening of those bonds, a challenge to those principles, a decay of faith, an abridgement of hope on which structure & the ultimate existence of civilized society depends. We have seen in every part of the globe one country after another which had erected an orderly, a peaceful, prosperous structure of civilised society, relapsing in hideous succession into bankruptcy, barbarism or anarchy. (Addison 1980: 63)

As we will see, this perception is critically important for understanding Churchill's approach to Nazi Germany.

Churchill also loved struggle; he thrived on contestation and tribulation. He explained, "Politicians rise by toil and struggles. ... They expect to fall; they hope to rise" (James 1970: 314). He relished the "trial," as he puts it. Churchill was happiest in adversity, writing that "it is impossible to quell the inward excitement which comes from a prolonged balance of terrible things" (James 1970: 367). According to Rubin (2003), "While others shrank from battle, Churchill embraced it"; fighting allowed him to "channel his belligerency into the flood of something finer, something real, historic" (93). Berlin (1949) connects this with other elements of Churchill's romanticism: "His world is built ... upon the supreme value of action, of the battle between simple good and simple evil, between life and death; but above all, battle. He has always fought."

This was a consistent theme throughout his career. Churchill delighted in his position as First Lord of the Admiralty during World War I because it presented him with an opportunity to participate directly in world events and leave his mark: "This, this is living History! Everything we are doing and saying is thrilling – it will be read by a thousand generations. ... Why, I would not be out of this glorious delicious war for anything the world could give me" (Rubin 2003: 94). Harold Nicolson, the British diplomat and politician, reported that when a colleague spoke of the desperation of Britain's predicament: "Winston takes a long puff at his cigar, smiles and answers: 'Myself I always find that occasions which demand the display of great moral and physical courage are very invigorating occasions. ...' There we were in the Smoking Room terrified and depressed by the alternatives between a disastrous war and the surrender of our independence. And this old battlehorse remains

determined and imperturbable" (CC: 943). This is the "blood" of
"blood, toil, tears, and sweat."

Churchill placed enormous emphasis on will and resolve (Rubin 2003:
42). "At the heart of his story is an irrepressible spirit. ... It arose from a
powerful concept of personal will that Churchill embraced early in adult-
hood," writes Shelden (2003: 5). Leo Amery, his longtime Conservative
colleague, described his "power of nervous output and will power"
(James 1970: 373). Churchill frequently "excoriated lesser men for lack
of will power, convinced that this deficiency was at the basis of British
weakness" (Charmley 1993: 367). One of his favorite sayings was "Here
firm, though all be drifting" (James 1996: 137). Churchill sweated and
toiled.

Lacking "Judgment": Churchill's Thinking Style

Consistent with his romanticism, Churchill's thinking was more like
System I than System II processing. Observes James (1970), "Churchill
was a romantic. ... He reacted from the heart and not the head" (205).
Rubin (2003) writes that he "drank constantly, cried frequently, painted
pictures ... and recited poetry at the slightest encouragement" (36). As
he once told his secretary, "I blub an awful lot" (Manchester and Reid
2015: 32). Churchill was most moved by tails of sacrifice for ideals and
courage under fire – his personal, and very romantic, virtues. He shed
tears for those who shed blood for England. "He was a highly emotional
man, easily touched to tears and profoundly stirred by glamorous and
ardent actions" (James 1970: 383). This distinguished him from his
peers, Rubin (2003) notes: At the time, "adult Englishmen did not often
weep" (132).

Both friends and foes regarded Churchill as emotional, impulsive, and
reckless, inclined toward action without proper deliberation and sober
calculation (Arnett 1991: 609; Baxter 1983: 7; Gilbert 1977: 557; Rubin
2003: 28, 43). He did not regulate his emotions through the use of
System II processing. The longtime Secretary to the Cabinet, Maurice
Hankey, called him "unreliable," a "rogue elephant" (Charmley 1993:
408). Lloyd George, Churchill's close ally in Britain's National Government that ruled during and after World War I, described him as a "wild
and dangerous fellow," who, "to secure his own ends ... becomes
reckless" (Charmley 1993: 161). Even Duff Cooper, also opposed the
appeasement of Germany, said Churchill's "enthusiasms carried him
away" (Charmley 1993: 306).

Above all, Churchill was said to lack "judgment," a conclusion reached
by many historians as well (Ball 2001: 310; Charmley 1993: 97;

James 1970: 334; Rubin 2003: 28). In 1928, his colleague Quintin Hogg said of Churchill that he had "the greatest respect for his brilliant abilities" but "none for his judgment" (Charmley 1993: 224). F. E. Smith famously said, "When Winston is right he is very right. But when he is wrong – Oh My God" (James 1996: 135). Stanley Baldwin, the prime minister, said privately in 1936 to a colleague:

One of these days I'll make a few casual remarks about Winston. . . . I've got it all ready. I am going to say that when Winston was born lots of fairies swooped down on his cradle gifts – imagination, eloquence, industry, ability, and then came a fairy who said 'No one person has a right to so many gifts,' picked him up and gave him such a shake and twist that with all these gifts he was denied judgment and wisdom. And that is why while we delight to listen to him in this House we do not take his advice. (CC: 166)

Chamberlain actually used this line of attack against Churchill in parliament (CC: 1280). This was not just posturing, but his private position as well: "[Former Foreign Secretary Herbert] Simon's judgment, and [former Foreign Secretary Samuel] Hoare's, might have been wrong at times, but Winston's was notorious" (CC: 1545).

We see this same type of criticism among Churchill's admirers. Clement Atlee, the leader of the Labour opposition who would go on to serve in Churchill's wartime cabinet, remembered, "He was brave, gifted, inexhaustible and indomitable. . . . Energy, rather than wisdom, practical judgement or vision, was his supreme qualification" (Best 2001: 334). Best (2001) asserts that Churchill was "by nature conceited, impetuous and self-willed. . . . [T]hough his mind was capacious, powerful and retentive, it had no training in critical method. . .and he was not always as well-informed as he felt himself to be" (10).

In criticizing his judgment, Churchill's contemporaries and later historians are commenting on his low levels of procedural and instrumental rationality. Sir Alan Brooke noted his inability to carefully consider the positives and negatives in his choices: "Winston was never good at looking at all the implications of any course of action which he favoured. . . . In fact, he frequently refused to look at them." He "showed no appreciation for practical difficulties" (Rubin 2003: 45). Churchill blurred desirability and feasibility. Charmley (1993) argues, "Churchill's ideas were always bold in conception and promised great results at little cost – and he always underrated the obstacles in the way of their achievement." He had a "fatal inability to distinguish between what was practicable and what was not" (108). Fittingly for a romantic, Addison (1980) compares him to a "great artist" who "produces odd results from the data." While the more rational thinker, like Chamberlain, "subordinates vision to matters of fact," Churchill instead subordinated "matters of fact to vision. Historians will recognize in him the inspired generalizer who begins with original ideas and ransacks the archives to prove them" (38). Churchill was, in Tetlock's (2005) terms, a hedgehog, not a fox. He was theory-driven rather than data-driven.

All of these characteristics of Churchill – his belief in agency, his emotion and passion, his love of action and adventure, and his refusal to capitulate and surrender his principles – are the foundation of the romantic myth that surrounds him. They are the essence of his perceived greatness, why so many loved (and still love) him. Yet they are also simultaneously his greatest personal flaws, a curse as well as a blessing. What appeared (and still appears) to some as bold and decisive leadership struck (and continues to strike) others as reckless, ill-considered, and impulsive action. The accounts of Churchill's greatest believers and his greatest detractors are therefore both accurate. Churchill had the courage of his convictions, which meant that he did not leave room for self-doubt and reflection.

"So Potent a Being as Myself": Churchill's Egotism and the Wilderness Years

Understanding Churchill as a romantic helps resolve the question raised by one historian: "Statesman or Opportunist?" (Neville 1996). Churchill was indeed a remarkably egotistical individual (James 1970: 16). He simply did not care about what his peers thought. His colleague Winterton (quoted in Eade 1953) recalls his reputation in the 1930s: "He was an erratic genius; he was utterly unreliable; he had caused unnecessary trouble to the prime minister and to all his colleagues in every Cabinet in which he had served by his volubility and persistence in disregarding every opinion except his own" (67). Lord Moran said at the time, "Winston is so taken up with his own ideas he is not interested in what other people think" (Manchester and Reid 2015: 16). Churchill's idea of a wonderful evening, he explained, was fine food followed by a good discussion "with myself as chief conversationalist" (Manchester and Reid 2015: 16). James (1970) notes that Churchill's own son commented that he "had no small talk and preferred to talk only about himself" (21).

Churchill critics, however, are confusing arrogance for unprincipled opportunism, egotism for egoism. Churchill thought that he was one of those romantic geniuses who would make history. He had a strong belief in his own personal fate, famously recalling in his memoirs of the moment when he became prime minister: "I felt as if I were walking with Destiny, and that all my past life had been but a preparation for this hour and this trial" (Churchill 1948: 409). One might discount such a post hoc and self-serving recollection were it not for the fact that he continually expressed this sentiment throughout his career (Addison 1980: 29). One observed in 1905: "Churchill ... feels upon himself the hand of destiny. He is the instrument of some great purpose of nature, only half disclosed as yet" (Addison 1980: 33). Bonham Carter (1965) recalls that at their very first meeting, he used an unusual metaphor, "We are all worms. But I do believe that I am a glowworm" (4). She continues, "I was conscious of his own ultimate confidence in himself. He had no doubts about his star. ... Even in those early days he felt that he was walking with destiny and that he had been preserved from many perils to fulfill its purpose" (10; see also Best 2001: 10, 330; James 1970: 383; Rubin 2003: 87).

It seems impossible for a man who had such a strong belief in his destiny, typical of a romantic, to be anything other than an egomaniac. The line between righteousness and self-righteousness was impossible not to cross. As Rubin (2003) observes, "Churchill's greatest fault was the fault of his greatest virtue: he was sufficient for himself. His disdain for others' opinion gave him his own clear vision" (91). Churchill himself saw this disagreeable combination, remarking as early as 1897: "*I am so conceited* I do not believe the Gods would create so potent a being as myself for so prosaic an ending" as dying on the battlefield as an ordinary soldier (Rubin 2003: 179 [emphasis added]). His historian admirers also admit this fault. Best (2001) writes, "[T]hese great achievements in the field of international relations ... were the work of a human being whom it is impossible to describe as other than extraordinary in his mixture of qualities. Not all of them were attractive. Egotism is not usually counted among the moral pluses. ... He was better at saying he could admit error than at actually admitting it. He was spoiled and self-indulgent" (333).

Churchill was, consistent with this romantic temperament, simply not a team player. He was loyal only to his own personal sense of right and wrong. The young star had switched parties twice in his career, leaving the Conservative party for the Liberals in 1904 and then returning to the Conservatives in 1924 (Addison 1980: 25; Ball 2001: 307; James 1970: 35). Winterton described him at the turn of the century: "Churchill made no attempt to dispel the suspicion and dislike with which he was regarded by the majority of the House of Commons. He seemed to enjoy causing resentment. He appeared to have ... a 'chip on his shoulder' when in the Chamber itself or in the Lobbies'" (Eade 1953: 63). This was extremely uncommon in British politics and earned him a reputation as an egoistic, self-aggrandizer lacking political principles (Addison 1980; Rubin 2003: 25). Bonham Carter (1963) remembers how he was regarded: "He was an outsider, a pusher, thruster and self-advertiser. After he crossed the Floor, he became, in addition, a rat, a turncoat, an *arriviste*" (7).

In fact, principles were all Churchill had; they were the source of his disloyalty. Approaching ideals in a deontological rather than a utilitarian fashion, he was loath to compromise. Some of Churchill's greatest critics and his greatest proponents agree that Churchill was remarkably consistent in his political beliefs (James 1970: 384). Winterton remembers, "His father had great ideals for which he was prepared to risk his career, so had he. His father was a rebel, so would he be. His father never cared whether he caused offense in public or private, nor would he" (Eade 1953: 64). As Manchester (1988) writes, "He had always nailed his colors to the mast, but not always to the same mast" (203). During his wilderness period, Churchill wrote to a colleague, "It may be possible to fight within the ranks of the Conservative Party to defend our rights and possessions, and to make the necessary sacrifices and exertions required for our safety, or is it all to go down the drain ... through the influence of the Central Office and the Government Whips? If so, I know my duty" (CHAR: 2/332).

Churchill's egotism, self-righteousness, and self-assuredness actually inhibited his ability to opportunistically promote his career (James 1970: 20, 25). He was unable to act strategically. Churchill lacked the patience that comes with long-term thinking and the ability to constrain himself when he disagreed with the party elders who could block his path to the top, casting fire indiscriminately. "A stinging snub is just as likely to be administered to one of his own supporters as to an 'honorable gentleman opposite," remembered Eden (Eade 1953: 82). Manchester (1988) notes, "Any other politician twice faced with uprisings in his own constituency would have trimmed his sails, if ever so slightly" (415). Stanley Baldwin noted that Churchill "cannot really tell lies. That is what makes him so bad a conspirator" (Charmley 1993: 392; also Rubin 2003: 133). His colleague, Lord Beaverbrook, said the same: "He is strictly honest and truthful to other people, down to the smallest detail of his life. ... Yet he frequently deceives himself" (James 1970: 327).

Romanticism in Action: Churchill on History and Making History

We can see Churchill's romanticism and nonrational thinking style in both his views of history and his behavior when holding his first major position in government, that of the First Lord of the Admiralty during World War I. Churchill was a prolific historian, which gives us an insight into how he viewed the forces guiding human events. His understanding of history was thoroughly romantic, driven by great men doing great deeds in great struggles over great ideals. And he wanted to be such a great man – a romantic quality that colored his first major post in government.

"In his views of history as in politics, he was a romantic, with a romantic's eye on men and events," writes James (1970: 347). Agency was featured over structure. "Churchill avoided introspection, held colourful but cardboard views of individual character, and believed very simply in the role of great men and heroic deeds in history," writes Addison (1980: 36). Reynolds (2001) summarizes "Churchill's principles of interpretation: contingency, not determinism, an emphasis on individuals rather than broad forces" (232). Best (2001) writes that Churchill's famous *History of the English-Speaking Peoples* was "willing to retain national stories and legends of doubtful historicity" but "included virtually none of the economic and demographic history that alone made serious historical sense of the whole. ... Concept and substance were both familiar in the standard 'Whig history of England. ... Churchill perhaps understood little of the deeper currents and manifold complexities that shape historical development" (319–20).

His agents were not realistically drawn or carefully observed but rather resembled caricatures.

Mr. Churchill sees history – and life – as a great Renaissance pageant: when he thinks of France or Italy, Germany or the Low Countries, Russia, India, Africa, the Arab lands, he sees vivid historical images. His eye is never that of the neatly classifying sociologist, the careful psychological analyst, the plodding antiquary, the patient historical scholar. The units out of which his world is constructed are simpler and larger than life, the patterns vivid and repetitive like those of an epic poet, or at times like those of a dramatist who sees persons and situations as timeless symbols and embodiments of eternal, shining principles. (Berlin 2014)

His histories pitted alternative ideals against one another in a black-and-white, and overly simplistic, fashion. His work is "populated with the Good and the Bad" (James 1970: 342) and is "more emotional than intellectual" (343). Even his great admirers agree. Churchill could not capture moral grays.

So long as the events or the human reactions were on a bold scale – dealing with courage, endurance, misery or defeat – he wrote with authority and with deep understanding: often his words clothed his feelings in majestic and memorable phrases. If the human or political situation became complex – a mixture of conscious or unconscious motives, of good and evil, of treachery and patriotism, existing side by side – then he tended to stumble or to evade the issues. (James 1970: 342)

Churchill applied this conception of history to the international politics of his time as well. He predicted that peace in his time "will be achieved only when in a favourable atmosphere half a dozen great men, with as many first class powers at their back, are able to lift world affairs out of their present increasing confusion" (Gilbert 1977: 445–6). The problem, according to Churchill, was that the "pedestals have for some years been vacant" of these "great men" (Charmley 1993: 251).

As First Lord of the Admiralty during World War I, Churchill was the prime planner and backer of a bold naval operation to seize control from the Turks of the Dardanelles, the narrow straits connecting the Mediterranean and the Black Sea. The idea was extremely attractive to a romantic. According to James (1970), "the sheer imaginativeness of the concept invested it with an attraction that was in sharp contrast with the dreary and bloody slogging-match on the western front" (98). Frustrated with the stagnation in the trenches on the European continent, Churchill was looking for action of any kind, which "led his restless imagination to toy with many ideas before it alighted on the Dardanelles" (Charmley 1993: 105). He wrote Prime Minister Asquith at the time, "We ought not to drift" but instead to "form a scheme for a continuous and progressive offensive" (James 1970: 73). The Dardanelles promised action and drama (James 1970: 88–9). Lord Selbourne complained, "The fundamental fault of his system is his restlessness" (James 1970: 70).

Churchill pushed the idea of a naval attack on the straits. Even when it was decided that ground troops would not be forthcoming, he decided they were unnecessary against much military advice. One of his colleagues grumbled, "Winston, very, very ignorant, believes he can capture the Dardanelles without troops" (James 1970: 82). Churchill was wrong: two British battleships and eight other allied ships were sunk. Ground troops were eventually brought in, beginning the Battle of Gallipoli, one of the greatest military defeats in British history, with more than 70,000 British casualties.

Although James (1970) circumspectly concludes that the fault was not the First Lord's alone, he writes, "Churchill was to a very real extent deeply responsible. He had at no stage conducted anything approaching a really thorough examination of the manifold problems involved in such an operation" and "had entered the naval operation without adequate realization of the very serious problems involved, and with insufficient contact with his service advisers; the War Council had not been adequately informed of the doubts that existed in the Admiralty about the operation" (86). In other words, Churchill's nonrational cognitive style was largely to blame. Historians accuse him of motivated bias, premature closing, and misplaced certainty. He overstated the possibility of success, did not listen to expert advice, and understated the obstacles (Charmley 1993: 107–9; James 1970: 99). Churchill considered criticism to be symptomatic of a lack of resolve rather than indicative of a hard-headed analysis of the situation. He was "apt to confuse critical comment on his tribe of brain-children with a lack of intestinal fortitude. Critical of the lack of initiative of others, Churchill never appreciated that the offensive spirit, when carried to excess, simply turned into a frenetic desire to be doing something" (Charmley 1993: 107).

"Cutting the Coat to the Cloth": Realpolitik and Rationalism in Chamberlain's Foreign Policy

Having established Churchill's romanticism – importantly, prior to his behavior in the 1930s and 1940s – we can compare it to the cognitive style underlying the rational appeasement policy of Neville Chamberlain and his cabinet. It was indeed a Realpolitik strategy. The government was promoting Britain's egoistic interest (and only Britain's egoistic interests) in light of the environmental constraints. Any war, even a winning one, would be devastating, likely bringing down the British Empire. More-over, the country was weak vis-à-vis the Germans given the jump on rearmament that the Nazis had. As Thompson (1971) notes, "the terms 'realism' and 'appeasement' were practically synonymous for Conserva-tives in the 1930s and the leaders of the National Government took special pride in their claim to be realists" (29–30).

Chamberlain's cabinet was egoistic, uninterested in the fate of any other country except insofar as it affected British security. The prime minister declared proudly of the prospect of fighting in Eastern Europe, "I am not going to get this country into a war with anybody for the League of Nations or anybody else or for anything else" (Charmley 1993: 309; Gilbert 1977: 777). He thought Britain should "enter such pacts as directly concern our interests, e.g. Locarno or Fear East, but should leave Eastern Europe to others" (Charmley 1993: 324). Chamberlain was concerned that "lest out of loyalty [to France] we should be led into a quarrel over causes which are of little interest to us, and for which she could not give us decisive aid" (Feiling 1946: 324). This pure egoism is, of course, perfectly reflected in Chamberlain's characterization of Czechoslovakia after returning home from Munich: "a quarrel in a far-way country between people of which we know nothing" (Charmley 1993: 349). This little country simply did not matter to Britain. At the time of Munich, Chamberlain confessed "my personal opinion was that on principle I didn't care two hoots whether the Sudetens were in the Reich or out of it" (DL, 19 September 1938).

Chamberlain was, like the League activists and pacifists who were so powerful at the time in British domestic politics, eager to avoid war, but largely because of its potentially devastating costs to Britain (Layne 2008). Chamberlain wrote of the need "to be sure in my own mind that the cost of war is not greater than the price of peace," while emphasizing he was not a "'peace at any price' man" (DL: 21). At Munich, Chamberlain believed Britain had "averted a catastrophe" (Gilbert 1977: 992–3). He wrote of the need "to avoid another Great War" (DL, 27 February 1938).

Chamberlain was highly attuned to structural constraints. He recognized that Britain's present military weakness relative to Germany in the late 1930s limited its options. The Conservative cabinet adjusted its policy to fit the situation in an instrumentally rational fashion. In September 1937, Chamberlain stated, "the proposition that our foreign policy must be, if not dictated, at least limited by the state of National Defences, remains true" (James 1970: 361). In his diary letters, Chamberlain wrote privately to his sister in January 1938:

[A]s a realist, I must do what I can to make this country safe. . . . Until we are full rearmed, our position must be one of great anxiety . . . we are in no position to enter lightheartedly upon war with such a formidable power as Germany. . . . [I]n the absence of any powerful ally, and until our armaments are completed, we must adjust our foreign policy to our circumstances, and even bear with patience and good humor actions which we should like to treat in a very different fashion. (DL: 21; Feiling 1946: 324)

Later in the year, he wrote privately that one "should never menace unless you are in a position to carry out your threats . . . if we have to fight we should be able to give a good account of ourselves . . . [W]e are certainly not in a position in which our military advisers would feel happy in undertaking to begin hostilities if we were not forced to do so" (DL, 11 September 1938). Germany was aware of this, he believed: [T]he Germans . . . are too conscious of their strength and our weakness and until we are as strong as they are we shall always be kept in this state of chronic anxiety" (DL, 22 May 1938). At the time of Munich, Chamberlain stated that Britain "could not think of [war] unless we had a reasonable prospect of being able to beat her to her knees in a reasonable time and of that I see no sign" (DL, 20 March 1938).

The military situation was not easy to rectify because of another constraint: Britain lacked the money to pay for rearmament. Chamberlain and his colleagues were highly attuned to what he called the "fourth arm of defence." The prime minister spoke of how it was necessary to "cut our coat according to the cloth" – in other words, to make policy in light of existing constraints (Gilbert 1977). To his cabinet, the prime minister stated, "Admittedly national safety comes before finance but the bill for armaments was running up very heavily ... and the danger of overloading the programme beyond the material capacity of the country had to be considered" (Self 2017: 40). Chamberlain contrasted his position with Churchill's: "[I]f we were to follow Winston's advice and sacrifice our commerce to the manufacture of arms we should inflict a certain injury upon our trade which it would take generations to recover, we should destroy the confidence which now happily exists and we should cripple our revenue" (DL, 14 November 1936). The Chamberlain government hoped to improve the situation gradually, in a way that would not cripple the economy, after which they would be in a better position to confront Germany more aggressively.

Given the potential costs of conflict and the poor odds of Britain prevailing at the time, Chamberlain devised a strategy of appeasing Germany through concessions while simultaneously building up the means to (he hoped – given the expected disastrous costs) deter conflict, strengthen the hand of Britain's diplomacy, and, if unsuccessful, give Britain the strength to win a war. In August 1937, Chamberlain referred to the "double policy of rearmament & better relations with Germany & Italy," which "will carry us through the danger period" (DL, 1 August 1937). Britain was temporarily weak, but it would have less need to appease its foes once it was stronger. Once Britain had rebuilt its defenses, this would "make our ordinary diplomacy effective," thought Chamberlain (Gilbert 1977: 992–3). He predicted that if the Germans "will presently come to realise that it never will be worth while [to go to war], then we can talk" (Gilbert 1977: 1091). This was Chamberlain's line of thinking as early as 1934, when he was still Chancellor of the Exchequer. "For the old aphorism 'force is no remedy' I would substitute 'the fear of force is the only remedy'... and so I have practically taken charge now of the defence requirements of the country" (Middlemas 1972: 50).

Ripsman and Levy (2008) argue that this is evidence of an instrumentally rational strategy of using appeasement to "buy time" for rearmament. There is much evidence for this argument in the archival record. For instance, Chamberlain wrote in February 1936 in a private letter:

I am pretty satisfied now that if we can keep out of war for a few years we shall have an air force of such striking power that no one will care to run risks with it. I cannot believe that the next war, if it ever comes, will be like the last one and I believe our resources will be more profitably employed in the air & on the sea than in building up great armies. (DL, 9 February 1936; also DL, 19 July 1936, 4 July 1937, 26 March 1939, 23 July 1939; DBFP 2(16): 251,746; Gilbert 1977: 992, 1091)

It is important to recognize that rearmament was not a resignation to an inevitable war, but rather an insurance policy in case Hitler could not be appeased. In the Commons in March 1938, Chamberlain stated his government's pithy policy: "By reason if possible – by force if not" (Charmley 1989: 69). This had been Chamberlain's line since he became Chancellor. In 1935, he explained "the way to talk to Hitler was to say that there were only two ways of getting security and peace. One: regional pacts. ... Two: Alliances and a balance of power. We wanted the first but could not get it without him and if he would not play we would be forced into Two" (Middlemas 1972: 53; also DL, 16 March 1935). He remembered the thinking of the cabinet at the time of Munich: "we did gain time at Munich for a good deal of rearmament, but that was not the main object of the settlement; it was, so to speak, a by-product of an agreement which Hitler felt it expedient to accept at this time" (DL: 24). Sir Horace Wilson recalled, "our policy was never designed just to postpone war, or enable us to enter war more united. The aim of appeasement was to avoid war" (DL: 24). "While hoping for the best it is also necessary to prepare for the worst," Chamberlain summarized in a private letter (DL: 6).

Advocates of the rational appeasement approach make a structural argument, claiming implicitly or explicitly that the British essentially had no choice. Chamberlain's biographer writes of the Munich settlement that arguments made by anti-appeasers "had much to do with the real options open to a responsible British statesman in September 1938 when confronting the prospect of a long, devastatingly costly and potentially unwinnable war on behalf of a state to which Britain had no formal treaty obligation, which it could not save and which would probably never be resurrected in its existing form – even if victory was eventually achieved" (DL: 32). According to Layne (2008), the "deck was stacked against grand strategic success because Britain's predicament was dire; it faced a surfeit of enemies, a paucity of allies, and a scarcity of resources" (433). These arguments draw on a historiographical turn in the 1970s following the release of documents that allow for a more nuanced assessment of the behavior of these "guilty men" – one that takes into account the "broader context of impersonal forces and structural constraints which limited the options open to British decision-makers in extraordinarily difficult circumstances," as Self explains in his expository essay at the beginning of the volume compiling Chamberlain's letters to his sisters (DL: 6).

What these accounts miss is that appeasement appealed to Chamberlain and his colleagues given their cognitive style. Realpolitik was the natural approach for a highly rational thinker like Chamberlain. It is true that he felt more constrained by structural features of this environment, but this is precisely because of his epistemic motivation. Chamberlain strived to see the environment objectively, admitting painful truths. At the time of the Munich conference, he declared, "I hope ... that my colleagues will not think that I am making any attempts to disguise the fact that, if we now possessed a superior force to Germany we should probably be considering these proposals in a very different spirit" (DL, 20 March 1938). He continued, emphasizing the need for objective analysis: "But we must look facts in the face."

Adjusting to the situation was a general principle of decision-making for Chamberlain:

Surely if you are going to have a policy you must take the particular situations and consider what action or inaction is suitable for those particular situations. That is what I myself mean by policy, and it is quite clear that as the situations and conditions in foreign affairs continually change from day to day, your policy cannot be stated once and for all, if it is to be applicable to every situation that arises. (Thompson 1971: 30)

In other words, the prime minister was a bottom-up, data-driven processor rather than a top-down, heuristic-driven thinker.

Chamberlain was unemotional and dispassionate, a marker of highly rational processing. Lord Strang described "a man of cool, calm mind" (James 1970: 358). Lord Salter wrote: "In debate and exposition his speech is lucid, competent, cogent, never rising to oratory, unadorned with fancy and rarely touched by perceptive emotion. But it gives a sense of mastery of what it attempts, well reflecting the orderly mind behind" (James 1970: 356). Chamberlain called his opponents, such as Foreign Secretary Anthony Eden, "feverish" and "alarmist" (DL: 31). When Chamberlain replaced Robert Vansittart, an aide to Eden and opponent of his policy, he wrote that "Anthony can work out his ideas with a sane slow man like ... [Alex] Cadogan" (DL, 12 December 1937).

Chamberlain engaged in global maximization. He thought of himself as a "practical operator ... who likes to see the whole picture ... as against Hitler, who looks out of the window at Berchtesgaden, dreamingly considering the future prospects of Germany without being very practical" (DL: 13). Rearmament was a concession to the constraints of the environment, a lesser evil. Chamberlain observed, "The very idea that the hard-won savings of our people ... should have to be dissipated upon the construction of weapons of war is hateful and damnable. But ... we have no alternative but to go on with it, because it is the very breath of our British being, our freedom itself, that is at stake" (Feiling 1946: 321).

Chamberlain also avoided cognitive "seizing," recognizing the uncertainty surrounding Hitler's intentions. This is a marker of procedural rationality. It is important to recognize that the extent of Nazi designs was unknown to British decision-makers. The "buying time" argument correctly points out that there was considerable concern about Nazi intentions all throughout the 1930s. Chamberlain and his colleagues were not naïve. They knew that Hitler was a revisionist of some kind, and they did not trust him. The Nazis were bullies, Hitler untrustworthy and likely mad (DL, 13 February 1938, 22 May 1938, 28 May 1938; 3 September 1938; 2 October 1938).

In November 1937, Chamberlain wrote:

Both Hitler & Goering said repeatedly & emphatically that they had no desire or intention of making war and I think we may take this as correct at any rate for the present. Of course they want to dominate eastern Europe; they want as close a union with Austria as they can get without incorporating her in the Reich and they want much the same things for the Sudetendeutsche as we did for the Uitlanders in the Transvaal. (DL, 26 November 1937)

Beyond that, however, the British were not certain what the Nazis had in mind. Hitler might be a garden-variety German nationalist, merely aiming to bring all ethnic Germans into a single Reich. This would include Austria, the parts of Poland taken from Germany in World War I, and the Sudetenland, but stop there. Chamberlain and his colleagues acknowledged this situation of incomplete information rather than denying it. The prime minister summarized the problem in September 1938: "The crucial question was whether Herr Hitler was speaking the truth when he said that he regarded the Sudeten question as a racial question which must be settled, and that the object of his policy was racial unity and not the domination of Europe. Much depends on the answer to this question" (Parker 1993: 169). While at Munich, Chamberlain tried to ascertain from Hitler whether his Czechoslovakian aims were limited to the Sudetenland (Gilbert 1977: 875).

Given the costs of the war, Chamberlain in particular felt he had to know with absolute certitude that Hitler had maximalist and hegemonic aims before confronting him more aggressively and rearming more quickly. He spoke of resisting war "until it becomes inevitable" (Gilbert 1977: 1056). This is, of course, consistent within an expected utility framework. Chamberlain stated that if he were "convinced that any nation had made up its mind to dominate the world by fear of its force, I should feel that it must be resisted" (DL: 22; also Welch 1993: 146). However, this was not established. Before Munich, Chamberlain lamented, "we have no definite knowledge of his intentions" (DL, 6 September 1938).

Welch concludes that Chamberlain was a "textbook realist" (Welch 1993: 145). Chamberlain explicitly accepted the label: "Yes, I am a realist," he declared to his sister (Gilbert 1977: 993). His "major object-ive" upon taking up his post was to bring policy "back to saner and more realistic grounds" (Charmley 1993: 358), by which he meant an increase in armaments (DL, 9 March 1935). Not surprisingly, Chamberlain complained that Churchill was "incapable of understanding how my mind works" (Charmley 1993: 224).

It cannot be argued that Chamberlain was a perfectly rational thinker, however. In fact, as I have maintained, likely no such thing exists. Rationality is a matter of degree, and previous chapters have shown that highly deliberative and objective thinkers are rare in international rela-tions. British politics in the 1930s is no exception. Both Holmes (2013) and Yarhi-Milo (2014) have recently noted that Chamberlain and his colleagues based many of their judgments not on considered analysis, but rather on their own vivid, personal experiences in face-to-face meetings with Hitler.

Chamberlain's greatest cognitive failure was his inability to update his beliefs about German intentions. While he did not "seize," he certainly did "freeze." More than his colleagues in cabinet, he persisted in the belief that Germany might come to terms. Chamberlain was consistently optimistic during 1938, even after the Anschluss and the first Czech crisis, that agreement could be reached (DL, 30 January 1938, 6 February 1938, 15 May 1938, 22 May 1938, 28 May 1938, 22 June 1938, 9 July 1938) at a time when doubts in his cabinet were rising (Parker 1993: 11, 345). After Munich, Chamberlain believed the German ambassador "was truthfully expressing his own views when he declared that he believed Hitler was not planning any aggressive moves" (DL, 28 January 1939), and he expressed frustration with those in his cabinet who would not believe this could be the case (DL, 8 January 1939, 5 February 1939; 12 February 1939, 26 February 1939). A speech in January 1939 called for "defence not defiance" (DL, 28 January 1939). Although Chamber-lain did express satisfaction, writing after Munich that "we have seen where our weak points were and have strengthened them, so that they could not make nearly a mess of us now as they could have then" (DL, 5 February 1939), he also complained of the "false emphasis" that had been "placed on rearmament, as though one result of the Munich agree-ment had been that it would be necessary for us to add to our rearma-ment programme" (DL: 26).

Chamberlain was also still willing to make further concessions. To his sister he wrote in February 1939: "All the information I get seems to point in the direction of peace. ... Of course that doesn't mean that

I want to bully them as they have tried to bully us; on the contrary, I think they have good cause to ask for consideration of their grievances" (DL, 19 February 1939). More problematically, Chamberlain's optimism persisted even after Hitler's greater ambitions were revealed. The Nazi seizure of Czechoslovakia demonstrated that Hitler's profession that German aims were limited to uniting ethnic Germans in one Reich was a lie (DL, 2 July 1939; 15 July 1939). However, as late as July 1939, Chamberlain thought that "Hitler has concluded that we mean business and that the time is not ripe for the major war" (DL, 23 July 1939). Historians make this critique as well (McDonough 1998: 47; Middlemas 1972: 46, 61; Parker 1993: 6–11).

My argument is only that Chamberlain was considerably more epistemically motivated in his effort to be objective and deliberative than his main opponent, Churchill. As argued earlier, procedural rationality is a question of degree. The epistemic motivation of Chamberlain becomes more evident when seen in relief. Indeed, demonstrating that Churchill was something other than a careful and calculating decision-maker is a necessary corollary of the rational appeasement argument. The most persuasive piece of evidence that Chamberlain's realism was not structurally determined is the very fact of Churchill. As we will see next, with his romantic temperament, he did not feel so hemmed in.

"In War, Resolution": Romantic or Rationalist in Disguise?

We cannot understand Churchill's famous resistance to Nazi aggression without reference to romanticism. Hitler and the Nazis were a danger to the civilization that in his eyes Britain epitomized and promoted. As early as November 1933, Churchill drew attention to "a philosophy of blood lust . . . being inculcated into [German] youth to which no parallel can be found since the days of barbarism (Hansard, 7 November 1933, c. 138; also CHAR: 9/132). This was a dominant motif in his speeches and writings: "When we read about Germany . . . we watch with surprise and distress the tumultuous insurgence of ferocity and war spirit, the pitiless ill-treatment of minorities, the denial of the normal protections of civilized society to large numbers of individuals solely on the ground of race" (Gilbert 1977: 459). On the BBC, he referred to the "most brutish methods of ancient barbarism" in Germany's domestic policies (Gilbert 1977: 567). These concerns were also evident in his private correspondence, in which he wrote of German "paganism." To his French colleague Flandin, Churchill expressed his worries: "I fear great the dangers which menace both our countries and indeed what is called civilization"

(Gilbert 1977: 656). He told his few anti-appeasement allies that "British leadership and action may yet save Europe and our grand civilization whose very existence is being threatened by the Nazis (CC: 162). The Nazis did not speak for the great German people, however, whom Churchill distinguished from the fascists (CHAR: 2/299).

By 1938, Churchill had concluded that this gulf in civilization between the British nation and the German regime gave the British little choice in policy:

You must have diplomatic and correct relations, but there can never be friendship between the British democracy and the Nazi Power, that Power which spurns Christian ethics, which cheers its onward course by a barbarous paganism, which vaunts the spirit of aggression and conquest, which derives strength and perverted pleasure from persecution, and uses, as we have seen, with pitiless brutality the threat of murderous force. That Power cannot ever be the trusted friend of the British democracy. (Hansard, 5 October 1938, col. 360–74)

He said the same privately, writing Lord Londonderry: "I am quite sure that there never was and there never will be any chance of a satisfactory arrangement between the German Nazi party and the British nation, and I am very sorry that we did not begin to arm on a great scale, especially in the air, when the menace of this violent party first appeared" (CHAR: 2/333).

Sure of Nazi intentions, Churchill vocally demanded more rapid rearmament, arguing that the best assurance of peace was through a preponderance of strength and the firm declaration that it would be used: "Our first supreme object ... is not to go to war. To that end we must do our best to prevent others from going to war" (Gilbert 1977: 459; also CHAR: 9/132, 7/46; Gilbert 1977: 452; Hansard, 26 March 1936, col. 1523–30). He expressed this opinion early on to Prime Minister Baldwin as well: "I certainly do not consider war with Germany inevitable, but I am sure the way to make it much less likely is to afford concrete evidence of our determination in getting about re-armament" (James 1970: 294). Weakness invited aggression.

Allies were also essential. Churchill declared, "Peace must be founded upon preponderance. There is safety in numbers" (Gilbert 1977: 567). He wrote privately, "I fear very gravely ... unless something happens to the Nazi regime in Germany there will be a devastating war in Europe. ... The only chance of stopping it is to have a union of nations, all well-armed and bound to defend each other, and thus confront the Nazi aggression with over-whelming force" (CHAR: 2/266; also 2/332). Churchill called for a "Grand Alliance" against German aggression, built on the cornerstones of France and Britain, which would deter German

aggression and magnetically attract other isolated countries menaced by
Germany (Hansard, 26 March 1936, col. 1523–30). This group should
include the Soviet Union if possible, but also any other small countries
that wished to join the alliance (Hansard, 14 March 1938, col. 93–103;
also 24 March 1938, col. 1444–55). At the time of the Sudeten crisis, he
proposed that this alliance issue a security guarantee to Czechoslovakia
(CHAR: 9/132); also Hansard, 24 March 1938, col. 1444–55).

Was Churchill actually more rational than his opponents? At first
blush, it seems that he, more than any other, saw things the way they
actually were – objectively, with no wishful thinking. The accuracy of
many of his prognostications and warnings is striking. Indeed, Churchill's official biographer entitled his volume on the 1930s *The Prophet of
Truth* (Gilbert 1977). After the Rhineland reoccupation, Churchill fore-
told Hitler's designs toward the east, asked whether Austria was next,
predicted that Eastern European countries would negotiate separate
peace treaties with Germany, and predicted that the Sudetenland was
only the first step in the eventual takeover of Czechoslovakia (Gilbert
1977: 718, 763; Hansard, 26 March 1936, col. 1523–30; 5 October
1938, 360–74). Churchill boasted he would "gladly submit my judgments about foreign affairs and National defence during the last five
years to comparison with his own" (CHAR: 9/133). He complained
during the 1930s, "The government was shutting its eyes to . . . disquiet-
ing facts" (CC: 161; see also CHAR: 2/270) and wrote to his wife that
Chamberlain "does not know the truth" about the woeful state of British
rearmament "& perhaps he does not want to" (CC: 878). He also excoriated the Baldwin government, telling Nicolson, "that in his long experience he has never known a Conservative Party composed of so many
blind and obstinate men" (CC: 940). His fawning biographer Manchester (1988) writes, "His perception was exceptional; an extraordinary
number of his peers were completely hoodwinked" (81). "The events
of September 1938 had proven him England's *most* sober statesman, as
well as its most prophetic" (Manchester and Reid 2015: 31). It is on this
basis that realist scholars have sought to appropriate Churchill's legend.
He was the perspicacious observer of their lessons about the dangers of
the anarchical international system, in which power is the ultimate arbiter
(Thompson 1983).[1]

---

[1] We can infer a similar conclusion from Schweller's (1996) argument about Britain's
"underbalancing" during the 1930s. While he makes little reference to Churchill, his
argument that domestic divisions prevented a unified and robust response to an obvious
German threat to the distribution of power implies that Churchill had it right. His policy
was the optimal, rational one for the situation that Britain faced.

However, the fact that Churchill turned out to be right about Nazi designs does not by itself indicate that his thought process was procedurally rational. It is not that Churchill did not act in a way consistent with his beliefs: He did. It is that his beliefs were formed without much thought, based on instinct rather than considered analysis. His thinking style was not deliberative. Consistent with his more intuitive, automatic, and impulsive cognitive style, Churchill diagnosed the Nazis as a threat with hegemonic ambitions immediately and without hesitation, without recognizing any uncertainty in his analysis, and in a manner that was consistent with his overall heuristic for understanding Britain in the world. Churchill penned a pamphlet called "The Truth About Hitler" in 1935 (CHAR: 8/518A/33). After war broke out, he indicated his, perhaps misplaced, certainty in a letter to his wife: "I have *no doubt* that a firm attitude by England and France would have prevented war" (CHAR: 1/344 [emphasis added]). This is in striking contrast to the uncertainty acknowledged by Chamberlain (and we will see, Halifax, in Chapter 8).

In diagnosing the accuracy of Churchill's predictions, his detractors *and* proponents make reference to his intuitive and emotional decision-making style, rather than pointing to a deliberative and objective one. James (1970) writes, "In a manner that perhaps owed as much to intuition as it did to actual knowledge, he saw the danger, and regarded the pace of British rearmament, substantial though it was, as inadequate to that danger" (308). According to Manchester and Reid (2015), "despite the fact that Churchill was prone to sentimentality, was mercurial, and at times lacked strategic military sense, he had, through intuitive leaps and careful analysis during the 1930s, arrived at an astonishingly accurate forecast of the calamity that had since befallen Europe and England. . . . Other sober and equable men, who lacked his imagination and penetrating vision, had allowed Britain to stumble unprepared into this war" (31).

Churchill's policy of accumulating strength as a way of deterring future aggression might be confused for instrumentally rational behavior given a superficial similarity to what has become known as "*rational* deterrence theory" (Aachen and Snidal 1989). However, a closer look reveals that Churchill's embrace of deterrence logic and his strategy of preponderance emerged not from a rational cognitive style, but rather from a romantic belief in the power of will and resolve. There was a rationalist deterrence strategy based on a cold and calculating poker game in which Britain sent costly signals of its determination, lest Germany form inferences about Britain's lack of commitment. However, this was not Churchill's approach.

For Churchill, the problem was not, as it is in rational deterrence theory, how to credibly demonstrate preexisting resolve to the enemy. That confidence and determination needed to be created and summoned in the first place through an act of agency. Churchill attributed the government's slow rearmament to a lack of resolution. He complained about the "helpless, hopeless mood" and despaired of England's "self-abasement" and "defeatist doctrines". "Nothing can save England if she will not save herself. If we lose faith in ourselves ... then indeed our story is told (Gilbert 1977: 486; Manchester 1988: 91). In a newspaper, he wrote: "It is a crime to despair. We must learn to draw from misfortune the means of future strength" (Gilbert 1977: 995). His country needed an emotional lift. "The world seems to be divided between the confident nations who behave harshly, and the nations who have lost confidence in themselves and behave fatuously" (Gilbert 1977: 686).

Churchill disliked how successive Conservative governments in Britain bowed to pacifist public opinion, rather than leading it. They were passive, not active, accepting Britain's circumstances and structural constraints rather than overturning them through agency and action. Whereas the government treated the public as a constraint, he sought it as something to be molded (Gilbert 1977: 669). Churchill stated in parliament, "Not only do we need a clear declaration of the Government's policy, but we require to get to work to rally the whole country behind that declared policy, in order that there shall not be shifts and changes, as well as that there shall not be any doubt or hesitation" (Hansard, 14 March 1938, col. 93–103). In romantic terminology, the Chamberlain government was not striving. Churchill wrote privately in September 1938:

The horrible positions into which the world has got is all due to lack of foresight and courage on the part of public men; and now perhaps the unfortunate peoples of the world may be hurled against each other in a meaningless and murderous confusion, whereas a firm, merciful and coherent action by the overwhelming forces on our side would have produced, and might still produce peace, progress and a prosperity unobtainable in former ages. (CHAR: 8/596)

He complained about the "inert personalities at [the government's] head" as early as March 1934. "The demand to-day is to have decided leadership" (CHAR: 2/137; also 2/182).

Churchill was advocating that Britain and its allies make up for material disadvantages in will and resolve. In a speech, he said:

If, through an earnest desire for peace, we have placed ourselves at a disadvantage, we must make up for it by redoubled exertions, and, if necessary, by fortitude in suffering. We shall no doubt arm. ... But arms – instrumentalities ... are not sufficient by themselves. We must add to them the power of ideas. ... It is this very conflict of spiritual and moral ideas which gives the free countries a great part of their strength. (CHAR: 9/132)

He warned of the need for a "supreme recovery of moral health and martial vigour" so that Britain would "arise again and take our stand for freedom as in the olden time" (Hansard, 5 October 1938, col. 360–74).

In other romantic flourishes, Churchill stressed that the road ahead would be arduous and that even if Britain were not to succeed, it should still fight. In this way, Churchill demonstrated the ethically deontological judgment of romantic, rather than the moral utilitarian logic of a realist. Consequences were unimportant. In remarks at a dinner, he spoke:

It may be true ... that this country will at the outset of this coming and to my mind almost inevitable war be exposed to dire peril and fierce ordeals. It may be true that steel and fire will rain down upon us day and night scattering death and destruction far and wide. ... Yes these trials and disasters ... will but serve to steel the resolution of the British people and to enhance our will for victory. ... I for one would willingly lay down my life in combat, rather than, in fear of defeat, surrender to the menaces of these most sinister men. (Manchester 1988: 440)

At another point, he said, "If the British Empire was fated to pass from life into history, we must hope it would not be by the slow process of dispersion and decay, but in some supreme exertion for freedom, for right and for truth" (CC: 1423).

Churchill argued that Britain's weakness, rather than justifying appeasement, actually required confrontation: "If things have got much worse, all the more must we try to cope with them" (CHAR: 9/132). As will be explored more extensively in Chapter 8, this is the very opposite of an instrumentally rational logic of adjusting to circumstances.

In another indication of Churchill's romanticism, his opposition to appeasement was much more than a simple critique that it signaled weakness to the adversary. He was disgusted by Britain's behavior, for not living up to his romantic image. During the Sudeten crisis, he wrote privately, "Owing to the neglect of our defences and the mishandling of the German problem in the last five years, we seem to be very near the bleak choice between War and Shame. My feeling is that we shall choose Shame, and then have War thrown in a little later" (CHAR: 2/331). Expressing frustration with his inability to convince other anti-appeasers to sign an open letter, he complained, "What are they made of? The day is not far off when it won't be signatures we'll have to give but lives – the lives of millions. Can we survive? Do we deserve to do so when there's no courage anywhere?" (James 1970: 371). At another point, he voiced similar feelings: "How ... could honourable men with wide experience and fine records in the Great War condone a policy so cowardly? It was sordid, squalid, sub-human and suicidal. ... The sequel to the sacrifice of honour would be the sacrifice of lives, our people's lives" (Gilbert 1977: 989). He predicted to his wife "further humiliations in which I rejoice to have no share" (CC: 1317). Charmley (1993) concludes that Churchill's "objections to Chamberlain's policy were visceral rather than intellectual" (346). To not stand up to aggression was cowardly (see also CHAR: 2/331). This was an emotional – not a deliberative – response. The rationalist would only focus instrumentally on the consequences of a perceived lack of resolve.

We see all of these same themes in Churchill's rearguard, backbench battle against the Conservative Baldwin government's moves to grant more self-government to India, which culminated in the Government of India Bill of 1935. Analysts have observed that Churchill's approach to India and Germany were essentially the same (Charmley 1993: 247; Tetlock and Tyler 1996: 167). He saw Britain as having brought civilization to India "far above anything they could possibly have achieved themselves or could maintain" (Rubin 2003: 188). He once proclaimed, "The rescue of India from ages of barbarism, internecine war, and tyranny, and its slow but ceaseless forward march to civilization constitutes upon the whole the finest achievement of our history" (James 1970: 217). The Indians "were humble primitives ... unable in 450,000 villages even to produce the simple organization of four or five people sitting in a hut in order to discuss their common affairs" (James 1970: 236–7).

Churchill derided the leaders of the Indian independence movement, denouncing the "evil and malignant Brahmins" with "itching fingers stretching and scratching at the vast pillage of a derelict Empire" (James 1970: 237). He accused Gandhi of "posing as a fakir," a religious ascetic who begged for food (Charmley 1993: 259). He argued that concessions would merely encourage more demands on their part, just as he did with the Nazis. "Appetite and demand in India have been raised to the highest pitch by sweeping concessions of principle," he warned (James 1970: 220). In the face of such demands, Britain must send signals of resolve. "The truth is that Gandhiism and all that it stands for, sooner or later, have to be grappled with and finally crushed. It is no use trying to satisfy a tiger by feeding him with cat's meat. The sooner that is realized, the less trouble and misfortune there will be for all concerned" (Gilbert 1977; James 1970: 219; Tetlock, and Tyler 1996: 165).

The problem, once again, was one of will and not of power. "The British lion, so fierce and valiant in bygone days, so dauntless and unconquerable through all the agony of Armageddon, can now be chased by rabbits from the fields and forests of his former glory. It is not that our strength is seriously impaired. We are suffering from a disease of the will," he declared (James 1970: 224; see also Charmley 1993: 256). Churchill complained of the "mood of unwarrantable self-abasement" and "defeatist doctrine" in regard to the Indian situation (Charmley 1989: 283).

Churchill's position on India makes sense given his set of beliefs. The question is whether he formed these beliefs based on careful deliberation or through a reliance on simple heuristics. The close parallels Churchill draws between the pacifist Indians and the militaristic Germans strongly suggests the latter. His knowledge of India, even according to his hagiographers, was minimal, extending only to the life of English elites on the subcontinent (Best 2001: 136–40; James 1970: 219, 231) and was based on "romanticized recollections of the 1890s" when he spent time there (James 1970: 223). When the Viceroy of India, Lord Irwin (later Viscount Halifax), who had proclaimed that the ultimate goal of the British government was eventual dominion status for India, offered Churchill a chance to personally meet Indian representatives attending negotiations over greater autonomy, he demurred:. "I am quite satisfied with my views of India. ... I don't want them disturbed by a bloody Indian" (Roberts 1991: 41).

Should the British government concede greater self-government, Churchill warned, there would be drastic consequences. Offering India dominion status of the kind that other former colonies had been given, Churchill argued, would lead to a famine in Britain in which "one-third of our population must vanish speedily from the face of the world" (James 1970: 223). He used the same language of moving toward an "abyss" that he would in 1940 (James 1970: 237) and called the nation to arms, just as he would against the Germans. The British must "fight with every scrap of strength we can command" against Indian autonomy (Charmley 1993: 269).

The difference between Churchill and the government was again largely one of cognitive style. The Baldwin government was also opposed to independence for India; given Indian resistance to British rule, key officials merely wanted to make concessions well short of dominion status while maintaining important safeguards. "Their policy was, as later historians have recognized, to concede where necessary but to retain control over the essentials of power for as long as possible," writes Charmley (1993: 246). The Baldwin government was acting pragmatically: "What divided Churchill from Baldwin and company over 'appeasement' was what divided them over India – attitude of mind. ... Despite Churchill's allegations to the contrary, Baldwin and Irwin were not trying to give away the Empire; they were trying to preserve it as best they could given these constraints. The same could be said of their policy towards Germany" (Charmley 1993: 287).

The government's position, in other words, was based on rational thinking in a way that Churchill's stance was not. Lord Irwin, the realist with whom we will become better acquainted in Chapter 8, "pursued a humane, enlightened, and, above all, a realistic policy. ... [W]hile maintaining law and order and acting firmly in the face of civil disobedience, Irwin realized that negotiation would have to come" (James 1970: 216). Even as the future Viscount negotiated greater autonomy with Indian politicians, he "was no starry-eyed idealist with visions of a better world. ... His mind ... was a well-tempered instrument. ... In the place of an unworldly saint they often encountered a logician," writes Birkenhead (1966: 263).

Churchill, in contrast, was a romantic with an intuitive and nonrational thinking style. He resisted any compromise, even the one in 1935. The Government of India Bill left Britain in control of the central government in India, while creating an all-India federation and conceding only greater self-government in local administration (Charmley 1993: 275). Churchill had reasons for all of his positions but "little inclination to make concessions to critics or to give serious weight to the possibility he might be wrong. In contrast his political foes continually invoked the need to strike reasonable balances between conflicting considerations" (Tetlock and Tyler 1996: 167).

The Wilderness: Churchill's Romantic Isolation

Churchill's cognitive style kept him out of the cabinet. By crying wolf on the Indian issue he became a lone wolf. It "debased the language of alarmism" and ruined his reputation (James 1996: 135). His position on India is one of the main reasons that he spent years in what he called the "wilderness," something that of course subsequently added to his reputation as a romantic hero. Chamberlain confided to his sister, "The question is whether Winston, who would certainly help on the Treasury bench in the Commons, would help or hinder in Cabinet or in Council. ... Would he wear me out resisting *rash* suggestions?" (CC: 1456 [emphasis added]). He was regarded as impulsive and emotional, not willing to retain an open mind and consider other points of view – and not just by Chamberlain (CC: 966–7; Eade 1953: 87). Another Chamberlain letter reads, "That is Winston all over. His are summer storms, violent but of short duration and often followed by sunshine. But they make him uncommonly difficult to deal with" (DL, 5 August 1939). After the remilitarization of the Rhineland, the prime minister wrote, "I am thankful in these circumstances we have not got Winston as a colleague. He is in the usual excited condition that comes on him when he smells war, and if he were in the Cabinet we should be spending all our time in holding him down instead of getting on with our business" (DL, 14 March 1936). Churchill would get in the way of the "careful diplomacy" necessary to avert war (DL, 14 November 1936). Chamberlain, as described earlier, did not oppose the use of threats, but Churchill was too "reckless" (DL, 9 April 1939). "There are more ways of killing a cat than strangling it and if I refuse to take Winston into the Cabinet to please those who say it would frighten Hitler it doesn't follow that the idea of frightening Hitler, or rather of convincing him that it would not pay him to use force, need be abandoned" (DL, 15 July 1939).

A newspaper article written in the 1930s summarized the prevailing image of Churchill at the time:

[A]s a statesman, Mr. Churchill is undoubtedly a conspicuous failure. Twenty years ago it was a fool-proof prophecy that one day he would be Prime Minister. But, in spite of his powerful mind and other dazzling gifts, in spite of his innumerable opportunities in a long and authoritative Ministerial career on one side or the other, in spite of the war itself . . . not one great or solid achievement stands to his name in any sphere of political endeavour. (CHAR: 2/576A-C)

The problem was his romanticism:

He is like a middle-aged schoolboy who cannot outgrow an early passion for colossal armies, mighty Empires, stupendous catastrophes, gigantic enemies in mass formation and a warrior's gleaming helmet under which he alone is to lead the armies, save the Empires, defy the catastrophes and annihilate his enemies over and over again. That is how he thinks and talks. (CHAR: 2/576A-C)

These are, of course, the downsides of the romantic according to the realist. Churchill, however, exposed the weaknesses of the highly rational thinker. Attempting to balance so many competing considerations and forces, the result was paralysis. In a famous speech to parliament made before Chamberlain became prime minister, Churchill complained, "The Government simply cannot make up their minds. . . . So they go on in strange paradox, decided only to be undecided, resolved to be irresolute, adamant for drift, solid for fluidity, all powerful-to be impotent. So we go on preparing more months and years – precious, perhaps vital, to the greatness of Britain – for the locusts to eat" (James 1970: 296). A few years later he sounded the same notes: "There is nothing to be said for not carrying out that policy [of rearmament] in all its vigour and integrity. To go thus far, and not to take all the consequential and logical steps which are required, would be to combine the dangers of both courses without the security of either" (CC: 1530); also Hansard, 24 March 1938, col. 1444–55; 14 March 1938, col. 93–103). In Chapter 8, we see whether Churchill would do the same when faced with the realities of governing.

8 "In Defeat, Defiance:" Churchill in Words (1935–1939) and in Deeds (1940)

Chapter 7 made the case that Churchill was a romantic and that this explains his opposition to the realist foreign policy response of Chamberlain's government to the rising German threat in the 1930s. What looks superficially like a standard deterrence approach – demonstrate resolve so as to send costly signals of credibility to Hitler – actually has its roots in Churchill's romanticism and his stress on will in addition to power. Nevertheless, readers might still be skeptical for two reasons.

First, as is the case with any piece of qualitative research, we run the risk of imposing our categories on the historical record, unconsciously picking those aspects of the story that work with our theory. Perhaps another analyst might find just as many instances of rational thinking on the part of Churchill and emotional, impulsive, or intuitive decisions by Chamberlain. Indeed, there is no such thing as a purely rational or completely irrational person, something our analysis of the prime minister's cognitive style in Chapter 7 demonstrates.

Second, it is all well and good to show that Churchill criticized the Chamberlain appeasement policy with romantic imagery and rhetoric. He had this luxury as long as he was out of government. The "wilderness" has its advantages. In this view, structural constraints both sharpen the mind and impose accountability. They make you think unromantically, in terms of the consequences – in other words, like an instrumentally rational realist. What do romantics do when they have the responsibility of governing? We must determine whether Churchill's romanticism influenced his behavior while in office. Did this realist–romantic divide persist past his inclusion into the cabinet? Many have accused Churchill of opportunism, unfairly castigating the government for something he would have been forced to do himself.

Mindful of the first problem, my co-author for part of this chapter, Therese Anders, and I conduct a quantitative analysis of the language used by Chamberlain and other government speakers, comparing it to that used by Churchill. Using "text as data" confirms the argument of Chapter 7. Chamberlain and Churchill have different cognitive styles, with the former's being much more procedurally and instrumentally rational in character – objective, deliberative, and consequentialist. By comparison, Churchill's syntax is much more emotionally laden, certain, and decisive. Chamberlain uses words that indicate a greater acknowledgment of and attention to structural constraints. Churchill's discourse indicates a belief in agency. It is romantic, marked by words associated with summoning energy and resolve in a fight for moral ideals. Both inductive and deductive textual analysis reveal the same results.

The approach to the second problem is considerably different. I go to the archives, most importantly transcripts of cabinet meetings in May 1940. Churchill took over as prime minister that month as France was collapsing, the bulk of the British army was trapped on the northern shores of France, and help from the United States was still nowhere on the horizon. This case is tailor-made for testing my argument. We can judge whether the romanticism of a leader matters when a state is up against a wall. During this period, Churchill shared office with both Chamberlain, who had been demoted, and Viscount Halifax, still foreign secretary. They now all had the same responsibilities for governing, allowing us to observe variation in their response to the same information and the same strategic situation. In this case there is even over-time variation in Britain's position, just prior to and immediately following the collapse of France.

There are clear expectations here. Realist thinkers will adjust goals to reflect current power realities. In case of impending defeat or major losses, they will seek accommodations that leave the country better off than if it were to continue to fight. In other words, they behave as instrumentally rational actors. We find the same insight in rationalist bargaining models. If war, which is costly, arises only when states disagree about who is stronger or more resolved to win, the act of fighting reveals what was previously private information (Fearon 1995; Goemans 2000). If we are losing, and we are epistemically motivated, we should adjust accordingly, becoming more likely to concede as our prospects deteriorate.

This, of course, does not capture how romantics will approach such a situation. As has been seen, romantics are not consequentialists who adjust their behavior depending on the structural environment. Instead, they seek to overcome obstacles through force of will. Romantics do not compromise on their ideals to save what they can. They would rather go down fighting, a tendency emblematic of deontological (not consequentialist) moral judgment. In Churchill's (1948) famous epigraph, he declared: "In Defeat, Defiance." "Defiance," of course, is a highly emotional word, not a cold and instrumentally rational one. It can be uttered only in those instances in which a more instrumentally rational individual would have cut his or her losses.

When Churchill became prime minister, he continued to behave in a way that was consistent with his romanticism. In May and June 1940, he successfully fought back efforts to explore a negotiated peace with the Nazis pushed by the highly rational foreign secretary, Viscount Halifax, in light of Britain's deteriorating position. The foreign minister was particularly important during this period. Halifax was Chamberlain's most important ally after he assumed his post in 1937 and the heir apparent to the prime minister. Halifax, rather than Chamberlain, was Churchill's main rival in the cabinet when the most fateful decisions in the war were made, although he received the support of the former prime minister. I therefore devote considerable attention to his cognitive style.

Churchill remained defiant even though he was no more confident about Britain's chances than his colleagues. His position actually inverted an instrumentally rationalist logic. Britain must continue fighting precisely because it was losing. Churchill argued that Britain could not get a better deal at that point, with its fleet intact, than if it were to lose the war. This is not consistent with any contortion of what might constitute rational thinking.

May 1940 is not just an ideal case methodologically; it was profoundly important historically. Had Churchill approached Hitler and Mussolini, it is quite possible that Germany would have allowed Britain to keep its fleet and its army, provided, of course, that it pulled out of the conflict and left the fascists to fight a single-front war against the Soviet Union. If the United States had still entered the war, it might have been only in the Pacific against Japan, since its ally in all but name had settled across the other ocean. The romanticism of one man seems to have been a necessary condition for the future direction of world history.

Churchill by the Numbers: A Quantitative Analysis of Parliamentary Speeches, 1934–1939 (with Therese Anders)

Quantitative discourse analysis using "text as data" is based on the idea that the way we talk reveals something about the way we think. Therese Anders and I composed a data set of all the speeches made by Churchill in the House of Commons from the beginning of the Baldwin government on 7 June 1935 until Churchill joined the cabinet as naval secretary on 3 September 1939. By focusing on parliamentary speeches rather than those made in other fora, we can develop a matching set of texts for the government. For every time that Churchill spoke, we also collected the speech made by the official government spokesperson in the debate, oftentimes Chamberlain but sometimes a surrogate. If the prime minister did not speak during a debate, the first comprehensive speech act of a high-ranking government representative was included. The total number of documents is 136, equally split between Churchill and the government. For the two instances in which the speech by Chamberlain was less than 100 words, we instead included the address of another government representative. All House of Commons speeches by Churchill were included, regardless of topic. We coded each speech based on whether it pertained primarily to foreign policy and on whether it referred to Germany. Approximately 91 percent of all speeches in the population are foreign policy speeches and 63 percent mention a word such as "Germany," "German," "Hitler," or "Nazi" at least each once. Of the government speeches, 32 percent were made by Chamberlain.

Discriminant Analysis

Our first cut at the data employs an inductive approach called discriminant analysis, which is based on a simple premise. We figure out the words that best discriminate between different speakers (Grimmer 2010). Words that discriminate are those that are used frequently by one type of speaker and not very much by the other type – in this case, Churchill and government speakers. We do this by calculating for every word used in any of these speeches a "mutual information" coefficient; these coefficients range from 0 to 1, with higher scores indicating more discrimination.

Mutual information is calculated using the following formula:

$$MI(X_j) = \frac{n_{j,chu}}{D} \log_2 \frac{n_{j,chu}D}{n_j n_{chu}} + \frac{n_{j,gov}}{D} \log_2 \frac{n_{j,gov}D}{n_j n_{gov}}$$
$$+ \frac{n_{-j,chu}}{D} \log_2 \frac{n_{-j,chu}D}{n_{-j} n_{chu}} + \frac{n_{-j,gov}}{D} \log_2 \frac{n_{-j,gov}D}{n_{-j} n_{gov}}$$

n_{chu} = Number of "Churchill" documents

n_{gov} = Number of "Government" documents

$D = n_{chu} + n_{gov}$

$n_j = \sum_{i=1}^{D} X_{i,j}$ (No. of documents that word $X_{i,j}$ appears)

n_{-j} = No. of documents that word $X_{i,j}$ does not appear

$n_{j,chu}$ = No. of "Churchill" documents that word $X_{i,j}$ appears

$n_{j,gov}$ = No. of "Government" documents that word $X_{i,j}$ appears

$n_{-j,chu}$ = No. of "Churchill" documents that word $X_{i,j}$ does not appear

$n_{-j,gov}$ = No. of "Government" documents that word $X_{i,j}$ does not appear

This equation produces a mutual information score closer to 1, as the number of speeches by a speaker (or type of speaker) include a particular word and the number of speeches given by another speaker (or type of speaker) do not include that word. However, it also matters how frequently that word appears in texts as a whole. If a word is used only once by one speaker over the course of several speeches and never by another speaker, its mutual information score will still be low. A word is non-discriminatory if it is used equally by two different speakers but also if it is never used at all. It should be noted that discriminant analysis does not distinguish between texts that use a word one time or more than one time. Either a text contains a word or it does not.

Mutual information scores tell us if a word discriminates, but not who is more likely to use it. To tell us which of the two types of speakers is particularly fond of a word, we calculate a difference score by subtracting the number of speeches in which a word is used by government speakers from the number of Churchill speeches in which it is used. If a word is used more by Churchill, the difference score will be negative; if it is used more by the government, the score will be positive.

$$\text{Difference} = n_{j,gov} - n_{j,chu}$$

When we plot words based on these two scores, we get a U-shaped curve with the words on the upper left most associated with Churchill and those on the upper right most associated with the government (Figure 8.1). The two most discriminating stems for the government are "ep" and "Churchill." The former is a shortening of Churchill's constituency – he was the Honorable Member from Epping. The high MI scores of the two terms show that in any debate involving Churchill, the government felt the need to address his claims.

Table 8.1 provides the list of words that best distinguish Churchill from the government up to and including a mutual information criterion value of .04, using a Porter stemmer so as to break down words into their etymological essence. For instance, "astonish" and "astonishment" are for our purposes the same word. Other stemmers yielded virtually identical results. *P*-values are calculated using a difference in proportion *z*-test based on the proportion of documents in which a specific word appears in government speeches and in Churchill speeches. They give a sense of the statistical significance of the results for each word since there is no commonly accepted benchmark for interpreting MI scores. Table 8.2 does the same for government speakers.

Looking first at the words that most distinguish government speakers, a number of things stand out in the results. First is the substantially higher use of words associated with instrumental rationality. These

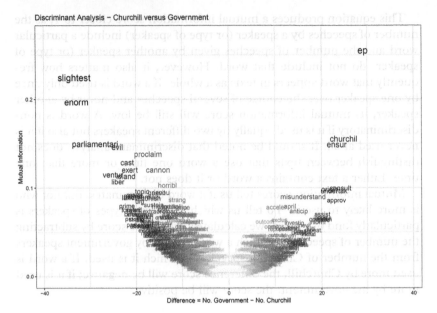

Figure 8.1 Graphical presentation of the discriminant analysis results. Words that distinguish Churchill are plotted on the left, words distinguishing government speakers on the right.

include words stressing interests and outcomes – desir, prefer, intent, intend, benefit, obtain, result, and outcom. Second, we observe words indicating deliberative thinking, such as anticip, base, conclus, investig, consider, determin, observ, report, review, conclud, envisage, approxim, research, inquir, revis, inspect, assumpt, and contempl. These terms include words indicating an emphasis on objective evaluation – awar, conscious, and accur. Third, words that indicate a greater acknowledgment and attention to structural constraints distinguish government speakers from Churchill – inevit, necess, necessity, and adjust. That the government's syntax is heavy on procedural rationality, instrumental rationality, and structure is highly consistent with the premise that Chamberlain and his colleagues were realists with a rational cognitive style and higher epistemic motivation.

Turning to Churchill, along with words that are associated with armed conflict – such as fire, captur, explos, strike, fight, die, quarrel, forc, violent, and injur – his use of terminology invoking the summoning of energy and strength for a struggle stands out: ventur, exert, endeavour, forward, strong, strength, mighti, urg, fight, confront, combin, command, vigour, embark, and spring. This is consistent with our

Table 8.1 *Words that distinguish Churchill.*

	Stemmed Word	Mutual Information	Difference	*p*-Value of Difference
1	slightest	0.225	−33	0.000
2	enorm	0.197	−33	0.000
3	parliamentari	0.150	−29	0.000
4	evil	0.146	−24	0.000
5	proclaim	0.138	−17	0.000
6	cast	0.129	−22	0.000
7	cannon	0.120	−15	0.000
8	exert	0.120	−21	0.000
9	ventur	0.115	−25	0.000
10	island	0.113	−22	0.000
11	liber	0.107	−24	0.000
12	horribl	0.103	−13	0.000
13	topic	0.096	−19	0.000
14	grievou	0.095	−15	0.000
15	excit	0.095	−15	0.000
16	mass	0.092	−20	0.000
17	gather	0.091	−21	0.000
18	nazi	0.090	−16	0.000
19	suprem	0.090	−19	0.000
20	land	0.089	−22	0.000
21	astonish	0.088	−17	0.000
22	strang	0.087	−11	0.001
23	urg	0.085	−19	0.000
24	sustain	0.081	−16	0.000
25	prime	0.080	−22	0.000
26	fortifi	0.079	−13	0.000
27	melancholi	0.079	−13	0.000
28	vigour	0.079	−13	0.000
29	crime	0.078	−10	0.001
30	injur	0.078	−10	0.001
31	grip	0.078	−10	0.001
32	flow	0.075	−14	0.000
33	forward	0.075	−21	0.000
34	safeti	0.075	−21	0.000
35	extraordinari	0.073	−15	0.000
36	agreeabl	0.071	−12	0.001
37	mood	0.071	−12	0.001
38	baltic	0.070	−9	0.002
39	unpleas	0.070	−9	0.002
40	god	0.070	−9	0.002
41	assign	0.070	−9	0.002
42	plead	0.070	−9	0.002
43	persever	0.070	−9	0.002
44	cruel	0.070	−9	0.002
45	subjug	0.070	−9	0.002
46	sphere	0.070	−18	0.000

Table 8.1 (*cont.*)

	Stemmed Word	Mutual Information	Difference	*p*-Value of Difference
47	britain	0.070	−21	0.000
48	life	0.070	−21	0.000
49	faith	0.069	−19	0.000
50	violent	0.067	−13	0.001
51	surviv	0.067	−13	0.001
52	unfold	0.067	−13	0.001
53	half	0.067	−18	0.000
54	bench	0.067	−18	0.000
55	credit	0.066	−14	0.001
56	master	0.066	−14	0.001
57	process	0.065	−20	0.001
58	law	0.064	−19	0.001
59	strong	0.064	−20	0.001
60	misfortun	0.063	−11	0.001
61	resist	0.063	−18	0.001
62	recov	0.061	−8	0.004
63	swept	0.061	−8	0.004
64	stream	0.061	−8	0.004
65	projectil	0.061	−8	0.004
66	disconcert	0.061	−8	0.004
67	strip	0.061	−8	0.004
68	highest	0.061	−17	0.001
69	conserv	0.060	−14	0.001
70	reproach	0.058	−15	0.001
71	parliament	0.058	−19	0.001
72	strength	0.058	−19	0.001
73	bound	0.057	−19	0.001
74	die	0.056	−10	0.003
75	dark	0.056	−10	0.003
76	fine	0.056	−10	0.003
77	armi	0.056	−18	0.001
78	undoubtedli	0.056	−18	0.001
79	injuri	0.055	−14	0.002
80	forc	0.055	−17	0.001
81	highli	0.054	−15	0.002
82	obstruct	0.053	−7	0.007
83	degener	0.053	−7	0.007
84	rifl	0.053	−7	0.007
85	illumin	0.053	−7	0.007
86	boast	0.053	−7	0.007
87	aspers	0.053	−7	0.007
88	improvid	0.053	−7	0.007
89	coher	0.053	−7	0.007
90	absurd	0.053	−11	0.003
91	prudent	0.053	−11	0.003
92	contrari	0.053	−17	0.002

Table 8.1 (*cont.*)

	Stemmed Word	Mutual Information	Difference	*p*-Value of Difference
93	confront	0.052	−14	0.002
94	reassur	0.052	−14	0.002
95	elect	0.052	−15	0.002
96	eye	0.052	−15	0.002
97	extrem	0.052	−18	0.002
98	fight	0.050	−17	0.002
99	admir	0.050	−17	0.002
100	neutral	0.049	−9	0.005
101	lobbi	0.049	−9	0.005
102	transform	0.049	−9	0.005
103	baffl	0.049	−9	0.005
104	triumph	0.049	−9	0.005
105	outrag	0.049	−9	0.005
106	hideou	0.049	−9	0.005
107	hundr	0.049	−13	0.003
108	quarrel	0.049	−14	0.003
109	freedom	0.049	−15	0.003
110	throw	0.049	−15	0.003
111	manner	0.049	−17	0.003
112	gain	0.048	−16	0.003
113	dwell	0.047	−12	0.004
114	interchang	0.046	−6	0.012
115	applianc	0.046	−6	0.012
116	tripl	0.046	−6	0.012
117	tardi	0.046	−6	0.012
118	murder	0.046	−6	0.012
119	cope	0.046	−6	0.012
120	darken	0.046	−6	0.012
121	gestur	0.046	−6	0.012
122	shift	0.046	−6	0.012
123	forbid	0.046	−6	0.012
124	miscalcul	0.046	−6	0.012
125	rail	0.046	−6	0.012
126	float	0.046	−6	0.012
127	stultifi	0.046	−6	0.012
128	molest	0.046	−6	0.012
129	imprud	0.046	−6	0.012
130	massiv	0.046	−6	0.012
131	vanquish	0.046	−6	0.012
132	captiou	0.046	−6	0.012
133	consensu	0.046	−6	0.012
134	unpopular	0.046	−6	0.012
135	deterr	0.046	−10	0.005
136	vagu	0.046	−10	0.005
137	lament	0.046	−10	0.005
138	virtu	0.046	−10	0.005

Table 8.1 (*cont.*)

	Stemmed Word	Mutual Information	Difference	*p*-Value of Difference
139	spring	0.046	−10	0.005
140	pariti	0.046	−11	0.004
141	democraci	0.046	−13	0.004
142	defens	0.046	−13	0.004
143	fire	0.046	−14	0.004
144	absolut	0.046	−17	0.003
145	occur	0.046	−17	0.003
146	man	0.046	−17	0.004
147	honour	0.045	−15	0.004
148	doubt	0.044	−14	0.005
149	thrown	0.043	−12	0.005
150	session	0.043	−13	0.005
151	contin	0.042	−8	0.009
152	conced	0.042	−8	0.009
153	humili	0.042	−8	0.009
154	preciou	0.042	−8	0.009
155	regain	0.042	−8	0.009
156	combin	0.042	−14	0.006
157	convict	0.042	−14	0.006
158	affair	0.041	−16	0.006
159	militari	0.041	−16	0.006
160	hitler	0.040	−9	0.009
161	artilleri	0.040	−9	0.009
162	path	0.040	−9	0.009
163	prescrib	0.040	−9	0.009
164	harbour	0.040	−10	0.008
165	enforc	0.040	−10	0.008
166	junctur	0.040	−10	0.008
167	embark	0.040	−10	0.008
168	moral	0.040	−12	0.007
169	fullest	0.040	−12	0.007
170	perfect	0.040	−13	0.006
171	sea	0.040	−15	0.006
172	germani	0.040	−16	0.006

All words with a mutual information criterion value of 0.04 and above using a Porter stemmer. Ordered for mutual information criterion and using difference as a tie breaker.

understanding of Churchill as a romantic who emphasizes agency. We also see words indicating resoluteness in the face of a great ordeal – sustain, stand, resist, fortif, persever, sacrifice, misfortune, and cope. Agency is also indicated in words indicative of action that affects the environment, rather than vice versa –vanquish, transform, decis, master, and triumph. Churchill uses more moralistic terms that indicate the kind

Table 8.2 *Words that distinguish government speakers.*

	Stemmed Word	Mutual Information	Difference	p-Value of Difference
1	ep	0.255	29	0.000
2	churchil	0.155	25	0.000
3	ensur	0.149	23	0.000
4	consult	0.100	24	0.000
5	origin	0.098	22	0.000
6	undertak	0.097	23	0.000
7	misunderstand	0.090	16	0.000
8	approv	0.086	23	0.000
9	april	0.079	13	0.000
10	acceler	0.078	10	0.001
11	anticip	0.073	15	0.000
12	assist	0.070	20	0.000
13	imposs	0.066	20	0.000
14	due	0.066	20	0.000
15	opportun	0.064	20	0.001
16	enter	0.064	20	0.001
17	gave	0.064	20	0.001
18	exclus	0.063	11	0.001
19	inform	0.061	19	0.001
20	outcom	0.061	8	0.004
21	investig	0.060	14	0.001
22	inevit	0.058	16	0.001
23	omit	0.056	10	0.003
24	compos	0.056	10	0.003
25	beg	0.055	14	0.002
26	fulli	0.054	18	0.002
27	perform	0.054	13	0.002
28	constantli	0.054	13	0.002
29	represent	0.053	11	0.003
30	repeat.	0.052	18	0.002
31	articl	0.051	16	0.002
32	previou	0.051	16	0.002
33	desir	0.049	16	0.003
34	prefer	0.049	15	0.003
35	includ	0.047	17	0.003
36	intend	0.047	17	0.003
37	length	0.046	13	0.004
38	entrust	0.046	11	0.004
39	output	0.046	10	0.005
40	commission	0.046	6	0.012
41	briefli	0.046	6	0.012
42	inspect	0.046	6	0.012
43	membership	0.046	6	0.012
44	recess	0.046	6	0.012
45	divers	0.046	6	0.012
46	perspect	0.046	6	0.012

Table 8.2 (*cont.*)

	Stemmed Word	Mutual Information	Difference	*p*-Value of Difference
47	hasten	0.046	6	0.012
48	evolv	0.046	6	0.012
49	slightli	0.046	6	0.012
50	optimist	0.046	6	0.012
51	expressli	0.046	6	0.012
52	intent	0.042	16	0.005
53	necess	0.042	14	0.006
54	alloc	0.042	8	0.009
55	X1st	0.042	8	0.009
56	candid	0.042	8	0.009
57	meantim	0.042	8	0.009
58	supplement	0.042	8	0.009
59	item	0.041	11	0.007
60	consciou	0.041	11	0.007
61	result	0.040	15	0.006
62	suggest	0.040	14	0.007
63	prospect	0.040	13	0.006
64	competit	0.040	9	0.009
65	shortli	0.040	9	0.009
66	absenc	0.040	9	0.009
67	allud	0.040	9	0.009

All words with a mutual information criterion value of 0.04 and above using a Porter stemmer. Ordered for mutual information criterion and using difference as a tie breaker.

of sharp good-versus-evil distinction we would expect from a moral deontic – molest, murder, dark, evil, liber, life, grievous, reproach, freedom, honour, horrible, democracy, moral, crime, virtu, cruel, hideous, mortal, convict, and peril.

We also observe a number of words indicating a System I decision-making style based on certain, decisive action, betraying an "implemental mindset" – bound, faith, undoubtedli, and absolut. Churchill's discourse is also one of dramatic extremes rather than utilitarian moderation ("on the one hand, on the other hand"), something indicated by the use of terms such as enorm, slightest, suprem, extrem, highest, vast, massiv, extraordinari, fullest, perfect, and prodig. Churchill's syntax is also much more emotionally laden, a sharp contrast to the government's cold calculativeness. Rather than "ask," he says "plead"; rather than being displeased, we see "outrage" and "lament." Rather than "lose," we see "humiliate" and "subjug." Rather than "consider," we have "dwell." Rather than being surprised, we see "astonish." Rather than being simply pleased, Churchill uses "revel." Rather than "fail," we have "stultif."

Rather than "say," we have "proclaim." Churchill also uses words such as excit, melancholi, and mood at much higher levels.

Analyses with "Diction"

Discriminant analysis is a largely inductive method that generates the words that are the best, most distinctive predictors of a particular speaker. Its results rely on the interpretation of the observer. Mindful of this potential source of bias, we undertake a more deductive approach based on a computer program known as *Diction*, developed by Roderick Hart (2009), which provides scores for texts on more than two dozen categories grounded in linguistic theory. In excess of 10,000 words are assigned to different "dictionaries," lists of words thought to capture a particular concept. *Diction* is specifically designed for political dialogue and has been used to study a diverse variety of political phenomena, particularly in American politics (see all the contributions in Hart 2014). More so than any other program, its categories allow us to judge the rationality and romanticism of specific leaders' syntax. Each text receives a score on different variables depending on the frequency of words uttered from that dictionary. This score is based on the assumption that the frequency of word use tells us something about the speaker – one (but not the only) approach in textual analysis.

This provides for a more explicit and deductive test of our hypotheses and a robustness check of the discriminant analysis. Table 8.3 shows the results of a regression with Churchill as a dummy variable, comparing his speeches to those of government speakers. We also include controls for year (with 1935 as the baseline), whether foreign policy was being discussed, and whether Germany was mentioned. Foreign policy speeches and those with references to Germany might be more likely to include certain words, and we have reason to believe that the deteriorating situation over the course of 1935–1939 would also affect discourse. For ease of interpretation, Figure 8.2 is a plot showing the effect of Churchill being the speaker, either yes or no, on scores for these variables. It presents coefficients with 90 and 95 percent confidence intervals. Each one of these lines is based on a separate regression analysis, with the score for each syntactical category as the dependent variable. All coefficients are standardized so as to facilitate comparison.

We can look at a number of variables to check the face validity of the results. Unsurprisingly, government speakers score more highly on "accomplishment" words, which indicate the completion of tasks, such as "establish," "finish," "influence" and "proceed." It is the government after all, that is engaging in foreign policy-making, and it has political

Table 8.3 *Regression results for the analysis of* Diction *scores comparing speeches*

	Accomplishment (1)	Aggression (2)	Ambivalence (3)	Blame (4)	Cognition (5)	Collectives (6)	Communication (7)
							Dependent Variable
Churchill	-0.56**	0.59***	-0.02	0.4*	-0.58**	-0.09	-0.51**
	(0.17)	(0.16)	(0.18)	(0.17)	(0.17)	(0.18)	(0.16)
Germany	0.15	0.47*	0.15	-0.10	-0.12	0.12	-0.24
	(0.20)	(0.18)	(0.21)	(0.20)	(0.20)	(0.21)	(0.20)
Foreign Policy	0.22	0.58	-0.38	-0.81*	0.32	0.66	-0.49
	(0.33)	(0.30)	(0.34)	(0.33)	(0.33)	(0.34)	(0.32)
1936	0.40	-0.32	0.27	-0.46	0.32	-0.39	0.57*
	(0.30)	(0.27)	(0.31)	(0.29)	(0.29)	(0.30)	(0.28)
1937	0.22	0.003	0.30	-0.60	0.21	-0.61	0.15
	(0.32)	(0.29)	(0.33)	(0.31)	(0.32)	(0.32)	(0.30)
1938	0.003	0.01	0.56	-0.58	0.49	-0.36	0.25
	(0.30)	(0.27)	(0.31)	(0.30)	(0.30)	(0.30)	(0.28)
1939	0.19	0.15	0.15	-0.45	0.34	-0.60	-0.02
	(0.34)	(0.30)	(0.35)	(0.33)	(0.33)	(0.34)	(0.32)
Constant	-0.20	-1.05**	-0.04	1.06**	-0.24	-0.22	0.60
	(0.40)	(0.36)	(0.42)	(0.40)	(0.40)	(0.41)	(0.38)
Observations	136	136	136	136	136	136	136
Adjusted R^2	0.06	0.23	-0.01	0.08	0.07	0.03	0.15

Note: * $p < 0.05$; ** $p < 0.01$; *** $p < 0.001$.
Independent variables are a dummy variable for Churchill as speaker, mention of Germany, foreign policy
OLS regression results with standard errors in parentheses. All dependent variable *Diction* values are expressed

reasons in a public forum to stress the actions it is taking on behalf of the nation-state. Government representatives score significantly higher on "communication" words referring to social interactions and intercourse, such as "listen," "speak," and "declare." This is in keeping with both the government's task of communicating with other nation-states and its preferred appeasement strategy. Also consistent with the latter is the government's higher score on "rapport" – a vocabulary that stresses similarities among groups of people. Examples of words in this dictionary include "consensus" and "camaraderie" as well as what Hart (2009) calls "cooperation" terms indicating interactions that result in a group product.

Churchill has higher "complexity" in his speech, measured by the average number of characters per word used.[1] This is what we would expect for someone known for his colorful and soaring rhetoric, and it

---

[1] This should not be confused with "cognitive complexity," a marker of epistemic motivation.

by Churchill to those of government speakers, 6/7/1935–9/2/1939. (Cond.)

Complexity (8)	Embellishment (9)	Hardship (10)	Inspiration (11)	Leveling (12)	Passivity (13)	Praise (14)	Rapport (15)	Variety (16)
0.32	0.40[*]	0.34[*]	−0.03	0.43[*]	0.04	0.75[***]	−0.50[**]	0.30
(0.18)	(0.17)	(0.17)	(0.18)	(0.17)	(0.18)	(0.16)	(0.17)	(0.18)
−0.12	−0.16	0.56[**]	0.17	−0.13	0.34	0.01	0.30	−0.08
(0.21)	(0.20)	(0.20)	(0.21)	(0.21)	(0.21)	(0.19)	(0.21)	(0.21)
0.82[*]	−0.50	−0.16	−0.22	−0.09	−0.15	0.18	−0.17	0.35
(0.34)	(0.33)	(0.33)	(0.34)	(0.33)	(0.34)	(0.32)	(0.34)	(0.34)
0.36	−0.29	0.24	−0.21	0.13	−0.71[*]	0.02	−0.19	0.04
(0.30)	(0.30)	(0.29)	(0.30)	(0.30)	(0.30)	(0.28)	(0.30)	(0.31)
0.45	−0.21	−0.07	−0.09	0.23	−0.35	0.33	−0.003	−0.11
(0.32)	(0.32)	(0.31)	(0.32)	(0.32)	(0.32)	(0.30)	(0.32)	(0.33)
0.44	0.22	0.12	0.001	0.18	−0.32	0.55	−0.40	0.02
(0.30)	(0.30)	(0.29)	(0.30)	(0.30)	(0.30)	(0.28)	(0.30)	(0.31)
0.25	−0.15	0.02	0.59	0.79[*]	−0.65	−0.02	−0.42	0.23
(0.34)	(0.34)	(0.33)	(0.34)	(0.34)	(0.34)	(0.32)	(0.34)	(0.35)
−1.17[**]	0.46	−0.47	0.11	−0.30	0.35	−0.74	0.43	−0.45
(0.41)	(0.40)	(0.40)	(0.41)	(0.40)	(0.41)	(0.38)	(0.41)	(0.42)
136	136	136	136	136	136	136	136	136
0.03	0.06	0.08	0.02	0.05	0.02	0.15	0.04	−0.01

focus, and year with 1935 as a baseline. Each column heading indicates a separate dependent variable. as z-scores with a mean of zero and a standard deviation of 1.

adds to the face validity of the results. The difference with the government, however, is significant only at the $p < 0.1$ level. Churchill also has a higher "embellishment" level, measuring the ratio of adjectives to verbs.

We turn now to the more important speech categories. The category of "cognition," words referring to cerebral processes, is best suited to judging variation in rationality. Hart (2009) notes that this includes "rationalistic" words such as "estimate," "examine," "reasonable," and "strategies" as well as "calculative" words such as "diagnose" and "analyze." Here the results are striking: *cognition is the variable that most distinguishes Churchill from those in the government.* The speaker, dichotomized as a dummy variable, accounts for 8 percent of the variance in use of these types of words and is significant at the $p < 0.001$ level.

To judge whether Churchill was a more romantic speaker than his government colleagues, I utilize the same categories employed by Bligh et al. (2004) in their study of "charismatic" leadership in American political discourse after the 9/11 attacks. Romantic leaders are charismatic leaders. Indeed, Max Weber, who first articulated this concept,

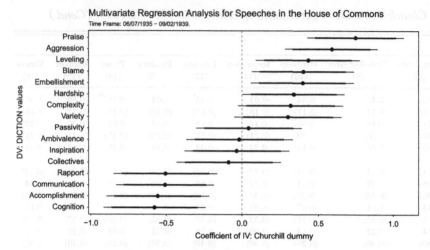

Figure 8.2 Churchill's romantic discourse.
Plotted are the OLS coefficients of the Churchill dummy for the
regression models in Table 8.3 with 90 percent and 95 percent
confidence intervals. All dependent variable *Diction* values are expressed
as z-scores with a mean of zero and a standard deviation of 1. All models
include binary variables for the following indicators: Germany dummy,
foreign policy dummy, and for the years 1936 through 1939. The
number of observations is 136.

sees charisma as a form of romantic authority based on emotional and
principled appeals that is antithetical to "rational" culture. Koch (1993)
writes that for Weber, charisma links "the creative, intuitive revelation of
individuals to the emotional longing of followers for change" (140).
Charisma is a creative force that transcends structural obstacles, "an
act of creative human intuition that is free from the confines of environmental necessity" (66). This is juxtaposed to instrumental rationality:
"Individuals may adjust themselves to the institutional structure but this
does not constitute revolutionary 'will'; it may merely be the instrumental calculation of the best means of survival within an already existing
social order" (141).

The results are consistent with the notion of Churchill as a romantic.
Churchill scores more highly than the government on what are called
"aggression" words in Diction. This is something of a misnomer, as the
category captures much more than physical violence. It measures "human
competition and forceful action," according to Hart (2009), with terms
connoting physical energy (e.g., blast, crash, explode, collide), social
domination (e.g., conquest, attacking), and goal-directedness (e.g.,

crusade, commanded, challenging, overcome), as well as words associated with personal triumph (e.g., mastered), excess human energy (e.g., pound, shove), and resistance (e.g., prevent, defend). "Aggression" words tap into romanticism, since they indicate dramatic tests of wills. Somewhat surprisingly, Churchill does not score any lower than Chamberlain and the government on "ambivalence" – that is, words indicating hesitation or uncertainty. These include hedges such as "perhaps" or inexactness such as "almost." Nor does he have a lower score for "passivity," which measures inactive words such as "submit" or "refrain."

As described earlier, romantics often describe a period of struggle for which a group's resolve must be steeled, but which will ultimately result in a triumph. We see this in the results. Churchill scores higher on "hardship" vocabulary. These words include "killers," "enemies," "betrayal," "slavery," and "exploitation." This seems to capture the grim picture that Churchill was painting of international affairs at the time. So too does Churchill's high use of "blame" vocabulary, which includes denigrating terms such as "mean," "naïve," "stupid," "cruel," and "malicious." Bligh et al. (2004) combine these two sets of terms in an "adversity" index on which charismatic speakers score more highly. Churchill fits this pattern.

However, Churchill combines this dire and negative picture of the present situation with a positive and hopeful future in a typically romantic fashion. While Churchill does not score higher on "inspiration" words measuring positive virtues such as honesty, virtue, courage, and patriotism, he does use many more "praise" words capturing positive personal or social qualities such as "beautiful," "might," "faithful," "noble," and "delightful." These are the opposites of "blame" terms and consistent with a romantic commitment to mobilizing a collectivity into a great national project of resistance (Bligh et al. 2004). This pattern is also in keeping with Churchill's very high score, relative to government speakers, on "leveling," words used to build a sense of social completeness by knocking down social hierarchies and divisions. These words include "totalizing" terms (everybody, each, fully), "permanence" adverbs (always, completely), and "resolute" adjectives (unconditional, absolute).

We note that the results should be biased against finding differences between the speakers given the public nature of the discourse. Government speakers can be expected to eschew uninspiring, cost–benefit analysis of the instrumentally rational variety in public settings, since one of their functions is to move and lead public opinion. In fact, Churchill spent significant time in his speeches on narrow technical issues such as the relative strengths of the German and British air forces, including numbers of reserve forces, training, and production. It was not all blood, toil, tears, and sweat. And yet the differences in syntax are strong and consistent with the argument. We also note that textual data are notoriously noisy, making the results all the more remarkable. Churchill's words were very different than those of the government.

Might these differences simply be a function of Churchill's lack of constraints as a backbencher? As mentioned earlier, it might be the case that those in the opposition, whether backbench insurgents or the government-in-waiting, have the luxury of speaking in romantic terms. If this is true, it should be the case that (1) Churchill's discourse during his wilderness years is no different than that of Labour speakers at the time and (2) his rhetoric demonstrates a marked change once he took the reins of power. Churchill joined the cabinet as First Lord of the Admiralty on 3 September 1939 and became prime minister on 11 May 1940.

Additional analyses show that neither seems to be the case, however. Table 8.4 compares Churchill's *Diction* scores during the debate following the Munich accord when a number of fellow Conservatives abstained from supporting the government and the Labour opposition voted against it. Speeches took place from 3–6 October 1938. The twenty Labour speakers score no higher than the twenty two loyal Conservatives who approved the government's policy on either "blame" (1.95–1.86, respectively), "denial" (6.35–5.34, respectively), or "cognition" (8.64–9.91, respectively). T-tests are not significant at the 95 percent level. Churchill, by comparison, scores 7.86 on blame, 4.58 on denial, and 4.39 on cognition. The difference between Labour (4.89) and loyal Conservatives (3.53) on "inspiration" is significant at the $p < 0.05$ level. However, Churchill is significantly more inclined toward inspirational rhetoric, scoring 9.36 on this measure. Labour is most distinctive in its use of "collectives" (11.60 compared to 6.67). However, Churchill has an even higher scorer on this dimension (15.32).

How did Churchill's discourse change over time? Table 8.5 extends the earlier analysis comparing Churchill to the government by adding in the speeches of Churchill as First Lord of the Admiralty ($N = 11$) and as prime minister from his ascension until December 1940, when the Battle of Britain is thought to have been finally won ($N = 20$). We use a set of dummy variables to estimate the discursive differences of Churchill in these different roles. The baseline category is Churchill in opposition. Regression results indicate that his scores on blame and cognition are not different. While his scores on "praise," "collectives," and "inspiration" did drop when he was brought into government, the differences with the wilderness period disappear when he becomes prime minister.

Table 8.4 *The Diction scores for speakers in the British House of Commons debate on the Munich agreement, 3–6 October 1938.*

	Means of Speakers		Two-Sided Student's T Test			
	Conservative Yes Voters	Labour	Difference	p-Value	Significant at 5%	Churchill
Accomplishment	0.05	0.11	−0.06	0.85	No	−1.53
Aggression	0.08	0.26	−0.19	0.55	No	−0.91
Ambivalence	0.34	−0.36	0.69	0.03	Yes	−0.54
Blame	−0.05	0.01	−0.06	0.83	No	4.00
Cognition	0.28	−0.05	0.33	0.29	No	−1.17
Collectives	−0.60	0.52	−1.12	0.00	Yes	1.36
Communication	0.31	−0.21	0.51	0.06	No	−0.85
Complexity	−0.12	0.12	−0.24	0.47	No	−0.61
Embellishment	−0.14	−0.14	0.00	0.98	No	0.91
Hardship	−0.02	0.23	−0.25	0.44	No	−1.04
Inspiration	−0.52	0.04	−0.55	0.04	Yes	1.85
Leveling terms	−0.17	0.01	−0.18	0.55	No	−1.51
Passivity	−0.28	0.06	−0.33	0.25	No	1.29
Praise	−0.16	−0.05	−0.10	0.72	No	2.59
Rapport	−0.13	0.28	−0.41	0.21	No	−0.96
Variety	−0.31	−0.18	−0.12	0.64	No	2.91

We conduct a difference in means test for Conservative speakers who voted "Yes" on the Munich Agreement ($N = 22$) versus Labour speakers ($N = 20$), for a total of 42 analyzed speeches. To allow for a comparison, we also present the *Diction* scores for Churchill in this debate. All *Diction* values are expressed as *z*-scores with a mean of zero and a standard deviation of 1.

When prime minister, Churchill scores even higher on hardship and aggression than in his wilderness period. It appears that while he had to toe the line somewhat as a mere cabinet member, when he became the leader of the government his rhetorical shackles were taken off. Churchill could be Churchill. The British politician talked less romantically when he first had to work with a cabinet of his former rivals but more romantically when he became the head of government. Therefore there is no consistent effect of governmental participation on his romantic discourse.

More Than Words?: Churchill in Action in May 1940

Textual analysis confirms the story told in Chapter 7 – that the conflict within the Conservative Party between Chamberlain and his allies on the one hand and Churchill (and no real allies) on the other hand was a

Table 8.5 *Regression results for the analysis of* Diction *scores of Churchill's*

	Accomplishment (1)	Aggression (2)	Ambivalence (3)	Blame (4)	Cognition (5)	Collectives (6)	Communication (7)
							Dependent variable:
Germany	0.09	0.06	0.56*	−0.15	−0.30	−0.33	−0.29
	(0.28)	(0.25)	(0.26)	(0.26)	(0.27)	(0.26)	(0.26)
Foreign Policy	0.35	0.89*	−0.81	−1.17**	0.26	0.96*	−0.76
	(0.44)	(0.39)	(0.41)	(0.42)	(0.44)	(0.42)	(0.42)
FLA	0.06	0.51	−0.72*	−0.31	0.23	−0.77*	−0.47
	(0.34)	(0.31)	(0.32)	(0.33)	(0.34)	(0.33)	(0.32)
PM	0.37	0.97***	−0.74**	0.05	−0.33	0.16	−0.44
	(0.26)	(0.23)	(0.24)	(0.24)	(0.26)	(0.25)	(0.24)
Constant	−0.48	−1.12**	0.53	1.23**	0.04	−0.59	1.07**
	(0.38)	(0.34)	(0.36)	(0.36)	(0.38)	(0.37)	(0.36)
Observations	98	98	98	98	98	98	98
Adjusted R^2	−0.005	0.20	0.13	0.09	−0.001	0.07	0.09

Note: * $p < 0.05$; ** $p < 0.01$; *** $p < 0.001$.

Included are dummy variables for speeches that make any reference to Germany, that pertain to a foreign policy OLS regression results with standard errors in parentheses. All dependent variable *Diction* values are expressed

divide between realists and a romantic, between deliberative and object-ive thinkers and an intuitive, impulsive, and emotional (non)thinker. I have not yet established, however, that Churchill's romanticism was decisive in actual practice. Churchill could say what he liked in oppos-ition because he did not face the real constraints of governing. Chamber-lain had complained of this very fact, writing to his sister, "In face of such problems to be badgered and pressed to come out and give a clear, decided, bold, unmistakable lead, show 'ordinary courage' and all the rest of the twaddle is calculated to vex the man who has to take the responsibility for the consequences" (DL: 20 March 1938). As Charmley (1993) puts it:

Churchill had long excoriated lesser men for lack of willpower, convinced that this was at the basis of British weakness. But was the lack of willpower a cause or effect? Had men come to lack the will to power because they lacked the means to it? What were the limits of willpower when faced with the economic "realities behind diplomacy"? Could the force of the human will prevail against the tides of history – or was the man who made the effort doomed to a Canute-like impotence? (367)

As prime minister, Churchill was in an incredibly constrained position. The new prime minister inherited in May 1940 a country on the ropes, a *speeches over time, 6/7/1935–12/19/1940.*

Complexity (8)	Embellishment (9)	Hardship (10)	Inspiration (11)	Leveling (12)	Passivity (13)	Praise (14)	Rapport (15)	Variety (16)
-1.17^{***}	-0.40	0.42	0.28	0.06	0.45	-0.15	0.61^{*}	-0.20
(0.23)	(0.27)	(0.25)	(0.27)	(0.28)	(0.27)	(0.26)	(0.27)	(0.28)
1.20^{**}	-0.66	-0.55	-0.58	-0.21	0.01	0.24	0.07	0.31
(0.37)	(0.42)	(0.40)	(0.42)	(0.44)	(0.43)	(0.41)	(0.43)	(0.44)
-0.23	-0.16	0.11	-0.89^{**}	-0.50	-0.61	-1.12^{***}	-0.13	0.40
(0.29)	(0.33)	(0.31)	(0.33)	(0.34)	(0.34)	(0.32)	(0.34)	(0.34)
0.86^{***}	-0.14	1.02^{***}	-0.09	-0.29	0.06	-0.47	-0.16	0.25
(0.22)	(0.25)	(0.23)	(0.25)	(0.26)	(0.25)	(0.24)	(0.25)	(0.26)
-0.35	0.97^{*}	-0.04	0.42	0.26	-0.32	0.11	-0.49	-0.22
(0.32)	(0.37)	(0.35)	(0.37)	(0.38)	(0.38)	(0.36)	(0.38)	(0.38)
98	98	98	98	98	98	98	98	98
0.29	0.05	0.17	0.05	-0.01	0.03	0.10	0.03	-0.01

topic, and that Churchill made while serving as First Lord of the Admiralty (FLA) or prime minister (PM). as z-scores with a mean of zero and a standard deviation of 1.

nation fighting one of the greatest military machines the world had ever seen, led by the most fanatical and bloodthirsty dictator the world might ever see. Just days after he took up the reins, the most powerful land army in Europe, that of France, was crumbling and the forces of the two countries were surrounded on the northern shores of France. In the wilderness, Churchill was free to sound off at will. Now he had the responsibility of governing, and Britain's position was worsening rather than improving. Churchill made decisions side by side with both Chamberlain, now Lord President, and Viscount Halifax, who stayed on as foreign secretary following the cabinet reshuffle. This allows for a direct comparison of politicians in the same structural position. In this part of the chapter, I offer more than just words. I focus closely on the cabinet deliberations, particularly those "five days in London" (Lukacs 1999) in which the fate of the world might have actually hung. First, though, we must consider the figure and mind of Viscount Halifax.

The "Holy Fox" and the Hedgehog

In May 1940, Prime Minister Neville Chamberlain became the political casualty of the fall of Norway to Nazi forces (another military catastrophe in which Churchill played a decisive role). Two alternatives emerged to lead the government. Although they shared party ties, writes Roberts (1991), "The two contenders ... could not have been more different. Halifax, the foreign secretary, was a calm, rational man of immense personal prestige and *gravitas*, his career and uninterrupted tale of achievement and promotion. ... Across the Cabinet table sat Churchill, the romantic and excitable adventurer, whose life was a ... story of cavalry charges, prison escapes and thirst for action" (1). Halifax was the preferred choice for prime minister of most Tories after Chamberlain resigned, having the support of the party establishment, most rank-and-file backbenchers. and the king. However, he declined the premiership and instead remained on as foreign secretary in a cabinet that was hardly hospitable to Churchill (Charmley 1993: 396–7; Reynolds 1985: 148–9). Unusually Chamberlain retained his role as head of the party and was given the post of Lord President of Council. Only one major appeaser was sacked. and none of the other anti-appeasers, like Anthony Eden, was given a cabinet position. The new prime minister acknowledged his weakness in a letter to Chamberlain: "To a large extent I am in your hands," he wrote (Costello 1991: 53; Roberts 1991; 210). This set the stage for a confrontation in the cabinet between a realist fox and a romantic hedgehog, to use the metaphor for thinking styles popularized by Tetlock (2005).

Halifax is universally regarded as having a highly rational cognitive style, both deliberative and objective. According to an old friend, Halifax built his career on his capacity for "assimilating information and analyzing it" (Costello 1991: 64). A contemporary who later wrote a biography of Halifax, Lord Birkenhead (1996), writes, "he wanted to listen and learn rather than to instruct" (190). Halifax analyzed information dispassionately and without bias. "He is so objective that we are left in some doubt as to what his own opinion is" (Birkenhead 1966: 79). Halifax strove to see where everyone, especially his political opponents, was coming from: "Edward once admitted that by the composition of his mind his tendency was to see both sides of any question that presented himself to him" (Birkenhead 1966: 606, also 112). Whereas Churchill's contemporaries frequently noted that he was only interested in hearing himself, Halifax was "receptive to advice but indifferent to criticism" (Birkenhead 1966: 190). Halifax avoided misplaced certainty and premature closure. He was aware of his ignorance. Birkenhead (1966) observes that Halifax found that the more he read, the more he realized how many questions there were of which he was "absolutely and completely in ignorance" and that "calmly, methodically and with no suggestion of panic he proceeded to remedy the defect" (60).

Given his rational cognitive style, it is not surprising that contemporaries of Halifax described him as a "cool, passionless, unemotional man" (Costello 1991: 41). Roberts (1991) writes of the "iron control he could exercise over his emotions" (211). Another friend remarked, "at times of great stress he was incapable of showing his pain or emotion" (Roberts 1991: 211). Chamberlain privately praised him as his "steady unruffled Foreign Secretary" (DL: 22 May 1938). During his time as the Viceroy of India, when he went by the title of Baron Irwin, his aides were "impressed by the incredible calm with which [he] confronted every situation, however critical. He seemed so completely balanced that it was almost unnatural, and he was only once seen to lose his temper in five years in India" (Birkenhead 1966: 188, also 606).

Halifax thought before he acted. He was not impulsive. Birkenhead (1966) notes his "caution" and "hatred of sudden instinctive action" (79). His wife observed, "He rarely acted on impulse or gave hasty answers, and usually, if asked his advice or opinion about something even quite unimportant, he would pause before he answered" (Birkenhead 1966: 84). He rigorously planned rather than spontaneously acted, even as a young man (Birkenhead 1966: 59).

In international politics, Halifax's rationalism made him a realist. His nickname was the "Holy Fox" (Roberts 1991): although he was very religious, the "ease with which he manipulated Christian moral tenets to rationalize the practical necessities of his Realpolitik made him by inclination a compromiser" (Costello 1991: 64; also Birkenhead 1966: 605). Halifax was a moral utilitarian, not a moral deontic – a pragmatist who made the best of the situation (Birkenhead 1966: 105). "Perhaps the greatest difficulty in the conduct of foreign affairs," he wrote, "is the fact that ideal policy is scarcely ever practicable," with compromises necessary in face of "harsh and obstinate realities" (Charmley 1993: 288). When he became foreign secretary, Halifax observed, "The world is a strangely mixed grill of good and evil. ... [F]or good or ill we have got to do our best to live in it" (Charmley 1993: 288; FO: 800/328, Hal/38/38, Halifax to Lumley, 21 March 1938). Halifax believed that tradeoffs, often painful ones, were necessary in international politics, saying at one point that "we go badly wrong if we allow our judgment of practical steps to be taken" to be "perpetually deflected by our moral reactions against wrong that we can in no circumstances immediately redress" (FO: 800/328, Hal/38/38, 21 March 1939). He analyzed each situation as it arose rather than trying to apply general principles, accommodating himself "to the new conditions by a change of colour as natural as that of a chameleon" (Birkenhead 1966: 487).

This flexibility led Halifax consistently toward mutually beneficial compromise rather than costly conflict (Birkenhead 1966: 112). "His instinct in an explosive situation was to conciliate. When nations or men became inflamed with passion, he did not catch fire. His first thought was to lower the temperature ... and some, more emotional than he, found something unnatural in the coolness which prevented him being easily moved by events which outraged others" (Birkenhead 1966: 606; also Roberts 1991: 116). Aware of constraints, "when confronted by an obstacle he always preferred to go round by the wings" (Birkenhead 1966: 113).

Not surprisingly, Halifax had been an initial supporter of appeasement based on his perceptions of British weakness, the terrible potential costs of modern war, and the uncertainty surrounding Hitler's intentions, which were the core of the rationalist case for seeking a modus vivendi with the Nazis. At the time of the Munich settlement, he wrote to a friend:

No one I imagine can think that the arrangements made at Munich were anything but the choice of the lesser of two horrible evils ... with the development of the air the capacity of this country as it existed in the XIX century, based on sea power ... no longer stands...we have not been as wrong and unprincipled as you think ... I could not have prevented a worse fate for Czechoslovakia ... and if I had sought that remedy, it would have been at the price of immeasurable suffering imposed on the world, and the probable disruption of the British Empire. (Roberts 1991: 124).

In March 1938, Halifax had said in the cabinet that putting pressure on the Czechs to make concessions to Germany was "a disagreeable business which had to be done as pleasantly as possible" (Gilbert 1977: 925). Privately, Halifax described Munich to a friend as a "horrid business and humiliating ... but yet better than a European war" (Roberts 1991: 125). He repeated this in his memoirs (Halifax 1957: 199).

Halifax also had a strong strategic sense as well, a recognition and awareness that it was important to judge British actions through German eyes. Rationalists call this an attentiveness to "higher-order beliefs." "The more we produced in German minds the impression we were plotting to encircle Germany the more difficult it would be to make any real settlement with Germany," he wrote (Charmley 1989: 17; Charmley 1993: 333; Gilbert 1977: 923). This factor influenced his position on Churchill's proposals. He worried that an alliance with France and the Soviet Union "would afford both a provocation and an opportunity to Germany to dispose of Czechoslovakia before the grand alliance had been organized" (Gilbert 1977: 923). Halifax had "security dilemma sensibility." Hostile actions might give Germany a reason to declare war, whether as pretext or out of security concerns (Charmley 1993: 310).

Although Halifax had suspicions about German intentions, he was extremely cognizant of his lack of complete information. Early on, before he took up his position as foreign secretary, Halifax rhetorically asked, "Are we in fact to judge the situation so serious that everything has to give way to military reconditioning of our Defence Forces? Such a conclusion in fact, appears to me to rest on premises not only of the inevitability but of a certain degree of certainty as to the early imminence of war, which I am not prepared to accept" (James 1970: 257). Several years later, he said in a cabinet meeting:

The ground upon which it is sought to justify the undoubted risk which we should be assuming is that unless we make a stand now, Germany will march uninterruptedly to hegemony in Europe, which will be but a first step towards a deliberate challenge to the British Empire. There is much force in this argument, and yet it may well be based upon a more confident prediction of future events than the experience of history will support. ... It cannot be contended that the future is not black, but there is at least an element of uncertainty in our diagnosis, and on the strength of that uncertainty we might at least refrain from embarking on the more hazardous courses. (Yarhi-Milo 2014: 71)

Halifax recognized Germany's "racial efforts" to unify all ethnic Germans "could not be doubted," but for him it was not clear whether Hitler had "lust for conquest on a Napoleonic scale" Charmley 1993: 335; (Gilbert 1977: 922). It was reckless to act, Halifax thought, before more evidence was accumulated. "It may well be true that Germany's superiority in arms may be greater a year or two or hence than it is now, but this is not a good argument for risking disaster now." He noted that the case for preventive war depended on predictions about the future that were inherently problematic. "Who is to say," Halifax asked, "what the future holds?" (Yarhi-Milo 2014: 71).

Halifax's thinking seems to have shifted following the Nazi seizure of the rest of Czechoslovakia. This is what we would expect from a realist, since this provocative act revealed credible information about what rationalists would call Hitler's "type." Whereas in February 1938 the foreign secretary did not think that "Hitler's racial ambitions are neces-sarily likely to expand into international power lust" (Roberts 1991: 301), he changed his mind in March 1939 when German troops entered Prague. For the foreign secretary, this was a genuine signal of German intentions, as heretofore Hitler had stressed that his ambitions were limited to merely uniting Germans in a single Reich. The "rape of Czechoslovakia" indicated instead that his goals were much grander in scope. On 16 March 1939, Halifax said in a cabinet meeting that he considered the military occupation of Czechoslovakia "significant" since "this was the first occasion on which Germany had applied her shock tactics to the domination of non-Germans" (Roberts 1991: 142). He wondered "if in fact events show that [Hitler] had reached already the decision to attempt at this moment the execution of a policy much wider than that of finding a remedy for the grievances of the Sudetendeutsch" (Roberts 1991: 116). As Halifax (1957) later wrote in his memoirs:

evidence seemed to accumulate that Hitler was not interested merely in the re-assembly of racial elements accidentally separated from the parent stock. Something much larger than this was being born and taking shape in that evil mind. After March and the final rape of Prague, it was no longer possible to hope that Hitler's purposes and ambitions were limited by any boundaries of race, and the lust of continental or world mastery seemed to stand out in stark relief. (207–8)

In light of this new information about German intentions, he advocated for all the measures that the anti-appeasers had long demanded : a Ministry of Supply, early movement toward eventual national conscription, staff talks with the French, and the designation of red lines to the Germans (Charmley 1993: 360; Roberts 1991: 129). He was a major force behind the British guarantee of Poland (Charmley 1989: 360). "[W]hat had *once seemed rational* and decent now looked base and craven" (Roberts 1991: 114 [emphasis added]). Halifax updated like a good fox, albeit a holy one, as we would expect given his high epistemic motivation.

"The One Firm Rock": British Decision-Making during the Fall of France

On the very day that Churchill became prime minister, the Germans invaded Belgium. In a few short weeks they had routed the French and driven the British Expeditionary Force to the northern shores of France, where it was feared it would be forced to surrender in totality, essentially eliminating Britain's entire land army. General Ironside, the Chief of Imperial General Staff, wrote in his diary that the British would be lucky to evacuate any more than 20 percent of its army from Dunkirk (Costello 1991: 210). France was on the brink of capitulating as well. The gravity of the situation was brought home to the cabinet in its discussion of a memorandum prepared by the Joint Chiefs entitled "British Policy in a Certain Eventuality" – with that eventuality being a war against Germany and probably Italy if France and Belgium fell (WP: (40) 138). Their prompt was explicit: "Can the Navy and the Air Force hold out reasonable hopes of preventing serious invasion, and could the forces gathered in this Island cope with raids from the air?" If the Germans could get land forces onto British shores, the report concluded, "the Army in the United Kingdom, which is very short of equipment, has not got the offensive power to drive it out." Preventing a land invasion hinged on winning the battle in the air, and the report noted "the concentration of the whole of our engine production for the fighter force in two factories" that a sustained attack could bring to a "standstill." Germany could be defeated even if France fell, but only if the "United States is willing to give us full economic and financial support, without which we do not think we could continue the war with any chance of success" (WP: (40) 138). The memo was at pains to "emphasise once more that these conclusions as to our ability to bring the war to a successful conclusion depend entirely upon full Pan-American economic and financial co-operation" (WP: (40) 138). The military situation in May 1940 was worse for Britain than at any time since the Napoleonic Wars.

The fall of France had a decisive impact on Halifax, as we would expect from a rational thinker highly attuned to structural circumstances. In December 1939, he had told the cabinet that if France ever sued for peace, "we should not be able to carry on the war by ourselves" (Reynolds 1985: 149). Halifax now wrote, "The one firm rock on which everyone was willing to build for the last two years was the French army and the Germans walked through it like they did through the Poles" (Roberts 1991: 211).

In November 1939, Halifax had expressed opposition to the convocation of a peace conference, as it would leave Britain vulnerable to a German double-cross (Roberts 1991: 184). Now, as France teetered on the edge, he broached the subject of approaching Italy. Mussolini, who had still not entered the war, might be kept neutral or brought over to the allied side provided that Britain made concessions in the Mediterranean. The French hoped that by keeping Italy out of the war, divisions might still be freed up from its southeastern borders to fight in the north. More controversially, Halifax thought Italy might be used as an intermediary to explore peace terms with the Germans. From 26 May through 30 May 1940, the British cabinet debated the issue, all before there was thought to be any real hope of rescuing the British Expeditionary Force.

Consistent with a deliberative and objective mindset, Halifax became more prone to negotiate and make concessions as Britain's position deteriorated. The foreign secretary stressed the importance of evaluating the situation objectively and realistically: "We had to face the fact that it was not so much now a question of imposing a complete defeat upon Germany but of safeguarding the independence of our own Empire and if possible that of France," he told his colleagues (WP: (40) 138). Anticipating a further decline in Britain's chances if France were to fall, Halifax believed this was the time to act. He told the War Cabinet "that we must not ignore the fact that we might get better terms before France went out of the war and our aircraft factories were bombed, than we might get in three months' time" (WP: (40) 145). Charmley (1993) concludes:

Halifax's very logical train of thought appears to have left him without an answer to the question of how Britain was going to survive to carry on the war if she also lost the best part of her army and France was forced to sue for peace. A rationalist like Halifax, who prided himself on putting logic before emotion, could not avoid the spectre of defeat. (207)

Halifax was not advocating the almost complete capitulation that France would offer the Germans several weeks later. He consistently stressed, in realist fashion, that Britain's independence must be guaranteed in any deal. Britain would not sacrifice its vital interests. In a desperate situation, the foreign secretary was simply engaging in the triage that we would expect from a highly rational thinker, recognizing the difficult tradeoffs that needed to be made: "We should say that we were prepared to fight to the death for our independence, but that, provided this could be secured, there were certain concessions that we were prepared to make to Italy" (WP: (40) 145; also Roberts 1991: 224; WP: (40) 138). Halifax was also willing to deal with Germany: "Assuming that Signor Mussolini wished to play the part of mediator, and that he could produce terms which would not affect our independence, he thought that we ought to be prepared to consider such terms" (WP: (40) 145). Possible concessions included acquiescence to German conquests in the east, the transfer of some colonies to Germany, and some Mediterranean concession to Italy such as Gibraltar, but not the dismantling of any portion of Britain's armed forces or its empire (Roberts 1991: 215). "If we got to the point of discussing the terms of a general settlement and found that we could obtain terms which did not postulate the destruction of our independence, we should be foolish if we did not accept them," he said to the War Cabinet (WP: (40) 140).

Chamberlain had also come to the conclusion that if France fell, Britain would be "fighting only for terms, not victory" (Costello 1991: 251) and that "logic and prudence" dictated that the allies should enquire about terms (Costello 1991: 252). On May 15 1940, he wrote of his meeting with the American ambassador:

I saw J. Kennedy this afternoon. He thought the French resolve was broken ... that they had no fight in them. He didn't see how we could fight on without them.

I told him I did not see how we could either. It seemed to me that if the French collapsed our only chance of escaping destruction would be if Roosevelt made an appeal for an armistice, though it did not seem likely that the Germans would respond. (CD: 15 May: 108)

In the War Cabinet, the new Lord President stated his conclusion:

that it was our duty to look at the situation. He felt bound to say that he was in agreement with the Foreign Secretary in taking the view that if we thought it was possible that we could now get terms which, although grievous, would not threaten our independence, we should be right to consider such terms. Again, looking at the matter realistically, he did not think it could be said that an approach to Signor Mussolini ... would be likely to produce an offer of decent terms, certainly not with Paris in Herr Hitler's grasp, but uncaptured. (WP: (40) 145)

Chamberlain agreed that Hitler's offer would likely be unacceptable (CD: 19 May 19: 110) but supported Halifax's position of seeking him out (CD: 26 May 1926: 114–6). Chamberlain complained that another War Cabinet member, Arthur Greenwood of the Labour Party, "argued that we had a good chance of outlasting Hitler but did not give me the impression that he had thought things out" (CD: 26 May: 114–6). Greenwood's thinking was not deliberative enough, in his opinion.

"We Shall Never Surrender"

In complete opposition to Halifax's rationalist logic that the fall of France necessitated a more serious contemplation of concessions, Churchill argued that because "Herr Hitler thought that he had the whip hand ... the only thing to do was to show him that he could not conquer this country" (WP: (40) 142). In other words, the only response to Britain's defeats was to keep fighting. He explained:

The best help we could give to [French premier] M. Reynaud was to let him feel that, whatever happened to France, we were going to fight it out to the end. At the moment our prestige in Europe was very low. The only way we could get it back was by showing the world that Germany had not beaten us. If, after two or three months, we could show that we were still unbeaten, our prestige would return. *Even if we were beaten, we should be no worse off than we should be if we were now to abandon the struggle.* (WP: (40) 142 [emphasis added])

Churchill was arguing that a decline in Britain's military fortunes would not affect its diplomatic bargaining power. A few days later, he repeated the sentiment: "We should get no worse terms if we went on fighting, even if we were beaten, than were open to us now. ... A time might come when we felt that we had to put an end to the struggle, but the terms would not then be more mortal than those offered to us now" (WP: (40) 145). "The only safe way," he claimed, "was to convince Hitler he couldn't beat us" (Roberts 1991: 215).

Churchill therefore favored fighting on, telling the War Cabinet that "peace and security might be achieved under a German domination of Europe. That we could never accept" (WP: (40) 140). The minutes revealed his deontological position. "The Prime Minister had said that we were not prepared to give in on any account. We would rather go down fighting than be enslaved to Germany. But in any case we were confident that we had a good chance of surviving the German onslaught" (WP: (40) 140). Churchill added a condition: " France, however, must stay in the war" (WP: (40) 140). Yet as it became clear that France would likely seek an armistice, he did not adjust his views at all (WP: (40) 142). He even convinced himself that "it was better that [France] should get out of the war rather than that she should drag us into a settlement which involved intolerable terms" (WP: (40) 140). Churchill was not updating but rather engaging in belief perseverance.

Halifax expressed great frustration with the prime minister's think-ing style. Churchill had "so disorderly a mind. I am coming to the conclusion that his process of thought is one that has to operate through speech. As this is exactly the reverse of my own it is irritating" (HD: 30 May 1940: 146). He wrote in his diary: "it does drive me to despair when he works himself up into a passion of emotion when he ought to make his brain think and reason" (HD: 28 May 1940: 142).[2] Alexander Cadogan, Permanent Undersecretary for Foreign Affairs, wrote that Churchill was seen as "too romantic and sentimental and temperamental" by his colleagues during this period (Charmley 1993: 404; Costello 1991: 222). Halifax was upset enough to threaten resig-nation (Roberts 1991: 221). The foreign secretary told Cadogan on May 27, "I can't work with Winston any longer" (Charmley 1993: 405; Costello 1991: 237). He wrote in his diary, "I thought Winston talked the most frightful rot. ... And after bearing it for some time I said exactly what I thought of them, adding that if that was really their view, and if it came to the point, our ways would separate" (HD: 28 May 1940: 142).

Historians also trace the differences to variation in rationality. Church-ill's argument to the cabinet was "calculated to appeal more to the heart

---

[2] This difference in cognitive styles was evident to Halifax at other points in the war, noting in 1942 his awareness of "how removed my mind and thoughts are from Winston's and Max's [Beaverbrook]. When they were here the other day I was profoundly conscious of how differently their minds worked to my own" (Birkenhead 1966: 536).

than the brain" (Robert 1991: 225), whereas "Halifax had attempted to bring logic and reason to a problem long since devoid of either" (Roberts 1991: 226). Roberts (1991) notes the importance of resolve in Churchill's romantic approach. He "put his faith in a combination of a short stretch of water and the sheer bloody-mindedness of the British people. Almost all the rational arguments were on Halifax's side" (216).

After a set of initial exchanges, Churchill called a meeting with the wider cabinet to lay out his case for fighting on, in what seems an effort to isolate Halifax (Charmley 1993: 406; also Costello 1991: 249). Churchill's argument was deontological rather than consequentialist. "He then said that he had no doubt that we could make peace with Hitler on some terms or other provided we made no attempt to interfere with the enslavement of Europe, but this he thought would be short-lived and he did not feel it compatible with his own conscience and honour to do it. And therefore we must fight on" (Halifax 1957: 227). Churchill stressed, in romantic fashion, the ordeal that Britain would endure: "[L]et us be quite plain what it would mean – the war would come home to women and children; there would be bitter suffering" (Halifax 1957: 227). And he imparted his own romantic willingness to sacrifice everything: "I am convinced . . . that every one of you would rise up and tear me down from my place if I were for one moment to contemplate parley and surrender. If this long island story of ours is to end at last, let it end only when each one of us lies choking in his own blood upon the ground" (Charmley 1993: 406; Costello 1991: 249).

In the War Cabinet session that immediately followed, in which the idea of considering any kind of negotiated settlement was finally laid to rest, Churchill reported on his preceding discussion with their colleagues: "They had not expressed alarm at the position in France, but had expressed the greatest satisfaction when he had told them that there was no chance of our giving up the struggle. He did not remember having ever before heard a gathering of persons occupying high places in political life express themselves so emphatically" (WP: (40) 145). Charmley (1993) concludes, "Churchill, whose imagination had long dwelt in regions unknown to sensible men like Halifax . . . through an effort of his own will . . . imposed his vision upon the Cabinet" (408). While we cannot be certain of whether the prime minister's romanticism was decisive in carrying his colleagues, we know that Halifax sat silent at this meeting (Costello 1991: 240). The notion of talking settlement to the Germans was never raised again.

By December 1940, Chamberlain was dead, Halifax had been sent (or exiled) to Washington as ambassador to the United States, and Churchill's fellow anti-appeasers such as Anthony Eden had been brought in to fill key posts. Bankrupt for all intents and purposes, Britain endured the Blitz until something did indeed turn up: Pearl Harbor.

Alternative Explanations: Preferences and Probabilities

Can we just as easily explain Churchill's positions by reference to a different utility function? Was he as instrumentally rational as Halifax and Chamberlain, simply with different inputs? We might argue that Churchill was more risk-acceptant. He valued the ends more than others; therefore he was more likely to gamble on securing them. Yet it seems difficult to argue that he was somehow more interested in survival and protecting Britain's vital interests than his colleagues, particularly given the evidence that Halifax was determined to protect the Empire. Churchill certainly made risky choices, in the sense that they had little chance of succeeding; yet he did not do so out of greater risk-acceptance. He was risk-indifferent. He did not seem to measure the odds at all. At no point do we see Churchill make a statement to the effect that great chances have to be taken given the importance of the ends.

Nor did the two sides have different preferences. Churchill did not have a higher "reservation price." For instance, Churchill did not insist on a total victory, such as the complete liberation of Europe. His goal was also, as Halifax paraphrased him, to preserve British independence and retain "the essentials and the elements of our vital strength, even at the cost of some territory," most notably Gibraltar, Malta, and some African colonies (WP: (40) 142; also CD: 26 May 1940, 114–6). Chamberlain claims Churchill even said he was "willing to make peace on the terms of the restoration of German colonies and the overlordship of Central Europe" (Reynolds 1985: 152).

Did Churchill have a different estimate than others about whether Hitler would settle? It does not seem so. Rather, because of his cognitive style, he was unwilling to find out. Although pessimistic about the chances of a mutually agreeable settlement, Halifax consciously sought to avoid premature closure, the "freezing" that marks a departure from procedural rationality. It was "very likely nothing will come of all this" (WP: (40) 138) because "we were unlikely to receive any offer which would not come up against the fundamental conditions which were essential to us" (WP: (40) 142). However, he "could see no harm in trying this line of approach" (WP: (40) 140). Churchill, in contrast, presupposed that Hitler would offer unacceptable terms, so there was little point in exploring mediation. He was as pessimistic as Halifax, but not as open-minded, an element of epistemic motivation. "There was no limit to the terms which Germany would impose upon us if she had her way," he argued (WP: (40) 140). Churchill thought "the chances of decent terms being offered to us at the present time were a thousand to one against" (WP: (40) 145), "the terms offered would certainly prevent us from completing our re-armament" (WP: (40) 140), and it was "impossible to imagine that Herr Hitler would be so foolish as to let us continue our re-armament" (WP: (40) 145).

We might be tempted again to think of Churchill's position through a rationalist, deterrence lens. Perhaps the prime minister simply wanted to convey Britain's resolve. A diplomatic approach would have signaled weakness that would have undermined Britain's bargaining position. However, as was the case while he was in opposition, Churchill was equally concerned about the effect of an overture on the morale of the government and the British public. Again, resolve was not something already there to signal; he was trying to create it in the first place (Costello 1991: 237). The minutes of the War Cabinet read:

To him the essential point was that [French Prime Minister] M. Reynaud wanted to get us to the Conference-table with Herr Hitler. If we once got to the table, we should then find that the terms offered us touched our independence and integrity. When, at this point, we got up to leave the Conference-table, we should find that all the forces of resolution which were now at our disposal would have vanished. (WP: (40) 145)

"Once we started negotiating for a friendly mediation of the Duce we should destroy our powers of fighting on," he predicted (Costello 1991: 218). Steeled for a fight, the will of the British would dissipate were it not constantly stoked. Churchill, as always, was in an implemental mindset, insistent on fighting on.

The realists countered that Britain's weak position was obvious to everyone, which meant that approaching Italy did not undermine Britain's position. In rationalist terms, this was no longer "private information." Chamberlain stated, "It was clear to the world that we were in a tight corner, and he did not see what we should lose if we said openly that, while we would fight to the end to preserve our independence, we were ready to consider decent terms if such were offered to us" (WP: (40) 145). However, as we have seen, resolve for Churchill was not simply a means to an end. Giving in was cowardly. He thought that Mussolini would regard British overtures "with contempt" since they were unfitting of a great power (WP: (40) 142). Churchill also worried about coming across as weak to the Americans and refused at this point to make a plea for their help: "If we made a bold stand against Germany, that would command their admiration and respect; but a *groveling* appeal, if made now, would have the worst possible effect" (WP: (40)

145 [emphasis added]). Churchill argued that when countries made deals with the devil, they lost a part of themselves. The War Cabinet minutes read: "The Prime Minister said that the nations which went down fighting rose again, but those which surrendered tamely were finished" (WP: (40) 145).

Perhaps Churchill and others had different assessments of the probability of Britain prevailing in the end. Those who worked with Churchill refer to his constant optimism (Charmley 1993: 376; Costello 1991: 228). Churchill, however, was generally extremely pessimistic about the eventual outcome. In March 1938, he told a colleague "that the situation is worse than in 1914. 'We stand to lose everything by failing to take strong action. Yet if we take strong action, London will be a shambles after half an hour'" (CC: 941). At the time of the Munich settlement, Harold Nicolson reports him saying, "It is the end of the British Empire" (CC: 1173). Upon taking up his post, he said privately, "I hope that it is not too late. I am very much afraid that it is. We can only do our best" (Costello 1991: 51). To his military aide, Lord Ismay, he confided, "Poor people. They trust me, and I can give them nothing but disaster for quite a long time" (Costello 1991: 79). He wrote Baldwin, the former prime minister on 4 June 1940, "We're going through very hard times & I expect worse to come: but I feel quite sure that better days will come." He then added, however: "Though whether we shall live to see them is more doubtful" (Reynolds 1985: 154). To Ismay, he predicted just 10 days later, "You and I will be dead in three months time" (Reynolds 1985: 154).

When he was in the opposition, Churchill relentlessly criticized the government for inflating estimates of Britain's air superiority, cultivating sources in the war ministries who supplied him with figures to make his more pessimistic public case. His speeches in the 1930s are filled with references to aircraft production and pilot reserves (Charmley 1993: 347). Abruptly upon entering government, however, Churchill became the government's cheerleader, something that was bitterly noted by the former targets of his ire (Charmley 1993: 346; Costello 1991: 228). He put a positive spin on the military's dire prognostications and analysis. After having complained of how far Britain had fallen behind in the arms race before the war, in the War Cabinet Churchill challenged the numbers that gave Germany a decisive air superiority, eventually having the military reduce the ratio from 4:1 to 2.5:1. He questioned pessimistic predictions that France would be occupied (WP: (40) 141). The point is not that Churchill did not have good reasons for drawing his particular conclusions; it is that he did so on every issue, demonstrating a lack of integrative complexity that suggests motivated bias and low procedural rationality.

When we understand Churchill as a romantic, this reversal makes complete sense. When Britain was behind in the arms race in the 1930s, he likely exaggerated Britain's poor position so as to create the will to make up the gap. This was romantic, but nevertheless purposive behavior. Once the war started, Churchill was engaging in the creative act of bolstering resolve. The day before Halifax relented in his bid to make overtures to Italy, Churchill produced the draft of a memorandum to be distributed throughout the government instructing ministers to use "confident language." While "not minimizing the gravity of events," they should show "confidence in our ability and inflexible resolve to continue the war. . . . Whatever may happen on the Continent we cannot doubt our duty and we shall certainly use all our power to defend the Island, the Empire and our Cause." He warned them "not to talk or look defeatist" (Costello 1991: 241; Reynolds 1985: 153).

The prime minister set out to do this in parliament as well. On the same night that the French asked for a ceasefire, he made perhaps his greatest and most famous speech and the clearest statement of his romantic ethos:

I have, myself, full confidence that if all do their duty, if nothing is neglected, and if the best arrangements are made, as they are being made, we shall prove ourselves once again able to defend our island home, to ride out the storm of war, and to outlive the menace of tyranny, if necessary for years, if necessary alone. . . . Even though large tracts of Europe and many old and famous States have fallen or may fall into the grip of the Gestapo and all the odious apparatus of Nazi rule, we shall not flag or fail. We shall go on to the end. We shall fight in France, we shall fight on the seas and oceans, we shall fight with growing confidence and growing strength in the air, we shall defend our island, whatever the cost may be. We shall fight on the beaches, we shall fight on the landing grounds, we shall fight in the fields and in the streets, we shall fight in the hills; we shall never surrender. (Hansard, 4 June 1940, col. 787–98)

We see in one speech all of the elements of romanticism: the deonto-logical indifference to consequences, the arduous struggle, the poor odds and power asymmetries, and the idealistic framing of the fight.

Churchill's rhetoric was surely instrumental, meant to create the resolve he thought was so necessary. But this does not mean it was disingenuous. In a private letter in June 1938, he wrote, "I fear that no gt [sic] distances there lies before us a trial more grievous than any we have known – aye & surmounted. We have been cruelly mismanaged & chances wh [sic] are inestimable have been thrown away. Still let us proclaim the only hope that makes later life endurable –Never give in" (CC: 1059–60).

The last possibility is that Churchill's differences with his cabinet members simply reflected a set of different beliefs about the likelihood of American intervention on behalf of the British. Lukacs (1999) writes that "Churchill had no plan in May 1940, save the hope that, with the help of the United States, Britain could somehow go on" (127). Chamberlain was generally dismissive of the United States (DL: 16), famously saying that it is "always best and safest to count on nothing from the Americans but words" (Charmley 1989: 38).

This alternative explanation seems unlikely, however, for two reasons. First, Churchill was frustrated with the Americans at this point and any public confidence that he displayed in their intervention he betrayed in private. He complained in May 1940 in the War Cabinet that the "United States had given us practically no help in the war, and now that they saw how great was the danger, their attitude was that they wanted to keep everything which would help us for their own defence" (WP: (40) 141). Reynolds (1985) writes that "for domestic consumption he stressed that U.S. help was imminent, yet in secret he remained disappointed at the lack of assistance, and even suspicious that America was waiting on the sidelines to pick up the pieces" (117). Churchill was mainly interested at the time in signals that would bolster British resolve. He wrote Roosevelt in mid-June 1940:

When I speak of the United States entering the war I am of course not thinking in terms of an expeditionary force, which I know is out of the question. What I have in mind is the tremendous moral effect that such an American decision would produce, not merely in France but also in all the democratic countries of the world, and, in the opposite sense on the German and Italian peoples. (Reynolds 1985: 100)

Second, although Churchill did seem to think that the United States would eventually enter the war, this belief was not based on a careful appraisal of the signals being sent by the United States. Rather, it was driven by his own romantic thinking style. All observers note that Churchill "romanticized the relationship" between the two countries, even before the war (Best 2001: 214; Reynolds 1985: 264). De Gaulle later recalled, "I can still see him at Chequers ... raising his fists towards the sky as he cried: '[T]he bombing of Oxford, Coventry, Canterbury, will cause such a wave of indignation in the United States that they'll come into the war" (Reynolds 195: 162; also Costello 1985: 249). Churchill thought this effect would be particularly strong in those American towns in New England with English namesakes. This belief was not based in careful deliberation, conclude his biographers. "The idea seems to have been in his head since the early 1920s, when the common interests and values of the English-Speaking Peoples became a recurrent theme in his writing and speech-making. That it stayed so despite a verity of Anglo-American diplomatic contretemps throughout that decade ... must be counted as a triumph of faith over experience," writes Best, a Churchill believer (2001: 214–5; also Reynolds 1985: 264). To the extent that Churchill believed American intervention was more likely and this affected his decision-making in the early days of the war, it was a motivated perception consistent with his romanticism and nonrational cognitive style.

"Finest Hour"?: Churchill's Place in History

The romantic myth of Winston Churchill is that through his bold leadership he summoned the will of the British people to fight a battle that they had no business fighting, much less winning. Through the power of his beautiful words, he increased their resolve, which held them steady through the lean year and a half before the Americans entered the war. We cannot assess this myth, however, as it involves an investigation of the effect that the prime minister had on millions of British citizens. It might be that they would have never surrendered, flourishing phrases or no.

However, it does appear possible to confirm a more modest version of this romantic account, that the course of history would have been very different had it been someone other than Churchill making the decisions in May 1940 – for instance, a much more procedurally rational and utilitarian leader like Viscount Halifax. As Charmley (1993) writes, "At his trial, the French collaborationist leader, Pierre Laval, excused his actions in June 1940 by asking who, in their right minds, could then have believed in anything save a German victory? The answer was Churchill" (400). He concludes: "It was by this margin that Britain stayed in the war." And by fighting on, Churchill put Britain in a position to win the war, if only by luck and highly improbable events – just those factors that no highly rational thinker would rely on.

Consider this hypothetical. Hitler followed a very particular blueprint in his quest for European domination that he set out in an unpublished book (Hitler 1983). In this manuscript, we find his strategy to knock out the French and then turn toward Eastern Europe in a final struggle against the Soviet Union. The battle was to be fought over the *Lebensraum* between those two countries that was so important for the literal cultivation of a new master race. Even so, that same book, as well as *Mein Kampf*, continually stress that Hitler hoped for a modus vivendi with Britain in which the English would maintain their empire and dominance of the seas while the Germans attained mastery on the Continent. Indeed, Hitler's perplexing decision to halt the German advance in France in May 1940, which gave the remainders of the British and

French armies just enough time to escape from Dunkirk, is consistent with the idea that Hitler was seeking such an accommodation with Britain (Costello 1991). Therefore there is a strong reason to believe that a diplomatic approach would have yielded the kind of deal that Halifax and Chamberlain hoped for. Had there been such a deal, Germany would not have gotten bogged down in a two-front war. If the Japanese in this scenario had still bombed Pearl Harbor, the Americans might have still entered the war, but it seems inconceivable that they would have fought to liberate Europe as well. The course of European history would have been very different and considerably darker.

This romantic understanding of what Churchill predicted would be Britain's "finest hour" holds true precisely because Churchill himself was a romantic who believed that individuals could resist, through force of will and resolve, what were perceived as immovable structural obstacles. Romantic outcomes depend on romantic individuals willing to defy the odds at all costs. Of course, Churchill got lucky: the Americans entered the war; the Nazis, inexplicably, declared war on the United States. However, Churchill's romanticism put Britain in a position to take advantage of these fortuitous moments.

Does this mean that romanticism, including its emotional and intuitive style of judgment, is a normatively good thing? Romanticism has as many downsides as upsides, tradeoffs that historians and Churchill contemporaries recognize and recognized. Colville (1996) believed, "Among Churchill's most powerful armaments was simplicity. Simplicity of aim, simplicity of thought, simplicity of expression" (113). "Only Churchill's magnificent and courageous leadership compensated for his deplorable strategic sense," noted his former Director of Military Operations (Baxter 1983: 10). Even critics of Churchill note that his vices were also virtues. James (1970) observes:

[H]is views on political matters had a strong tendency to the simplistic. He was not, politically or intellectually, a sophisticated man. Certainly his mind was not profound. In many respects this was a source of great strength, for he often cut through to the heart of the matter and was impatient of the quibblings and qualifications to which many politicians of superior intellectual ability are prone. It was not for nothing that one of his favorite maxims was "Here firm, though all be drifting." But there are occasions in which intellectual imagination is crucial. Churchill had much imagination and he was always fertile in ideas and projects. (381)

Eden reminded that "even his best enemies did not deny that he had ideas" (quoted by Eade 1953: 89).

The same is true of the appeasers as well, of course. We have seen how Chamberlain and Halifax's epistemic motivation, particularly their acknowledgment of uncertainty, paralyzed them from acting. At any other time, we might have been happy to have been governed by the appeasers. Uncertain of Hitler's ambitions, concerned that he could be needlessly provoked, they kept waiting for the information that would justify a confrontation. In 1940, there was a fortuitous meeting of the man and the moment. James (1970) writes, "Churchill's faith in his own star and his desire for direction led him into hasty conclusions, unwise interventions and some serious errors. In war conditions these were serious enough in all conscience, but in these conditions the credit side – the energy, the application and the boldness – was perhaps of greater importance" (382).

9 "Beginning the World All Over Again": Resolving the Paradox of Ronald Reagan

Ronald Reagan is a riddle. How is it that the president who denounced the Soviet Union as an "evil empire" in some of the most confrontational rhetoric ever used in the Cold War could go on to negotiate with Soviet leader Mikhail Gorbachev a nuclear arms reduction treaty that was the first step in ending the Cold War? Why did a president who famously hated nuclear weapons begin his presidency with the greatest peacetime build-up in American history? How could the president who famously wanted to build a shield against nuclear weapons offer to share it with the Soviets? (Shimko 1991: 118; Wilson 2014: 5). Reagan was a Cold Warrior who wanted to abolish nuclear weapons. The Kremlin could not understand "this strange, exasperating U.S. President, who was strident one day and seemed to be sending feelers for negotiation the next" (Oberdorfer 1991: 37). Before the Moscow summit in 1988, the Soviet premier asked, "Who would have thought in the early eighties that it would be this President who would sign with us the first nuclear-arms reduction agreement in history?" (Cannon 1991: 792). Anatoly Dobrynin, Russian's ambassador to the United States, famously called Reagan a "paradox" (Diggins 2007: 265; Farnham 2001: 198; Oberdorfer 1991: 22), both something and its opposite.

Reagan perplexes Americans as well, even those who knew him best. Fitzgerald (2001) writes, "To most of his aides and advisers Reagan was an enigma" (219). Greenstein (2000), a longtime observer, calls Reagan an "interpretive puzzle" (115). Jack Matlock, a former aide, says that "President Reagan, particularly among other intellectuals, is simply not understood" (Wohlforth 1996: 113).

I argue that Reagan was a romantic, and that many of these contradictory impulses can be traced to that fact. Reagan thought that the United States – in the words of Thomas Paine that he often quoted – "had the power to begin the world all over again." Like Churchill, Reagan believed in the power of agency. In his mind, his first job as president was to inspire a sense of confidence and possibility in a United States suffering from self-doubt and hopelessness. This was as

246

true for the domestic economy as it was in foreign affairs, where Reagan believed the United States had abdicated its place of leadership and its sense of righteousness. His framing of the Cold War as a battle of good versus evil, in which the United States would prevail over – not manage or tolerate – the Soviet Union, was decidedly romantic. For Reagan, the arms build-up was not just about reestablishing security; it was an expression of American will, resolve, and purpose, aimed at reinvigorating America's faith in itself.

Reagan also had the romantic's thinking style – intuitive and emotional by observers' accounts, rather than deliberative and objective. The president was not reflective and made sense of the world through heuristics that came in the form of anecdotes. He used stories to make sense of the world, choosing them not after a careful study of their truth, but based on whether they appealed to his preexisting prejudices. Reagan demonstrated considerable "freezing" tendencies. He did not agonize over decisions and never second-guessed himself afterward. It is this cognitive style that has – mistakenly, in my mind – earned him the reputation of being unintelligent, an "amiable dunce." Reagan might have been uninformed, but this was a function of his lack of epistemic motivation, not a lack of cognitive capacity. He made decisions based on gut instinct. He was not rational, but was not stupid either.

Reagan's romantic framing of the Cold War appealed to conservatives and neoconservatives. However, his romanticism manifested itself in other ways that made Reagan truly unique, drawing conservative criticism. Most importantly, Reagan detested nuclear weapons. This is, of course, true of almost everyone, given their tremendously destructive potential. What made Reagan romantic was his unwillingness to accept the highly consequentialist logic of mutually assured destruction, which accepted the existence of nuclear weapons as a lesser evil that kept the peace. As a nonrational thinker, Reagan could never come to terms with this utilitarian understanding of their benefits.

The president tried to begin the world all over again in two ways that, in most eyes, were mutually contradictory. First, he advocated for a strategic defense system that could provide a shield against an incoming nuclear strike. The Strategic Defense Initiative (SDI) was a bold, romantic plan for an invention that would save civilization from nuclear terror, allowing for a defense that did not require threatening the lives of millions of people. The president believed the system could make nuclear weapons "obsolete," rendering this lesser evil unnecessary. Reagan endorsed the concept of strategic defense after little deliberation and believed in its promise despite overwhelming technical evidence to the contrary. This acceptance, I argue, is due to his nonrational cognitive style, which went hand in glove with the very romanticism that made him love the idea of SDI so much in the first place.

Reagan's second romantic bid was to reach dramatic news arms-control agreements with the Soviet Union. Like Churchill, Reagan thought that history could be made and remade by great efforts on the part of individuals even in the face of massive structural obstacles. Churchill's task was to win a war, Reagan's to avoid one, which meant engaging Soviet leaders. As we will see, from the very beginning of his presidency, Reagan expressed his desire to radically reduce nuclear weapons directly to Soviet premiers in personal letters, even though relations with the Soviet Union were poor and progress in arms-control talks was nonexistent. Reagan does not seem to have realized at first how his moralistic framing of the Cold War, pursuit of an arms build-up, and quest for a space shield undermined these efforts. However, this is evidence of the president's nondeliberative cognitive style.

In this chapter, I establish Reagan's romanticism, his intuitive and nonrational thinking style, and the ways in which it manifested itself in his foreign policy agenda. In establishing the president's degree of rationality, I rely on both critics and admirers of Reagan. As will be seen, they are of one mind about how Reagan thought; they simply disagree about whether this was a good or bad thing. The same was, of course, true of Churchill. I am not the first to characterize Reagan as a romantic. Both admirers (D'Souza 1999: 43) and harsh critics (Talbott 1988) describe him in this way. However, we lack a firm understanding of what this means.

"Dreamer-in-Chief": Reagan's Romanticism

Perhaps more than anything, Reagan believed in the power of agency. On his desk, a number of aides have noted, were two plaques. One stated, "There is no limit to what a man can do or where he can go if he doesn't mind who gets the credit" (Cannon 1991: 183). The other read, "It CAN be done" (Adelman 2014: 204). Talbott (1988) writes, "Reagan believed that if a leader dared to ask elementary questions, the most intractable problems could become amenable to solution. . . . He prepared to say, in effect: 'Here's the problem (poverty, inflation, international terrorism, nuclear war); now here, in a simple declarative sentence, is the solution: Let's do it'" (195). He would refer frequently to a Thomas Paine quote: "We have it within our power to begin the world over again" (Public Papers of the President [PPP]: 8 March 1983, 21 January 1985, and 24 September 1984). In a speech, Reagan remarked, "I do not dismiss the dangers of big deficits, nuclear conflict, or international terrorism.

Each could destroy us if we fail to deal with them decisively. But we can and will prevail if we have the faith and the courage to believe in ourselves and in our ability to perform great deeds, as we have throughout our history" (Garrison 2013: 48). At another point he declared, "[A]ll we need to begin with is a dream that we can do better than before. All we need to have is faith, and that dream will come true. All we need to do is act, and the time for action is now" (Garrison 2013: 49). Cannon (1991) writes that Reagan "had a sense of the world as it would and as it might be, not merely of the way it was. Reagan wanted a world without nuclear weapons, and a world without walls and iron curtains" (281).

With this romanticism came an emphasis on vision, creativity, and imagination, but little attention to practicability and implementation (Diggins 2007: 13; Farnham 2001: 134). Garrison (2013) refers to Reagan's "chimeric imagination" that "has a great deal in common with the romantic/idyllic varieties" (14). According to Cannon (1991), "He was a dreamer, preoccupied with ultimate destinations" rather than the practical steps of getting there (503). Abshire and Neustadt (2005), in describing Reagan's romanticism, note its core element: "[A]ny ought-to-be that can be dreamed can be made into reality" (203–4). Strobe Talbott (1988) has pejoratively called him the "dreamer-in-chief."

Many scholars juxtapose this romanticism against conservative realism (Diggins 2007: 16, 191). Wolfe (1981) argues, "Ronald Reagan is not a conservative ... his program is romantic. Reality, as romantics know, resists change. Dreams change all the time" (37–9). To Diggins (2007), "Reagan ... was a romantic who drew from the fountain of life and the ideals of youth ... and stood ready to believe in every possibility. ... A conservative takes pride in having a firm grasp on reality, while a romantic is impatient with reality and reaches out to the impossible to make it possible" (72).

Reagan thought individuals could bring about change even in the face of great structural obstacles. As it was for Churchill, history itself was a story of individual agency, although Reagan knew far, far less about the subject than the British romantic. In his second inaugural address, the president noted that:

[W]hat shines out from the pages of history is the daring of the dreamers and the deeds of the builders and the doers. These things make up the stories we tell and pass on to our children. They comprise the most enduring and striking fact about human history – that through the heartbreak and tragedy man has always dared to perceive the outline of human progress, the steady growth in not just the material wellbeing, but the spiritual insight of mankind. (PPP: 21 January 1985)

This was more than rhetoric. "His entire foreign policy was aimed at reversing history," recalled Robert Gates, who served as the deputy chief of the Central Intelligence Agency (CIA) during the Reagan administration (Pemberton 2015: 149). Robert "Bud" McFarlane, who served as National Security Advisor during the critical mid-1980s period, noted Reagan's "self-confidence in the ability of a single heroic figure to change history" and his belief that he was himself such an individual (Oberdorfer 1991: 22). Diggins (2007) writes, "Reagan saw himself as a rescuer, the romantic hero who saves life from the treacherous currents of nature and politics. He saw himself doing so as an individual ... who ... headed history in the right direction" (41).

Reagan's stoking of confidence and America's belief in itself leads all observers to comment on his optimism (Wilson 2014: 45, 50). Cannon observes that Pangloss looked like a pessimist by comparison (Garrison 2013: 47). Reagan (1990) later explained his mission at the beginning of his presidency: "We had to recapture our dreams, our pride in ourselves and our country, and regain that unique sense of destiny and optimism that had always made America different from any other country in the world" (219). Rather than responding to America's crisis of confidence by setting realistic goals, Erikson maintains that Reagan "sought just the opposite ... to believe in even more splendid visions. Rather than force people to face the constraints of life in our world, Reagan stressed their capabilities" (quoted in Garrison 2013: 50).

Achieving one's goals in the face of structural obstacles requires great will, determination, and resolve – romantic attributes that Reagan had and admired in others (Anderson 1990: xxvi; Garrison 2013: 49; Talbott 1988: 195). Reagan described his own process of mind over matter: "If you have something you believe in deeply, it's worth repeating time and again until you achieve it" (Cannon 1991: 93). After Reagan lost his insurgent 1976 presidential bid to unseat President Gerald Ford, Reagan described his state of mind:

It's just one battle in a long war and it will go on as long as we all live. ... You just stay in there and you stay there with the same beliefs and the same faith that made you do what you're doing here. ... The cause is there and the cause will prevail because it is right. Don't give up your ideas. Don't compromise. Don't turn to expediency. (Anderson 1990: 46)

Many note that the president's romanticism reflected the very roles that he played as an actor. Cannon (1991) explains: "The Reagan role had been created in Hollywood, out of material he brought with him from the Middle West. It was the role of The Gipper, symbolized by the insouciance of halfback George Gipp. When coach Knute Rockne asks

Gipp if he can carry the football and Gipp answers, 'How far?' . . . It was a role, but it was also Reagan" (41). As a Sunday School teacher, Reagan loved to tell tales of courage and individual initiative by those trapped in floods or lost in the jungle (Fitzgerald 2001: 58). He venerated ordinary Americans "who by their moral courage and persistence had triumphed against all odds" (Fitzgerald 2001: 36).

Amiable Dunce?: Reagan's Thinking Style

As a romantic, Reagan's decision-making style was distinctly nonrational – lacking in objectivity and deliberation and marked instead by intuition and emotion. Reagan earned the reputation of being an "amiable dunce," uninformed about even the most important issues, such as distinctions between the various arms of the American "nuclear triad" (Cannon 1991: 101; Oberdorfer 1991: 19). Talbott (1988) complains, "When drawn into the realm of facts, he often displayed stunning ignorance about the capabilities of the weapons over which he had authority" (5). He even apparently thought that ballistic missiles could be recalled (Shimko 1991: 111). For our purposes, however, the issue is not what or how much Reagan knew, but rather how and whether he went about actively thinking. Reagan's lack of knowledge on crucial subjects was a by-product of his cognitive style. He lacked epistemic motivation.

Reagan did not care for painstaking deliberation. His former economic adviser explained: "Reagan is not an analytic person. He was bored with argument, and he made it clear he was bored with argument" (Cannon 1991: 238). Adelman (2014) describes Reagan similarly, as "neither inwardly reflective nor outwardly revealing" (65). As Anderson (1990) explains, "He makes decisions promptly and decisively, and then goes on to something else" (279). Alexander Haig, Reagan's first secretary of state, compared him to Nixon, who would "sit in anguish for hours over a decision before it was made. . . . I never sensed that with Reagan. He was the most graceful and easy decision-maker I've ever seen" (Cannon 1991: 151).

By all accounts, Reagan did not seek out information to make judgments, a part of the deliberative process (Farnham 2001: 226; Weinberger 1990: 11). Reagan was not interested in what he called the "details" of government, which as Cannon (1991: 94) notes, included most of the business of governing. Anderson recalled, "He does not actively and constantly search out and demand things. He must rely on what is or is not brought to him" (Cannon 1991: 181). Even when information was made available, such as at Cabinet meetings, Reagan rarely asked questions, leading aides to wonder if he had been paying attention (Anderson 1990: 218; Cannon 1991: 135; Farnham 2001: 251). He rarely commented on memoranda (Mann 2009: 267). Cannon (1991: 181) cites a Reagan staffer who estimates that Reagan did not react to 95 percent of the material brought to him. Reagan did not even glance at his briefing book before hosting his first major summit, the G-7 meeting in 1983. He explained to his chief of staff, James Baker, "Well, Jim, the *Sound of Music* was on last night" (Cannon 1991: 57; also Adelman 2014: 11).

The president famously carried with him small blue index cards that he used as crib notes for a particular subject (Wohlforth 1996: 107). Kissinger hated this practice, complaining that in his meetings with the president, "He would try to avoid policy discussions. ... If he couldn't he'd resort to his cue cards" (Fitzgerald 2001: 175; also Cannon 1991: 132). This was not a time-saving exercise, a bounded rationality strategy for a busy man. The president's workday was also notoriously short (Cannon 1991: 55–6). Yet Reagan did not lack cognitive capabilities. Indeed, he was generally regarded by the same aides as highly intelligent, and he had a fantastic memory. In the terms of this book, as a thinker, he relied heavily on System I processing.

Reagan relied heavily on heuristics. Every work on the president, whether by journalists or by former colleagues, seems to mention his dependence on anecdotes. Reagan made sense of the world through stories that he had picked up throughout his years as an actor and politician (Fischer 1997: 117). Pemberton (2015) writes, "Reagan's mind seemed to work in terms of such stories. ... He transformed complex political problems or policies into anecdotes always involving concrete, easily visualized individuals or situations, whether the subject was 'welfare queens' abusing a social support system or young American and Soviet citizens discussing their dreams of a better world" (18).

Reagan frequently resorted to telling anecdotes when he was asked to analyze an issue or explain details about a policy, tasks with which he struggled (Cannon 1991: 136, 361). When asked in 1980 whether his policy of an arms build-up might have the opposite effect of its intent, inducing fear on the part of the Soviet Union that would decrease security, Reagan replied: "The great American humorist, Will Rogers, some years ago had an answer for those who believed that strength invited war. ... He said, 'I've never seen anyone insult Jack Dempsey,'" the great boxer of Reagan's youth (Glad 1983: 64). Cannon (1991) concludes that Reagan "did not know enough," so his "consistent inclination was to fall back on the store of anecdotes and information he had acquired on the banquet circuit" (154). They acted as cognitive shortcuts.

The president liked anecdotes and stories because they were vivid and concrete. This is typical of an intuitive thinker. His former chief of staff, Donald Regan, wrote, "Reagan shunned the abstract, the theoretical, the cold and impersonal approach to problems. His love of stories was connected to his tendency to see everything in human terms" (Fischer 1997: 117). Reagan was bored by a series of briefings on the Soviet Union, for instance, except for one that described the social stresses of alcoholism, crime, and corruption in contemporary Russian life. Gates remembers, "He was riveted I think because [the briefing] described the Soviet Union in terms of human beings, everyday life, and the conditions under which they lived. It was all far more real to the president than the strategic concepts and broad geopolitics the others of us went on about" (Brands 2015: 504). Clark, finding that Reagan (in his words) knew "next to nothing about what was going on in many corners of the globe," sought out films to educate Reagan, knowing that he would respond to their narrative form and visual impact. He even asked the CIA to produce documentaries on leaders whom Reagan would be meeting since he would not read memoranda (Cannon 1991: 158).

Successful aides exploited these characteristics of Reagan's thinking. His first national security advisor coached others on how to reach Reagan: "If you think there are particular points that you really want to score, you're going to have to dress them up a little bit, tie them to a metaphor or an analogy and put a little sex appeal in it" (Cannon 1991: 152). Casper Weinberger used cartoons to persuade Reagan (Cannon 1991: 153). This "made him vulnerable to arguments that were short on facts and long on theatrical gimmicks," writes Fischer (1997: 118).

Reagan did not demonstrate any commitment to objectivity. In a conversation with a journalist who had confided in him, he once said, "You believed it because you wanted to believe it. There's nothing wrong with that. I do it all the time" (Cannon 1991: 39). Kissinger was frustrated by this tendency. "What he said was what he believed. He didn't stand in front of his mirror in the morning while he shaved wondering whether that was the truth or not" (Fitzgerald 2001: 175). Colleagues note that Reagan would frequently conflate fact and fiction in the anecdotes that he accumulated (Cannon 1991: 60), forgetting that the fictional stories had never occurred in reality, even those drawn from movies in which he had starred as an actor (Fitzgerald 2001: 22).

Reagan instead engaged in bolstering behavior, choosing bits of information that reinforced previously held beliefs (Fitzgerald 2001: 57; Garthoff 1994: 9; Talbott 1988: 5). His thinking demonstrated considerable motivated bias. Colin Powell, who served as Reagan's national security advisor, later noted that aides could reach Reagan only when they touched on what the general called a "built-in transistor" in Reagan's mind, some central theme or memory that served as a heuristic (Cannon 1991: 181). Cannon (1991) explains:

When Reagan received new information, he mentally scanned stored files much as if he had hit the "search" key of the computer. If the new information touched what Colin Powell called a "transistor," Reagan responded to what he was being told with one of his old stories. If it didn't, he would wait, usually saying nothing, until something that was said to him struck one of his mental buttons. (292).

His economic advisor agreed: "He wanted to hear the conclusions and check to see if they agreed with his priors" (Cannon 1991: 238). When Reagan read, he looked at conservative columns, the highly conservative periodical *Human Events*, as well as the comics (Fitzgerald 2001: 215; Glad 1983: 66) and did not heavily scrutinize the arguments. Anderson complained of Reagan's gullibility: "If he read it, in the newspaper or in an article, and it sounded reasonable, he accepted it as true" (Cannon 1991: 180).

Once Reagan made a decision, he also was extremely unlikely to revise his beliefs (Brands 2015: 382). The president demonstrated "freezing" tendencies. His former treasury secretary and chief of staff, Donald Regan, observed, "The President has a unique talent. He is serene internally. When he has made a decision, he lives with it. He doesn't fret over it. And most of all, he doesn't change his mind" (Anderson 1990: 286). Haig, too, noticed that Reagan could make decisions easily without second-guessing himself, again comparing him favorably to Nixon, albeit with the caveat that Reagan did not always understand the full consequences of what he had decided (Cannon 1991: 151). Many of his top officials observed the same. Secretary of State George Shultz (1993) later wrote, "Many times I would try to correct the president on particular facts of a favorite story. It rarely worked. Once a certain arrangement of facts was in his head, I could hardly ever get them out" (601). Former national security advisor John Poindexter told his colleagues in 1986, "I have watched Ronald Reagan for two decades. ... When he gets an idea in his head, it stays there" (Shultz 1993: 778).

By all accounts, Reagan relied on instinct, intuition, and his "gut" in making decisions (Cannon 1991: 34, 304; Farnham 2001: 246). First "taken aback by Reagan's intellectual emptiness," French President Francois Mitterrand concluded that "beneath the surface you find someone who isn't stupid, who has great good sense and profoundly good intentions. What he does not perceive with his intelligence, he feels by nature" (Farnham 2001: 246). The long-serving Soviet ambassador, Anatoly Dobrynin, observed the same. Reagan was "a man of finer instincts than intelligence" who "grasped matters in an instinctive way but not necessarily in a simple one" (Farnham 2001: 246). Lord Carrington, defense secretary to Margaret Thatcher, compared Reagan and the Iron Lady: "The difference between them was that while he had gut feelings, she had an intelligence that he did not have" (Adelman 2014: 93). Cannon (1991) recalls what he learned while covering Reagan as a journalist: "What I knew was that he understood all manner of things that suggested powers of analysis without possessing any visible analytical ability" (138).

Reagan is also often described as an emotional thinker (Farnham 2001: 247). According to Cannon (1991), "what Reagan saw and felt as an actor and a politician frequently did not correspond to the facts. Reagan recognized this and, in a conflict between feelings and facts, usually gave greater weight to his feelings" (39). Like Churchill, Reagan was an "an unabashed sentimentalist" (Cannon 1991: 338).

Reagan's nonrational cognitive style and his romanticism went hand-in-hand. As argued previously, romantics do not behave based on reason and instrumental rationality. A number of scholars and observers make this connection in their descriptions of Reagan. Abshire and Neustadt (2005) write, "Whether or not he ever read much of the nineteenth-century American romantic novelists, poets and philosophers, he had their romantic themes," which include that "intuition often overrides reason" (203–4). Diggins (2007) evokes both when he writes of Reagan, "He stood for freedom peace, disarmament, self-reliance, earthly happiness, the dreams of the imagination and the desires of the heart" (xvii). Wolfe (1981), in commenting on Reagan as the "latest Romantic hero," writes: "To think or dream – that was the question. . . . [T]o Reagan, the gap between appearance and reality is to be cherished. . . . [I]t is far better to work with dreams, for in that realm – and not in the realm of reason – human imagination truly hold sway" (37–9). Pemberton (2015) notes that Reagan's favorite anecdotes always had a romantic quality; they "usually involved people triumphing over evil or adversity" (18).

As we will see, this lack of epistemic motivation meant that Reagan's decision-making was not instrumentally rational. A former political consultant complained that he "doesn't have the knack for weighing alternatives" – that is, for performing the cost–benefit analysis that is part of utility maximization (Fitzgerald 2001: 65). Nor did the president deliberately lay out the steps to reach his goal. A staffer remembered:

He never sat down, at least to my knowledge, in the campaign or the administration and said, "Now here is my grand design, what I want to do and all the theory." . . . And yet, if you stepped back and added up all the specific things he said and looked at them, it formed a grand design. In other words, he did it by inference rather than deduction. It's a different way of thinking. (Cannon 1991: 140)

Anderson (1990) says the same, comparing Reagan to his fellow Republican and predecessor, the realist Richard Nixon: "Nixon's instinct is to plan and plot, the kind of man who thinks seven or eight moves ahead in a chess game. . . . Reagan was just the opposite" (279).

This same intuitive thinking style, however, had important advantages. It was part of what gave Reagan the reputation of the "Great Communicator." In an interview, the pragmatic Secretary Shultz recounted a story of running a speech explaining a recent foreign policy decision by Reagan:

"Perfect." Then a moment of silence. "Of course if I was doing it, I wouldn't do it this way.". . . In one place he put a little story. He had personalized it. He said, "That's the most important point on this page. It's not enough to get it into people's head. You got to get it into their gut if they are really going to understand it. And the way that you do that is you tell a story that they can relate to." (Interview with the author)

Reagan also stuck to his guns, which even rational thinkers admired. Shultz remembered, "He had a consistency about him, and he would stick with things. Sometimes you'd wish that he wouldn't. On the other hand, there was a presidential instinct that was very strong" (Wohlforth 1996: 104).

Reagan's intuitive thinking style and romanticism were ultimately a double-edged sword. Shultz (1993) concludes:

Ronald Reagan had visionary ideas. In pursuing them, he displayed some of his strongest qualities: an ability to break through the entrenched thinking of the moment to support his vision of a better future, a spontaneous, natural ability to articulate the nation's most deeply rooted values and aspirations, and a readiness to stand by his vision regardless of pressure, scorn or setback. At the same time, he could fall prey to serious weakness: a tendency to rely on his staff and friends to the point of accepting uncritically – even wishfully – advice that was sometimes amateurish and even irresponsible. (263)

The "Ashheap of History": Romanticism in Foreign Affairs

Reagan's political program rested primarily on infusing Americans with the same spirit of agency that he had (Diggins 2007: 17). Taking office in the midst of a terrible recession marked by rampant inflation, the new president saw his country as afflicted by a sense of hopelessness, a belief that things could not improve (Garrison 2013: 45). While noting in his inaugural address the "economic affliction of great proportions," he observed:

It is time for us to realize that we're too great a nation to limit ourselves to small dreams. We're not, as some would have us believe, doomed to an inevitable decline. I do not believe in a fate that will fall on us no matter what we do. I do believe in a fate that will fall on us if we do nothing. (PPP: 20 January 1981)

Action and agency were necessary. Fittingly for a romantic, he made reference to heroes who overcome obstacles:

We have every right to dream heroic dreams. Those who say that we're in a time when there are not heroes, they just don't know where to look. You can see heroes every day going in and out of factory gates. Others, a handful in number, produce enough food to feed all of us and then the world beyond. (PPP: 20 January 1981)

Reagan's view of the presidency was "essentially inspirational" (Garthoff 1994: 7).

Reagan had a particular view of the United States as a country that constantly overcame structural constraints, one with "a history that has been the story of hopes fulfilled and dreams made into reality" (PPP: 8 March 1983). "To me," he declared, "our country is a living, breathing presence, unimpressed by what others say is impossible" (Cannon 1991: 793). In concluding his inaugural address, Reagan urged Americans "to believe in ourselves and to believe in our capacity to perform great deeds, to believe that together with God's help we can and will resolve the problems which now confront us. And after all, why shouldn't we believe that? We are Americans" (PPP: 20 January 1981). He believed that "America has always been greatest when she dared to be great. ... The American people would rather reach for the stars than reach for excuses why we shouldn't" (Cannon 1991: 495).

This would require will and resolve: "So, with all the creative energy at our command, let us begin an era of national renewal. Let us renew our determination, our courage, and our strength. And let us renew our faith and our hope" (PPP: 20 January 1981; also 21 January 1985). Diggins (2007) notes, "Reagan's most biting critique of Jimmy Carter was that the president tried to make the people feel contrite. Carter asked them to think small, to face an era of limits. Reagan proposed to save American from such sickness of will" (31). Reagan was not just critical of Democrats, however. He regarded the Vietnam War as perhaps most responsible for sapping the feeling of purpose from the United States. It was a failure of "striving." The American government was "afraid to win" (Cannon 1991: 335; Glad 1983: 46). "The real crisis we face today is a spiritual one; at root, it is a test of moral will and faith," he declared (PPP: 8 March 1983; also 8 June 1982).

Of course the greatest challenge the United States faced, besides its faltering economy, was the threat posed by the Soviet Union and its formidable arsenal of nuclear weapons. The president had long believed that the Soviet Union was committed to worldwide socialist revolution and territorial expansion. All Soviet leaders were, in his mind, similarly driven by the ideological aims of Marx and Lenin (Shimko 1991: 102–6). Their arms build-up could be understood only as offensive in nature, driven by a desire for superiority (Shimko 1991: 109).

Reagan is perhaps best known for his framing of the Cold War as a Manichean fight between good and evil rather than a simple geopolitical rivalry (Mann 2009: 23), a theme he sounded from the beginning of his political career (Wilson 2014: 13). His most famous statement to this effect was his speech before an evangelical forum in 1983:

So, I urge you to speak out against those who would place the United States in a position of military and moral inferiority ... the temptation of blithely declaring yourselves above it all and label both sides equally at fault, to ignore the facts of history and the aggressive impulses of an evil empire, to simply call the arms race a giant misunderstanding and thereby remove yourself from the struggle between right and wrong and good and evil. (PPP: 8 March 1983)

The Soviets were the "focus of evil in the modern world" (PPP: 8 March 1983).

Less noticed is the romantic character of Reagan's foreign policy narrative. The Cold War was an epic struggle with clear moral sides (Wilson 2014: 15). In describing Reagan as a romantic, Wolfe (1981) notes "there can be no epics without Evil. The Russians fill the role in the opera of American foreign policy" (37–9). The United States had to be the hero. "We stand here on the only island of freedom that is left in the world. There is no place to flee to ... no place to escape to. We defend freedom here or it is gone. There is no place for us to run, only to make a stand," Reagan wrote as early as 1968 (Glad 1983: 43), a sentiment he repeated in office (PPP: 31 March 1983). Cannon (1991) argues that this was Reagan's most important story: "He made sense of foreign policy through his long-developed habit of devising dramatic, all-purpose stories with moralistic messages, forceful plots and well-developed heroes and villains" (364).

Reagan began the largest arms peacetime arms build-up in American history, arguing that previous presidents had left the United States weak.

Improving the military balance in the United States' favor was the only way to force the Soviet Union, intent in his eyes on world domination, to make concessions. Reagan sought preponderance, not balance (Wilson 2014: 17). Less than two weeks after entering office, he approved an increase in the defense budget of $32.6 billion over the $200.3 billion that Carter had approved in his last week in office, which itself was an increase of $26.4 billion over the year before. Reagan pledged to increase the military budget from one fourth to one third of federal spending (Garthoff 1994: 34). His arms program totaled $1.5 trillion over five years and included 50 MX missiles each with 10 MIRVs, the B-1 bomber, the Trident submarine, the neutron bomber, the F-14 fighter, and two new aircraft carrier groups (Wilson 2014: 18).

Arms were not enough, however. In romantic fashion, Reagan never stopped stressing the importance of will and resolve in confronting the Soviets (PPP: 16 October 1981, 8 January 1983, and 16 January 1984). In his inaugural address, he proclaimed:

Our reluctance for conflict should not be misjudged as a failure of will. . . . We will maintain sufficient strength to prevail if need be, knowing that if we do so we have the best chance of never having to use that strength. Above all, we must realize that no arsenal or no weapon in the arsenals of the world is so formidable as the will and moral courage of free men and women. (PPP: 20 January 1981).

In his famous "Evil Empire" speech, he said the same (PPP: 8 March 1983; also 8 June 1982).

Of course, the arms build-up was a means to an end. The president believed in "peace through strength," one of the most consistent themes of his administration (PPP: 23 March 1983, 6 April 1984, and 8 March 1983). "Weakness only invites aggression," he asserted (PPP: 23 March 1983). The Soviets "respect only strength and resolve in their dealings with other nations" (Shimko 1992: 368). Reagan, however, was trying to inspire resolve as much as credibly signal it. This is the difference between the rationalist and the romantic. For Reagan, the decline in American arms spending was symptomatic of a failure of will. He complained in the late 1970s that the United States had "abdicated [its] historical role as the spiritual leader of the Free World and its foremost defender of democracy. Some of our resolve was gone, along with a part of our commitment to uphold the values we cherished" (Farnham 2001: 229; see also Garthoff 1994: 97; PPP: 6 April 1984). Following the build-up, he expressed satisfaction: "We've come a long way since the decade of the seventies, years when the United States seemed filled with self-doubt and neglected its defenses" (PPP: 16 January 1984). The president proclaimed, "Peace through strength is not a slogan. It's a fact of life.

And we will not return to the days of handwringing, defeatism, decline and despair" (PPP: 6 April 1984).

Armed with resolve, Reagan claimed that United States would eventually prevail over the Soviet Union (although not through military means, an important point we will see later), a view he expressed before becoming president (Glad 1983: 64; Mann 2009: 23). Unlike a realist, Reagan "conveyed no sense of the tragic, no reason why the world had to remain in a state of perilous conflict," writes Diggins (2007). "The march of freedom and democracy" would "leave Marxism–Leninism on the ash-heap of history," he famously predicted before the British House of Commons in 1982 (PPP: 8 June 1982). "I believe that communism is another sad, bizarre chapter in human history whose last pages even now are being written," he proclaimed to the evangelicals the next year (PPP: 8 March 1983; also WC: 1985, p. 865). Unlike Nixon, his Republican predecessor who grudgingly accepted the permanence of the Soviet Union, Reagan saw the potential for transformation (Mann 2009: 19). Shultz notes Reagan's opposition to structural thinking: "The concept of détente was, 'We are here, they are here, that's life, and the name of the game is peaceful coexistence and the avoidance of war. ... Reagan rejected that concept" (Mann 2009: 24). In a subsequent interview with the author, Shultz said, "Reagan thought, 'We're here, but they're not as strong as they look and if we work at it right, things can change.'" He reminded, "That was very controversial" (interview with the author).

Readers will note the strong parallels between Churchill and Reagan. The president recognized as much, making frequent references to the British hero and using his conception of "civilization" (PPP: 8 June 1982). Like Churchill, he was also fond of employing metaphors of sunlight and darkness, which represented the opposing forces of good and evil (Glad 1983: 43; PPP: 21 January 1985; Wilson 2014: 18).

It is easy to establish that Reagan's perceptions of the Soviet Union were simplistic and one-sided. Matlock, who admires Reagan greatly, nevertheless estimated his knowledge of the Soviet Union to be "just about the same as that of the average man in the street" (Fitzgerald 2001: 304). McFarlane observed the president's reliance on simplifying heuristics: "Dealing as he did with Reagan every day, he was struck by the president's spotty command of historical facts. Reagan had very few contacts with Soviet officials and still tended to base many of his judgments more on generalities, even slogans, than on a nuanced understanding of Soviet reality" (Matlock 2004: 132). Reagan commonly picked up from conservative news outlets quotes attributed to Marx or Lenin claiming that lying, cheating, and stealing were acceptable if they served the broader goal of world revolution and the creation of a universal communist state (Cannon 1991: 282; Diggins 2007: 352; Glad 1983: 33; PPP: 8 March 1983; Shimko 1992: 361). When a Soviet journalist asked Reagan to identify the passages in Marx that he frequently invoked, he had no answer: "Oh my, I don't think I could recall and specify here and there" (Shimko 1992: 364). Matlock remembers, "He had various ideological assumptions, and he had read some book by someone which had a lot of pseudo-quotes from Lenin, most of which were false ... which we finally had to demonstrate to him" (Wohlforth 1996: 114). Matlock recalled that McFarlane told him in 1985, "The President, he has a jumble of things, including these false statements about what Lenin had said that he got from some right-wing literature." The national security advisor asked Matlock to have them vetted. Most were not authentic (interview with the author).

However, as was the case with Churchill, I do not judge Reagan's thinking style on the basis of whether these beliefs accurately reflected reality; I only evaluate the process by which they were formed. Even Reagan's closest aides and admirers argue that his views of the Soviet Union were not the product of intense engagement with the subject. Instead, they were a reflection of a nondeliberative cognitive style. It is not so much that Reagan's views of the Soviets were simplistic, but that he was comfortable in his ignorance and made no serious effort to rectify it.

The Nightmare: Reagan's Rejection of Consequentialist Nuclear Strategy

From the beginning of his presidency, years before his dramatic summits with Gorbachev, Reagan identified his desire to completely abolish nuclear weapons, although he never promised to deliver on this ambitious aim during his administration. In the same speech in which he railed against the Soviets as an "evil empire," he spoke of negotiating "real and verifiable reductions in the world's nuclear arsenals and one day, with God's help, their total elimination" (PPP: 8 March 1983). In a famous speech in Japan, he declared: "A nuclear war can never be won and must never be fought" (PPP: 11 November 1983). Both in public and in private, he consistently called his "dream" one of a world free of these most destructive of armaments (Anderson 1990: 72–3; Oberdorfer 1991: 97; PPP: 8 June 1982, 11 November 1983, 16 January 1984, 21 January 1985, 14 November 1985; Reagan 1990: 550; Shultz 1993: 484). At the 1976 presidential convention, where Reagan gave an impromptu speech, he lamented "a world in which the great powers have poised and aimed at each other horrible missiles of destruction, that can, in a matter of minutes, arrive in each other's country and destroy virtually the civilized world we live in" (Anderson 1990: xxxix; Cannon 1991: 295). Reagan frequently confided to his advisors his fear of a coming Armageddon (Wilson 2014: 67). He did not keep his dream to radically reduce nuclear weapons to himself, and consistently mentioned this goal in correspondence with Soviet leaders (Letters: 24 April 1981, 7 May 1982). At this time, of course, Reagan was pursuing a modernization program of the American nuclear arsenal, as he and aides believed that the United States had fallen dangerously behind. Not surprisingly, his antinuclear attitude was largely ignored at the time, both by the Soviets and, as we will see, by his own administration.

Reagan deeply disliked the underlying nuclear strategy of the United States, that of "mutually assured destruction." "MAD stands for mutual assured destruction, but MAD is also a description of what the policy is," Reagan once remarked in a speech (PPP: 19 June 1986; see also Cannon 1991: 320). Under this logic, nuclear weapons were less likely to be used and a nuclear war less likely to be fought if each side could survive a first strike and retaliate against its foe. The prospect of losing millions of civilians should deter any leader from beginning a nuclear war. Somewhat counterintuitively, the best way to prevent a nuclear war was for both sides to be defenseless against the other's missiles. Efforts at defense were destabilizing because they suggested an effort to develop a first-strike capability and shield against retaliation. In any case, MAD was the basis of American nuclear strategy, and was the foundation of the Anti-Ballistic Missile (ABM) Treaty of 1972, which placed restrictions on the ability of the Soviets and the Americans to develop defensive systems against nuclear weapons.

MAD is a consequentialist strategy. Nuclear weapons, although capable of horrible destruction, nevertheless create stability and peace. Nixon had embraced this doctrine and its utilitarian logic, saying: "Although every instinct motivates me to provide the American people with complete protection against a major nuclear attack, it is not now within our power to do so. And it might look to an opponent like the prelude to an offensive strategy threatening the nuclear deterrent" (Cannon 1991: 236). MAD was a pragmatic choice in light of structural constraints and one that demonstrated security dilemma sensibility. However, Reagan was not a consequentialist. In doubting the strategy, he "questioned the foundations of modern deterrence" (Cannon 1991: 64; also Talbott 1988: 5).

Reagan thought the strategy of securing peace by threatening to kill millions of others was unethical. In a speech in 1985, he asked, "Is there either logic or morality in believing that if one side threatens to kill tens of millions of our people our only recourse is to threaten killing tens of millions of theirs?" (PPP: 21 January 1985), a sentiment he continually expressed both in public (PPP: 23 March 1983; 21 January 1985, and 17 September 1985) and in private (Adelman 2014: 142; Fitzgerald 2001: 256; Matlock 2004: 142), including in summits with the Soviets (Reykjavik: second meeting, Soviet transcript; Geneva: second plenary session).

Of course, there was a moral justification for MAD, but it was a consequentialist one of lesser evils. While it was certainly horrible to point weapons at millions of citizens of other countries, it served the greater good of preventing war for both sides. As a nonrational thinker, however, Reagan thought in morally deontological terms. Frank Carlucci, who served first as national security advisor and later as secretary of defense, recalled, "He would say to me that nuclear weapons are inherently evil" (Cannon 1991: 291). Shultz recalled: "I heard him say many times, what's so good about keeping peace by the ability to wipe each other out?" (interview with the author). In other words, Reagan refused to accept MAD simply by virtue of its consequences. It is not enough to say that Reagan hated nuclear weapons and the idea of using them, as almost everyone did. Reagan did not have different preferences; he thought differently.

Reagan frequently likened the nuclear stalemate to a pistol standoff between two gunslingers, another indication of his attraction to analogies and metaphors (Cannon 1991: 320; Fitzgerald 2001: 208; PPP: 25 March 1983). "I thought that was the most ridiculous thing I had ever seen," he remembered later.

It's like two guys with guns pointed at each other's heads and cocked and thinking that neither one of them will take a chance and pull the trigger. But to have the power to destroy, literally, the civilized world, and it would only take somebody pushing a button. ... If they launched theirs first, you know that ours would be on their way even though we'd be blown up too. (Anderson 1990: xxxiii)

He used the exact same analogy in a National Security Planning Group (NSPG) meeting (NSPG: minutes, 10 December 1984). Reagan's gunslinger analogy, however, missed the logic of MAD entirely. If a sharp shooter draws first (and has good aim), he wins. The entire point of MAD was to avoid such a situation. Any first strike would only wound, not kill.

Reagan's distaste for MAD was largely emotional in nature, not cold and calculating, as many have noted (Farnham 2001: 247). Adelman (2014: 58) pithily observes, "[T]here was some logic to MAD, but there was no comfort in MAD. ... Americans were scared to death by it." Reagan wrote in his memoirs, "Somehow this didn't seem to be something that would send you to bed feeling safe" (Reagan 1990: 547).[1]

Another element of MAD troubled the president greatly: he would have no ability to defend the United States in the event of a Soviet nuclear strike (Diggins 2007: 36; Fitzgerald 2001: 106). All he could do was retaliate in turn (Fitzgerald 2001: 28). This denied the president the agency that he so valued. Reagan's frustration with the structural constraints of MAD is most evident in the frequently told story of his visit, as a presidential candidate, to the North American Aerospace Defense Command (NORAD) in 1979, where he observed the nuclear operations center. When asked what the response would be to a Soviet nuclear attack, the Air Force general briefing Reagan responded, "We can't stop it." Reagan complained directly after, "We have spent all that money and have all that equipment and there is nothing we can do to prevent a nuclear missile from hitting us" (Anderson 1990: 83; Cannon 1991: 319; Diggins 2007: 288; Fitzgerald 2001: 20ff). Of course, by the logic of MAD, it is precisely the lack of agency that makes the situation stable. Leaders have no other choice but to retaliate against a nuclear strike, which is why no one will start a war in the first place provided the opponent has first-strike survivability.

A realist would (and as we will see, did) argue that MAD provided security, even if it was distasteful. Reagan was not such a consequentialist, however, but a romantic. This is crucial for understanding Reagan's crusade to radically reduce nuclear weapons during his presidency (Cannon 1991: 323). McFarlane later observed that the "President saw himself as a heroic figure on the order of one of his more dramatic motion picture roles, destined to change history by rescuing mankind from the deadly threat of nuclear weapons and ballistic missiles" (Oberdorfer 1991: 141). As Cannon (1991) writes, Reagan "had a sense of world as it would be and as it might be, not merely of the way it was. Reagan wanted a world without nuclear weapons" (281). The president believed "that history was not predetermined ... and that a world without nuclear weapons could be possible because it could be imagined" (Diggins 2007: 266).

---

[1] At Reykjavik, Reagan said, "It would be better to eliminate missiles so that our populations could sleep in peace" (Reykjavik: White House transcript). At Geneva, he said the American people "look at the sky and think what might happen if missiles suddenly appear and blow up everything in our country" (Geneva: second plenary session). He spoke of the "world's nightmare about nuclear weapons" to Gorbachev (Geneva: third plenary session).

The Dream: Reagan's Commitment to Strategic Defenses

Reagan's reaction to these structural obstacles was a romantic one – to exercise agency. When he visited the NORAD facility and saw the American reliance on MAD, Anderson reported him as saying, "There must be something better than this" (Reagan 1990: 547; Shultz 1993: 262). He was literally trying to will a different outcome. His solution became known as the Strategic Defense Initiative (SDI), quickly dubbed "Star Wars" by its critics. The idea was to create a shield against intercontinental ballistic missiles (ICBMs), the most powerful and numerous type of nuclear weapon.

SDI was Reagan's attempt to escape the consequentialist logic of MAD (Garthoff 1994: 99). Rather than accept the unpleasant reality of relying on nuclear weapons for security, Reagan strove to remake it. "The main reason for his sudden, and tenacious, attraction to the idea was a strong desire to escape the *confines* of mutual deterrence and mutual dependence for survival" (Garthoff 1994: 99 [emphasis added]). In announcing the program publicly, the president declared, "We must not *resign* ourselves to a future in which security on both sides depends on threatening the lives of millions of innocent men, women, and children" (PPP: 31 March 1983 [emphasis added]). In a later speech he offered the hope that nations "could defend themselves against missile attack and mankind, at long last, escape the *prison* of mutual terror. And this is my dream" (PPP: 21 November 1985 [emphasis added]). Talbott (1988) contrasts Reagan's vision with the pragmatic, utilitarian view that prevailed before him:

For decades, the twofold object of American defense and diplomacy had been to make sure that the Soviet Union did not take over the world and that the thermonuclear bomb did not blow it up. These goals amounted to making the best of two bad but inescapable realities: the existence of the Soviet Union and the existence of the Bomb. That was not good enough for Reagan. He saw himself as ... a dreamer who could get things done, or at least could inspire the hope that they could be done someday. (3)

SDI, if successful, would absolve leaders of the moral weight of killing millions of Soviet citizens. No American president would have to order a retaliatory nuclear strike, which appealed greatly to Reagan (Diggins 2007: 292; see also PPP: 21 January 1985 and 26 August 1987). As he would later pithily put it, "Wouldn't it be better to save lives than to avenge them?" (PPP: 23 March 1983), something he said in high-level meetings as well. "We must be prepared to make clear to the American people that this is a system which does not kill people, that it would free the world from the threat of nuclear weapons" (NSPG: 17 December 1984; also Geneva: third plenary session). Reagan spoke of a "change from a policy of assured destruction to one of assured survival" (Cannon 1991: 741).

Reagan hoped that a successful shield would render nuclear weapons "obsolete," a term he consistently used, even in private meetings (NSPG: 5 December 1984, 23 March 1983, 21 January 1985, and 26 August 1987; Reagan 1990: 608). SDI provided a path to his dream of the "complete elimination of nuclear weapons" (NSPG: 20 September 1985). In an NSPG meeting, Reagan said, "To take an optimistic view, if the US is first to have both offense and defense we could put the nuclear genie back into the bottle by volunteering to eliminate offensive weapons" (NSPG: 30 November 1983).

The problem was that there was no real promise of SDI offering anything like the protection Reagan was hoping for, a "shield that could protect us from nuclear missiles just as a roof protects a family from rain" (PPP: 19 June 1986). Soviet land-based intercontinental ballistic missiles (ICBMs) were outfitted with "multiple independently targetable reentry vehicles" (MIRVs) – in other words, with several warheads per missile that would shortly after launch break off into different directions with different targets. Because of this technology, a successful strategic defense system would need a "boost-phase interceptor" that could destroy 2000 missiles in 3 to 5 minutes before the MIRVs could be released. American missiles would have to be stationed in space so as to catch the ICBMs early – so early, in fact, that it was an open question as to whether there would even be time for a presidential authorization. In addition, the Soviets could easily knock out these satellites preemptively in the first phase of a nuclear strike so they would have to be protected somehow. Moreover, SDI could not stop bombers, cruise missiles, or submarine missiles, which packed enough force to do tremendous damage to the United States. Supercomputers not yet invented would need to be able to coordinate the interception of several thousand missiles and would have to be almost perfect to be successful. If the system destroyed 90 percent of an attack using only 10 percent of the Soviet arsenal, the largest cities in the United States would still be destroyed, with tens of millions of casualties (Fitzgerald 2001: 246–8; Talbott 1988: 196ff).

Almost all works on Reagan, whether by historians, journalists, or former colleagues, stress how the president was impervious to evidence demonstrating the infeasibility of a space-defense shield. Lacking epistemic motivation, remaining open to incoming information that might undermine his beliefs and hopes was not part of his cognitive style.

Matlock (2004) writes, "One thing should have been clear from the beginning of the SDI debate: there was no possibility that any country could devise an impenetrable missile-defense shield so reliable that it could be counted on to repel a massive retaliatory attack." Carlucci said, "After each of those briefings, I would go in to the president ... and try to put it in perspective. Mainly I would tell him, 'Look, this thing cannot be deployed in the time frame that the Defense Department was telling you.'" Weinberger's claim of a two-year time frame was "unimaginable from a technical point of view" (Wohlforth 1996: 57).

Anderson (1990) knew that whenever Reagan "decided to move forward on such an important policy path he rarely looked back or changed his mind" (96). Shultz (1993) observed the same: "Once he was sold on this idea, he stuck with it and looked for ways to persuade others that his idea was right. It was a Reagan characteristic that I would observe again and again" (263). The secretary later commented, "He was conditioned in his mind to seize on a report that strategic defense was possible" (Wohlforth 1996: 35). Carlucci remembered, "Obviously, as everybody knows, he was not a person who wanted to get into the technicalities" (Wohlforth 1996: 43). More neutral biographers are much less charitable about Reagan's persistent belief in SDI (Adelman 2014: 109; Cannon 1991: 321; Garthoff 1994: 99; Oberdorfer 1991: 25).

The president's faith was reinforced by his own romantic understanding of the United States as the "can do" nation where technological marvels were always around the corner (Cannon 1991: 333; see also PPP: 31 March 1983). Matlock said: "He had almost a romantic belief in American technology and inventiveness. And he said [to scientists], 'You have to find a way to defend us'" (interview with the author). Talbott (1988) notes that Reagan "always enjoyed a story about an eccentric inventor who tinkers for years in his garage with a gadget the neighbors chuckle over – until it whirs and takes flight, changing the face of civilization" (195).

This lack of deliberation and objectivity about SDI's feasibility is evident in the process by which it was conceptualized and developed. The president's speech announcing the program was arranged hastily, with no consultation with either the secretary of defense or the State Department (Cannon 1991: 331). Initial assessments of the feasibility of the program involved only a few scientists who were deeply committed to the idea and whose work was funded by conservative donors. Their visits to the White House were not recorded in the official list (Anderson 1990: 95). Carlucci later complained that "a whole organizational structure had been set up outside the procurement mechanism, outside the control of the JCS [Joint Chiefs of Staff]" (Wohlforth 1996: 45). A number of government panels, both before and after the announcement, concluded that the SDI did not have enough promise to justify major government expenditures (Fitzgerald 2001: 119ff, 137, 204, 210–1, 244ff; Talbott 1988: 196).

This cognitive style was a part of Reagan's romanticism, which is essential for understanding his commitment to SDI (Abshire and Neustadt 2005: 203–4). When announcing the program, he told the public that "tonight we're launching an effort which holds the promise of changing the course of human history. There will be risks, and results take time. But I believe we can do it" (PPP: 23 March 1983). Talbott (1988: 186) calls SDI the "most vivid and enduring example of Reagan's proclivity for grand gestures of political imagination, and a refusal to let discouraging facts ... get into the way" (also Cannon 1991: 333; Diggins 2007: 288).

Dear Chairman: Reagan's Romantic Belief in Personal Engagement

Another manifestation of Reagan's romanticism, albeit one that is typically overlooked, was his faith in personal diplomacy, his belief that personal contact (his efforts in particular) could break through previous obstacles to agreement (Oberdorfer 1991: 22; Wohlforth 1996: 16). Reagan wrote later, "I felt that if I could ever get in a room alone with one of the top Soviet leaders, there was a chance the two of us could make some progress in easing tensions between our two countries" (Reagan 1990: 566). From the beginning of his presidency, even as he was launching a massive arms build-up and decrying the evils of the Soviet system, Reagan was writing personal letters to the Soviet premiers, often in longhand, and leaving the door open to personal diplomacy (Mann 2009: 31; Wilson 2014: 5). "I tried to send signals to Moscow indicating we were prepared to negotiate a winding down of the arms race if the Soviets were also sincere about it," he recalled (Reagan 1990: 548).

When I asked Matlock whether Reagan could be characterized as a romantic, the former adviser answered affirmatively, noting Reagan's nuclear abolitionist streak but also his belief in negotiation: "He really did think that if we went about it the right way, we could eliminate nuclear weapons. He really did think that if you go about it the right way there are very few people who can't be influenced by reason and good will. In that sense you could say he was a romantic" (interview with the author). The realist Kissinger expressed frustration with this very tendency of the president, which he regarded as simplistic (Diggins 2007: xix, 412). Shultz recalled a now famous dinner he had with Reagan at the White House following a snowstorm at which the president first revealed to him his desire to directly engage with the Soviets: "I'm thinking, this guy has never had a real conversation with a big-time communist leader and he's dying to have one. . . . That was blinding news. Nobody had any idea that was what was in his gut" (interview with the author).

The president believed that he had a special talent in this regard (Wilson 2014: 85). Matlock later commented on Reagan's

strong confidence in his ability to convince. And this confidence in his ability to communicate and convince was one of the sources of his strength. In the final analysis, I don't know to what degree he was convincing, but his confidence did lead him to take chances because he felt that the Soviet system could change. He did think that it was an "evil empire," but he also thought it was one that could change, and that we could influence that change. (Wohlforth 1996: 22)

Mann (2009: 19) notes how Reagan's belief that the Cold War could be transformed helps explain how the president was even more willing than Nixon to do business with a Soviet leader.

Oberdorfer (1991) notes the "dichotomous nature of Reagan's views. On the one hand, he could condemn the Soviet leaders with sincerity and zeal, using the harshest rhetoric ever heard from a U.S. President, and on the other he could express a persistent willingness, even an eagerness, to reach out to them in constructive discussions" (22). Even as he denounced the Soviet Union as an "evil empire," the president stressed in the same speech, "This doesn't mean we should isolate ourselves and refuse to seek an understanding with them. I intend to do everything I can to persuade them of our peaceful intent" (PPP: 8 March 1983). Understanding Reagan as a romantic makes this seeming contradiction more understandable. The president believed in the power of "charismatic leadership" to make history (Diggins 2007: 198). He said, "Systems may be brutish. Bureaucrats may fail. But men can sometimes transcend all that, transcend even the forces that seemed destined to keep them apart" (Diggins 2007: 392; Farnham 2001: 248). Present from the very beginning of his presidency, this other side of Reagan's romanticism did not, and still does not, receive nearly the same attention as his dramatic rhetoric. In Chapter 10, we will see Reagan's romanticism in practice and in interaction with the very different approaches of his advisers.

Dear Chairman: Reagan's Romantic Belief in Personal Engagement 269

tendence of the president, which he regarded as simplistic (Diggins 2007:
xix, 413). Shultz recalled a now famous dinner he had with Reagan at the

10   Winning One as the Gipper?: Reagan's Administration and American Engagement with the Soviet Union

Ronald Reagan's romanticism made him completely unique in his own administration, something that impacted his pursuit of a world without nuclear weapons and a United States protected by a strategic defense system. By comparing the president to his key aides, we are able to see his thinking style more clearly. Two factions predominated in his administration: a highly hawkish conservative (and neoconservative) group that opposed rapprochement with the Soviet Union and a collection of pragmatic realists who wanted to negotiate mutually beneficial accords on nuclear weapons. Each seized on one prong of Reagan's romanticism. The conservatives loved his tough talk and moralistic framing of the Cold War as well as the arms build-up; the realists seized upon Reagan's desire to personally engage Soviet leaders so as to bring about arms control.

Neither side, however, truly embraced all of Reagan's goals. Both sides found instrumental uses for the Strategic Defense Initiative (SDI), but neither was genuinely committed to its realization. For the conservatives, it facilitated a new arms race they thought the United States would win and posed an obstacle to any new treaty. For the pragmatists, it was a bargaining chip for precisely such an agreement. And neither faction believed in total nuclear abolition. The highly consequentialist realists were taken aback by Reagan's opposition to mutually assured destruction and wanted the president to scale back his plans for SDI since the program gave the false impression that the United States was pursuing a first-strike capability. They pushed Reagan in the direction of ensuring a survivable second-strike capability by reducing the growing number of Soviet intercontinental ballistic missiles (ICBMs) through a treaty. The conservatives did not seem to want to bring the number of nuclear weapons down at all.

In 1983, the president, dissatisfied with the state of relations with the Soviet Union, empowered pragmatists in his administration to engage the Soviet Union in a series of summit meetings. Pragmatists pushed the president (over conservative objections) to trade away the testing of a strategic defense system that could not promise what Reagan hoped in exchange for a significant reduction in strategic nuclear weapons. Reagan resisted, however, instead coming up with yet another romantic solution to the problems at hand. To convince the Soviets that SDI was meant as a shield and not as a sword, he proposed sharing any system with them and even the international community, to be deployed only after major reductions in offensive nuclear weapons. His audacious plan, meant to preserve his bold dreams, was rejected by both the Soviets and his own administration as unrealistic.

This chapter shows how Reagan's romanticism set him apart in his cabinet and administration, with his uniqueness being the source of the Reagan riddle. Different factions aimed to maneuver the president in their preferred direction in regard to Soviet policy and nuclear weapons. The chapter also shows how Reagan brought his nonrational thinking style to the summits with the Soviet Union. I end with a discussion of the impact of Reagan's romanticism on the course of events.

I do not try to establish Reagan's precise role in "winning" the Cold War in the sense of establishing whether his arms build-up forced Soviet acquiescence and ultimately the regime's collapse (Brooks and Wohlforth 2000; Lebow and Risse-Kappen 1995; Risse-Kappen 1991; Wohlforth 1994). Nor do I seek to uncover the sources of the personal bond that developed between Reagan and Gorbachev, although this too was certainly important (Holmes 2018; Wheeler 2013). I offer only some thoughts about the contribution of Reagan's romanticism to the American ability to come to terms with the Soviet Union, which was obviously also driven by internal and external forces in the direction of rapprochement. The president's unique approach seems to have both promoted and hindered the pursuit of his goals at various times. It is possible that were he not a romantic, there would have never been an Intermediate Nuclear Forces Treaty, which eliminated all such nuclear weapons from Europe, ending the Euromissile crisis. In this way, Reagan set the agenda. However, it also seems possible that his commitment to his dream of SDI denied him the ability to exploit the program as a bargaining chip in a grand compromise at Reykjavik that would have reduced the world's stockpile of strategic nuclear weapons dramatically – perhaps more than the reduction that his successor, George H. W. Bush, ultimately negotiated after Reagan left office. Reagan's romanticism caused him to think big, giving him what Bush later called the "vision thing." However, it also blinded him.

"The Ship of Feuds": Reagan's Divided Cabinet

Reagan's administration was terribly divided, one of the most dysfunctional in modern American history. This was partly a function of his delegatory and often indifferent leadership style, but also a reflection of his ideology and cognitive style. Observers consistently note a cleavage in the administration between the "pragmatists" or "realists" on the one hand and the "conservatives," "neoconservatives" or "ideologues" on the other hand (Brands 2015: 500; Cannon 1991: 306–7; Farnham 2001: 233; Fitzgerald 2001: 64, 157, 215; Shultz 1993: 165). The former were located primarily in the State Department, led from 1982 on by George Shultz; the latter dominated the National Security Council in Reagan's first term, as well as the Central Intelligence Agency (CIA), the Arms Control and Disarmament Agency (ACDA), and the Department of Defense, where Caspar Weinberger served as Secretary for almost all of Reagan's tenure. This gave the administrative a heavy conservative, hardliner tilt, especially in the early years. The divisions were most pronounced over how to manage relations with the Soviet Union and the related question of the role that nuclear weapons should play in America's defense.

Reagan, however, never fully identified with either group (Diggins 2007: 412; Wilson 2014: 22). As Fitzgerald (2001) writes, "Both sides claimed Reagan as their own, but he never decided between them" (17). I argue that this was a result of Reagan's romanticism, something that becomes evident when we compare the preferences of the different factions on the issue of negotiating arms control agreements with the Soviets as well as SDI. According to Cannon (1991), "Reagan did not fit the neat ideological stereotype that was presented in alternative forms by movement conservatives and liberal activists. He was an American original, both in form and substance" (185).

The conservatives in Reagan's administration were actually radicals with grand ambitions of rolling back the Soviet empire and winning the Cold War. They had an image of the Soviet Union as an intractable foe bent on spreading its influence and ideology, one that responded only to pressure and coercion. In their eyes, the Soviet Union was consistently cheating on previous arms agreements in an effort to create a nuclear superiority that would give the country a first strike capability (Diggins 2007: 352; Garthoff 1994: 35; Shimko 1991: 69). The détente that had been pushed by Nixon and Kissinger was a dangerous delusion, limiting American but not Soviet power. The only option for the United States was to match and surpass the Soviet build-up, which had in their eyes given the Russians military superiority. Neoconservatives emphasized the "barbaric" nature of the Soviet regime more than more traditional hawk-ish conservatives, who thought more in terms of power and interests. In addition, the former were fiercer supporters of Reagan's interventions in the developing world to stem Soviet influence. However, in terms of nuclear and arms control issues they generally acted as a single block (Diggins 2007: 192, 196, 287; Fitzgerald 2001: 17, 79, 108, 172, 176; Garthoff 1994: 309; Shimko 1991: ch. 5). Instead of mutual restraint, they wanted to fight the Cold War and win it (Diggins 2007: 357).

Conservatives therefore embraced Reagan's rhetoric about the Soviet Union wholeheartedly, as well as his pledge to restore American confi-dence, his arms build-up, and the nuclear modernization program. In this sense, Reagan was their hero and most charismatic voice. However, this faction, which dominated the administration in its early years, opposed other products of Reagan's romantic approach to international relations: his desire to personally engage Soviet leaders, his plans for a major reduction in America's nuclear stockpile, and his dreams of abol-ishing the nuclear weapons that were such an important part of American power (Adelman 2014: 66; Cannon 1991: 742; Diggins 2007: 287; Oberdorfer 1991: 16; Shultz 1993: 274).

Conservatives in the administration showed no interest in seriously engaging the Soviet Union in arms-control talks, insisting that any engagement with the Russians would require prior "restraint" on their part. Anything else would amount to appeasement, thereby legitimizing and rewarding bad Soviet behavior (Diggins 2007: 205; Matlock 2004: 102; Shimko 1991: 64–7, 74; Weinberger 1990: 347ff). Matlock describes Weinberger as "very wary about negotiations with the Soviet Union. He realized you got to do it, as a show. He was convinced it was not going to bring anything whatsoever" (interview with the author). Hardliners were concerned that Reagan's romanticism would be exploited by the Soviets and sought to prevent the president from meeting the Soviets for fear he would surrender too much (Wilson 2014: 85). As an example, on 11 July 1983 Reagan sent a longhand letter to Soviet leader Andropov that did not go through the normal staffing and clearance process. Nevertheless his conservative national security advisor William Clark, had him remove two sentences: "If we can agree on mutual, verifiable reductions in the number of nuclear weapons we both hold could this not be a first step toward the elimin-ation of all such weapons? What a blessing this would be for the people we both represent" (Anderson 1983: xxxix; Cannon 1991: 742; Ober-dorfer 1991: 38; Shultz 1993: 358). Reagan complained in his diary, "Some of the N.S.C. [National Security Council] staff are too hardline and don't think any approach should be made to the Soviets. I think I'm hardline and will never appease. But I do want to try to let them see there is a better world if they'll show by deed they want to get along with the free world" (quoted in Reagan 1990: 572). When Reagan first met the Soviet ambassador, he had to be smuggled into the White House so as not to alert conservative NSC staffers (Fitzgerald 2001: 221; Oberdorfer 1991: 17–8).

The difference between the conservatives and the president was Reagan's romanticism. Even though they held the same views of the Soviet Union, the president saw "history as open to change," while the conservatives regarded the world as "dark and foreboding" (Diggins 2007: 218). Reagan was agentic; the conservatives were structuralists.

The conservatives liked the SDI program, albeit for different reasons than Reagan. Rather than opening up the possibility of nuclear abolition, it offered, in the unlikely chance it worked, a chance at superiority. If it did not, it would nevertheless disrupt or prevent any arms-control talks or agreements given its destabilizing effect on deterrence and Soviet opposition to the program (Cannon 1991: 760; Fitzgerald 2001: 108, 257). Moreover, the Soviets were thought to be working on a system of their own. Weinberger acknowledged that SDI "runs against conventional MAD [mutually assured destruction]. ... There will be doubters who will say a DABM [defensive anti-ballistic missile] program will frighten Europe, or not be technically doable or unwise for lots of other reasons" and would "need work on Capitol Hill." Even so, he supported moving forward "because it would be disastrous if the Soviets were to develop effective missile defense and we did not" (NSPG: 30 November 1983). According to Matlock, "Most of the people were pushing it for tactical reasons. Weinberger thought they would never accept it. He originally did not think much about it, but he saw it as a brilliant way of preventing any agreement from being signed" (interview with the author). Schultz and Carlucci concur (Wohlforth 1996: 34). Weinberger and other conservatives tried consistently throughout the decade to legally reinterpret the Anti-Ballistic Missile (ABM) Treaty in a less restrictive way so as to open up possibilities for the testing of SDI.

The pragmatic alternative to conservative hardliners was a grudging acceptance of certain unalterable structural features of the world – the Soviet Union, the nature of its regime, and its gigantic nuclear arsenal. This faction's leader was Secretary of State Shultz (Larson 1997: 191), who embraced the label: "I was in no closet. I was proud to be a pragmatist," he writes, although "it amused me to think of my State Department arms control colleagues as a bunch of 'fire-in-the-belly' pragmatists" (Shultz 1993: 508). Pragmatists believed, as Shultz tells it, "A return to predétente estrangement would be unwise and self-defeating. This was the country that could wipe us out in thirty minutes with strategic nuclear missiles" (117).

In a speech in October 1984, he laid out his pragmatic philosophy:

We are left with two inescapable truths: in the nuclear age we need to maintain a relationship with the Soviet Union. Yet we know that they have acted in ways that violate our standards of human conduct and rule by law and that are repugnant to use. ... A sustained and sound relationship, therefore, will confront the fact that the Soviets can be expected periodically to do something abhorrent to us or threaten our interests. ... Should we refuse to conclude agreements with the Soviets in one area when they do something outrageous in some other area? ... We do not seek negotiations for their own sake. We negotiate when it is in our interest to do so. Therefore, when the Soviet Union acts in a way we find objectionable, it may not always make sense for us to break off negotiations or suspend agreements. If those negotiations or agreements were undertaken with a realistic view of their benefits for us, then they should be worth maintaining under all but exceptional circumstances. (Shultz 1993: 490; also Oberdorfer 1991: 96)

Shultz was arguing against what he called "light switch diplomacy," what he thought to be the self-defeating tendency of the United States to quickly break off talks whenever the Soviet Union did something it did not like. This would inevitably happen quite often given the nature of the regime. Thinking about foreign affairs in this morally deontological way was leading the United States to cut off its nose to spite its face.

Consistent with the argument of this book, the realist Shultz had a cognitive style marked by epistemic motivation. Matlock (2004) writes that Shultz was "able to probe the details of a subject without losing sight of the big picture" (25). He was "a good listener" who "sought differing points of view before every important decision and, when possible, took time to reflect before making up his mind" (25) and "rarely showed emotion" (68) (also Oberdorfer 1991: 45). Kissinger admired Shultz for this reason, writing: "Highly analytical, calm and unselfish, Shultz made up in integrity and judgments for his lack of flamboyance" (Adelman 2014: 18). This gave rise to his nickname, the Sphinx: Shultz could not be easily read.

The result was a highly instrumentally rational foreign policy focused on egoistic interests, one that separated vital from peripheral considerations and that was oriented toward the long term. As Shultz (1993) admonished, "We should not sacrifice long-term interests in order to express immediate outrage. ... Sudden shifts in policy, stemming from emotional and perfectly understandable reactions to Soviet behavior, are not the way to pursue our interests" (488). Oberdorfer (1991) observes that the secretary had a "patience for long-term enterprises and objectives that was unusual" (45). In high-ranking meetings, Shultz consciously avoided cognitive closure and misplaced certainty. In response to Weinberger's assertion that the Soviets had no interest in concluding an arms-control agreement, he laid out his "list of ten do's and don'ts," which included "Don't base policy on speculations about the Soviet Union" (NSPG: 27 March 1984). Shultz cautioned equanimity. Before Congress, he advised, "We should not allow ourselves ... if something positive happens somewhere to get carried away with euphoria. Nor, given our strength and the Soviet interest in working with a strong country like the United States, should we go into paroxysms of despair either" (Shimko 1991: 83).

As a realist and therefore a consequentialist decision-maker, Shultz and other pragmatists disliked Reagan's early rhetoric (Matlock 2004: 62; Shultz 1993: 267) and, at least initially, his pursuit of both SDI and nuclear abolition. Shultz believed in MAD, as it had kept the peace; the ABM was a "milestone of central importance," as it enhanced MAD's credibility (Shultz 1993: 247). The realists were consequentialists interested in results and outcomes (Cannon 1991: 113; Fitzgerald 2001: 17).

Shultz came out strongly against SDI behind closed doors when he was belatedly informed of the program, just a few days before the speech revealing it to the public. The highly rational Shultz could not believe how little deliberation and thought had gone into the project. He remembered, "I did not know much about the science involved in possible strategic defenses, but from what little I knew, it seemed to present huge, perhaps insuperable problems" (Shultz 1993: 246). As Shultz tried to gather information about how extensively the idea had been vetted, he was not reassured. "The chiefs are not equipped to make this kind of proposal. They are not scientists," he told NSC staff. "We don't have the technology to do this." The secretary of state also had great concerns that the speech oversold the shield. He told William Clark, "This is so sweeping that it must be carefully considered" (Shultz 1993: 249–51).

Perhaps most importantly, Shultz was worried about the program's effect on nuclear strategy (Fitzgerald 2001: 205): "This changes the whole strategic view and doctrine of the United States," he told the White House. Shultz was thinking about how the Soviets would react, demonstrating the security dilemma sensibility more characteristic of a rational thinker. The secretary worried that the "initiative will not be seen as a peaceful gesture" but rather "will be seen as destabilizing." It raised the specter of an American first strike, a sword rather than a shield. He complained at the time:

[I]f we put a defensive system in place and continue to maintain our offensive weapons, the result is destabilizing. The Soviets will assume that we are on to something more than the president reveals in his address. Ironically, the address may make more dangerous our "window of vulnerability" because the Soviets will see this as an effort to render their offensive capability obsolete by the end of the century. (Fitzgerald 2001: 250–2)

According to Shultz, SDI, although an attempt at defense, could actually decrease American security. In the NSPG in November 1983, Schultz said, "We should go easy on throwing out a deterrence strategy that has worked well in favor of something new and immature. . . . We should not become confident that we can develop a defense that could not be countered . . . the U.S. should not send the wrong message that we think our current strategy is wrong; to do so would be disastrous" (NSPG: 30 November 1983).

Shultz tried to convince the president of the merits of MAD, making a pragmatic case that stressed structural realities: "[N]uclear weapons cannot be uninvented," he stressed (Shultz 1993: 466). Some number of nuclear weapons that could withstand a first strike were a necessary evil (Wohlforth 1996: 176; also 172). The secretary of state notes, however, that "I made no real impact on the president with this argument" (Shultz 1993: 466). He implies that Reagan was engaging in wishful thinking, a kind of motivated bias: "I could see the depth of his feelings about this issue, his abhorrence of reliance on the ability to 'wipe each other out' as the means of deterring war, and, of course, I could agree that if we could learn how to defend ourselves, that would be wonderful" (253). In his memoirs, the former secretary of state writes of the president's cognitive closure:

Ronald Reagan's views were definite: all nuclear weapons should be eliminated, and strategic defense should take over the role of deterrence. He was annoyed with me for expressing reservations. I pointed out that offensive weapons were needed and that even the most far-reaching version of his dream of strategic defense was incomplete. . . . The president listened, but he didn't give any ground. (Shultz 1993: 505)

However, the pragmatists supported direct diplomatic engagement with the Soviets in an effort to reduce the proliferation of Soviet ICBMs with more and more warheads, thereby eroding the stability of deterrence and MAD (Fitzgerald 2001: 267; Shimko 1991: 93; Shultz 1993: 497). According to Shultz (1993), this "meant that we and the Soviets were increasingly able to threaten all of the other's land-based intercontinental launches of ballistic missiles with only a fraction of our own" (248). The United States still had an advantage in bombers as well as nuclear submarines, the latter of which were highly invulnerable. Nevertheless, given the contentious domestic politics surrounding where to base the weapons, it was hard for the United States to keep up in land-based ICBMs (Shultz 1993: 248). Meeting with the president in 1984, Shultz (1993) told him, "Standing still with the Soviets is not an option. The choice is to negotiate new agreements or enter a world with no arms limitations" (497).

Thus Reagan's inclination to seek out Soviet leaders met with favor by the pragmatists over the strenuous objections of conservatives who consistently tried to sabotage his efforts (Diggins 2007: 169, 176; Oberdorfer 1991: 35; Shultz 1993: 166, 264, 268, 491, 497, 503). Shultz (1993) recognized that arms-control talks "meant we would have to compromise and have to realize that nothing is perfect or airtight" (503). In other words, one had to be realistic.

Only One Supports Zero: Reagan and the Euromissile Crisis

Between the resistance of pragmatists and conservatives, Reagan was alone in his advocacy of a nuclear weapon–free world created through a strategic defense shield and personal engagement with the Soviets (Cannon 1991: 301; Larson 1996: 207; Farnham 2001: 247; Mann 2009: 42; Oberdorfer 1991: 26; Reagan 1990: 550; Shultz 1993: 376; Talbott 1988: 7). His romanticism isolated him. Shultz (1993) admits, "Reagan was consistently committed to his personal vision of a world without nuclear weapons; his advisers were determined to turn him away from that course" (360). He later recalled that "all along President Reagan stated his vision and his dream that nuclear weapons be eliminated, and nobody took that seriously. ... [H]e said it during his election campaign, he said it endless numbers of times, and practically everybody, all the arms control people, tried to talk him out of it" (Wohlforth 1996: 170–2). Anderson (1983) writes, "[W]hen Reagan began to talk privately of a dream he had when someday we might live in a world free of all nuclear missiles, well, we just smiled" (73). Kenneth Adelman recalled, "All of us who were conservatives thought that when [President Jimmy] Carter said, 'I want to eliminate nuclear weapons,' that was the stupidest thing we'd ever heard. We all made fun of it, and then we have our hero who says things really more extreme than Carter ever does" (Mann 2009: 40). A quip by a State Department staff member puts Reagan's romanticism in relief. "Let's start with eliminating just one missile" (Shultz 1993: 512).

SDI also had very few true (but many instrumental) believers in the bureaucracy and attracted public scorn from six former Secretaries of Defense (Cannon 1991: 300; Garthoff 1994: 100, 230; Wohlforth 1996: 38). Talbott (1988) concludes, "Virtually no one in the U.S. Government except Reagan believed in the vision of an America so thoroughly defended that nuclear weapons would rust away. SDI in its purest, presidentially sanctioned form was, from the outset, simultaneously a sacred cow and an embarrassment" (7).

All of these divisions over Soviet policy were evident early in Reagan's first term in the American handling of the "Euromissile crisis." Soviet deployment of 360 SS-20 intermediate-range nuclear missiles in Eastern Europe in 1979 had disrupted the balance of forces on the continent and led, at European request, to a North Atlantic Treaty Organization (NATO) pledge to deploy countervailing American weapons in Western Europe: 464 hard-to-detect cruise missiles in five countries, and 108 Pershing II ballistic missiles in Germany that could strike the Soviet Union in less than 20 minutes (Shultz 1993: 347). Along with the Soviet invasion of Afghanistan, the Euromissile crisis ended the détente, ushering in one of the most confrontational periods of the Cold War. The SS-20s were not ICBMs, the heavy weapons launched in the Soviet Union that could reach the United States. However, they were particularly threatening because, armed with three warheads each, they could quickly strike NATO allies. They were also highly mobile, making it difficult to target them in a retaliation; in arms-control jargon, they were "survivable." The counter-deployment would be a significant upgrade from the Pershing I missiles that could not reach Soviet soil; Pershing II's reach would encompass Moscow's command-and-control centers (Garthoff 1994: 291). Given pressure from the peace movement, however, NATO countries simultaneously agreed to try to engage the Soviets in arms-reduction talks, the second track of NATO's "dual track" decision.

The original decisions were made by President Carter. When Reagan took office, he had to come up with a specific proposal. The enterprising and highly conservative Richard Perle devised what became known as the "zero option": the Soviets would remove all Intermediate-Range Nuclear Forces (INF) from both Europe and Asia (so as to prevent the Soviets from simply storing the mobile missiles off of the continent) in exchange for an agreement by the United States not to deploy its own counterforces. Hawks in the Reagan administration believed that the offer was "non-negotiable"; in other words, it so heavily favored American interests that it had no chance of being accepted by the Soviets, since the Soviet Union would be trading real weapons for hypothetical ones.

However, for conservatives this was the zero option's charm (Fitzgerald 2001: 178; Talbott 1988: 170). As Weinberger explained forthrightly in a national security meeting:

If refused by the Soviets, they would take the blame for its rejection. If the Soviets agreed, we would achieve the balance that we've lost. Such a plan would be to propose a "zero option." ... The Soviets will certainly reject an American zero-option proposal. But whether they reject it or they accept it, they would be set back on their heels. We would be left in good shape and would be shown as the White Hats. (NSPG: 13 October 1981)

Pragmatists, whose only real home in Reagan's first term was the State Department, opposed the zero-option precisely because it had no chance of succeeding (Fitzgerald 2001: 179). When Shultz took over from Alexander Haig, he advised Reagan, "Let's make it our preferred outcome and ultimate goal, even when, as I feel is inevitable, we propose intermediate possible outcomes" (Shultz 1993: 160). They pushed instead a "zero-plus" option, an acknowledgment that the administration would have to come off of zero with a specific number of warheads that could potentially be reduced to zero in subsequent agreements (Cannon 1991: 303–5; Fitzgerald 2001: 178, 227; Shultz 1993: 348ff). Paul Nitze, American envoy to the arms-control talks in Geneva during the 1980s, tried to find some mutual reduction short of zero that would appeal to both sides, although often without sanction from the government. Unsurprisingly, Nitze was a renowned rational thinker. According to his biographer and son-in-law, Strobe Talbott (1988), "Nitze prided himself on his pragmatism, his love of rigor, his reliance on the facts, no matter how dry, mind-numbing or discouraging" (186).

Reagan ultimately backed the zero option, but out of genuine conviction, rather than the instrumental approach of the conservatives. Indeed, Reagan "alone may have believed in his proposal for a zero option for INF in 1981," writes Garthoff (1994: 327). The president wrote later: "I viewed the zero–zero proposal as the first step toward the eventual elimination of all nuclear weapons from the earth; the Soviets saw it as an attempt by us to reduce the immense Soviet imbalance of nuclear missile power in Europe – which it was" (Reagan 1990: 550–1). Reagan expressed this sentiment in private, too, saying, "We need to emphasize the idea of elimination of nuclear weapons in the end; the zero option for INF would be a great step in that direction" (NSPG: 17 December 1984). As a romantic, the president appreciated the offer's boldness and simplicity. "Give me a proposal that can be expressed in a single sentence and that sounds like real disarmament," he had ordered (Fitzgerald 2001: 179; see also Talbott 1988: 170).

Reagan endorsed the zero option publicly on November 18, 1981. The Soviets, as expected, responded negatively. Arms negotiations in Geneva went nowhere, and when in November 1983 the Americans introduced their own INF forces to Western Europe, the Soviets walked out of arms talks. This was a nadir in the Cold War.

In a Room Alone: Reagan Engages the Soviets

Beginning sometime late in 1983, Reagan began to push his advisers more aggressively to directly engage the Soviets on arms control (Yarhi-Milo 2014: 192). What Oberdorfer (1991) calls "the turn" and Fischer (1997) the "Reagan reversal" has long puzzled observers. It is part of the paradox of Ronald Reagan, the Cold Warrior who also extended the olive branch of peace. As noted, the Soviets had recently walked out of talks following the deployment of American INF missiles to Western Europe. Reagan seems to have come to the realization that Soviet leaders were genuinely afraid of the United States and a preemptive nuclear strike (Reagan 1990: 588). He had developed "security dilemma sensibility." In 1984, Reagan consistently expressed concerns about Soviet perceptions of American intentions (NSPG: 27 March 1984, 5 December 1984). At a national security meeting, he said, "I'm willing to admit that the USSR is suspicious of us" (NSPG: 10 December 1984). Matlock remembers a meeting during this period in which Reagan "started talking about how he needed to meet the Soviet leaders to convince them that I am not the sort of person that would eat their grandchildren. Weinberger started talking about all the reasons why they shouldn't. Reagan said, 'Cap, we're not going that route'" (interview with the author).

A number of accounts claim that crucial events that year increased the president's security dilemma sensibility – the Able Archer incident, the accidental downing of a Korean airliner over Soviet airspace, and the television movie entitled *The Day After* (Fischer 1997: 102ff; Garthoff 1994: 167; Mann 2009 42; Oberdorfer 1991: 66–7; Shimko 1991: 107; Shimko 1992: 356). After a NATO exercise gave the Soviets the impression that the Americans were beginning a nuclear attack, Reagan remembered thinking, "Well, if that was the case, I was even more anxious to get a top Soviet leader in a room alone and try to convince him we had no designs on the Soviet Union and Russians had nothing to fear from us" (Reagan 1990: 589). Matlock recalled Reagan asking, "Do they really think that we would start a nuclear war. Jesus, that isn't true. I got to meet with these guys" (interview with the author). The president wrote in his diary in September 1984:

I have a feeling we'll get nowhere with arms reductions while they are as suspicious of our motives as we are of theirs. I believe we need a meeting to see if we can't make them understand we have no designs on them but we think they have designs on us. If we could once clear the air maybe reducing arms wouldn't look so impossible to them. (Reagan 1990: 603; see also Shimko 1992: 370)

Some claim that during this period Reagan's fear of nuclear war overcame his strident anticommunism, leading him to emphasize the shared interests of the two countries rather than their differences. This thaw was accelerated by Gorbachev's arrival (Cannon 1991: 292; Diggins 2007: 354; Farnham 2001: 232). Reagan transformed from an "essentialist" who believed that the Soviet Union was an intractable foe governed by ideological goals incompatible with American interests, to an "interactionist" who saw the conflict in terms of mutual misperception (Farnham 2001: 225). This change is all the more striking given my argument that Reagan's cognitive style would seem to inhibit this type of learning (Farnham 2001: 242).

This raises the question: was Reagan reacting to information in the way that a normatively rational thinker should, updating his understanding of the Soviet Union by putting himself in its shoes and adjusting his strategy in a more cooperative direction as a result? During his first three years in office, Reagan indeed demonstrated little understanding that the Soviets might genuinely fear the United States. "Since when has it been wrong for America to be first in military strength? How is military superiority dangerous?" he asked rhetorically (Fitzgerald 2001: 110; Glad 1983: 46; also Garthoff 1994: 105; Oberdorfer 1991: 23; Talbott 1988: 198). In his "Evil Empire" speech, he referenced the "fact" that "the Soviet Union is acquiring what can only be considered an offensive military force" (PPP: 23 March 1983).

However, the degree of change should not be overstated, and the shift took place in a manner consistent with Reagan's thinking style. To start with, Reagan did not rethink his approach based on a cold and analytical effort to put himself in the Soviets' shoes. The events thought to have brought about a change in his beliefs are exactly the kind that should appeal to Reagan's cognitive style. Intuitive thinking, as argued earlier, is affected more by concrete cases experienced directly by participants, which evoke intense emotions. Reagan seems to have had difficulty understanding Soviet fears abstractly and analytically, as a more procedurally rational thinker would be able to do; he had to have a personal experience. The Able Archer incident provided a concrete example of the possibility of nuclear escalation, not a theoretical one. *The Day After* affected Reagan emotionally, likely due to the fact that visual representations of nuclear destruction are more vivid than dry, factual accounts.

To the extent that Reagan became more considerate of Soviet perceptions, he replaced one essentialism with another. The president was
taken with the idea that the Soviet people as a whole had a fearful and
even paranoid character borne out of their history, something encapsu-
lated in a few anecdotes that he frequently recounted. Many of these
were false. Reagan constantly maintained that the Soviets did not allow
their wartime American allies to land in Soviet-occupied Eastern
Europe during bombing missions against Nazi Germany (NSPG:
18 September 1984, 20 September 1985). In March 1984, Reagan
asked, "Have we given enough attention to the fact that they have a
climate of insecurity?" (NSPG: 27 March 1984). "Just think about the
Soviets' historical fear of invasions and suspicion of foreigners that
reaches extreme paranoia in some cases," he instructed his aides
(NSPG: 20 September 1985).

Reagan also seemed to easily hold contradictory ideas simultaneously. He remarked that the Soviets were said to still have barbed wire
up near Moscow to remind the population of how close Hitler came,
something that German foreign minister Hans-Dietrich Genscher told
him. "How do you argue with this fear?" he asked his colleagues
(NSPG: 18 September 1984). In the same meeting he summarily
declared: "I have to believe that the USSR (mainly its leaders) has a
world aggression program." A month later he said the same: "Everything they have said says that they are looking at a first-strike because it
is they, not we, who have built up both offensive and defensive systems"
(NSPG: 5 December 1984).

Although Reagan seems to have become more aware of Soviet perceptions, he made no effort to understand them – a critical element of
genuine security dilemma sensibility. In fact, Reagan's response was to
try to convince Soviet leaders that their views were wrong. Reagan
consistently accompanied his expressions of concerns about Soviet fears
with an assertion that American fears were much better founded in the
historical record. In recounting his first meeting with the Soviet foreign
minister Gromyko, his first conversation with a Soviet official other than
the Russian ambassador, he remembered: "I opened with my monologue
and made the point that perhaps both of us felt the other was a threat,
then explained that by the record we had more reason to feel that way
than they did" (Reagan 1990: 604). At another point he observed, "I
think there is great mutual suspicion between the two countries even if
ours is more justified than theirs" (Shimko 1992: 369). This view persisted even following sustained engagement with the Soviets. Each side
mistrusted the other, Reagan said at Reykjavik, but the "facts were all on
our side" (Reykjavik: third meeting). Reagan even does this in his

memoirs, well after his supposed reversal. He wrote that Americans had "limitless reasons to be wary of the Red Bear because from the day it was born on the streets of Russia it was dedicated to consuming the democracies of the world" (Reagan 1990: 588).

In his efforts at persuasion, the president relied consistently on a simple, concrete argument to make his case – that of American restraint after World War II when it had a nuclear monopoly. This was a common theme that littered both his speeches and his interventions in national security meetings (Fitzgerald 2001: 222; Letters: 24 April 1981 and 16 April 1984; PPP: 14 November 1985; Wilson 2014: 99–100). For instance, in a handwritten postscript in his letter to Chernenko, Reagan expressed sympathy with Soviet fears given its tragic history:

Surely those losses which are beyond description, must affect your thinking today. I want you to know that neither I nor the American people hold any offensive intentions toward you or the Soviet people. The truth of that statement is underwritten by the history of our restraint at a time when our virtual monopoly on strategic power provided the means for expansion had we so chosen. (Letters: 16 April 1984)

For Reagan, this simple fact was supposed to reassure the Soviet Union of American intentions.

In reality, Reagan never truly changed his mind that the Soviet system was evil and America was good (Marlo 2016: 6; Wilson 2014: 84), something he himself stressed (Shimko 1991: 104–5). What changed over time were his views on Gorbachev. His was not a rational updating process, however, based on what rationalists would regard as costly signals. Instead, Reagan set great store in what the Soviet premier said and did not say. Most importantly, Reagan consistently stressed in both public and private that Gorbachev was the only Soviet leader never to have stated the Soviet aim was worldwide revolution and a one-world socialist state (Diggins 2007: 385; Farnham 2001: 240; Shimko 1992: 361–3). This might be regarded as a rational process of intention inference had Reagan noted that Gorbachev must have been under constant pressure domestically to make such a statement. However, he did no such thing, seeming to change his beliefs based on a piece of vivid information. Reagan's more optimistic view was ultimately validated by events, but again judging accurately is not a marker of rationality. Reagan reached his conclusion in an intuitive fashion.

Finally, an important part of Reagan's motivation for greater engagement had nothing to do with his views about the Soviets. He simply believed the United States was in a better bargaining position as a result of the massive arms build-up of the previous three years (Farnham

2001: 238; Fitzgerald 2001: 110). The president thought increasing Soviet flexibility was a response to that new leverage (Cannon 1991: 74, 510; Garthoff 1994: 207, 250, 316). Reagan (1990) recalled in his memoir that "something else had changed: I felt we could now go to the summit, for the first time in years, from a position of strength" (594; also 548–50, 634). This does not appear to have been a post hoc rationalization. Indeed, in April 1982, the president asserted: "A vigorous defense buildup will also be a great help at arms control talks. The Soviets do not believe that they can keep up with us" (NSPG: 16 April 1982). Even as he called for the Soviets and the Americans to "approach each other with ten-fold trust and thousand-fold affection," Reagan stressed that "America has repaired its strength. . . . We are ready for constructive negoti-ations with the Soviet Union" (Garthoff 1994: 161; see also Garthoff 1994: 247; PPP: 29 March 1983). This is Matlock's understanding of "the turn": "He thought of it as chips. . . . He wanted to negotiate from a position of strength. We hadn't had enough to cut [before]" (interview with the author). Shultz concurs, telling the author in an interview: "All the way through, he had the strategy that things could change, and you had to have strength, but once you got to that point when the strength paid off, then if you had a chance to talk to someone you would. So there was nothing that changed about him" (interview with the author).

"The Greatest Sting Operation in History":
The Pragmatists Push a Grand Compromise

Reagan put Shultz in charge of re-engaging with the Soviets, something that had become significantly easier with the departure of his first national security adviser. William Clark was replaced by the more prag-matically minded Robert McFarlane (Cannon 1991: 509; Garthoff 1994: 106; Oberdorfer 1991: 98). Jack Matlock, a top State Department Russian expert serving at the time as ambassador to Czechoslovakia, was brought in to replace the neoconservative NSC staffer in charge of Russian relations, Richard Pipes, precisely to prepare for summit meet-ings (Garthoff 1994: 105). According to Matlock, McFarlane told him, "Nobody here knows how to do it. Your job is to tell us how to do it" (interview with author). The ambassador had turned down a similar offer the year before because there was no real chance of success given the politics within the administration (interview with the author).

McFarlane and Shultz encouraged the president to consider a grand compromise – a drastic reduction in strategic nuclear weapons in exchange for restrictions on American development of strategic defenses. This was a classic pragmatic compromise. Although Reagan would not get everything he wanted, he would get what was most important – the reduction of Soviet ICBMs. McFarlane had been instrumental in pushing forward SDI (as we have seen, without Shultz's knowledge), but he did not truly believe the program was feasible. Instead, it served as a "bargaining chip" of little value to the United States but of great value to the Soviets, one that could be used to induce the latter to bring down their number of ICBMs and warheads (Shultz 1993: 246; Talbott 1988: 204, 213; Wohlforth 1996: 36). The national security adviser asserted that if the strategy worked, it would be the "greatest sting operation in history" (Cannon 1991: 326; Fitzgerald 2001: 195; Talbott 1988: 204). He later claimed, "The idea of SDI, that is, providing a shield for Americans against nuclear attack, was Ronald Reagan's idea absolutely. The idea – a different idea—to use high technology in the form of SDI to leverage Russian behavior to reduce nuclear weapons, was my idea" (Cannon 1991: 236). McFarlane was not a nuclear abolitionist (Cannon 1991: 326); indeed, he cautioned against undermining MAD in national security meetings (NSPG: 17 December 1984). However, McFarlane generally tried to keep his true objectives hidden lest he undermine his influence with the president (Talbott 1988: 204).

Although Shultz had initially been highly resistant to SDI, given its destabilizing effects and false promise, the realist found the silver lining in McFarlane's idea of using it for leverage (Shultz 1993: 516). The secretary of state said at the time that "the Soviets will assume that we are on the verge of some special technical innovation. Maybe that is the great benefit" (251). Later he remembered, SDI "in fact proved to be the ultimate bargaining chip. And we played it for all it was worth" (264). Shultz even used the president's romanticism to his advantage: "I came to feel that utopian though [Reagan's] dream might be, the shared view of Reagan and Gorbachev on the desirability of eliminating nuclear weapons could move us toward the massive reductions in medium-range and strategic ballistic missiles that Reagan had proposed back in 1981 and 1982. I supported those goals wholeheartedly" (700).

Shultz told the president that strategic defenses should be "positioned in the agreement as the key to implementation of the offensive nuclear reductions" (Shultz 1993: 575). He pushed for "umbrella talks" with the Soviets in which strategic weapons and "space" weapons would be negotiated simultaneously, so as to facilitate a linkage. In an NSPG meeting, he was explicit: "We must reach arms control agreements because it is not clear that we can contemplate an unrestrained race with the Soviet Union. We need reductions and we need to trade for them. They won't come for free" (NSPG: 17 December 1984). Shultz also tried to manage Reagan's expectations for strategic weapons reductions.

"Defense is important," he said, "even if you don't have the elimination of nuclear weapons" (NSPG: 17 December 1984). The realists tried to convince Reagan that he could live with limitations on SDI if the number of weapons the system needed to intercept was lower as a consequence of an arms reduction agreement (Fitzgerald 2001: 280). Indeed, offensive weapon reduction was necessary so that any shield would not be overwhelmed (NSPG: 5 December 1984).

Reagan, however, was uninterested in such a pragmatic compromise. He wanted both radical reductions in nuclear weapons and unfettered ability to develop strategic defenses (Oberdorfer 1991: 128). McFarlane later noted how his realist, consequentialist argumentation was ineffective with Reagan: "I went all through this reasoning but he did not understand my investment strategy. For him the idea of anti-missile defenses had an appeal in itself. My own concepts for leveraging Soviet behavior were lost on him" (Fitzgerald 2001: 198). In the NSPG, Reagan stated categorically: "There is no price on SDI. We must be frank with the Soviet Union on the need to go down the path towards defense, to eliminate nuclear weapons, but clearly we are not going to give up SDI" (NSPG: 17 December 1984). At the very same meeting, Reagan declared, "My goal is the total elimination of nuclear weapons," but also, "Whatever we do, we must be resolved among ourselves that SDI is not the price for reductions." The president publicly declared his opposition to a grand compromise in September 1985 (PPP: 17 September 1985), supported by conservatives who opposed arms control in general. Weinberger resisted even the discussion of SDI in arms-control talks with the Soviets, which Shultz thought unrealistic (Cannon 1991: 760; Fitzgerald 2001: 280; Oberdorfer 1991: 102; Shultz 1993: 577).

Reagan did propose a way to have his cake and eat it too, in a proposal that was as radical and romantic as SDI and nuclear abolition: the United States could share its strategic defense technology with the Soviet Union and perhaps even the international community as a whole. In his memoirs, the president reveals that he made up his mind in November 1985, just before the Geneva summit: "This, I thought, should convince them it would never be a threat to them" (Reagan 1990: 631). Reagan had first mentioned the possibility publicly in March 1983, the same month he announced the program. He repeated the offer in 1984 during an election debate with Walter Mondale (PPP: 29 March 1983; also Shultz 1993: 260).

Sharing SDI was one of the most consistent themes voiced by Reagan in those national security meetings in which he was so notoriously reticent. As Matlock (2004) observed, "Once he had an idea in his head, it was might hard to dislodge it. Sharing SDI was one of those ideas, and it was just about as immovable as the idea of SDI itself" (168). In December 1984, Reagan said, "It is important to link research on SDI to making nuclear weapons obsolete. ... I still wonder whether or not we could give them the technology" (NSPG: 5 December 1984). That same month he hypothesized that "international control of SDI for world protection might be possible at some point" (NSPG: 17 December 1984). Just before the Geneva meeting, he declared:

I am prepared, once any of our SDI programs prove out, to then announce to the world that integrating these weapons in our respective arsenals would put international relations on a more stable footing. In fact, this could even lead to a complete elimination of nuclear weapons. We must be prepared to tell the world we are ready to consult and negotiate on integrating these weapons into a new defense philosophy, and to state openly that we are ready to internationalize these systems. (NSPG: 20 September 1985)

In no minutes can I find any mention of sharing technology with the Soviets by any other participant. "Such sharing of sophisticated technology seemed fanciful to politicians of every description, from Richard Perle to Walter Mondale, but Reagan meant it," writes Cannon (1991: 293; also Oberdorfer 1991: 145–6). Carlucci remembered that Reagan did "sincerely believe that he could give [SDI] to the Russians and everything would be fine. I and others would try to explain to him that, technically, that was just not feasible" (Wohlforth 1996: 43). Matlock concurred: "He was definitely a true believer in sharing. This was something that virtually the entire bureaucracy that dealt with these things said we couldn't do" (interview with the author). Matlock told an anecdote of Reagan's inclusion of a reference to sharing in his letter to Gorbachev in summer 1986:

He wanted a section on sharing. We sent a draft in, and he changed it and made a very strong commitment to sharing. I checked this out, and all the experts said, "We can't do that." So I changed it back, and sent it to him. It went back to him four times. Finally, he called me in and said, "Jack, is this my letter?" I said, "Yes, sir, Mr. President." He said, "This is what I want to say." And I said, "Look, Mr. President, everybody tells me we can't do that." He said, "Damn it, it is my letter, that's what I am going to do." And that's the letter he sent. (Wohlforth 1996: 43–4)

"The Fate of the World in Their Hands": Reagan and Gorbachev Meet in Geneva

Ronald Reagan and Mikhail Gorbachev first met in November 1985 in Geneva. Reagan's romanticism stands out in the transcripts. The president saw to it that in his first meeting with Soviet leader it would be just the two of them, another indication of Reagan's belief in personal diplomacy. Reagan also made arrangements so that after the first morning session and lunch the two leaders would be left completely alone except for their interpreters. He even had a fireplace lit. In their conversation, Reagan stressed the potential for agency: "[N]ow the two of them were here with the fate of the world in their hands so to speak. The U.S. and the Soviet Union were the two greatest countries on Earth, the superpowers. They were the only ones who could start World War III, but also the only two countries that could bring peace to the world" (Geneva: first private meeting). Oberdorfer (1991) reports that Reagan said, "There are all these people sitting in the next room. . . . They've programmed us – they've written your talking points, they've written my talking points. We can do that, or we can stay here as long as we want and get to know each other and we can create history and do something that the world will remember in a positive way" (144). Shultz (1993) even maintains that the president said to Gorbachev, "You know, people have come to think of us as enemies. We don't have to be" (602).

Before the summit, the Soviets had made a proposal to reduce strategic nuclear weapons by 50 percent in exchange for a ban on space-based weapons – in other words, SDI – that also included research otherwise allowed under most interpretations of the ABM Treaty (Garthoff 1994: 228; Oberdorfer 1991: 130). Gorbachev repeated this offer in Geneva (Geneva: second private meeting). Over Weinberger's objections, the United States had responded with its own plan for halving this most dangerous type of weapon but with no mention of strategic defenses (Fitzgerald 2001: 302). In Geneva, Reagan laid out his vision for sharing the technology with the Soviets. He told Gorbachev, "If both sides continue their research and if one or both come up with such a system then they should sit down and make it available to everyone so no one would have a fear of a nuclear strike" (Geneva: first private meeting). He stressed that even if both sides completely eliminated their nuclear arsenals, a "mad man might come along with a nuclear weapon. If we could come up with a shield and share it, then nobody would worry about the mad man. He didn't even want to call this a weapon; it was a defense system" (Geneva: first private meeting). The president likened the technology to a more modern "gas mask," defensive in orientation and necessary as an insurance policy in case of an "unforeseeable return to nuclear missiles" (Geneva: second private meeting), an analogy he used over and over both at the meeting and at other points (Geneva: third plenary meeting). Just as countries had not disposed of their masks when chemical weapons were banned, neither could they dispense with a protection against nuclear weapons when these were abolished (Talbott 1988: 217; Weinberger 1990: 309).

Reagan was thereby showing consideration for Soviet fears that strategic defense might be used by the United States for offensive purposes (Geneva: second plenary session), something he repeated in multiple sessions (Geneva: second private meeting). However, simultaneously Reagan made the case that the Soviets had nothing to fear from the United States. He repeated his favorite anecdotes about how the United States had not exploited its nuclear monopoly after World War II and instead proposed to eliminate these weapons of mass destruction weapons entirely (Geneva: first and second plenary sessions).

Gorbachev accused the United States of trying to use SDI to gain a first-strike capability, which would unleash a new arms race in space and on the ground (Geneva: second plenary session and second private meeting). "If the goal was to get rid of nuclear weapons," he asked, "why start an arms race in another sphere?" (Geneva: second private meeting). It seems that because Gorbachev could not accept that Reagan truly believed in an impenetrable shield, he falsely maligned the president's intentions. The Soviet premier argued that a "defense against once certain level of strategic missiles was one thing, but a defense against a much larger number of such missiles would not be reliable at all. This could only lead to the conclusion that the only possible use of a strategic defense was to defend against a weakened retaliatory strike, not against a first strike" (Geneva: third plenary meeting). The same was true of Reagan's plan to share SDI technology. The minutes read: "Gorbachev questioned the sincerity of the President's willingness to share SDI research, pointing out that the U.S. did not share its most advanced technology even with its allies. Gorbachev called for a more realistic discussion" (Geneva: third plenary meeting).

McFarlane later tried to imagine what Gorbachev must have been thinking when meeting Reagan: "I'm talking to a man who is not hearing me intellectually. He's dismissing my kind of sensible criticisms of his program and he keeps coming back to me with this rather romantic image of a future that is disconnected from reality" (Oberdorfer 1991: 150). In McFarlane's estimation Gorbachev would have "had to conclude one of two things: either Reagan was being cynical with all his preaching about eliminating nuclear weapons, and his real intention was to bankrupt the Soviet system; or he was incredibly ignorant" (Fitzgerald 2001: 310). As Diggins (2007) writes, "The romantic Reagan must have been an enigma to the realist Gorbachev" (380). However, the Soviet premier seemed to pick up on the president's nonrational cognitive style. "To a certain extent ... he could understand that the idea of strategic defense had captivated the President's imagination," he said at one point. However, Reagan's arguments "contained many emotional elements, elements which were part of one man's dream" (Geneva: third plenary meeting). Gorbachev "said that there were dreams of peace and there were realities" (Geneva: third plenary meeting).

Although the two sides made no headway on the SDI issue, they did agree on the principle of a 50 percent reduction in strategic nuclear weapons that would be defined more precisely later. Both sides also adopted a joint communiqué containing Reagan's formula that a nuclear war could never be won and could never be fought (Garthoff 1994: 240; Matlock 2004: 165; Shultz 1993: 605).

The "Sleeves from the Vest": Reagan Resists a Grand Compromise

Just a few months after the Geneva summit, Gorbachev made an even more radical proposal in January 1986 – the complete elimination of nuclear weapons by 2000. But it had the same catch. The United States would have to formally give up the pursuit of a strategic defense system. Most Reagan officials were dismissive of the idea, thinking it a public relations stunt by the Soviet leader (Cannon 1991: 755; Garthoff 1994: 265). Reagan asked instead of this far-fetched idea: "Why wait until the end of the century for a world without nuclear weapons?" (Oberdorfer 1991: 157; Shultz 1993: 700; also Wilson 2014: 104). In an interview with the author, Matlock recalled:

When that came in, everyone said, "It's pure propaganda," but Reagan said, "Wait a minute. This seems to be the first time that a Soviet leader seems to be serious about eliminating nuclear weapons. We are not going to knock this. It is OK to say a lot of these details we don't agree with but we're not going to try to downplay it." At first his advisers were really shocked" (interview with the author).

Matlock (2004) noted: "Though specialists on both sides considered the idea impractical ... it fitted Reagan's dream of putting the world on the road to abolishing nuclear weapons" (178). Weinberger seemed nervous about Reagan's affinity for nuclear abolition, saying that the government "should keep the focus away from the date for abolishing nuclear weapons" (NSPG: 3 February 1986). In any case, SDI was still a sticking point.

By June the Soviets had given up on banning SDI programs entirely and settled on a new strategy – ensuring American compliance with the ABM Treaty for long enough to ensure that any reduction in offensive weapons would not leave the Soviets vulnerable to a strike. During a period of 15 years the United States would be allowed to research strategic defense in the laboratory (Garthoff 1994: 279; Shultz 1993: 718). After the end of that period each side could do what it liked. Schultz wanted to jump at the opportunity. Since it was extremely unlikely that there would be anything worthwhile to test over the next decade at least, the Soviet proposal entailed no cost. The United States "should give them the sleeves from our vest on SDI and make them think they got our overcoat" (Shultz 1993: 716; also 718), receiving large cuts in Soviet nuclear weapons without limiting SDI in practice. The secretary had even suggested at an earlier meeting an indefinite ABM Treaty extension using this same logic: "Since the time period under discussion is when SDI deployments won't occur anyhow, we could propose that the ABM Treaty remain in force so long as reductions go on" (NSPG: 3 February 1986). Nitze also supported such a deal (Wohlforth 1996: 40).

This pragmatic argument did not move Reagan, who, in Shultz's words, "was afraid that any discussion with the Soviets about strategic defense would be used as a way to scuttle SDI. I tried to convince him that we could give up those deployment rights that we could not exercise anyway – we lacked the technical capability – and hold the line there. That would be giving the Soviets the sleeves from our vest! But he remained apprehensive" (Shultz 1993: 718). Instead, "The President talked only about going ahead full steam on SDI and then sharing it with the Soviets" (Shultz 1993: 721), receiving the support of Weinberger, who was always looking for a way to scuttle any arms-control deal (NSPG: 3 February 1986). Reagan decided:

The U.S. will not give up SDI. We should point out that SDI is not for the U.S. alone – we seek a mutual shift from sole reliance on offensive weapons to an offense–defense mix. We should remember the principle of sharing SDI at the deployment stage. . . . As we continue to develop SDI we need to find a way for SDI to be a protector for all – perhaps the concept of a common trigger where some international group, perhaps the UN, could deploy SDI against anyone who threatens use of nuclear weapons. (NSPG: 3 February 1986)

Reagan tried to add some meat to the bones of this radical idea in June, telling his advisers:

I'm thinking of something like an agreement now, that if SDI research proves out, and recognizing that both sides are now free to conduct research under the ABM treaty, we would, when we get to the point of needing to test, invite the Soviets to observe our test, but that actual deployment by either side would depend on movement towards total elimination of strategic nuclear missiles. In this way, both sides would see SDI not as a threat, but as a defense against a madman. (NSPG: 6 June 1986)

No one commented on the president's idea. "The meeting ended before general discussion could continue" read the minutes (NSPG: 6 June 1986).

Weinberger suggested a different approach, one in which each side would agree not to test or deploy strategic defenses for five years. After this period, if either side wanted to develop a defensive system it need only submit a plan for sharing the benefits and for eliminating all ballistic missiles, nuclear or non-nuclear. If no agreement could be reached, however, either side could go forward as soon as 7½ years from the ratification of the treaty. The logic was that ballistic missiles, being "fast flyers" in comparison to the slower bombers and cruise missiles, were the most dangerous weapons because they posed a first-strike threat (Cannon 1991: 760; Garthoff 1994: 280; Matlock 2004; Shultz 1993: 754; Talbott 1988: 307ff). Weinberger reasoned that the Soviets depended more on ballistic missiles than the United States so his proposal would improve American security (Weinberger 1990: 340). Moreover, the plan had little chance of being accepted because it allowed the United States to move forward at its own pace on SDI. The tactics were identical to the INF zero option, proposing a plan that the Soviets would never accept.

However, the zero ballistic missile idea (ZBM, as it became known) had a "strong appeal to the visionary and romantic side of Ronald Reagan," writes Oberdorfer (1991). It was incorporated into American plans (NSPG: 12 June 1986; also Cannon 1991: 760) but blended with the president's desire to share SDI. Reagan gave "official guidance" on 12 June 1986 instructing officials to develop a "new initiative" in which "actual deployments of ABM systems would be linked and phased to actual ballistic missile reductions by both sides." In stark contrast to Weinberger's proposal, if testing proved successful, there would be "no deployment of an ABM system by either side until agreement is reached on reductions of ballistic missiles." And each country would agree to "share its ABM system with the other side. ... Eventually our goal would be sharing the ABM systems with all responsible nations of the world" (NSPG: 12 June 1986; also Reagan 1990: 665). The president was excited: "[Gorbachev] gets his precious ABM Treaty, and we get all his ballistic missiles. And after that we can deploy SDI in space" (Oberdorfer 1991: 199). This was the proposal that Reagan brought to Reykjavik, one much more audacious, bold, and romantic than Weinberger's.

Again with the Gas Masks: The Reykjavik Summit

One is struck by the similarity of the Reykjavik and Geneva summit transcripts. Reagan again made an impassioned plea for SDI as a defense against "a madman such as Hitler" armed with nuclear weapons, to be deployed only after the complete elimination of strategic nuclear weapons[1] and with a treaty obligation to share the technology with the Soviet (Reykjavik: first meeting, Soviet transcript[2]). These stipulations would, according to Reagan, alleviate any possibility of using SDI offensively.

Reagan made his case using the exact same analogies and anecdotes that he had in Geneva. He recognized Soviet fears but stressed that the United States had exercised restraint when it had the nuclear monopoly after World War II, demonstrating its trustworthiness (Reykjavik: second meeting). According to a participant at the summit, the president "spoke in stories, almost in parables – extolling the wonders of the Baruch plan, the shrewdness of making gas masks, the hostility of Russia's denying U.S. pilots airfields, the duplicity of the Soviet test moratorium in the 1950s – really anything taken from the well-stocked shelves of his mental warehouse" (Adelman 2014: 153). He surmised, "A collective groan must have filled the room, as the President told his gas mask tale, with the same expression and most of the same words, unabridged, yet again" (148). Indeed, the minutes show that Gorbachev, exasperated, called out, "I've heard all about gas masks and maniacs, probably ten times already. But it still does not convince me" (Reykjavik: fourth meeting, Soviet transcript).

Gorbachev asked Reagan for a ten-year commitment to the ABM Treaty so as to "have the confidence needed while reducing" its nuclear weapons (Reykjavik: second meeting, White House transcript). It would be politically impossible to explain to the Soviet people that "they should be prepared to begin reductions while the ABM Treaty is being destroyed" (Reykjavik: second meeting, White House transcript). In a Soviet concession, Gorbachev would allow laboratory research during this period, but there could be no testing or deployment of strategic defenses (Reykjavik: second meeting). Reagan did not want to wait a decade to put up a defense shield, even though there was no chance it would be ready even in this time frame, demonstrating his nonrational thinking style: "Why the Hell should the world have to live for another ten years under the threat of nuclear weapons if we have decided to eliminate them?" (Reykjavik: third meeting, White House transcript).

In response to the bold but perhaps impractical idea of Reagan to share SDI technology, the Soviet General Secretary replied, as he himself put it, "in a less philosophical spirit, more on the practical plane"

---

[1] Here Reagan seems to have confused ballistic missiles and strategic nuclear weapons.
[2] All references refer to US State Department transcripts unless otherwise noted.

(Reykjavik: second meeting, Soviet transcript). "Excuse me, Mr. President," Gorbachev said, "but I do not take your idea of sharing SDI seriously. You don't want to share even petroleum equipment, automatic machine tools or equipment for dairies, while sharing SDI would be a second American revolution. And revolutions do not occur all that often. Let's be realistic and pragmatic" (Reykjavik: second meeting, Soviet transcript). Adelman (2014) describes the scene, noting the difference in cognitive styles as well as Reagan's romanticism: "Gorbachev acted like a capitalistic CEO trying to analyze and solve the issues at hand. Reagan resembled a Russian artist, flitting here and there, following his imagination about" (152).

In the dramatic fourth session that has made Reykjavik the source of such great historical interest, the Soviets proposed a complete elimination of strategic nuclear weapons over ten years, conducted in two stages, with a 50 percent reduction in the first five years. The Americans countered with a proposal to eliminate all ballistic missiles over ten years and to halve the number of strategic nuclear weapons during the first five years of this period. In terms of what would be permanently scrapped, the two sides were talking about slightly different things. The Soviets had in mind the entire nuclear triad of the United States, the Americans only ballistic missiles (Reykjavik: fourth meeting). However, Reagan agreed to the Soviet concept, saying, "If we agree that by the end of the 10-year period all nuclear weapons are to be eliminated, we can turn this agreement over to our delegations in Geneva so that they can prepare a treaty which you can sign during your visit to the U.S."[3] (Reykjavik: fourth meeting, Soviet transcript).

What would have been one of the most momentous agreements in international relations history ultimately faltered over differences on SDI. Gorbachev predicated his proposal on an American agreement to limit strategic defense to laboratory research for the ten years it took to dismantle nuclear arsenals. Reagan insisted on maintaining rights to the research, development, and testing permitted by the ABM Treaty (Reykjavik: fourth meeting, Soviet transcript). However, the president, a nonrational thinker, would not make the utilitarian tradeoff between his two visions. Pragmatists like McFarlane were distraught. Matlock recalled that "later, when he was no longer in office, McFarlane told me that he was appalled that the president had turned down the offer at Reykjavik. He said, 'What Gorbachev offered at Reykjavik was exactly what I was aiming for. Once we had an agreement on reductions, ten

---

[3] Gorbachev was to visit Washington in 1987.

years [of delay on SDI testing] was fine. It was crazy to turn that down'"
(Wohlforth 1996: 58). Shultz later remarked, "It would take forever in
laboratories" (Wohlforth 1996: 58). Subsequent comments seem to
suggest that while the secretary of state would not have supported a
radical plan for eliminating nuclear weapons, he was disappointed that
Reagan did not agree to a delay on SDI deployment in exchange for deep
cuts in ICBMs (Wohlforth 1996: 176).

No, It Isn't Romantic: The INF Treaty and Conservative Resistance to Reagan's Program

The consolation prize of the Reykjavik summit was a tentative agreement
on intermediate nuclear forces based on the zero option, the supposedly
impractical and "non-negotiable" proposal of 1981. Initial Soviet resistance, before Gorbachev came to power, had led the United States to
come off the zero proposal in 1985 (Cannon 1991: 764). At Reykjavik,
the General Secretary put it back on the table, even agreeing to not
include British and French forces in the deal. After Reykjavik, the two
sides agreed on Gorbachev's suggestion of "global zero" – all of these
weapons would be destroyed, whether deployed in Asia or Europe. The
two sides signed the INF treaty at a 1987 summit in Washington, the first
major reduction of nuclear arms in history and the first to eliminate an
entire class of weapons. More than 800 American missiles and
1800 Soviet missiles were to be destroyed, with on-site monitoring
(Cannon 1991: 775; Garthoff 1994: 305, 315, 327, 338; Shultz 1993:
767). Perhaps more importantly, although they accounted for only 5 percent of the superpowers' arsenals, an exchange of intermediate-range
weapons was considered particularly dangerous, the most plausible path
to a total nuclear war.

Now it was the Americans and Europeans who were having second
thoughts. Allies and NATO commanders questioned the wisdom of a
treaty that eliminated all but smaller battlefield nuclear weapons from
Western Europe. Even though the Soviets gave up more in absolute
terms, NATO INF missiles were seen as a necessary counterweight to
massive Soviet superiority in conventional forces – tanks, artillery, and
ground forces (Garthoff 1994: 291; Matlock 2004: 252; Oberdorfer
1991: 244; Shultz 1993: 767). German Chancellor Kohl, French President Mitterrand, and British Prime Minister Thatcher all had concerns
about the deal (Adelman 2014: 221; Mann 2009: 48).

Conservative hawks and neoconservatives also felt betrayed by a major
arms deal with the Soviets (Cannon 1991: 779; Mann 2009: 49, 232;
Wilson 2014: 139). Intellectuals like George Will, Irving Kristol,

Norman Podhoretz, William Buckley, Richard Pipes, and Elliot Abrams were all critical (Cannon 1991: 779; Garthoff 1994: 202, 249, 334; Matlock 2004: 272–5). Will complained Reagan was "elevating wishful thinking to the status of political philosophy" (Diggins 2007: 384) and "that the day Reagan signed the INF Treaty was the day that the Cold War was lost" (Wilson 2014: 139). Shultz remembered, "Nixon was against it. Kissinger was against it. Scowcroft was against it. All of the far right was against it. The NATO commander was against it" (Wohl-forth 1996: 105). Conservatives in the Senate such as Jesse Helms tried to block ratification of the treaty through poison pill amendments but were fought back (Cannon 1991: 781). During the 1988 presidential campaign, George Bush, the vice president, was the only Republican candidate to support it (Mann 2009: 263–4). Reagan complained to his chief of staff at the time: "I think I'm the only person left in this government who wants to try to see the completion of an INF Treaty with the Soviets" (Oberdorfer 1991: 244). Diggins (2007) observes, "Many of those who later credited Reagan with defeating communism had first claimed that he had lost the Cold War" (384).

In the end, the treaty passed overwhelmingly in the Senate. "Managing the right wing of the Republicans was a big problem," Matlock remembered, but "politically you couldn't outflank Ronald Reagan from the right. Some of them tried. Like George Will" (interview with the author; also Mann 2009: 237). Reagan's longstanding reputation as a Cold Warrior and a guiding light for the New Right helped in this regard, as did the knowledge that Reagan could ultimately rely on Democratic votes if necessary. Reagan's treaty had more enthusiastic backing from the left than the right.

The opposition shows again how Reagan's romanticism differentiated him from other conservatives. Reagan pinpointed the difference as belief in agency:

I think that some of the people who are objecting the most and just refusing to accede to the idea of ever getting any understanding, whether they realize it or not, those people basically down in their deepest thoughts have accepted that . . . there must come to be a war between the superpowers. Well, I think as long as you've got a chance to strive for peace you strive for peace. (Cannon 1991: 779; Matlock 2004: 272)

After Reykjavik, resistance also hardened to Reagan's bold plans for strategic weapons reductions. The president himself thought that had there been an agreement at Reykjavik: "[T]he world would have greeted it with great joy." However, his proposal to do away with most nuclear weapons in ten years had "scandalized many of Reagan's associates, who didn't want to admit it," Matlock writes (2004: 239; also Mann 2009: 47; Oberdorfer 1991: 183). Colin Powell remembered, "The chiefs thought they had dodged a bullet when Gorbachev insisted that the price had to be SDI" (Mann 2009: 48). "Reykjavik scared everyone. It was seen as scary proof that Ronald Reagan might do something terribly reckless," explained a staffer (Mann 2009: 48). The secretary of state gave a public speech calling on the two sides to develop "something other than the total elimination of nuclear weapons – that goal was too idealistic" (Shultz 1993: 778). Weinberger finally came out against Reagan's abolitionist goals, a position he had always privately harbored (Reagan 1990: 685). In response to Reagan's plea "to remember that the whole thing was borne of the idea that the world needs to get rid of nuclear weapons," Weinberger responded with an endorsement of MAD logic: "We can't live with nuclear weapons if they are used. We can't get rid of them because there are no defenses against them. We must do nothing to inhibit our ability to defend against nuclear weapons" (NSPG: 8 September 1987). Reagan's nuclear abolitionism was simply not taken seriously by American foreign policy elites (Wilson 2014: 140).

Following the summit, Reagan pushed ahead in an effort to realize the zero ballistic missile plan put together before Reykjavik, signing National Security Decision Directive (NSDD) 250 just days after his return. The NSDD tasked the Joint Chiefs of Staff (JCS) with developing a plan for eliminating all offensive ballistic missiles by 1996, provided that the Soviets accepted the plan. According to the document, these missiles were the most threatening to the United States, given their fast speed, making them "uniquely suited for an attempted first-strike by an aggressor," as opposed to bombers and cruise missiles, which were "slow-flying systems ... better suited for deterrence though the prospect of retaliation" (NSC: National Security Decision Directive 250). Anticipating resistance, the NSC staff took into account suggestions made by Admiral Crowe, the Chairman of the JCS, "except those which would change the tone to suggest that the issue was *whether* the objective of eliminating ballistic missiles in ten years was an appropriate objective rather than *how* best to achieve that objective" (Reagan Library [RL]: "NSDD on Post-Reykjavik Follow-Up Activities," 1 November 1986).

Somewhat predictably, the JCS responded by arguing that the United States could not eliminate all ballistic missiles within ten years without either a major increase in the defense budget or increased risk (RL: Linton Brooks, "Memorandum for Frank Carlucci," 23 February 1987). In an October 1986 national security meeting, Admiral Crowe had already declared that he opposed the ZBM idea (Oberdorfer 1991: 208). Weinberger was particularly resistant to ZBM, even though he had originated the plan – an irony that was not lost on the NSC staff. A joint memo to the NSC adviser, Frank Carlucci, reads:

While no useful purpose will be served by raising this point with the President, it does seem to us that if this were a football game Secretary Weinberger's repudiation of a proposal which grew out of *his* concept of eliminating ballistic missiles, and which was tabled in Iceland with the encouragement and support of *his* senior arms control representative, would lead to a 15 yard penalty for piling on. (RL: Clinton Brooks/Bob Linhard, Memorandum for Frank Carlucci, "JCS Response to NSDD-250," 31 March 1987)

Of course, the ZBM proposal had been a way to derail arms talks, not something to seriously negotiate.

The defense secretary based his opposition on his belief that the Soviets continued to have aggressive designs. He wrote, "The Soviets would strive," among other goals, "to dominate the post-war world, which is expected to adopt eventually some form of Soviet socialism or at least to submit to Soviet domination. ... The Soviets view the capability to preempt enemy use of nuclear weapons as the highest goal" (RL: Caspar Weinberger, Memorandum for the President, "Post-Reykjavik Activities," 5 December 1986).

Reagan had no real support from any part of the bureaucracy, including Shultz and his own NSC staff. Shultz pushed Weinberger to consider the potential public relations breakthrough of eliminating ballistic missiles, arguing that the increased financial costs and enhanced security would be worth it (NSC: William Cockell, Memorandum for Record, "JCS Briefing on Response to NSDD 250," 26 February 1987). However, ever the pragmatist, Shultz was advising Reagan immediately after Reykjavik to scale down his ambitions, suggesting again the alternative of drawing down strategic weapons by 50 percent over 5 years and eventually to a small residual force (JM: George Shultz, Memorandum to the President, "Strategy for the Soviets," 14 November 1986, Box 19). The NSC staff, even while complaining about the speciousness of the JCS objections, recommended to Carlucci that the issue be quietly shelved. By simply acknowledging receipt of the JCS report and not formally responding, the press could not report that the military blocked consideration of such a drastic proposal (NSC: Clinton Brooks/Bob Linhard, Memorandum for Frank Carlucci, "JCS Response to NSDD-250," 31 March 1987).

The ZBM idea seems to have died there, with Carlucci recommending that the president drop the issue entirely (NSC: Frank Carlucci, Memorandum for the President, "Elimination of Ballistic Missiles," 7 April 1987). Only Matlock seems to have genuinely pushed Reagan's bolder ideas, even drafting for the president a "National Plan for Elimination of Nuclear Weapons" (JM: Box 19) that drew the ire of others on the staff for being unrealistic. It went nowhere (JM: Bob Lindhard, Memorandum for Jack Matlock, "Your Paper, dated 25 November," 2 December 1986, Box 19).

With the ZBM proposal dismissed, the two sides reverted to previous plans for a 50 percent strategic arms reduction. SDI remained a sticking point. The President persisted in pushing an "international SDI and international defense against any ballistic missile" and sharing technology (NSPG: 10 November 1987; also 8 September 1986). After Reykjavik, his administration finally put its foot down. Weinberger said bluntly, "I don't believe that we could ever do that" (NSPG: 8 September 1987). The always more careful Shultz put it more diplomatically: The "idea needs to be made more concrete before it can be fully evaluated. It must have sufficient detail to be as realistic as cuts in START and INF. ... I don't think that this is the moment to spring a new concept on the Soviets, but we need to be ready to deal" (NSPG: 10 November 1987). The neoconservative Adelman warned, "Mr. President, that would be the most massive technical transfer the western world has ever known" (NSPG: 8 September 1987).

The "Vision Thing": The Upsides and Downsides of Reagan's Romanticism

With support from neither conservatives nor realists, Reagan would have to be content with the INF Treaty. Consumed by the Iran contra scandal, hampered by his lame duck status, and unwilling to bridge differences with the Soviets, the president did not successfully negotiate any major reduction in strategic nuclear weapons.

What do we make of Reagan's romanticism, its impact on relations with the Soviet Union, and its contribution to the arms-control breakthroughs of the period? It seems unlikely that another president would have so passionately sought major reductions in nuclear stockpiles. Yet at the same time, at Reykjavik, Reagan's radical and romantic dream of a world without nuclear weapons (or at least far fewer of them) was undermined by his other radical and romantic dream of a space shield protecting the United States from attack. Still, without Reagan's romanticism, the two sides would likely not have been talking about such steep reductions in the first place.

Matlock (2004) doubts that what was narrowly missed at Reykjavik could have been implemented:

It is simply not plausible to think that the much more radical changes that Reagan and Gorbachev discussed in Reykjavik, some of which were vehemently opposed by powerful interests in both countries and by America's closest allies, could have been put in acceptable treaty language, ratified and implemented in the short period of time they postulated. The program in its entirety was too ambitious to be practical. (241)

As we have seen, one of romanticism's virtues is to test whether what realists regard as insurmountable obstacles are, in fact, so immovable. The same had been said about the complete elimination of INF forces, something that Reagan himself noted. In his victory lap after the Moscow summit in 1988, Reagan stopped in London to give a speech, asserting:

The history of our time will undoubtedly include a footnote about how, during this decade and the last, the voice of retreat and hopelessness reached a crescendo in the West. ... These same voices ridiculed the notion of going beyond arms control, the hope of doing something more than merely establishing artificial limits within which arms buildups could continue all but unabated. ... And yet it was our double-zero option, much maligned when first proposed, that provided the basis for the INF treaty, the first treaty ever that did not just control offensive weapons but reduced them and, yes, actually eliminated an entire class of U.S. and Soviet nuclear missiles. (PPP: 3 June 1988)

In any case, although the Washington and Moscow summits passed without any major agreement on ICBMs, the meetings did pave the way for a START agreement under President George H. W. Bush. Shultz credited the president for these successes: "Remember that Ronald Reagan's initial proposals for strategic arms talks and for the intermediate-range INF talks were for massive reductions. That is where he started. And at Reykjavik, in a sense, that's what Gorbachev put on the table. So if you want to look at the lineage, I think that's a handy place to start" (Wohlforth 1996: 47). Former Soviet officials also acknowledge Reagan's contribution (Wohlforth 1996: 109).

Asking whether Reagan's romanticism helped or hindered arms control brings up again the normative question of whether rational thinking is good or bad. Reagan's cognitive style, decidedly nonrational, is frequently denigrated in historiographies and tell-all books from aides who were fired. Indeed, even the president's admirers were often frustrated by it. However, it is important to note that procedurally rational thought is not necessarily normatively superior or more successful in practice. Reagan did, by virtue of his cognitive style, often combine "ignorance and insistence," as Neustadt notes (Farnham 2001: 226). Nevertheless, calling Reagan nonrational is not an insult, and in some ways it might be a compliment.

Former aide Jack Matlock (2004) writes positively, "He did not think in neat, analytical categories, but in a general, almost impressionistic way. Yet he managed to grasp simultaneously the various dimensions of an activity: goals, tactics that work and don't work, the mind-set and political needs of his interlocutor" (154). McFarlane remarked, "He knows so little, and accomplishes so much" (Diggins 2007: 12; Wohlforth 1996: 103). Anderson (1983) remembers, "Rarely did he ask searching questions ... he would act, quickly, decisively, and usually, very wisely" (290). Farnham (2001) refers to his "intuitive intelligence" (247). Diggins (2007) even sees a positive in Reagan's tendency to believe his own fictional stories: "The stories he learned in his youth might not have been literally true, but they taught a deeper truth. ... His associates realized that the first victim of his ability to reinvent or enhance reality was Reagan himself, for his ability to convince others rested on his unshakable belief in his own stories. He was a romantic ... not an impostor" (18).

Even the pragmatist Shultz came to see this positive aspect of Reagan's style of thinking. Reagan "used a story to impart a larger message and sometimes that message was simply more important to him than the facts. He was a gifted storyteller, who could use a story effectively to make his point take on a deeper and more vivid meaning or to defuse a tense situation" (Shultz 1993: 1133). The secretary noted that Reagan "manages to get the essence of the problems pretty well. ... And often times the people who are immersed in the detail sort of lose the essence" (Cannon 1991: 134). This is one of the downsides of rational deliberation seen in this book.

Reagan supposedly once told a political adviser that he wanted to be president so he could "end the Cold War" (Wilson 2014: 9). Was this all a master plan on the part of Reagan? It does not seem so. Reagan felt his way through the process rather than designing a master plan, as some have suggested (Streusand et al. 2016). Wilson's (2014) case for the "triumph of improvisation" captures the process best, and this experimentation is consistent with an understanding of Reagan as a romantic. When asked how he would end the Cold War, Reagan responded in a way that revealed both his sense of agency and his intuitive thinking style: "I'm not sure, but there has got to be a way" (Wilson 2014: 9).

Conclusion

The Irrationality of Rational Choice Theory: Saving a Paradigm from Itself

Drawing on Isaiah Berlin's famous metaphor, Tetlock (2005) distinguishes between two different styles of thinkers – foxes and hedgehogs. Foxes are the procedurally rational, epistemically motivated leaders of the preceding chapters. Indeed, Tetlock makes use of the "need for cognition" construct I rely on so heavily in developing the traits of his different animals. Hedgehogs "know one big thing" that they apply to as many cases as possible. In Tetlock's research on elites, when compared to foxes, these hedgehogs are not particularly good forecasters and adjust their beliefs less in light of disconfirming evidence. They bolster rather than update. They are bold but often wrong. Foxes, in contrast, tend to hedge their bets. Rather than trying to cover all cases with a single heuristic, they approach each one separately, bringing all relevant information to bear.

For international relations scholars, this discussion might call to mind the role that paradigms play in theorizing. In essence, the criticism of paradigmatic adherents, whether they be realists or constructivists or something else, is that they are hedgehogs. David Lake's broadside against the role that these schools of thought play in international relations scholarship – that "'isms' are evil" – parallels the critiques made of hedgehogs. Lake (2011: 467) worries that paradigms tell us the answers going in, guiding our selection of evidence and even telling adherents what constitutes an interesting question. "Having adopted a tradition," he writes, "we then look only for evidence that affirms our prior belief in the rightness of that tradition. Practice becomes not an attempt to falsify theories through ever more demanding tests, but to support theories that were adopted prior to their confrontation with evidence" (470). He complains that those who identify with paradigms or research traditions in international relations engage in "self-affirming research and then wage theological debates between academic religions" (465).

The critique is familiar, but the implications have not been properly drawn out. We can train our lessons about rationality onto scholarship itself. *In the terms that we have used in this book, paradigmatic international relations research is often not rational.* If we accept Lake's critique, para-digms lead scholars to engage in theory-driven rather than data-driven research and biased assimilation of new evidence. In an ironic twist, those who should be the most objective observers of international politics suffer from serious cognitive shortcomings. If objectivity is the hallmark of science, then we are failing. What is a paradigm if not a heuristic that simplifies the world? Most paradigmatic pushers who would accept this definition of what paradigms do seem to miss the implication.

Lake's frustration with "isms" emerges out of a particular notion of how social science should proceed, what Patrick Thaddeus Jackson (2008) has recently called "dualist." It is marked by the "drive for classical objectivity" (132). In this way of thinking, good scientific prac-tices are those that better "guarantee that knowledge of the world corres-ponds to the world itself; valid knowledge means mirroring the world, representing it accurately, and not ignoring any of its important and essential features" (133). The virtues of the good academic are being an even-handed, balanced, and objective observer of what the data tell us. The social scientist is "merely a neutral conduit for 'the facts'" (132). Paradigms impede this objectivity, which represents one of the founda-tions of procedural rationality.

Indeed, Mearsheimer and Walt (2013), in defending the "big ideas" approach to international relations, accept the notion of paradigms as a heuristic, thereby offering an implicit endorsement of a kind of System I academic research: "There is simply no way to understand an infinitely complex world just by collecting facts," they write (435). "Because the world is infinitely complex, we need mental maps to identify what is important in different domains of human activity" (430). Nisbett and Ross (1980) could not have said it better. However, they were describing the "intuitive science" of "laypersons," not those with doctorates and fancy academic titles.

Is paradigmatic research by definition less rational than other types? Not necessarily. The problem is one of premature closure and a lack of humility. Paradigmatic research is not inherently evil. However, it involves dangerous temptations and becomes uncomfortably irrational when it loses sight of what it does not know. As we saw in this book, a hallmark of the rational thinker is acceptance (rather than avoidance and denial) of uncertainty. This is the problem of reification, drawn to our attention most forcibly by critical theorists. Levine and Barder (2014) write:

[T]heorists tend to forget the artificiality of the simplifying assumptions on which their grand theories are predicated. Over time, the maps become more than a guide through which a complicated and essentially indeterminate world is disclosed; they come, rather, to be conflated with that world. This process is known as *reification*: the tendency to forget that concepts and theories cannot capture the full, dynamic, constantly changing nature of things-as-such. Such forgetting has particular consequences. When the contours of a conceptual map can no longer be held distinct from the world that map purports to describe, its partiality falls out of view: the theorist no longer sees what is excluded from it, nor feels any need to reflect on what might fall under erasure by that forgetting. ... In this way, reification gives particular, contingent, and contestable agendas a false sense of necessity, inevitability, scientific objectivity, or naturalness. (869)

Rational thinking in foreign policy-making requires statesmen to keep in mind what they do not know, avoiding cognitive closure and misplaced certainty. The same is no less true of scholars. Using paradigms can help us simplify the world so as to make our jobs more tractable. However, once we lose sight of the fact that we are engaging in simplification, irrational tendencies easily creep in.

Rational Choice Theory: The Lady Doth Protest Too Much

Rational choice theory cannot escape this critique. Indeed, it might be more culpable than most other paradigms. Rationalists (and even others) often claim that rationalism's virtue is that it is non-paradigmatic. Perhaps most prominently, Fearon and Wendt (2002) make the case for seeing both rationalism and constructivism as something other than realism, liberalism, or other international relations traditions: "[R]-ationalism seems to refer to a methodological approach that may imply a philosophical position on what social explanation is and how it ought to work, the nature of which is debated. ... If the field does focus on rationalism versus constructivism, then the central debate in [international relations] will not be about international relations but rather about how to study international relations" (52). In this view, rationalism implies no substantive commitments or assumptions about the nature of world politics.

Although the 2011 TRIP (Jordan et al. 2009) survey of several thousand international relations scholars does not specify rationalism as a paradigm, a separate question asks respondents whether they assume the rationality of actors in their research. A greater percentage (30.6 percent) of those who employ a rational choice framework in their work identify as non-paradigmatic compared to those whose work does not assume the rationality of actors (20.9 percent) or who take a position in the middle (22.9 percent). Similarly, the same TRIP survey reveals that 70 percent of formal modelers identify as non-paradigmatic. They assume strict rationality at a much higher level than the overall sample, 50 percent as compared to 7 percent. Thus there is a clear relationship between assuming rationality and feeling as if one is avoiding the "isms" altogether (Rathbun 2017).

However, this claim does not withstand any kind of careful scrutiny. Rationalists have an easily identifiable ontology that differentiates their perspective from other approaches. Rationalism is based on a particular microeconomic building block – namely, the assumption of individualistic and egoistic actors seeking to maximize their personal interests, generally but not exclusively material in nature, through rational calculation. Firms seek profits, leaders seek office, and militaries seek larger budgets. Benefits of different choices are weighed against costs in a utilitarian fashion.

While at first glance the claim seems somewhat banal, from this assumption rationalists are able to develop a distinct vision of what international politics looks like that directly challenges other approaches in international relations. Institutions and strategic settings determine whose interests are privileged over others (Lake and Powell 1999; Milner 1998). The classic example is rent-seeking behavior by protectionist interests with privileged access to the policy-making process. Although free trade is in the public's interest, ordinary citizens have less incentive and ability to effectively lobby for their interests (Lake 2009). Since the choices of others often affect political actors' ability to get what they want, individualistic units interact with one another strategically, making judgments in situations of incomplete information as to the preferences, strategies, and power of others (Lake and Powell 1999; Milner 1998).

The problem is, as critical theorists have warned, one of reification. Rational choice began as a largely normative theory but morphed into a positive one (Mercer 2005; Stein 1999). Rationalists went from explaining how decisions should be made, to convincing themselves somewhere along the way that this was how decisions were actually made. Stein (1999) notes that rationalism was originally formulated as a way to improve (generally less than rational) decision-making, to advocate for logic rather than explain it. We can partially trace this process by looking at the approach to rationality taken by Keohane (1984), who played a more important role than anyone else in deriving value from thinking about international relations in microeconomic, utilitarian terms. Nevertheless, Keohane recognized the stylization of the approach and warned against reification: "The assumption of rational egoism creates an abstract, unreal world for analysis. It can mislead us if we take premises for reality and seek to apply our conclusion in a simple-minded way to the world that we observe. ... assumptions can easily be distorted in such a way as to do violence to reality" (70).

The very resistance by rationalists to the idea that their research is paradigmatic is actually evidence of reification. Moreover, rationalism's claim to purely objective, non-paradigmatic theorizing becomes even more potentially pernicious to the extent that rationalists believe it. This is surely ironic, as rationalists seem fiercely committed to the idea that they are doing proper, positivistic social science. Three fourths of hard rationalists in the 2011 TRIP survey identify as positivists, compared to 39 percent in the sample as a whole and 25 percent of nonrationalists. The key to using paradigms responsibly is remaining objective about one's own subjectivity.

Willful Ignorance

Once reification is in place, the familiar dynamics kick in. The same criticisms about theoretical belief perseverance and top-down reasoning made of laypersons in the heuristics and biases tradition have long been applied to rational choice theory. Green and Shapiro (1996) write of

[a] debilitating syndrome in which theories are elaborated and codified in order to save their universal character, rather than by reference to the requirements of viable empirical testing. When this syndrome is at work, data no longer test theories; instead, theories continually apace and elude data. In short, empirical research becomes theory driven rather than problem driven, designed more to save or vindicate some variant of rational choice theory rather than to account for any specific set of political phenomena. (6)

Rational choice theorists dig in like hedgehogs, collecting evidence to bolster their approach rather than rationally updating their approach to reflect the accumulated data that should generate doubts about their assumptions.

Rationalists aspire to develop universal theories of politics, predisposing them to search for a single decision-making style. This creates a temptation to engage in post hoc theorizing, premised on the notion of revealed preferences, in which theorists work backward from observed behavior to posit a set of interests, probability estimations, and other beliefs that make any behavior rational. In Almond and Genco's (1977) terms, rationalists put epistemology before ontology. One can reasonably ask what would amount to a falsification of a rational choice theory. "To the extent that theorists exploit the ambiguity in the meaning of rationality to transform successive disconfirming instances into data consistent with a newly recast theory, one most question whether the succession of theories is susceptible to empirical evaluation in any meaningful sense" (Green and Shapiro 1996: 36).

Rationalists take advantage of the difficulty in directly observing the processes they presuppose. As Green and Shapiro (1996) write, the "most important source of slipperiness in model building is the multiplication of unobservable terms, which causes the complexity of a theory to outstrip the capacity of the data to render an informative test" (39). Rationalists seem to be content to believe that any behavior can be explained as rational; they see no need to develop a set of tests of their very assumptions (35). Rationalism's insistence that it makes no claims about thinking processes means that rationality is judged by whether political actors made choices that made sense in light of their goals. As the latter are generally unobservable, however, there is always a post hoc story that makes behavior rationally understandable. That is not a good thing, methodologically. One can always work backward, changing preference functions and beliefs to make political behavior understandable.

The problem of observing cognitive processes is certainly not unique to rational choice. Indeed, psychological researchers contend with this problem every day. What is singular is the willful resistance to any attempt at observing the very cognitive process on which the rationalist paradigm rests. In the terms of this book, that means the lack of attention to, or concern for, the procedural rationality of the political actors under study.

As seen earlier, rationalists might fall back on the claim that, unlike others who engage in paradigmatic research, they are different in that they are not truly internalizing their assumptions. The presumption of expected utility maximization is simply useful for generating hypotheses (MacDonald 2003). We have seen how far this gets the approach, however. When subjected to empirical testing, the key claim, that how actors actually think in practice is immaterial, does not hold up. This was true in the preceding chapters at the level of both college undergraduates and heads of state.

This book shows that cognitive processes are not completely unobservable: They are unobserved. While it is difficult to observe exactly what goes on in the mind of political actors, or any individual for that matter, approximations can be made. Rationalists are just not looking. This is another example of the irrational tendencies of rational choice theory – an ostrich-like tendency to not seek out information that is there for the taking, which violates the very foundations of rational thought.

Given the fact that any behavior or choice can be made rational after the fact by positing a set of unobserved preferences and beliefs, rationalists simply have no choice but to observe procedural rationality if they want falsifiable theories. By specifying the characteristics of rational decision-makers a priori, we avoid this post hoc rationalization of rationalism. This has the advantage of making the very construct on which the approach is based empirically real. It makes little sense to speak of rationality if there is no irrationality or, in the terms used in this book, variation along a continuum. The key question is, as Lupia et al. (2000) put it, "What then would distinguish rational choice from irrational choice?" (11).

A rationalism willing to examine and test the very decision-making processes it assumes will likely entail jettisoning any aspirations of a universal theory of politics for a more conditional one in which rational choice offers an appropriate model when decision-makers have a procedurally rational decision-making style by virtue of the psychological dispositions highlighted in this book or, alternatively, owing to situational factors that incentivize deliberation and objectivity, such as environments in which the stakes are high. We are left with the much more modest claim, formulated by Stein (1999: 213): "Strategic-choice explanations will certainly be correct in explaining the choice of actors who self-consciously and correctly use strategic-choice theory in making their decisions" (see also Lebow and Stein 1989).

Of course, I might appear as the wolf in sheep's clothing, leading the rationalist lamb to its demise. Why would anyone trust me? Perhaps I have my own paradigmatic inclinations, convinced that psychology will always win the day and driven to evaluate the evidence as always showing irrationality rather than rationality. This book, however, shows that I have no such universalist goals. Some political actors better approximate the ideals of System II theorizing than others, since rational thought can be envisioned as a spectrum with no clear break between irrationality and rationality. My surmise is that rationality will be an appropriate characterization of decision-making in some instances but not others. Just as it appears empirically unsustainable to assume rationality, it is equally at odds with reality to assume there is no such thing. Little lamb, you have nothing to fear.

To save rational choice, rationalists must become more rational in their epistemological approach – open to disconfirming evidence, driven by empirical testing rather than paradigmatic confirmation, voracious in the collection of information about processes that have heretofore been simply assumed. This requires them to allow the possibility that those same cognitive processes might not occur in their objects of study and to grapple with the consequences, rather than hoping that everything will turn out all right. A focus on the psychology of rationality helps save rational choice from itself.

References

Archival Sources and Abbreviations

CD: Neville Chamberlain diary, 1937–1940. Chamberlain archives, University of Birmingham.

CHAR: Chartwell papers. Winston Churchill archives, Churchill College, University of Cambridge.

FO: Foreign Office papers. Public Record Office, London.

Geneva: National Security Archive, "To the Geneva Summit: Perestroika and the Transformation of U.S. Soviet Relations," http://nsarchive.gwu .edu/NSAEBB/NSAEBB172/index.htm.

HD: Viscount Halifax Diaries, 1940–1946. Halifax archives, University of York.

JM: Jack Matlock. Chronological Files, Ronald Reagan Presidential Library.

Letters: Letters from Reagan to Soviet Premiers. Boxes 37–40, Ronald Reagan Presidential Library.

NSC: NSC Executive Secretariat. Box 92185, National Security Decision Directives, Ronald Reagan Presidential Library.

NSPG: National Security Planning Group Records. Box 90318, Ronald Reagan Presidential Library.

Reykjavik: National Security Archive, "The Reykjavik File: Previously Secret Documents from U.S. and Soviet Archives on the 1986 Reagan–Gorbachev Summit, http://nsarchive.gwu.edu/NSAEBB/NSAEBB203/.

WC: William Cockell files. Box 91296, Ronald Reagan Presidential Library.

WP: War Cabinet minutes. Public Record Office, London.

Document Collections and Abbreviations

CC: Gilbert, Martin, ed. *Volume V, Companion Part 3, Documents, The Gathering Storm.*

DBFP: *Documents on British Foreign Policy.* London: Her Majesty's Stationery Office.

DL: Self, Robert, ed. 2000. *The Neville Chamberlain Diary Letters.* Aldershot, UK: Ashgate.

GW: Bismarck, Otto Fürst von. 1977. *Die gesammelten Werke.* Nendeln, Liechtenstein: Kraus Reprint.

Hansard. London: Her Majesty's Stationery Office. (British parliamentary record.)

Lettres: Richelieu, Armand Jean Du Plessis, Cardinal de. 1853–1877. *Lettres, instructions diplomatiques et papiers d'état du Cardinal de Richelieu*, edited by D. L. M. Avenel. Paris.

Papiers: Richelieu, Armand Du Plessis, Cardinal de. 1975. *Les Papiers de Richelieu*, edited by Pierre Grillon. Paris.

PPP: Public Papers of the President, http://presidency.proxied.lsit.ucsb.edu/ws/.

Memoirs and Other Writings

Adelman, Ken. 2014. *Reagan at Reykjavik: Forty-Eight Hours That Ended the Cold War*. New York: Harper Collins.

Anderson, Martin. 1990. *Revolution: The Reagan Legacy*. Stanford, CA: Hoover Press.

Bismarck, Otto Fürst von. 1966. *The Memoirs, Being the Reflections and Reminiscences of Otto, Prince von Bismarck, Written and Dictated by Himself after His Retirement from Office*. Vols. 1–2. New York: Fertig.

Churchill, Winston. 1948. *The Gathering Storm*. Boston: Houghton Mifflin.

Halifax, Edward Frederick Lindley Wood. 1957. *Fullness of Days*. New York: Dodd, Mead.

Jansenius. 1637. *Alexandri Patricii Armacani: theologi Mars gallicus sev De ivstitia armorum et foederum regis Galliæ libri duo*. [Anonymous pamphlet.]

Reagan, Ronald. 1968. *The Creative Society*. New York: Devin-Adair Publishing.

1990. *An American Life: The Autobiography*. New York: Simon and Schuster.

Richelieu, Armand Jean Du Plessis, Cardinal de. 1618. *Les principaux points de la foi d l'église catholique, deffendus contre l'escrit addressé au Roy par les quatre ministers de Charenton*. Paris.

1651. *Traité qui contient la méthode la plus facile et la plus asseurée pour convertir ceux qui se sont separez de l'église*. Paris.

1907–1931. *Mémoires du Cardinal de Richelieu*, edited by Société de l'Histoire de France. Paris. (Referred to as Mémoires.)

1961. *The Political Testament of Cardinal Richelieu*. Madison: University of Wisconsin Press (referred to as TP).

Shultz, George P. 1993. *Turmoil and Triumph: My Years as Secretary of State*. New York: Scribner's.

Weinberger, Caspar W. 1990. *Fighting for Peace*. Leeds: University of Leeds.

Secondary Sources

Abshire, David M., and Richard E. Neustadt. 2005. *Saving the Reagan Presidency: Trust Is the Coin of the Realm*. College Station, Texas: A&M University Press.

Achen, Christopher H., and Duncan Snidal. 1989. "Rational Deterrence Theory and Comparative Case Studies." *World Politics* 41(2): 143–69.

312   References

Addison, Paul. 1980. "The Political Beliefs of Winston Churchill." *Transactions of the Royal Historical Society*, Fifth Series 30: 23–47.

2007. *Winston Churchill*. Oxford: Oxford University Press.

Alkon, Paul K. 2006. *Winston Churchill's Imagination*. Lewisburg, PA: Bucknell University Press.

Almond, Gabriel A., and Stephen J. Genco. 1977. "Clouds, Clocks, and the Study of Politics." *World Politics* 29(4): 489–522.

Anker, Elisabeth. 2005. "Villains, Victims and Heroes: Melodrama, Media and September 11." *Journal of Communication* 55(1): 22–37.

Appel, Willi, and Ralph T. Daniel. 1961. *The Harvard Brief Dictionary of Music*. New York: Washington Square Press.

Arad, Ayala, and Ariel Rubinstein. 2012. "The 11–20 Money Request Game: A Level-*k* Reasoning Study." *American Economic Review* 102(7): 3561–73.

Arkes, Hal R., and Peter Ayton. 1999. "The Sunk Cost and Concorde Effects: Are Humans Less Rational than Lower Animals?" *Psychological Bulletin* 125 (5): 591–600.

Arnett, Jeffery. 1991. "Winston Churchill, the Quintessential Sensation Seeker." *Political Psychology* 12(4): 609–21.

Axelrod, Robert M. 2006. *The Evolution of Cooperation*. New York: Basic Books.

Ball, Stuart. 2001. "Churchill and the Conservative Party." *Transactions of the Royal Historical Society*, Sixth Series 11: 307–30.

2003. *Winston Churchill*. New York: New York University Press.

Bargh, John A., and Tanya L. Chartrand. 1999. "The Unbearable Automaticity of Being." *American Psychologist* 54(7): 462–79.

Baron, Jonathan. 1982. *Thinking and Deciding*. Cambridge: Cambridge University Press.

1985. *Rationality and Intelligence*. Cambridge: Cambridge University Press.

Bartels, D. M. 2006. "Proportion Dominance: The Generality and Variability of Favouring Relative Savings Over Absolute Savings." *Organizational Behavior and Human Decision Processes* 100: 76–95.

Barzun, Jacques. 1944. *Romanticism and the Modern Ego*. Boston: Little, Brown and Co.

Baumeister, Roy F. C., Nathan DeWall, and Liqing Zhang. 2007. "Do Emotions Improve or Hinder the Decision Making Process." In *Do Emotions Help or Hurt Decisionmaking?: A Hedgefoxian Perspective*, ed. Kathleen D. Vohs, Roy F. Baumeister, and George Loewenstein New York: Russell Sage Foundation, pp. 11–31.

Baxter, Colin F. 1983. "Winston Churchill: Military Strategist?" *Military Affairs* 47(1): 7–10.

Bazerman, Max H., Ann E. Tenbrunsel, and Kimberly Wade-Benzoni. 1998. "Negotiating with Yourself and Losing: Making Decisions with Competing Internal Preferences." *Academy of Management Review* 23(2): 225–41.

Bechara, Antoine, Hanna Damasio, Antonio R. Damasio, and Gregory P. Lee. 1999. "Different Contributions of the Human Amygdala and Ventromedial Prefrontal Cortex to Decision-Making." *Journal of Neuroscience* 19(13): 5473–81.

Bechara, Antoine, Hanna Damasio, Daniel Tranel, and Antonio R. Damasio. 1997. "Deciding Advantageously before Knowing the Advantageous Strategy." *Science* 275(5304): 1293–5.

2005. "The Iowa Gambling Task and the Somatic Marker Hypothesis: Some Questions and Answers." *Trends in Cognitive Sciences* 9(4): 159–62.

Beersma, B., and Carsten K. W. De Dreu. 1999. "Negotiation Processes and Outcomes in Prosocially and Egoistically Motivated Groups." *International Journal of Conflict Management* 10(4): 385–402.

Berlin, Isaiah. September 1, 1949. "Mr. Churchill." *The Atlantic.* www .theatlantic.com/magazine/archive/1949/09/mr-churchill/303546/

2014. *Political Ideas in the Romantic Age: Their Rise and Influence on Modern Thought.* Princeton: Princeton University Press.

Berzonsky, M. D., and C. Sullivan. 1992. "Social-Cognitive Aspects of Identity Style: Need for Cognition, Experiential Openness, and Introspection." *Journal of Adolescent Research* 7: 140–55.

Best, Geoffrey. 2001. *Churchill: A Study in Greatness.* London: Hambeldon and London.

Bickerton, Derek. 1994. *Language and Human Behavior.* Seattle: University of Washington Press.

Birkenhead, Frederick Winston Furneaux Smith. 1966. *Halifax: The Life of Lord Halifax.* Boston: Houghton Mifflin.

Blanchard, Jean-Vincent. 2011. *Eminence: Cardinal Richelieu and the Rise of France.* London: Bloomsbury Publishing.

Bligh, Michelle C., Jeffrey C. Kohles, and James R. Meindl. 2004. "Charisma under Crisis: Presidential Leadership, Rhetoric, and Media Responses before and after the September 11th Terrorist Attacks." *Leadership Quarterly* 15(2): 211–39.

Booth, Ken, and Nicholas J. Wheeler. 2008. *The Security Dilemma: Fear, Cooperation and Trust in World Politics.* New York: Palgrave.

Brands, H. W. 2015. *Reagan: The Life.* New York: Doubleday.

Brooks, Stephen G., and William C. Wohlforth. 2000. "Power, Globalization, and the End of the Cold War: Reevaluating a Landmark Case for Ideas." *International Security* 25(3): 5–53.

Bueno de Mesquita, Bruce. 2014. *Principles of International Politics.* 5th ed. Thousand Oaks, CA: Sage/Congressional Quarterly Press.

Byman, Daniel L., and Kenneth M. Pollack. 2001. "Let Us Now Praise Great Men: Bringing the Statesman Back In." *International Security* 25(4): 107–46.

Cacioppo, John T., and Richard E. Petty. 1982. "The Need for Cognition." *Journal of Personality and Social Psychology* 42(1): 16–131.

Cacioppo, John T., Richard E. Petty, Jeffrey A. Feinstein, W. Blair, and G. Jarvis. 1996. "Dispositional Differences in Cognitive Motivation: The Life and Times of Individuals Varying in Need for Cognition." *Psychological Bulletin* 119(2): 197–253.

Cacioppo, John T., Richard E. Petty, and Katherine J. Morris. 1983. "Effects of Need for Cognition on Message Evaluation, Recall, and Persuasion." *Journal of Personality and Social Psychology* 45(4): 805–18.

Cannon, Lou. 1991. *President Reagan: The Role of a Lifetime*. New York: Public Affairs.

Carr, Edward Hallett. 1946. *The Twenty Years' Crisis*. London: Macmillan.

Carlton, David.1964. *The Twenty Years' Crisis*. London: Macmillan.

1993. "Churchill in 1940: Myth and Reality." *World Affairs* 156(2): 97–103.

2001. "Churchill and the Two 'Evil Empires.'" *Transactions of the Royal Historical Society*, Sixth Series 11: 331–51.

Carter, Violet Bonham. 1965. *Winston Churchill: An Intimate Portrait*. New York: Harcourt, Brace & World.

Catherwood, Christopher. 2009. *Winston Churchill: The Flawed Genius of WWII*. New York: Berkley.

Chaiken, Shelly. 1980. "Heuristic versus Systematic Information Processing and the Use of Source versus Message Cues in Persuasion." *Journal of Personality and Social Psychology* 39(5): 752–66.

Charmley, John. 1989. *Chamberlain and the Lost Peace*. Chicago: Ivan Dee.

1991. "Essay and Reflection: Churchill as War Hero." *International History Review* 13(1): 96–104.

1993. *Churchill: The End of Glory*. New York: Harcourt Brace.

Chatterjee, Subimal, Timothy B. Heath, Sandra J. Milberg, and Karen R. France. 2000. "The Differential Processing of Price in Gains and Losses: The Effects of Frame and Need for Cognition." *Journal of Behavioral Decision Making* 13(1): 61–75.

Chong, Dennis. 2013. "Degrees of Rationality in Politics." In *The Oxford Handbook of Political Psychology*, ed. Leonie Huddy, David O. Sears and Jack S. Levy, Oxford: Oxford University Press, pp. 96–129.

Church, William F. 1972. *Richelieu and Reason of State*. Princeton: Princeton University Press.

Colville, John R. 1996. "The Personality of Winston Churchill." In R. Crosby Kemper III, ed., *Winston Churchill: Resolution, Defiance, Magnanimity, Good Will*. Columbia: University of Missouri Press, pp. 108ff.

Costello, John. 1991. *Ten Days That Saved the West*. London: Bantam Press.

D'Agostino, Paul R., and Rebecca Fincher-Kiefer. 1992. "Need for Cognition and the Correspondence Bias." *Social Cognition* 10(2): 151–3.

Damasio, Antonio. 1994. *Descartes' Error: Emotion, Reason, and the Human Brain*. New York: Avon Books.

De Callières, Francois. 2000. *On the Manner of Negotiating with Princes*. Boston: Houghton Mifflin.

De Dreu, Carsten K. W., Bianca Beersma, Katherine Stroebe, and Martin C. Euwema. 2006. "Motivated Information Processing, Strategic Choice, and the Quality of Negotiated Agreement." *Journal of Personality and Social Psychology* 90(6): 927–43.

De Dreu, Carsten K. W., and Terry L. Boles. 1998. "Share and Share Alike or Winner Take All?: The Influence of Social Value Orientation upon Choice and Recall of Negotiation Heuristics." *Organizational Behavior and Human Decision Processes* 76(3): 253–76.

De Dreu, Carsten K. W., and Peter J. Carnevale. 2003. "Motivational Bases of Information Processing and Strategy in Conflict and Negotiation." *Advances in Experimental Social Psychology* 35: 235–91.

De la Croix, Horst and Richard G. Tansey. 1986. *Gardner's Art through the Ages.* New York: Harcourt Brace Jovanovich.

Dessler, David. 1989. "What's at Stake in the Agent–Structure Debate?" *International Organization* 43(3): 441–73.

Diggins, John P. 2007. *Ronald Reagan: Fate, Freedom, and the Making of History.* New York: W. W. Norton & Company.

Dijksterhuis, Ap, Maarten W. Bos, Loran F. Nordgren, and Rick B. Van Baaren. 2006. "On Making the Right Choice: The Deliberation-without-Attention Effect." *Science* 311(5763): 1005–7.

Donnelly, Jack. 2000. *Realism and International Relations.* Cambridge: Cambridge University Press.

Dorra, Henri. 1972. *Art in Perspective.* New York: Harcourt Brace Jovanovich.

D'Souza, Dinesh. 1999. *Ronald Reagan: How an Ordinary Man Became an Extraordinary Leader.* New York: Simon and Schuster.

Eade, Charles, ed. 1954. *Churchill, by His Contemporaries.* London: Hutchinson.

Einhorn, Hillel J., and Robin M. Hogarth. 1981. "Behavioral Decision Theory: Processes of Judgment and choice." *Journal of Accounting Research* 19(1): 1–31.

Elliott, John H. 1991. *Richelieu and Olivares.* Cambridge: Cambridge University Press.

Elster, Jon. 1979. *Ulysses and the Sirens: Studies in Rationality and Irrationality.* Cambridge: Cambridge University Press.

Elster, Jon. (ed.). 1986. *Rational Choice.* New York: New York University Press.

1989. *Nuts and Bolts for the Social Sciences.* Cambridge: Cambridge University Press.

1999. *Alchemies of the Mind.* Cambridge: Cambridge University Press.

2009. *Reason and Rationality.* Princeton, NJ: Princeton University Press.

Epstein, Seymour, Rosemary Pacini, Veronika Denes-Raj, and Harriet Heier. 1996. "Individual Differences in Intuitive-Experiential and Analytical-Rational Thinking Styles." *Journal of Personality and Social Psychology* 71(2): 390–405.

Erlanger, Philippe. 1968. *Richelieu: The Thrust for Power.* New York: Stein and Day.

Evans, Jonathan S. B. 1984. "Heuristic and Analytic Processes in Reasoning." *British Journal of Psychology* 75(4): 451–68.

2008. "Dual-Processing Accounts of Reasoning, Judgment and Social Cognition." *Annual Review of Psychology* 59: 255–79.

Evans, Jonathan, and David E. Over. 2013 [1996]. *Rationality and Reasoning.* London: Psychology Press.

Farnham, Barbara. 2001. "Reagan and the Gorbachev Revolution: Perceiving the End of Threat." *Political Science Quarterly* 116(2): 225–52.

Fearon, James D. 1994. "Domestic Political Audiences and the Escalation of International Disputes." *American Political Science Review* 88(3): 577–92.

1995. "Rationalist Explanations for War." *International Organization* 49(3): 379–414.

Fearon, James, and Alexander Wendt. 2002. "Rationalism vs. Constructivism: A Skeptical View." In *Handbook of International Relations*, ed. Walter Carlnaes, Thomas Risse-Kappen, and Beth Simmons. London: Sage, pp. 52–72.

Feiling, Keith Grahame. 1946. *The Life of Neville Chamberlain*. London: Macmillan & Co.

Fettweis, Christopher J. 2013. *The Pathologies of Power: Fear, Honor, Glory, and Hubris in US Foreign Policy*. Cambridge: Cambridge University Press.

Feuchtwanger, E. J. 2002. *Bismarck*. London: Routledge.

Finnemore, Martha. 2004. *The Purpose of Intervention: Changing Beliefs about the Use Of Force*. Ithaca, NY: Cornell University Press.

Finucane, Melissa L., Ali Alhakami, Paul Slovic, and Stephen M. Johnson. 2000. "The Affect Heuristic in Judgments of Risks and Benefits." *Journal of Behavioral Decision Making* 13(1): 1–17.

Fischer, Beth A. 1997. *The Reagan Reversal: Foreign Policy and the End of the Cold War*. Columbia: University of Missouri Press.

Fischhoff, Baruch, Paul Slovic, and Sarah Lichtenstein. 1977. "Knowing with Certainty: The Appropriateness of Extreme Confidence." *Journal of Experimental Psychology: Human Perception and Performance* 3(4): 552–64.

Fischhoff, Baruch, Paul Slovic, Sarah Lichtenstein, Stephen Read, and Barbara Combs. 1978. "How Safe Is Safe Enough? A Psychometric Study of Attitudes towards Technological Risks and Benefits." *Policy Sciences* 9(2): 127–52.

Fiske, Susan T., and Shelley E. Taylor. 1984. *Social Cognition*. New York: McGraw-Hill.

Fitzgerald, Frances. 2001. *Way out There in the Blue: Reagan, Star Wars and the End of the Cold War*. New York: Simon and Schuster.

Frank, Elisabeth, and Veronika Brandstätter. 2002. "Approach versus Avoidance: Different Types of Commitment in Intimate Relationships." *Journal of Personality and Social Psychology* 82(2): 208–21.

Frye, Northrop. 1947. *Anatomy of Criticism: Four Essays*. Princeton, NJ: Princeton University Press.

Gall, Lothar. 1986. *Bismarck: The White Revolutionary*. London: Allen and Unwin.

Garrison, Justin D. 2013. *"An Empire of Ideals": The Chimeric Imagination of Ronald Reagan*. New York: Routledge.

Garthoff, Raymond. 2000. *The Great Transition: American–Soviet Relations and the End of the Cold War*. Washington, DC: Brookings Institution Press.

Gawronski, Bertram, and Galen V. Bodenhausen. 2006. "Associative and Propositional Processes in Evaluation: An Integrative Review of Implicit and Explicit Attitude Change." *Psychological Bulletin* 132(5): 692–731.

George, Alexander L.1969. "The 'Operational Code': A Neglected Approach to the Study of Political Leaders and Decision-Making." *International Studies Quarterly* 13(2): 190–222.

Gigerenzer, Gerd. 2007. *Gut Feelings: The Intelligence of the Unconscious*. London: Penguin.

Gigerenzer, Gerd, and Daniel G. Goldstein. 1996. "Reasoning the Fast and Frugal Way: Models of Bounded Rationality." *Psychological Review* 103(4): 650–69.

Gilbert, Martin. 1977. *Winston Churchill: Prophet of Truth, 1922–1939*. Boston: Houghton Mifflin.

Glad, Betty. 1983. "Black-and-White Thinking: Ronald Reagan's Approach to Foreign Policy." *Political Psychology* 4(3): 33–76.

Glaser, Charles L. 1994. "Realists as Optimists: Cooperation as Self-Help." *International Security* 19(3): 50–90.

2010. *Rational Theory of International Politics: The Logic of Competition and Cooperation*. Princeton, NJ: Princeton University Press.

Goddard, Stacie E. 2009. "When Right Makes Might: How Prussia Overturned the European Balance of Power." *International Security*, 33(3): 110–42.

Goddard, Stacie E., and Daniel H. Nexon. 2005. "Paradigm Lost? Reassessing Theory of International Politics." *European Journal of International Relations* 11(1): 9–61.

Goemans Hein. 2000. *War and Punishment: The Causes of War Termination and the First World War* Princeton, NJ: Princeton University Press.

Gollwitzer, Peter M., and Ronald F. Kinney. 1989. "Effects of Deliberative and Implemental Mind-Sets on Illusion of Control." *Journal of Personality and Social Psychology* 56(4): 531–42.

Green, Donald, and Ian Shapiro. 1996. *Pathologies of Rational Choice Theory: A Critique of Applications in Political Science*. New Haven, CT: Yale University Press.

Greene, Joshua D., R. Brian Sommerville, Leigh E. Nystrom, John M. Darley, and Jonathan D. Cohen. 2001. "An fMRI Investigation of Emotional Engagement in Moral Judgment." *Science* 293(5537): 2105–8.

Greene, Joshua D., Leigh E. Nystrom, Andrew D. Engell, John M. Darley, and Jonathan D. Cohen. 2004. "The Neural Bases of Cognitive Conflict and Control in Moral Judgment." *Neuron* 44(2): 389–400.

Greenstein, Fred I. 2000. "Reckoning with Reagan: A Review Essay on Edmund Morris's Dutch." *Political Science Quarterly* 115(1): 115–22.

Grieco, Joseph M. 1988. "Anarchy and the Limits of Cooperation: A Realist Critique of the Newest Liberal Institutionalism." *International Organization* 42(3): 485–507.

Grimmer, Justin. 2010. *Representational Style: The Central Role of Communication in Representation*. Dissertation (Cambridge, MA: Harvard University).

Gross, James J. 1998. "The Emerging Field of Emotion Regulation: An Integrative Review." *Review of General Psychology* 2(3): 271–99.

Haas, M. L. 2005. *The Ideological Origins of Great Power Politics, 1789–1989*. Cornell University Press.

Hall, Todd A. In press. "On Provocation: Outrage, International Relations, and the Franco-Prussian War." *Security Studies*.

Hamilton, Eric, and Brian C. Rathbun. 2013. "Scarce Differences: Towards a Material and Systemic Foundation for Offensive and Defensive Realism." *Security Studies* 22(3): 436–35.

318   References

Hanson, Stephen. 2010. *Post-Imperial Democracies: Ideology and Party Formation in Third Republic France, Weimar Germany, and Post-Soviet Russia*. Cambridge: Cambridge University Press.

Hart, Roderick P. 2009. *Campaign Talk: Why Elections Are Good for Us*. Princeton, NJ: Princeton University Press.

  2014. *Communication and Language Analysis in the Public Sphere*. Hershey: Information Science Reference.

Haslam, Jonathan. 2002. *No Virtue Like Necessity: Realist Thought in International Relations since Machiavelli*. New Haven, CT: Yale University Press.

Hermann, Margaret G., Thomas Preston, Baghat Korany, and Timothy M. Shaw. 2001. "Who Leads Matters: The Effects of Powerful Individuals." *International Studies Review* 3(2): 83–131.

Herrmann, Richard K., Philip E. Tetlock, and Penny S. Visser. 1999. "Mass Public Decisions to Go to War: A Cognitive–Interactionist Framework." *American Political Science Review* 93(3): 553–73.

Hitler, Adolf. 1983. *Hitler's Secret Book*. New York: Grove/Atlantic.

Holborn, Hajo. 1960. "Bismarck's Realpolitik." *Journal of the History of Ideas* 21 (10): 84–98.

Holmes, Marcus. 2013. "The Force of Face-to-Face Diplomacy: Mirror Neurons and the Problem of Intentions." *International Organization* 67(4): 829–61.

  2015. "Believing This and Alieving That: Theorizing Affect and Intuitions in International Politics." *International Studies Quarterly* 59(4): 706–20.

  2018. *Face-to-Face Diplomacy: Social Neuroscience and International Relations*. Cambridge: Cambridge University Press.

Holmes, Marcus, and David Traven. 2015. "Acting Rationally without Really Thinking: The Logic of Rational Intuitionism for International Relations Theory." *International Studies Review* 17(3): 414–40.

Holsti, Ole R. 1962. "The Belief System and National Images: A Case Study." *Journal of Conflict Resolution* 6(3)244–252.

Holsti, Ole R., and James N. Rosenau. 1988. "The Domestic and Foreign Policy Beliefs of American Leaders." *Journal of Conflict Resolution* 32(2): 248–94.

Hsee, Christopher K., and Yuval Rottenstreich. 2004. "Music, Pandas, and Muggers: On the Affective Psychology of Value." *Journal of Experimental Psychology: General* 133(1): 23–30.

Huddy, Leonie, David O. Sears, and Jack S. Levy. 2013. "Introduction: Theoretical Foundations of Political Psychology. In *The Oxford Handbook of Political Psychology*, ed. Leonie Huddy, David O. Sears, and Jack S. Levy. 2d ed. Oxford: Oxford University Press, pp. 1–19.

Hymans, Jacques E. C. 2006. *The Psychology of Nuclear Proliferation: Identity, Emotions and Foreign Policy*. Cambridge: Cambridge University Press.

Jackson, Patrick T. 2008. "Foregrounding Ontology: Dualism, Monism and IR Theory." *Review of International Studies* 31(1): 129–53.

James, Robert Rhodes. 1970. *Churchill: A Study in Failure*. New York: World Publishing. Co.

Janson, Horst Woldemar. 1991. *History of Art*. New York: Abrams.

Jervis, Robert. 1970. *The Logic of Images in International Relations*. New York: Columbia University Press.

1976. *Perception and Misperception in International Politics*. Princeton, NJ: Princeton University Press.

1978. "Cooperation under the Security Dilemma." *World Politics* 30(2): 167–214.

1994. "Hans Morgenthau, Realism and the Scientific Study of International Politics. " *Social Research* 61(4): 853–76.

Johnson, Dominic, and Dominic Tierney. 2011. "The Rubicon Theory of War." *International Security* 36(1): 7–40.

Johnson-Laird, Philip Nicholas. 1983. *Mental Models: Towards a Cognitive Science of Language, Inference, and Consciousness*. Cambridge, MA: Harvard University Press.

Jolls, Christine, Cass R. Sunstein, and Richard Thaler. 1998. "A Behavioral Approach to Law and Economics." *Stanford Law Review* 1471–550.

Jones, Reginald. 1996. "Churchill as I Knew Him." In *Winston Churchill: Resolution, Defiance, Magnanimity, Good Will*, ed. R. Crosby Kemper III. Columbia: University of Missouri Press.

Jordan, Richard, Daniel Maliniak, Amy Oakes, Susan Peterson, and Michael J. Tierney. 2009. *One Discipline or Many? TRIP Survey of International Relations Faculty in Ten Countries*. Williamsburg, VA: College of William and Mary. http://irtheoryandpractice.wm.edu/projects/trip/

Jost, John T., Jack Glaser, Arie W. Kruglanski, and Frank J. Sulloway. 2003. "Political Conservatism as Motivated Social Cognition." *Psychological Bulletin* 129(3): 339.

Kahneman, Daniel. 2011. *Thinking, Fast and Slow*. New York: Farrar, Straus and Giroux.

Kahnemann, Daniel, Paul Slovic, and Amos Tversky. 1982. *Judgment under Uncertainty: Heuristics and Biases*. Cambridge: Cambridge University Press.

Kahneman, Daniel, and Amos Tversky, A. 1972. "Subjective Probability: A Judgment of Representativeness." *Cognitive Psychology* 3(3): 430–54.

Kalberg, Stephen. 1980. "Max Weber's Types of Rationality: Cornerstones for the Analysis of Rationalization Processes in History." *American Journal of Sociology* 1145–79.

Keegan, John. 2002. *Winston Churchill*. New York: Viking.

Kelley, H. H., and Stahelski, A. J. 1970. "Social Interaction Basis of Cooperators' and Competitors' Beliefs about Others." *Journal of Personality and Social Psychology* 16(1): 66–91.

Kemper, R. Crosby. 1996. "The Rhetoric of Civilization." In *Winston Churchill: Resolution, Defiance, Magnanimity, Good Will*, ed. R. Crosby Kemper III. Columbia: University of Missouri Press.

Keohane, Robert O. 1984. *After Hegemony: Cooperation and Discord in the World Political Economy*. Princeton, NJ: Princeton University Press.

Kertzer, Joshua. 2016. *Resolve in International Politics*. Princeton, NJ: Princeton University Press.

Kertzer, Joshua D., Kathleen E. Powers, Brian C. Rathbun, and Ravi Iyer. 2014. "Moral Support: How Moral Values Shape Foreign Policy Attitudes." *Journal of Politics* 63(3): 825–40.

Kertzer, Joshua D., and Brian C. Rathbun. 2015. "Fair Is Fair: Social Preferences, Bargaining and Reciprocity and International Politics." *World Politics* 67(4): 613–55.

Khong, Yuen Foong. 1992. *Analogies at War: Korea, Munich, Dien Bien Phu, and the Vietnam Decisions of 1965*. Princeton, NJ: Princeton University Press.

Kissinger, Henry. 1994. *Diplomacy*. New York: Simon and Schuster.

Klaczynski, Paul A., and Kristen L. Lavallee. 2005. "Domain-Specific Identity, Epistemic Regulation, and Intellectual Ability as Predictors of Belief-Biased Reasoning: A Dual-Process Perspective." *Journal of Experimental Child Psychology* 92(1): 1–24.

Knecht, Robert Jean. 2014. *Richelieu*. London: Routledge.

Koch, Andrew M. 1993. "Rationality, Romanticism and the Individual: Max Weber's 'Modernism' and the Confrontation with 'Modernity.'" *Canadian Journal of Political Science* 1: 123–44.

Kokis, Judite V., Robyn Macpherson, Maggie E. Toplak, Richard F. West, and Keith E. Stanovich. 2002. "Heuristic and Analytic Processing: Age Trends and Associations with Cognitive Ability and Cognitive Styles." *Journal of Experimental Child Psychology* 83(1): 26–52.

Koopman, Cheryl, Jack Snyder, and Robert Jervis. 1990. "Theory-Driven versus Data Driven Assessment in a Crisis," *Journal of Conflict Resolution* 34(4): 694–722.

Koremenos, Barbara, Charles Lipson, and Duncan Snidal. 2001. "The Rational Design of International Institutions." *International Organization* 55(4): 761–99.

Krebs, Ronald. 2015. *Narrative and the Making of US National Security*. Cambridge: Cambridge University Press.

Krebs, Ronald R., and Patrick Thaddeus Jackson. 2007. "Twisting Tongues and Twisting Arms: The Power of Political Rhetoric." *European Journal of International Relations* 13(1): 35–66.

Kruglanski, Arie W., and Donna M. Webster. 1996. "Motivated Closing of the Mind: 'Seizing' and 'Freezing.'" *Psychological Review* 103(2): 263–83.

Ku, Kelly Y. L., and Irene T. Ho. 2010. "Dispositional Factors Predicting Chinese Students' Critical Thinking Performance." *Personality and Individual Differences* 48(1): 54–8.

Kuhlman, D. Michael, and Alfred F. Marshello. 1975. "Individual Differences in Game Motivation as Moderators of Preprogrammed Strategy Effects in Prisoner's Dilemma." *Journal of Personality and Social Psychology* 32(5): 922–31.

Kuhlman, D. Michael, and David L. Wimberley. 1976. "Expectations of Choice Behavior Held by Cooperators, Competitors, and Individualists across Four Classes of Experimental Games." *Journal of Personality and Social Psychology* 34(1): 69–81.

Kydd, Andrew H. 2005. *Trust and Mistrust in International Relations*. Princeton, NJ: Princeton University Press.

Laibson, David. 1997. "Golden Eggs and Hyperbolic Discounting." *Quarterly Journal of Economics* 112(2): 443–77.

Lake, David A. 1999. *Entangling Relations: American Foreign Policy in its Century.* Princeton, NJ: Princeton University Press, 1999.

2009. "TRIPs across the Atlantic: Theory and Epistemology in IPE." *Review of International Political Economy* 16(1): 47–57.

2011. "Why 'Isms' Are Evil: Theory, Epistemology and Academic Sects as Impediments to Understanding and Progress." *International Studies Quarterly* 55(2): 465–80.

Lake, David A., and Robert Powell. 1999. *Strategic Choice and International Relations.* Princeton, NJ: Princeton University Press.

Lane, Robert E. 2003. "Rescuing Political Science from Itself." In *Oxford Handbook of Political Psychology*, ed. David O. Sears, Leonie Huddy, and Robert Jervis. Oxford: Oxford University Press, pp. 755–793.

Langer, Ellen J. 1975. "The Illusion of Control." *Journal of Personality And Social Psychology* 32(2): 311–28.

Larson, Deborah W. 2000. *Anatomy of Mistrust: US–Soviet Relations during the Cold War.* Ithaca, NY: Cornell University Press.

2011. "The Origins of Commitment: Truman and West Berlin." *Journal of Cold War Studies* 13(1): 180–212.

Layne, Christopher. 2008. "Security Studies and the Use of History: Neville Chamberlain's Grand Strategy Revisited." *Security Studies* 17: 397–437.

Leary, Mark R., James A. Shepperd, Michael S. McNeil, T. Brant Jenkins, and Byron D. Barnes. 1986. "Objectivism in Information Utilization: Theory and Measurement." *Journal of Personality Assessment* 50(1): 32–43.

Lebow, Richard Ned. 1981. *Between Peace and War.* Baltimore: Johns Hopkins University.

2008. *Cultural Theory of International Politics.* Cambridge: Cambridge University Press.

Lebow, Richard Ned, and Janice Gross Stein. 1989. "Rational Deterrence Theory: I Think, Therefore I Deter." *World Politics* 41(2): 208–24.

Lebow, Richard Ned, and Thomas Risse-Kappen (eds.). 1995. *International Relations Theory and the End of the Cold War.* New York: Columbia University Press.

Lerner, Jennifer S., and Philip E. Tetlock. 1999. "Accounting for the Effects of Accountability." *Psychological Bulletin* 125(2): 255–75.

Levi, Anthony. 2000. *Cardinal Richelieu and the Making of France.* New York: Carroll and Graf.

Levine, Daniel J., and Alexander D. Barder. 2014. "The Closing of the American Mind: 'American School' International Relations and the State of Grand Theory." *European Journal of International Relations* 20(4): 863–88.

Levy, Jack S. 2013. "Psychology and Foreign Policy Decision-Making. In *Oxford Handbook of Political Psychology*, ed. Leonie Huddy, Davoid O. Sears, and Jack S. Levy. Oxford: Oxford University Press, pp. 301–33.

Lovejoy, Arthur. 1924. "On the Discrimination of Romanticisms." *Proceedings of the Modern Language Association* 39(2): 229–53.

1941. "The Meaning of Romanticism for the Historian of Ideas." *Journal of the History of Ideas* 2(3): 257–78.

Luce, Mary Frances, James R. Bettman, and John W. Payne. 1997. "Choice Processing in Emotionally Difficult Decisions." *Journal of Experimental Psychology: Learning, Memory, and Cognition* 23(2): 384–405.

Ludwig, Emil. 2013. *Bismarck: Story of a Fighter*. New York: Skyhorse Publications.

Lukacs, John. 2001. *Five Days in London, May 1940*. New Haven, CT: Yale University Press.

Lumsdaine, David Halloran. 1993. *Moral Vision in International Politics: The Foreign Aid Regime, 1949–1989*. Princeton, NJ: Princeton University Press.

Lupia, Arthur, Mathew D. McCubbins, and Samuel L. Popkin. 2000. *Elements of Reason: Cognition, Choice, and the Bounds of Rationality*. Cambridge: Cambridge University Press.

MacDonald, Paul K. 2003. "Useful Fiction or Miracle Maker: The Competing Epistemological Foundations of Rational Choice Theory." *American Political Science Review* 97(4): 551–66.

Manchester, William. 1988. *The Last Lion, Vol 2: Alone, 1932–1940*. Boston: Little, Brown.

Manchester, William, and Paul Reid. 2012. *The Last Lion, Vol. 3: Defender of the Realm, 1940–1965*. Boston: Little, Brown.

Mann, James. 2009. *The Rebellion of Ronald Reagan: A History of the End of the Cold War*. New York: Viking Press.

Marlo, Francis H. 2016. "The Historiography of the End of the Cold War." In *The Grand Strategy That Won the Cold War*, ed. Douglas E. Streusand, Norman A. Bailey, and Francis H. Marlo. Lanham, MD: Lexington Books, pp. 3–10.

Matlock, Jack F. 2004. *Reagan and Gorbachev: How the Cold War Ended*. New York: Random House.

Mayseless, Ofra, and Arie W. Kruglanski. 1987. "What Makes You So Sure? Effects of Epistemic Motivations on Judgmental Confidence." *Organizational Behavior and Human Decision Processes* 39(2): 162–83.

McClintock, C. G. 1972. "Social Motivation: A Set of Hypotheses." *Behavioral Science* 17(5): 438–54.

McClintock, C. G., and W. B. Liebrand. 1988. "Role of Interdependence Structure, Individual Value Orientation, and Another's Strategy in Social Decision Making: A Transformational Analysis." *Journal of Personality and Social Psychology* 55(3): 396–409.

McCubbins, Matthew D., and Mark Turner. 2012. "Going Cognitive: Tools for Rebuilding the Social Sciences." In *Grounding Social Sciences in Cognitive Sciences*, ed. Ron Sun. Cambridge, MA: MIT Press, pp. 387–414.

McDaniels, Timothy L., Lawrence J. Axelrod, Nigel S. Cavanagh, and Paul Slovic. 1997. "Perception of Ecological Risk to Water Environments." *Risk Analysis* 17(3): 341–52.

McDermott, Rose. 1998. *Risk-Taking in International Politics*. Ann Arbor: University of Michigan Press.

2004. "The Feeling of Rationality: The Meaning of Neuroscience for Political Science." *Perspectives on Politics* 2(4): 691–706.

McDonough, Frank. 1998. *Neville Chamberlain, Appeasement and the British Road to War*. Manchester: Manchester University Press.

McElroy, Todd, and John J. Seta. 2003. "Framing Effects: An Analytic–Holistic Perspective." *Journal of Experimental Social Psychology* 39(6): 610–17.

Mearsheimer, John J. 1994. "The False Promise of International Institutions." *International Security* 19(3): 5–49.

2005. "Hans Morgenthau and the Iraq War: Realism versus Neo-Conservatism." opendemocracy.com.

Mearsheimer, John J., and Stephen M. Walt. 2013. "Leaving Theory Behind: Why Simplistic Hypothesis Testing Is Bad for International Relations." *European Journal of International Relations* 19(3): 427–57.

Meinecke, Friederich. 1957. *Machiavellianism: The Doctrine of Raison D'État and Its Place in Modern History*. New Haven, CT: Yale University Press.

Mercer, Jonathan. 1996. *Reputation and International Politics. Ithaca, NY*: Cornell University Press.

2005. "Rationality and Psychology in International Politics." *International Organization* 59(1): 77–106.

2010. "Emotional Beliefs." *International Organization* 64(1): 1–31.

Metcalfe, Janet, and Walter Mischel. 1999. "A Hot/Cool-System Analysis of Delay of Gratification: Dynamics of Willpower." *Psychological Review* 106 (1): 3–19.

Middlemas, Keith. 1972. *The Diplomacy of Illusion: The British Government and Germany, 1937–1939*. London: Weidenfeld and Nicolson.

Milner, Helen V. 1998. "Rationalizing Politics: The Emerging Synthesis of International, American, and Comparative Politics." *International Organization* 52(4): 759–86.

Mitzen, Jennifer, and Randall Schweller. 2011. "Knowing the Unknown Unknowns: Misplaced Certainty and the Onset of War." *Security Studies* 20(1): 2–35.

Monteiro, Nuno P., and Keren G. Ruby. 2009. "IR and the False Promise of Philosophical Foundations." *International Theory* 1(1): 15–48.

Morgenthau, Hans J. 1946. *Scientific Man vs. Power Politics*. Chicago: University of Chicago Press.

1948. *Politics among Nations: The Struggle for Power and Peace*. New York: A. A. Knopf.

Murray, A. J. H. 1996. "The Moral Politics of Hans Morgenthau." *Review of Politics* 58(1): 81–107.

Newstead, Stephen E., Simon J. Handley, Clare Harley, Helen Wright, and Daniel Farrelly. 2004. "Individual Differences in Deductive Reasoning." *Quarterly Journal of Experimental Psychology Section A* 57(1): 33–60.

Nisbett, Richard E., and Lee Ross. 1980. *Human Inference: Strategies and Shortcomings of Social Judgment*. Englewood Cliffs, NJ: Prentice Hall.

Oberdorfer, Don. 1991. *The Turn: From the Cold War to a New Era: The United States and the Soviet Union, 1983–1990*. New York: Simon & Schuster.

Onea, Tudor. 2016. "Immoderate Greatness: Is Great Power Restraint a Practical Grand Strategy." *European Journal of International Security* 2(1): 111–32.

Orcibal, Jean. 1948. "Richelieu, homme d'église, homme d'état: À propos d'un ouvrage récent." *Revue d'histoire de l'Église de France* 34(124): 94–101.

Oye, Kenneth A. 1985. "Explaining Cooperation under Anarchy: Hypotheses and Strategies." *World Politics* 38(1): 1–24.

Pacini, Rosemary, and Seymour Epstein. 1999. "The Relation of Rational and Experiential Information Processing Styles to Personality, Basic Beliefs, and the Ratio-Bias Phenomenon." *Journal of Personality And Social Psychology* 76 (6): 972–87.

Pagès, G. 1937. "Autour du 'grand orage': Richelieu et marillac, deux politiques." *Revue historique*: 63–97.

Parent, Joseph M., and Joshua M. Baron. 2011. "Elder Abuse: How the Moderns Mistreat Classical Realism." *International Studies Review* 13(2): 193–213.

Parker, Andrew M., and Baruch Fischhoff. 2005. "Decision-Making Competence: External Validation through an Individual-Differences Approach." *Journal of Behavioral Decision Making* 18(1): 1–27.

Parker, R. A. C. 1993. *Chamberlain and Appeasement: British Policy and the Coming of the Second World War*. Basingstoke, UK: Macmillan.

Parsons, Craig. 2007. *How to Map Arguments in Political Science*. Oxford: Oxford University Press.

Peckham, Morse. 1951. "Toward a Theory of Romanticism." *Proceedings of the Modern Language Association* 66(2): 5–23.

Pemberton, William E. 2015. *Exit with Honor: The Life and Presidency of Ronald Reagan*. London: Routledge.

Perkins, David N., and Ron Ritchhart. 2004. "When Is Good Thinking." In *Motivation, Emotion, and Cognition: Integrative Perspectives on Intellectual Functioning and Development*, ed. David Y. Dai and Robert J. Sternberg. London: Routledge, pp. 351–384.

Pflanze, Otto. 1955. "Bismarck and German Nationalism." *American Historical Review* 60(3): 548–66.

  1990. *Bismarck and the Development of Germany*. Princeton, NJ: Princeton University Press.

Ponting, Clive. 1991. *1940: Myth and Reality*. Chicago: I. R. Dee.

Posen, Barry R. 2014. *Restraint: A New Foundation for US Grand Strategy*. Ithaca, NY: Cornell University Press.

Pouliot, Vincent. 2008. "The Logic of Practicality: A Theory of Practice of Security Communities." *International Organization* 62(2): 257–88.

Press, Daryl. 2005. *Calculating Credibility: How Leaders Assess Military Threats*. Ithaca, NY/London: Cornell University Press.

Priester, Joseph R., and Richard E. Petty. 1995. "Source Attributions and Persuasion: Perceived Honesty as a Determinant of Message Scrutiny." *Personality and Social Psychology Bulletin* 21(6): 637–54.

Quattrone, George A., and Amos Tversky. 1988. "Contrasting Rational and Psychological Analyses of Political Choice." *American Political Science Review* 82(3): 719–36.

Quinault, Roland. 2001. "Churchill and Democracy." *Transactions of the Royal Historical Society* 11: 201–20.

Rapport, Aaron. 2012. "The Long and Short of It: Cognitive Constraints on Leaders' Assessments of "Postwar" Iraq, *International Security* 37(3): 133–71.

2015. *Waging War, Planning Peace: US Noncombat Operations and Major Wars.* Ithaca, NY: Cornell University Press.

Rathbun, Brian C. 2004. *Partisan Interventions: European Party Politics and Peace Enforcement in the Balkans.* Ithaca, NY: Cornell University Press.

2007a. "Hierarchy and Community at Home and Abroad Evidence of a Common Structure of Domestic and Foreign Policy Beliefs in American Elites." *Journal of Conflict Resolution* 51(3): 379–407.

2007b. "Uncertain about Uncertainty: Understanding the Multiple Meanings of a Crucial Concept in International Relations Theory." *International Studies Quarterly* 51(3): 533–57.

2008. "A Rose by Any Other Name: Neoclassical Realism as the Natural and Necessary Extension of Neorealism." *Security Studies* 17(2): 294–321.

2012. *Trust in International Cooperation: International Security Institutions, Domestic Politics and American Multilateralism.* Cambridge: Cambridge University Press.

2014. *Diplomacy's Value: Creating Security in 1920s Europe and the Contemporary Middle East.* Ithaca, NY/London: Cornell University Press.

2017. "Subvert the Dominant Paradigm: A Critical Analysis of Rationalism's Status as a Paradigm of International Relations." *International Relations* 31 (4): 403–25.

2018. "The Rarity of Realpolitik: What Bismarck's Rationality Tells Us about International Politics." *International Security* 43(1): 7–55.

Rathbun, Brian C., Joshua D. Kertzer, and Mark Paradis. 2017. "Homo Diplomaticus: Mixed-Method Evidence of Variation in Strategic Rationality." *International Organization* 71(S1): S33–60.

Rathbun, Brian C., Joshua Kertzer, Jason Reifler, Paul Goren, and Thomas Scotto. 2016. "Taking Foreign Policy Personally: Personal Values and Foreign Policy Attitudes." *International Studies Quarterly* 60(1): 124–137.

Reber, Arthur S. 1989. "Implicit Learning and Tacit Knowledge." *Journal of Experimental Psychology* 118(3): 219–35.

Rescher, Nicholas. 1988. *Rationality: A Philosophical Inquiry into the Nature and the Rationale of Reason.* Oxford: Clarendon Press.

Reynolds, David. 1985. "Churchill and the British 'Decision' to Fight on in 1940." In *Diplomacy and Intelligence during the Second World War*, ed. R. Langhorne. Cambridge: Cambridge University Press, pp. 147–67.

2001. "Churchill's Writing of History: Appeasement, Autobiography and 'The Gathering Storm.'" *Transactions of the Royal Historical Society*, Sixth Series 11: 221–47.

Rickert, William E. 1977, Summer. "Winston Churchill's Archetypal Metaphors: A Mythopoetic Translation of World War II." *Central States Speech Journal* 28: 106–12.

Ripsman, Norrin M., and Jack S. Levy. 2008. "Wishful Thinking or Buying Time?: The Logic of British Appeasement." *International Security* 33(2): 148–81.

Risse-Kappen, Thomas. 1991. "Did 'Peace through Strength' End the Cold War? Lessons from INF." *International Security* 16(1): 162–88.

1997. *Cooperation among Democracies: The European Influence on US Foreign Policy.* Princeton, NJ: Princeton University Press.

Roberts, Andrew. 1991. *The Holy Fox: A Biography of Lord Halifax.* London: Weidenfeld and Nicolson.

Rogers, Robert D., Adrian M. Owen, Hugh C. Middleton, Emma J. Williams, John D. Pickard, Barbara J. Sahakian, and Trevor W. Robbins. 1999. "Choosing between Small, Likely Rewards and Large, Unlikely Rewards Activates Inferior and Orbital Prefrontal Cortex." *Journal of Neuroscience* 19 (20): 9029–38.

Rosenthal, Leon. 2008. *Romanticism.* New York: Parkston Press International.

Ross, Lee, and Andrew Ward. 1996 "Naive Realism: Implications for Misunderstanding and Divergent Perceptions of Fairness and Bias." In *Values and Knowledge,* ed. Terrance Brown, Edward Reed, and Elliot Turiel. Hillsdale, NJ: Erlbaum, pp. 103–37.

Rubin, Gretchen. 2003. *Forty Ways to Look at Winston Churchill: A Brief Account of a Long Life.* New York: Ballantine Books.

Sambanis, Nicholas, Stergios Skaperdas, and William C. Wohlforth. 2015. "Nation-Building through War." *American Political Science Review* 109(2): 279–96.

Schelling, Thomas. 1966. *Arms and Influence.* New Haven, CT: Yale University Press.

Schultz, Kenneth A. 1999. "Do Democratic Institutions Constrain or Inform? Contrasting Two Institutional Perspectives on Democracy and War." *International Organization* 53(02): 233–66.

2001. *Democracy and Coercive Diplomacy.* Cambridge: Cambridge University Press.

Schweller, Randall. 2006. *Unanswered Threats: Political Constraints on the Balance of Power.* Princeton, NJ: Princeton University Press.

Scott, Alexander Maccallum. 1905. *William Spencer Churchill.* London: Methuen Publishing.

Self, Robert. 2017. *Neville Chamberlain: A Biography.* London: Routledge.

Shelden, Michael. 2013. *Young Titan: The Making of Winston Churchill.* New York: Simon and Schuster.

Shiffrin, Richard M. , and Walter Schneider. 1977. "Controlled and Automatic Human Information Processing: II. Perceptual Learning, Automatic Attending and a General Theory." *Psychological Review* 84(2): 127–90.

Shiloh, Shoshana, Efrat Salton, and Dana Sharabi. 2002. "Individual Differences in Rational and Intuitive Thinking Styles as Predictors of Heuristic Responses and Framing Effects." *Personality and Individual Differences* 32(3): 415–29.

Shimko, Keith L. 1991. *Images and Arms Control: Perceptions of the Soviet Union in the Reagan Administration.* Ann Arbor: University of Michigan Press.

1992. "Reagan on the Soviet Union and the Nature of International Conflict." *Political Psychology* 13(3): 353–77.

Simon, Andrew F., Nancy S. Fagley, and Jennifer G. Halleran. 2004. "Decision Framing: Moderating Effects of Individual Differences and Cognitive Processing." *Journal of Behavioral Decision Making* 17(2): 77–93.

Simon, Herbert A. 1955. "A Behavioral Model of Rational Choice." *Quarterly Journal of Economics* 69(1): 99–118.

  1978. "Rationality as Process and as Product of Thought." *American Economic Review* 68(2):1–16.

  1983. *Reason in Human Affairs*. Stanford, CA: Stanford University Press.

Sloman, Steven A. 1996. "The Empirical Case for Two Systems of Reasoning." *Psychological Bulletin* 119(1): 3–22.

Slovic, Paul, Nancy Kraus, Henner Lappe, and Marilyn Major. 1991. "Risk Perception of Prescription Drugs: Report on a Survey in Canada." *Canadian Journal of Public Health/Revue Canadienne de Sante'e Publique* 82(3): 15–20.

Smith, Eliot R., and Jamie DeCoster. 2000. "Dual-Process Models in Social and Cognitive Psychology: Conceptual Integration and Links to Underlying Memory Systems." *Personality and Social Psychology Review* 4(2): 108–31.

Smith, Michael Joseph. 1986. *Realist Thought from Weber to Kissinger*. Baton Rouge: Louisiana State University Press.

Smith, Stephen M., and Irwin P. Levin. 1996. "Need for Cognition and Choice Framing Effects." *Journal of Behavioral Decision Making* 9(4): 283–90.

Snidal, Duncan. 2002. "Rational Choice and International Relations." In *Handbook of International Relations*, ed. Walter Carlsnaes, Thomas Risse, and Beth A. Simmons. London: Sage, pp. 73–94.

Snyder, Jack. 2013. *Myths of Empire: Domestic Politics and International Ambition*. Ithaca, NY: Cornell University Press.

Spencer, Alexander. 2016. *Romantic Narratives in International Politics: Pirates, Rebels, and Mercenaries*. Manchester: Manchester University Press.

Stankiewicz, W. J. 1955. "The Huguenot Downfall: The Influence of Richelieu's Policy and Doctrine." *Proceedings of the American Philosophical Society* 99(3): 146– 68.

  1960. *Politics and Religion in Seventeenth-Century France*. Berkeley: California University Press.

Stanovich, Keith E. 1999. *Who Is Rational?: Studies of Individual Differences in Reasoning*. Mahwah, NJ: L. Erlbaum Associates.

  2011. *Rationality and the Reflective Mind*. New York: Oxford University Press.

Stanovich, Keith E., and Richard F. West. 1997. "Reasoning Independently of Prior Belief and Individual Differences in Actively Open-Minded Thinking." *Journal of Educational Psychology* 89(2): 342–57.

  1998. "Individual Differences in Rational Thought." *Journal of Experimental Psychology: General* 127(2): 161–88.

  2000. "Individual Differences in Reasoning: Implications for the Rationality Debate?" *Behavioral and Brain Sciences* 23(5): 645–65.

Stein, Arthur A. 1999. "The Limits of Strategic Choice: Constrained Rationality and Incomplete Explanation." In *Strategic Choice and International Relations*, ed. David A. Lake and Robert Powell. Princeton, NJ: Princeton University Press, pp. 197–228.

Stein, Janice Gross. 1988. "Building Politics into Psychology: The Misperception of Threat." *Political Psychology* 9(2): 245–71.

Steinberg, Jonathan. 2012. *Bismarck: A Life*. Oxford: Oxford University Press.

Stokstad, Marilyn. 2005. *Art History*. Upper Saddle River, NJ: Pearson/Prentice Hall.

Strack, Fritz, and Roland Deutsch. 2004. "Reflective and Impulsive Determinants of Social Behavior." *Personality and Social Psychology Review* 8(3): 220–47.

Streusand, Douglas E., Norman A. Bailey, and Francis H. Marlo (eds.). 2016. *The Grand Strategy That Won the Cold War*. Lanham, MD: Lexington Books.

Suedfeld, Peter, and Philip Tetlock. 1977. "Integrative Complexity of Communications in International Crises." *Journal of Conflict Resolution* 21(1): 169–84.

Talbott, Strobe. 1988. *The Master of the Game: Paul Nitze and the Nuclear Peace*. New York: Alfred Knopf.

Taliaferro, Jeffrey W. 2004. *Balancing Risks: Great Power Intervention in the Periphery*. Ithaca, NY: Cornell University Press.

Tapié, Victor Lucien. 1967. *La France de Louis XIII et de Richelieu*. Paris: Flammarion.

Tetlock, Philip E. 1983. "Cognitive Style and Political Ideology." *Journal of Personality and Social Psychology* 45(1): 118ff.

    1984. "Cognitive Style and Political Belief Systems in the British House of Commons." *Journal of Personality and Social Psychology* 46(2): 365ff.

    1998. "Social Psychology and World Politics." In *Handbook of Social Psychology*, ed. D. Gilbert, S. Fiske, and G. Lindzey. New York: McGraw-Hill, pp. 870–82.

    2005. *Expert Political Judgment: How Good Is It? How Can We Know?* Princeton, NJ: Princeton University Press.

Tetlock, Philip E., and Barbara A. Mellers. 2002. "The Great Rationality Debate." *Psychological Science* 13(1): 94–9.

Tetlock, Philip E., Randall S. Peterson, and James M. Berry. 1993. "Flattering and Unflattering Personality Portraits of Integratively Simple and Complex Managers." *Journal of Personality and Social Psychology* 64(3): 500–11.

Tetlock, Philip E., and Anthony Tyler. 1996. "Churchill's Cognitive and Rhetorical Style: The Debates Over Nazi Intentions and Self-Government of India." *Political Psychology* 17(1): 149–70.

Thompson, Kenneth. 1983. *Winston Churchill's World View: Statesmanship and Power*. Baton Rouge: Louisiana State University Press.

Thompson, Neville. 1971. *The Anti-Appeasers: Conservative Opposition to Appeasement in the 1930s*. Oxford: Clarendon Press.

Tingley, Dustin H. 2011. The Dark Side of the Future: An Experimental Test of Commitment Problems in Bargaining." *International Studies Quarterly* 55(2): 521–54.

Toates, Frederick. 2006. "A Model of the Hierarchy of Behaviour, Cognition, and Consciousness." *Consciousness and Cognition* 15(1): 75–118.

Toplak, Maggie E., and Keith E. Stanovich. 2003. "Associations between Myside Bias on an Informal Reasoning Task and Amount of Post-Secondary Education." *Applied Cognitive Psychology* 17(7): 851–60.

Trachtenberg, Marc. 2003. "The Question of Realism." *Security Studies* 13(1): 156–94.

Treasure, Geoffrey Russell Richards. 1972. *Cardinal Richelieu and the Development of Absolutism*. New York: St. Martin's Press.

Tversky, Amos, and Daniel Kahneman. 1973. "Availability: A Heuristic for Judging Frequency and Probability." *Cognitive Psychology* 5(2): 207–32.

    1983. "Extensional versus Intuitive Reasoning: The Conjunction Fallacy in Probability Judgment." *Psychological Review* 90(4): 293–315.

Tziampiris, Aristotle. 2009. *Faith and Reason of State: Lessons from Early Modern Europe and Cardinal Richelieu*. New York: Nova Science Publishers.

Varshney, Ashutosh. 2003. "Nationalism, Ethnic Conflict, and Rationality." *Perspectives on Politics* 1(1): 85–99.

Verplanken, Bas. 1993. "Need for Cognition and External Information Search: Responses to Time Pressure during Decision-Making." *Journal of Research in Personality* 27(3): 238–52.

Verplanken, Bas, Pieter T. Hazenberg, and Grace R. Palenewen. 1992. "Need for Cognition and External Information Search Effort." *Journal of Research in Personality* 26(2): 128–36.

Waltz, Kenneth. 1959. *Man, the State and War*. New York: Columbia University Press.

    1979. *Theory of International Politics*. Boston: McGraw Hill.

    1998. "The Origins of War in Neorealist Theory." *Journal of Interdisciplinary History* 18(4): 615–28.

Weber, Hermann. 1992. "'Une Bonne Paix': Richelieu's Foreign Policy and the Peace of Christendom." In *Richelieu and His Age*, ed. Joseph Bergin and Laurence Brockliss. Oxford: Clarendon, pp. 45–70.

Webster, Donna M., and Arie W. Kruglanski. 1994. "Individual Differences in Need for Cognitive Closure." *Journal of Personality and Social Psychology* 73 (4): 733–46.

Welch, David. 1993. *Justice and the Genesis of War*. Cambridge: Cambridge University Press.

Wendt, Alexander. 1987. "The Agent–Structure Problem in International Relations Theory." *International Organization* 41(3): 335–70.

Wheeler, Nicholas J. 2013. "Investigating Diplomatic Transformations." *International Affairs*, 89(2): 477–96.

    2018. *Trusting Enemies: Interpersonal Relationships in International Conflict*. Oxford: Oxford University Press.

Wilson, James Graham. 2014. *The Triumph of Improvisation: Gorbachev's Adaptability, Reagan's Engagement, and the End of the Cold War*. Ithaca, NY/ London: Cornell University Press.

Wittkopf, Eugene R. 1990. *Faces of Internationalism: Public Opinion and American Foreign Policy*. Durham, NC: Duke University Press.

Wohlforth, William C. 1994 "Realism and the End of the Cold War." *International Security* 19(3): 91–129.

Wohlforth, William C. (ed.). 1996. *Witnesses to the End of the Cold War*. Baltimore: Johns Hopkins University Press.

Wolfe, Alan. 1981, December. "Ronald, the Romantic Radical." *Mother Jones* 37–40.

Wright, Anthony D. 2011. *The Divisions of French Catholicism, 1629–1645: "The Parting of the Ways."* Burlington, VT: Ashgate Publishing.

Wrigley, Chris. 2001. *"Churchill and the Trade Unions." Transactions of the Royal Historical Society*, Sixth Series 11: 273–93.

Yarhi-Milo, Keren. 2014. *Knowing the Adversary: Leaders, Intelligence, and Assessment of Intentions in International Relations.* Princeton, NJ: Princeton University Press.

Zacher, Mark, and Richard Matthew. 1995. "Liberal International Relations Theory: Common Threads, Divergent Strands." In *Controversies in International Relations Theory*, ed. Charles Kegley. New York: St. Martin's Press, pp. 107–50.

Zagare, Frank C. 1990. "Rationality and Deterrence." *World Politics* 42(2): 238–60.

Zarnett, David. 2017. "What Does Realist Foreign Policy Activism Tell Us about Realist Theory?" *Foreign Policy Analysis* 13(3): 618–37.

Ziblatt, Daniel. 2006. *Structuring the State: The Formation of Italy and Germany and the Puzzle of Federalism.* Princeton, NJ: Princeton University Press.

Index

Cambridge Studies in International Relations